Lesbian, Gay, and Bisexual
Identities in Families

D0714073

Lesbian, Gay, and Bisexual Identities in Families

Psychological Perspectives

Edited by

Charlotte J. Patterson
University of Virginia

Anthony R. D'Augelli
The Pennsylvania State University

New York   Oxford
OXFORD UNIVERSITY PRESS
1998

284778

Oxford University Press

Oxford   New York

Athens   Auckland   Bangkok   Bogotá   Buenos Aires   Calcutta
Cape Town   Chennai   Dar es Salaam   Delhi   Florence   Hong Kong   Istanbul
Karachi   Kuala Lumpur   Madrid   Melbourne   Mexico City   Mumbai
Nairobi   Paris   São Paulo   Singapore   Taipei   Tokyo   Toronto   Warsaw

and associated companies in
Berlin   Ibadan

Copyright © 1998 by Oxford University Press, Inc.

Published by Oxford University Press, Inc.
198 Madison Avenue, New York, New York 10016

Oxford is a registered trademark of Oxford University Press, Inc.

Library of Congress Cataloging-in-Publication Data
Lesbian, gay, and bisexual identities in families :
psychological perspectives / edited by Charlotte J. Patterson,
Anthony R. D'Augelli.
p. cm.
Includes bibliographical references and index.
ISBN 0-19-511049-8 (cloth).—ISBN 0-19-511050-1 (pbk.)
1. Gays—Family relationships—psychological aspects.
2. Bisexuals—Family relationships—Psychological aspects.
3. Gays—Identity.   4. Sexual orientation—Psychological aspects.
I. Patterson, Charlotte.   II. D'Augelli, Anthony R.
III. D'Augelli, Anthony R.   Lesbian, gay, and
bisexual identities over the lifespan.
HQ76.25.L485 1998
155.3'4—DC21   97-44736

1   3   5   7   9   8   6   4   2

Printed in the United States of America
on acid-free paper

Preface

Cultural understandings of families have traditionally been intertwined with heterosexist assumptions. Not only does society generally presume children to be heterosexual unless otherwise specified but also parents and other family members are usually expected to be heterosexual. Only quite recently has research and scholarship examined lesbian, gay, and bisexual lives within the context of families. Recent research has focused on lesbian and gay couples, and on their families of origin. Studies of lesbian mothers, gay fathers, and their children have also emerged, and a considerable research literature has accumulated. Given how new much of the relevant research and theory on this subject is, however, it is not surprising that authoritative reviews are rare and often difficult to locate.

Building on the work published in our earlier volume, *Lesbian, Gay, and Bisexual Identities Over the Lifespan: Psychological Perspectives* (Oxford University Press, 1995), which emphasized *individuals*, the present work takes families as its central focus. Families are significant contexts in which the development of sexual identity usually occurs and in which such identities are maintained over time. Families are also deeply influenced by the sexual identities of their members, as are the communities in which families are embedded. The chapters in this volume review the most important recent scholarship on lesbian, gay, and bisexual identities in families, and identify promising directions for future research and theory in this multifaceted area.

As our title is intended to suggest, we are interested here not in an abstract ideal of "the family" but, rather, in the multiplicity of actual families with which lesbian, gay, and bisexual individuals are connected in various ways. Our perspective is influenced by the need to recognize variations in lesbian, gay, and bisexual family lives that are associated with cultural, ethnic, racial, and social class differences, as well as to explore commonalities across the lifespan. An ecological perspective that views families in the context of their community and cultural environments is central to our approach. We hope to examine the many different kinds of family relationships sustained by lesbian, gay, and bisexual people.

The first section of the book is devoted to exploration of different perspectives on sexual orientation in families and consists of four chapters. The first chapter is authored by J. Michael Bailey and Khytam Dawood, and focuses on evidence relevant to genetic contributions to sexual orientation. The second chapter, by Angela M. L. Pattatucci, discusses biopsychosocial interactions and the development of sexual orientation. Both of these chapters highlight important and controversial new research on sexual orientation that embodies a biobehavioral point of view and emphasizes the interplay of continuities and discontinuities across generations. In the third chapter, Beverly Greene presents work on ethnic identity and family dynamics in lesbian, gay, and bisexual development, and discusses the ways in which culturally diverse family settings may influence the development of sexual identities, and vice versa. Rounding out this section, Walter L. Williams describes some cultural influences on conceptions of sexual orientation and family lives.

The second section of the book focuses on key aspects of interpersonal relationships within the families of lesbians, gay men, and bisexual individuals. A chapter on lesbian, gay, and bisexual adolescents' relationships with parents is authored by Ritch C. Savin-Williams. In their chapter, Steven James and Bianca Cody Murphy discuss lesbian, gay, and bisexual couple relationships. The place of friendship in the family lives of lesbians and gay men is the subject of a chapter by Jacqueline S. Weinstock. Charlotte J. Patterson's chapter concerns the family lives of children with lesbian and gay parents. Gilbert Herdt and Jeff Beeler consider the positions of older gay men and lesbians in families. Completing this section, Joan Laird's chapter explores a variety of intergenerational processes in lesbian-headed families.

Consistent with our ecological approach, community and contextual issues are the focus of the third and final section of the book. M. Lee Badgett discusses economic issues that are important to the families of lesbians and gay men. A chapter on cultural heterosexism and the family by J. Roy Gillis explores antigay attitudes, policies, and social structures as these affect lesbian and gay family lives. The final chapter in this section is by April Martin, and it explores clinical issues for the families of lesbians and gay men.

We hope that this volume will contribute to an understanding of the role of sexual orientation in family lives, as well as to setting the research agenda relevant to lesbian, gay, and bisexual issues in families for future years. We also hope that this book will enhance the training of the next generation of social science researchers, who will learn more about the role of sexual orientation in family lives. We expect that the book's primary audience will be advanced undergraduate students, graduate students, and faculty in fields such as developmental, social, clinical, community, counseling, and family psychology. In addition, we hope the book will be useful to those in related disciplines such as social work, sociology, anthropology, education, gay and lesbian studies, family studies, and women's studies. It may also be valuable to professionals in various fields such as law, nursing, psychiatry, and education who seek current knowledge of family lives from lesbian, gay, and bisexual perspectives.

We are very grateful to the contributors, whose efforts have made this volume possible. We also want to thank Joan Bossert, at Oxford University Press, for her editorial support and enthusiasm, our anonymous reviewers for their helpful suggestions about this project, and Alice Saxion, at Pennsylvania State University, for her assistance with preparation of the manuscript. Our most heartfelt thanks go to members of our families, especially to our partners, Deborah Cohn and George Dempsie, who have taught us so much about the topic of this book.

July 1997   *C.J.P.*
                                                                                                         A.R.D.

Contents

III Community and Contextual Issues

I

Perspectives on the Families of Lesbians, Gay Men, and Bisexuals

1

Behavioral Genetics, Sexual Orientation, and the Family

J. Michael Bailey and Khytam Dawood

Explanations of individual differences in sexual orientation have often involved the family. For example, psychoanalytic hypotheses have emphasized the importance of parental personality (Bell, Weinberg, & Hammersmith, 1981; Bieber et al., 1962). Genetic hypotheses are obviously relevant to the family; genetic traits often run in families. Although the precise nature of the family's influence on sexual orientation remains unknown, we have begun to make progress, largely owing to the discipline of behavioral genetics.

Behavioral genetics comprises a set of techniques from genetics in order to elucidate the origins of behavioral variation. Behavioral geneticists have primarily focused on what might be called quantitative genetics, including family, twin, and adoption studies, but more recently there has been great interest in molecular genetics studies (Hamer, Hu, Magnuson, Hu, & Pattatucci, 1993). The aim of quantitative genetics, generally, is to estimate the magnitude of genetic and environmental influences on a trait. Most behavior genetics studies of sexual orientation have been of this type, and there is now a reasonably large and consistent body of studies to review. Quantitative genetics methods are rather blunt instruments because the questions they attempt to answer are generally broad. For example, quantitative studies estimate the magnitude of all genetic influences on sexual orientation. This might be distinguished from more conceptually ambitious goals such as determining precisely which genes affect sexual orientation, or elucidating how they do so. The latter goals require the techniques of molecular genetics, such as linkage analysis. Molecular genetics has great promise, and for some traits, especially genetic diseases, molecular techniques have yielded important breakthroughs. However, in the early stages of genetic investigation, such as is the status of sexual orientation research at present, even answers to broad, imprecise questions will measurably advance knowledge.

It is important to emphasize that a trait need not have any genetic influences at all to be usefully illuminated by behavioral genetics methods. For example, in order to demonstrate that a trait is entirely environmentally determined, it is necessary to falsify genetic hypotheses. Behavioral genetics designs, including twin and adoption studies, are ideally suited to do this.

In this chapter, we have two main goals. First, we explicate some key behavioral genetics concepts and research strategies. Second, we review the behavioral genetics literature of sexual orientation. Our review is not a comprehensive, study-by-study examination (for such an examination, see Bailey & Pillard, 1995), but rather, a consideration of several key issues concerning the role of the family in the origins and development of sexual orientation.

Behavioral Genetics

Geneticists study the reasons why traits vary in a population. They cannot study traits that do not vary. Thus, behavior geneticists can study why some people are taller or more intelligent than others, or why some people are schizophrenic and others are not, or why some people are heterosexual and others homosexual. They cannot study why, for example, all people have cells. Observable trait variation is *phenotypic variation* and can be quantified as the variance of the trait. One goal of quantitative geneticists is to decompose the phenotypic variance into proportions of variance due to three broad but distinct sets of causes: genetic factors, shared environmental factors, and nonshared (or unique) environmental factors.

Heredity

Genetic factors are those that are transmitted via genes, or segments of DNA that affect the synthesis of proteins. "Genetic" is often assumed to refer to the influence of any biological factor, but strictly speaking (as we are here), it does not. For example, maternal hormonal perturbations in utero, viral infections, injuries, and diet are all nongenetic biological factors. The importance of genetic factors can be illustrated most neatly by studies of monozygotic (MZ) twins separated at birth. Such twins are nearly identical genetically, and typically have rearing environments that are no more similar than those of unrelated individuals. Thus, any resemblance between separated MZ twins must be due to genetic factors. (We are assuming here that prenatal environmental factors shared by twins are not responsible for trait similarity.) Geneticists quantify the importance of genetic factors as a trait's *heritability*. Heritability is a number ranging from 0 (genetic factors unimportant) to 1 (genetic factors all important). The conceptually simplest way to compute heritability is as the correlation between separated MZ twins. Fortunately, because separated twins are so rare, there are several other more commonly used (if less conceptually straightforward) ways to compute heritability (Plomin, DeFries, & McClearn, 1990).

All heritability calculations require assumptions: about sampling, the underlying distribution of the trait being decomposed, the comparability of environments for different types of relatives, and the absence of the (typically more complex) causal components not included in the model. Furthermore, precise heritability estimates require large samples. In our view, once a trait has been established as having nontrivial heritability (which in our view, would exceed .20), there are diminishing returns to efforts for more precise estimates, owing to the logistical problems in obtaining them. We believe that resources are better spent on attempting to characterize the nature of genetic and environmental influences in greater detail. That is, instead of estimating the proportions of variance associated with genes and environments, it would be better to identify relevant genes and environments, or to elucidate how they affect sexual orientation.

We note one more complication concerning genetic variation, which can be divided into additive and nonadditive variance (Falconer, 1989). Additive genetic variance reflects genetic factors that cause parents and their children to resemble each other. However, some genetic effects decrease the resemblance between parents and offspring, and variance due to these effects is nonadditive. For example, a trait that develops only when a child inherits the same rare gene (i.e., a rare recessive allele) from each parent may be entirely genetic, but children with the trait will usually differ from their parents, who will usually not have the trait. Our main point here is that a trait can in principle be highly genetic and yet be only weakly familial. Indeed, nonadditive genetic effects are most likely to occur for traits associated with reproduction or survival (Falconer, 1989), as sexual orientation probably is.

Environment

Behavioral geneticists divide environmental factors into two categories. Shared environmental factors are those typically shared by siblings reared together. These include, for example, family's religious affiliation, exposure to alcoholic parents, parental income, and neighborhood attributes. In contrast, nonshared environmental factors are those that are uncorrelated between siblings reared together. These would include idiosyncratic experiences with peers, parental favoritism, and order of birth. The importance of the shared environment is most directly assessed as the correlation of genetically unrelated siblings reared together. The importance of the nonshared environment is reflected most clearly in the degree of dissimilarity between MZ twins reared together. That is, for example, if individual differences in a trait were completely due to nonshared environmental factors, then the MZ trait correlation should average zero. It is important to emphasize that environmental factors can be biological as well as psychosocial. For example, over half the time, an MZ twin born with major brain anomalies will have a normal co-twin (Torrey, 1994). Such differences must be environmentally caused, but they are clearly not psychosocial in origin.

Behavior Genetics Methodologies

The simplest kind of behavioral genetics studies are attempts to determine if a trait or characteristic runs in families, and if so, to quantify the degree to which the trait is aggregated in the family. Typically, for categorically assessed traits, index subjects (probands) with and without the trait are recruited, and their close relatives (siblings, parents, and children) are assessed for the trait. If the trait is familial, it will be more common in relatives of probands with the trait. (For a thorough introduction to behavioral genetics concepts and methods, see Plomin et al., 1990.)

Familiality suggests, but does not prove, a genetic contribution to the characteristic because some characteristics (e.g., religious affiliation, last names) run in families for environmental reasons. In order to disentangle genetic and familial environmental effects, more sophisticated designs are necessary, including twin and adoption studies. We have already mentioned the study of separated MZ twins, which exemplifies both twin and adoption methodologies, and is the most conceptually appealing strategy. Unfortunately for science, separated MZ twins are rare, and this is especially limiting with relatively rare traits such as homosexuality; there are fewer than ten separated twin pairs with homosexuality (i.e., at least one twin in the pair is gay or lesbian) known in the literature. Thus, a more common strategy is to compare similarity of unseparated MZ and dizygotic (DZ) twins. DZ twins are less similar genetically than MZ twins, but both types of twins were reared together. Thus, it is assumed that MZ and DZ twins have equally similar environments. If so, and if genes contribute to a trait's variation, then MZ twins will be more similar on the trait compared with DZ twins.

Finally, adoption studies may focus either on biological relatives separated early in life (whose similarity reflects the importance of genes) or on biologically unrelated individuals reared together (whose similarity reflects the importance of shared environment).

Behavioral Genetics Findings

There have by now been thousands of behavioral genetics studies of hundreds of traits. Obviously, these studies have not all found exactly the same results; however, it is possible to reach a couple of very general conclusions about the literature (Bailey, in press). First, studies of adequate statistical power nearly always find evidence for heritability, which is typically in the moderate range (.30–.70). Second, traits that run in families usually do so primarily for genetic reasons. The bulk of environmental variance appears to be of the nonshared type (Plomin & Daniels, 1987). In other words, for most behavioral traits, the most powerful environmental determinants are those not shared by even identical twins reared in the same family. What is the nature of environmental influences that cause genetically identical people reared in the same family to differ? We do not know. They could be either psychosocial, such as the effects of subtle differences in parental socialization, or biologic, such as differences in the intrauterine environment.

Although we feel certain that these generalizations apply to most traits studied by behavioral geneticists, they do not necessarily apply to all traits. Thus, one cannot merely assert that because most traits are moderately heritable, no other traits need be studied. Characteristics strongly associated with diminished reproduction, such as homosexuality (Bell & Weinberg, 1978) are especially likely candidates to have low heritabilities; genes causing homosexuality should, all else equal, be selected against. We thus begin our review of the sexual orientation literature.

Behavioral Genetics of Sexual Orientation

We have organized this section of the chapter around several questions that have motivated much of the behavioral genetics research on sexual orientation.

Does Homosexuality Run in Families?

Magnus Hirschfeld, an early proponent of biological explanations of sexual orientation, observed in 1936 that male homosexuality has a "familial taint" (Hirschfeld, 1936), but it was not until 1986 when this observation was investigated empirically. Pillard and Weinrich (1986) recruited homosexual and heterosexual male probands using newspaper advertisements that did not mention the nature of the study. Probands were asked about both their own and their siblings' sexual orientations (in this study, these reflected both sexual attraction and sexual behavior). The investigators also contacted the large majority of probands' brothers, in order to verify proband reports. Gay male probands had an excess of gay brothers (22 percent) compared to heterosexual male probands' brothers (4 percent). Subsequent studies have used similar methodologies, with the exception of a study by Bailey, Bobrow, Wolfe, & Mikach (1995), who recruited gay and bisexual (based on sexual identity or, when unavailable, sexual attraction) men from consecutive admissions at an HIV outpatient center. (In most studies, both gay and bisexual men have been counted as "homosexual" probands; i.e., bisexual men and gay men have been considered as having the same sexual orientation.) This ascertainment strategy is more systematic than advertising for volunteers, and it may be less subject to self-selection biases. All available studies have focused on the rate of homosexuality in siblings rather than other first-degree relatives (e.g., parents or offspring).

Across available studies (Bailey & Bell, 1993; Bailey, Murphy, Ferrando, & Trivedi, 1995; Bailey & Pillard, 1991; Bailey, Willerman, & Parks, 1991; Hamer et al., 1993; Pillard & Weinrich, 1986), the median rate of homosexuality in brothers of gay male probands has been approximately 10 percent. These rates have exceeded those for heterosexual controls (median = 1 percent), as well as the prevalence estimates from recent large-scale epidemiological surveys (Billy, Tanfer, Grady, & Klepinger, 1993; Diamond, 1993; Johnson, Wadsworth, Wellings, Bradshaw, & Field, 1992), suggesting that male homosexuality is familial. Lesbians also appear to have more homosexual sisters (median = 13 percent) than do heterosexual controls (median = 2 percent), though the familiality estimates have varied more widely for women (Bailey & Bell, 1993; Bailey & Benishay, 1993; Bailey, Pillard, Neale, & Agyei, 1993; Pattatucci & Hamer, 1995; Pillard, 1990).

Do male and female homosexuality run in the same families? This question is important because its answer would reveal whether male and female sexual orientation have similar or different causes. For example, neurohormonal theories of male and female homosexuality posit that they are the result of opposite processes (diminished and elevated androgen action, respectively). Genes that cause an increase in androgen activity would presumably be different from the genes that cause diminished androgen activity. Thus, to the extent that familiality reflects genes operating through this route, male and female homosexuality should run in different families. Most family studies have reported information about sisters of gay men or brothers of lesbians. Although there was a trend in these studies for gay men to report an excess of lesbian sisters and lesbians to report an excess of gay brothers (both compared to same-sex controls), these trends are modest and based on relatively few families. Thus, the degree to which male and female homosexuality are cofamilial remains a very open question.

Is Sexual Orientation Genetically Influenced?

Virtually all evidence concerning genetic influences on sexual orientation comes from twin studies. Six separated MZ twin pairs with homosexuality have been reported in the literature (Bailey & Pillard, 1995). Both male pairs were concordant (i.e., similar) for adult homosexual feelings and behavior (though one pair differed in their degree of homosexual identity). Although it is tempting to dismiss this finding as based on too few subjects, it is a statistically very unlikely result. If we liberally assume the prevalence of male homosexuality to be 6 percent, which an American study (Laumann, Gagnon, Michael, & Michaels, 1994) found, as the rate for male homosexual attraction, the probability that both pairs would be concordant is less than one in two hundred. In contrast, all four female pairs were discordant (i.e., different) for sexual orientation. The results for men and women do not differ significantly; the sample size is too small to enable a statistically powerful test. (Because the male finding was significant, power was obviously sufficient.) Thus, it would be premature to declare female sexual orientation less heritable than male sexual orientation owing to findings for separated MZ twins.

There have been several studies of unseparated twins, in which the crucial comparison is between concordance rates for MZ and DZ twins. Regarding male studies (Bailey, Dunne, & Martin, 1996; Bailey & Pillard, 1991; Buhrich, Bailey, & Martin, 1991; Heston & Shields, 1968; Kallmann, 1952; King & McDonald, 1992; Whitam, Diamond, & Martin, 1993), the MZ concordance rate exceeded the DZ concordance rate in all but one study (King & McDonald, 1992). However, the specific concordance rates varied widely. For example, the MZ concordance rates varied from 100 percent (Kallmann, 1952) to 20 percent (Bailey, Dunne, et al., 1996), the latter figure being lower than some for DZ concordance rates. Nevertheless, a genetic hypothesis is clearly supported by the existing data There have been fewer twin studies of women (Bailey, Dunne, et al., 1996; Bailey et al., 1993; King & McDonald, 1992; Whitam, Diamond, & Martin, 1993), but these have yielded a similar picture, with all but one (Bailey, Dunne, et al., 1996) supporting a genetic hypothesis.

What is the heritability of sexual orientation? As we have noted, in order to estimate heritability, it is necessary to make a number of assumptions. One of the most important assumptions concerns the mode of genetic and environmental transmission. The most common assumption is that traits are multifactorial—that is, they are determined by a multitude of genetic and environmental factors, each with small effect. If so, then the underlying "liability" (Falconer, 1989) is normally distributed. If one knows the base rate, or prevalence, of the trait of interest, then calculating heritabilities from MZ and DZ concordance rates is fairly straightforward (though beyond the scope of this chapter; see Gottesman & Carey, 1983, for a clear exposition). One interesting consequence of this model is that even apparently modest concordances can yield high heritabilities. To see how this is so, assume that a trait is rare, with a prevalence of .001. Even an MZ concordance rate of .10 could yield a heritability as high as .60 (of course, heritability will also depend on the DZ concordance). To see why this might make sense, consider that an MZ concordance rate of .10 means that being genetically identical to someone who has the trait increases one's own chances of having the trait one hundred-fold. The mode of transmission of sexual orientation is unknown, but a multifactorial assumption is probably safe for most traits. Most genetic influence appears to be polygenic, the result of many genes with small effect rather than major genes with large effects (Bailey, in press). If this were the only important assumption, then it would be worth calculating heritabilities from available studies.

However, another important assumption, random (or at least representative) ascertainment, is certainly false. Most of the twin studies of sexual orientation recruited probands via advertisements in gay or lesbian publications or by word of mouth. This contrasts with the ideal, in which everyone from a well-defined population could be assessed about their twin status and their sexual orientation. The primary concern with unsystematic recruitment is ascertainment bias, in which one's results are affected by (typically unknown) biases. One kind of ascertainment bias, concordance-dependent bias (Kendler & Eaves, 1989), occurs when participants have been recruited in a way that inflates concordances (to an equal degree for MZ and DZ twins). If, for example, a gay twin who sees an advertisement for a study is less likely to call if his twin is heterosexual, this would cause concordance-dependent bias.

We suspect that concordance-dependent bias has occurred in most of the studies we cited. The study that used the least systematic recruitment procedure (Kallmann, 1952), yielded the highest MZ concordance figure (100 percent) and the study that arguably had the best sampling method (Bailey, Dunne et al., 1996; this study sampled a large number of twins from a twin registry) had the lowest figure (20 percent for strictly defined non-heterosexuality). Because by definition, concordance-dependent bias affects MZ and DZ concordances equally, it cannot cause a spurious heritability finding. One cannot know, however, that only concordance-dependent bias has occurred, and it remains possible (though there is no empirical evidence) that ascertainment bias has inflated MZ concordance relative to DZ concordance, and thus created spurious heritability findings. It is somewhat reassuring, then, that the study with the best sampling methods (Bailey, Dunne et al., 1996) also found evidence that male sexual orientation is heritable. The same study, however, did not support a genetic hypothesis for female sexual orientation.

We have focused considerable attention on the seemingly tangential issue of ascertainment bias because, in our view, it is the single greatest barrier to progress. One cannot appreciate the limitations of the existing genetic database without understanding it. The most plausible route by which this limitation can be reduced in the future is through the use of large, representative twin registries. Investigators using this approach can attempt to maximize participation, and just as importantly, can have some idea about the rate of nonparticipation. Concordance-dependent bias is likely to be less in registry studies. We noted that a recent study using the Australian Twin Registry obtained concordances somewhat lower than other studies (Bailey, Dunne et al., 1996). Although this study included responses from nearly 5,000 twins (not all of whom were matched with participating twins), the study had relatively low statistical power to detect heritability because the large majority (percentage) of twin pairs were concordant for heterosexuality and, hence, not very informative. Thus, very large samples will be needed.

Another potential methodological limitation concerns the "equal environments assumption" that the trait-relevant environment is no more similar for MZ twins than for DZ twins or adoptive siblings. A frequent objection to human twin studies is that parents treat MZ twins especially similarly and that this similar treatment, rather than the twins' similar genotype, could explain their similar behavior. Indeed, MZ twins are more likely to have been dressed alike and to have shared the same room as children, among other things. The question is whether such treatment makes them more similar, and the evidence suggests that this is not the case, at least for traits studied so far (Plomin et al., 1990). For example, MZ twins whose parents make an effort to treat them alike do not behave more similarly than do MZ twins whose parents make an effort to treat them differently. MZ twins whose parents mistakenly believe that they are DZ twins are as similar as they should be based on their true zygosity. A recent study tested the equal environments assumption for sexual orientation, and found that concordant MZ twins did not recall having been treated more similarly than discordant MZ twins (Bailey, Dunne et al., 1996).

In conclusion, we believe that there are almost certainly genetic influences on sexual orientation for men, somewhat less certainly so for women. The genetic evidence is certainly less strong for sexual orientation than for some other traits that have been studied longer and more carefully (and more easily), such as IQ, personality, and schizophrenia (Plomin et al., 1990). On the other hand, it is much stronger than it was a decade ago.

Is Sexual Orientation Environmentally Influenced?

Yes.

After our apparent equivocation in the previous section, our answer here may seem a bit abrupt, but it is warranted. How do we know that sexual orientation is environmentally influenced? We know it must be so because there are indisputable cases of MZ pairs in which twins have different orientations. In fact, results from the most careful studies suggest that homosexual twins will have heterosexual co-twins more than half the time. With rare exceptions, MZ twins can only differ for environmental reasons. (The rate of MZ discordance is much too high to be attributable to mutations.) Thus, although we believe the genetic evidence is strong (especially for men), the environmental evidence is definitive.

But what does it mean? What kind of environmental influence can make genetically identical twins reared in the same family have different sexual orientations? Note that the answer to this question will be different from the environment emphasized by social constructionists, who are usually concerned with environments shared by all members of a culture. Furthermore, to reemphasize, "environment" is not equivalent to "social influence." A recent review (Molenaar, Boomsma, & Dolan, 1993) found that a considerable amount of trait variance among nonhuman animals is due to poorly understood (and hence seemingly random) developmental perturbations. One relevant finding is that twins discordant for sexual orientation typically report that they were different as children, with the twin who is sexually attracted to women more masculine than the twin who is sexually attracted to men. If these memories are valid, they suggest that relevant environmental factors operate by childhood. In our view, the determinants of MZ discordance for sexual orientation is an important topic that has barely been explored.

MZ twin differences can only illuminate the nonshared environment. Is shared environment important for sexual orientation? The ideal design to answer this question would require a set of systematically ascertained homosexual probands with adoptive siblings. If shared environment were important, then adoptive siblings would have a higher rate of homosexuality than expected. The expected rate would equal the prevalence rate in the general population, and that rate remains somewhat controversial (Diamond, 1993). This ideal test has not been accomplished, and it is unlikely to be done in the near future. As we have noted, systematic ascertainment remains an elusive goal in behavioral genetics studies of sexual orientation.

However, two twin studies, one of men (Bailey & Pillard, 1991), the other of women (Bailey et al., 1993) included (unsystematically ascertained) probands with adoptive siblings. In the male studies, the rate of homosexuality among adoptive brothers, 11 percent, was higher than plausible prevalence rates (and indeed was higher than for biological siblings, whose rate was significantly lower than that for DZ twins, 23 percent). We suspect that the high adoptive rate is due to concordance-dependent ascertainment bias. (Because recruiting advertisements asked if readers had twins or adoptive siblings, probands would have been more likely to weigh the sexual orientations of their twins and adoptive siblings than of their nontwin biological siblings in making the decision to participate. We thus would expect the nontwin sibling rate to be less inflated.) A female study with an identical design yielded a 6 percent rate among adoptive sisters, which is somewhat higher than estimated prevalence rates of females homosexuality (Diamond, 1993), but again, we suspect that concordance-dependent bias caused the 6 percent rate to be inflated. Clearly, no firm conclusions can yet be drawn about shared environmental influences on sexual orientation.

Do Children of Gay Parents Become Gay?

A question that is somewhat related to (but also somewhat distinct from) shared environment concerns the sexual orientations of children raised by gay and lesbian parents. Are such children more likely to become gay or lesbian themselves?

One might expect elevated rates of homosexuality in children of homosexual people for either genetic or environmental reasons. To the extent that a trait has additive genetic variation, parents and offspring will resemble each other on the trait. Thus, additive genetic influences will cause gay men to have more gay sons, and lesbians to have more lesbian daughters, compared with heterosexual parents. We have noted that sexual orientation is a good candidate for nonadditive genetic effects, and thus even granting the validity of the genetic findings, it is not clear that homosexual parents should have higher rates of homosexual children on genetic grounds.

Gay and lesbian parents could be more likely to have gay or lesbian children for environmental reasons as well. At least three environmental transmission routes are conceivable: imitation, socialization, and lessening of antihomosexual stigma. By the first model, imitation, children may acquire their sexual orientations in part by imitating their parents. An immediate problem with this model is that most gay men and lesbians have heterosexual parents and thus develop opposite to the model's prediction. Psychoanalytic theorists (e.g., Bieber et al., 1962) have attempted to resolve this paradox by hypothesizing that as children, owing to atypical relationships with their parents, homosexual individuals identified with their opposite-sex parents. Although, to our knowledge, psychoanalytic writers have not extended this theory to the development of children of gay and lesbian parents, it would be consistent with an increased rate of homosexuality among the same-sex children of such parents. By a socialization hypothesis, gay and lesbian parents might conceivably either reinforce behavior that increases the probability of a homosexual outcome or else fail to discourage such behavior in their children. For example, one could speculate that gay and lesbian parents may discourage rigid gender role identification and encourage affectional openness, and that this is more likely to cause children to become homosexual. (This example is speculative because we do not know whether homosexual parents are more likely to socialize their children in these manners or children reared in these ways are more likely to become homosexual.) Finally, some writers (e.g., Arkes et al., 1994; Krauthammer, 1993; Pattullo, 1992) have suggested that destigmatizing homosexuality makes it easier for those who are so predisposed to become homosexual, and thus increases the rate of homosexuality in those cultures or subcultures in which it is destigmatized. It is at least plausible that being reared by a gay or lesbian parent has the effect of making homosexuality a more acceptable alternative. People who have gay or lesbian acquaintances are relatively tolerant of homosexuality (Herek & Glunt, 1993; Schmalz, 1993).

Patterson (Patterson, 1992) has reviewed the literature concerning development of children of homosexual parents, and the general picture of the literature has not changed since her review. Studies have typically found that approximately 10 percent of the children of homosexual parents become homosexual. The 10 percent figure is higher than population prevalence rates, and thus, if one could be confident about the figure's validity, would suggest that children of gay and lesbian parents are more likely to become homosexual. However, as in the twin studies, ascertainment bias makes acceptance of precise figures imprudent. Some of the relevant studies (e.g., Bailey, Bobrow, et al., 1995) recruited homosexual parents whose children were old enough to have known sexual orientations. Thus, parents in these studies would typically be aware of their children's sexual orientations and might well weigh that information in deciding whether to participate, thus inducing concordance-dependent bias. Based on our interactions with gay fathers, we would expect that on average, they are somewhat more hesitant to participate in such studies if their sons are heterosexual. If so, the typical 10 percent figure is likely to overestimate the true rate.

This particular problem is avoided by studies that recruit families before children's sexual orientations are known and then follow the children into adolescence or adulthood (e.g., Golombok & Tasker, 1996). Unfortunately, those studies are subject to a different kind of bias, differential attrition. Longiludinal studies almost always have significant attrition, and it is possible that the probability of a family's dropping out is related to children's sexual orientation.

It seems unlikely that any kind of bias is sufficiently large to threaten one very general conclusion from the parent-offspring studies. The large majority of children of homosexual parents grow up to be heterosexual. This conclusion is too general to satisfy those primarily interested in the scientific issues of whether there is (genetic or environmental) parent-to-child transmission of sexual orientation because it is consistent with a large range of possible transmission parameters. On the other hand, much of the interest in these studies stems from their relevance to social issues such as child custody rights of gay and lesbian parents. Anyone who regards as negative the possibility that being reared by a homosexual parent substantially increases the chance of one's becoming homosexual should be reassured. The absolute magnitude by which a child's chances of becoming homosexual increase as the result of being reared by a homosexual parent may be zero, and cannot be large.

Are There Different Types of Homosexuality?

On average, gay men were feminine boys and lesbians masculine girls, compared with same-sex heterosexuals (Bailey & Zucker, 1995), and some aspects of their "gender nonconformity" persist into adulthood (Bailey, Finkel, Blackwelder, & Bailey, 1996). However, there is substantial variation among homosexual people in childhood and adult gender nonconformity (Bailey, Finkel, et al., 1996; Bailey & Zucker, 1995; Bailey, Nothnagel, & Wolfe 1995), and some writers have hypothesized that it reflects etiologic heterogeneity of homosexuality. Karl Heinrich Ulrichs (1825–1895), an early theorist (and arguably the first gay liberationist), believed that there were two types of gay men: the *weibling*, or female-type, and the *mannling*, or male-type (LeVay, 1996, chap. 1). Bell and Weinberg (1978) entitled their book *Homosexualities: A Study of Diversity in Men and Women*, and in a subsequent book (Bell et al., 1981) explored the possibility that homosexuality associated with childhood gender nonconformity had different causes than homosexuality associated with gender-typicality. Meyer-Bahlburg (1993) has suggested that homosexuality associated with childhood gender nonconformity may be more explicable via endocrinologic theories than is other homosexuality.

Two possibilities are relevant to behavioral genetics. First, it is possible that homosexuality associated with gender nonconformity may be more, or less, biological than other kinds of homosexuality. Perhaps, for example, "feminine" male homosexuality is genetic homosexuality, and "masculine" male homosexuality is more environmentally induced. This possibility leads to the prediction that gay men with high genetic loading (as evidenced by their having a gay identical twin or other gay brothers) should be relatively feminine compared to other gay men. We have examined gender nonconformity, for both men (Bailey & Pillard, 1991) and women (Bailey et al., 1993), and it did not appear to be an indicator of genetic loading. For example, gay men who were feminine as children were no more likely to have gay identical twins than gay men who were typically masculine as children.

The second possibility is that while different "types" of homosexuality may not differ much in their heritabilities, different genes contribute to their expression. Relevant to this possibility, we also examined the degree of developmental similarity between twins in concordant MZ pairs (Bailey & Pillard, 1991; Bailey et al., 1993). That is, if both twins reached a similar (homosexual) endpoint, were their developmental histories similar? We found very high correlations in childhood gender nonconformity for both male and female concordant pairs. If both twins were homosexual, either both tended to recall a feminine childhood or both tended to recall a masculine childhood. This is consistent with the possibility that different "types" of homosexuality are influenced by different genetic and shared environmental factors.

It is possible, of course, that variables other than gender nonconformity are relevant in dividing homosexuality into etiologic subtypes. The analyses we have mentioned here can be modified appropriately to study alternative hypotheses.

Conclusions

It should be apparent from our review that few conclusions can yet be drawn with certainty regarding genetic and environmental determinants of sexual orientation. That is to be expected. Systematic study began scarcely a decade ago. The firmest conclusion that the present evidence supports is that environment affects sexual orientation. However, the best established environmental influence is that which causes MZ twins to differ, and no existing theory offers a compelling account of why this would happen. The genetic evidence is not definitive, primarily because of methodological limitations of existing studies, but the bulk of the evidence is consistent with some genetic influence. The question whether gay and lesbian parents influence their children's sexual orientation remains quite open, but it is clear that the large majority of children of homosexual parents become heterosexual. Finally, homosexuality may be etiologically heterogeneous, though it has not been clearly established as such. We know much more than we did ten years ago, but much work remains to be done.

The most potential important research innovations are methodological. For example, ascertainment bias must be reduced far more than in existing studies. Twin studies should use twin registries, and should strive to achieve high cooperation rates. Studies of children of gay parents should attempt to ascertain families when children are very young, and should strive to minimize attrition. Finally, studies of influences on sexual orientation could benefit greatly from more precise specifications, and tests, of the hypothetical mechanisms that lead to homosexual versus heterosexual outcomes.

References

Arkes, H., Berke, M., Bradley, G., Dalin, D., Fortin, E., Garcia, J., Gellman, M., George, R., Haffenreffer, H., Hittinger, J., Hittinger, R., Jenson, R., Meilaender, G., Muller, J., Neuhaus, R. J., Novak, D., Nuechterlein, J., Stackhouse, M., Turner, P., Weigel, G., & Wilken, R. (1994, February 24). Morality and homosexuality. *Wall Street Journal*.

Bailey, J. M. (1995). Sexual orientation revolution. *Nature Genetics*, 209.

Bailey, J. M. (in press). Can behavior genetics contribute to evolutionary behavioral science? In C. Crawford & D. Krebs (Eds.), *Evolution and human behavior: Ideas, issues and applications*. Hillsdale, NJ: Erlbaum.

Bailey, J. M., & Bell, A. P. (1993). Familiality of male and female homosexuality, *Behavior Genetics, 23*, 313–322.

Bailey, J. M., & Benishay, D. S. (1993). Familial aggregation of female sexual orientation. *American Journal of Psychiatry, 150*, 272–277.

Bailey, J. M., Bobrow, D., Wolfe, M., & Mikach, S. (1995). Sexual orientation of adult sons of gay fathers. *Developmental Psychology, 31*, 124–129.

Bailey, J. M., Dunne, M. P., & Martin, N. G. (1996). Sex differences in the distribution and determinants of sexual orientation. Manuscript submitted for publication.

Bailey, J. M., Finkel, E., Blackwelder, K., & Bailey, T. (1996). Masculinity, femininity, and sexual orientation. Unpublished manuscript.

Bailey, J. M., Murphy, R. L., Fernando, S., & Trivedi, S. (1995). Siblings of a systematically ascertained cohort of HIV-infected homosexual men. Unpublished manuscript.

Bailey, J. M., Nothnagel, J., & Wolfe, M. (1995). Retrospective measured individual differences in childhood sex-typed behavior among gay men: Correspondence between self- and maternal reports. *Archives of Sexual Behavior, 24*(6), 613–622.

Bailey, J. M., & Pillard, R. C. (1991). A genetic study of male sexual orientation. *Archives of General Psychiatry, 48*, 1089–1096.

Bailey, J. M., & Pillard, R. C. (1995). Genetics of human sexual orientation. *Annual Review of Sex Research.*

Bailey, J. M., Pillard, R. C., Neale, M. C., & Agyei Y. (1993). Heritable factors influence sexual orientation in women. *Archives of General Psychiatry, 50*, 217–223.

Bailey, J. M., Willerman, L., & Parks, C. (1991). A test of the maternal stress theory of human male homosexuality. *Archives of Sexual Behavior, 20*(3), 277–293.

Bailey, J. M., & Zucker, K. J. (1995). Childhood sex-typed behavior and sexual orientation: A conceptual analysis and quantitative review. *Developmental Psychology, 31*, 43–55.

Bell, A. P., & Weinberg M. S. (1978). *Homosexualities: A study of diversity among men and women.* New York: Simon & Schuster, pp. 160–170.

Bell, A. P., Weinberg, M. S., & Hammersmith, S. K. (1981). *Sexual preference: Its development in men and women.* Bloomington, IN: Alfred C. Kinsey Institute of Sex Research.

Bieber, I., Dain, H. J., Dince, P. R., Drellich, M. G., Grand, H. G., Grundlach, R. H., Kremer, M. W., Rifkin, A. H., Wilbur, C. B., & Bieber, T. B. (1962). *Homosexuality: A psychoanalytic study.* New York: Basic Books

Billy, J. O. G., Tanfer, K., Grady, W. R., & Klepinger, D. H. (1993). The sexual behavior of men in the United States. *Family Planning Perspectives, 25*, 52–60.

Diamond, M. (1993). Homosexuality and bisexuality in different populations. *Archives of Sexual Behavior, 22*(4), 291–310.

Falconer, D. S. (1989). *Introduction to quantitative genetics, third edition.* New York: Longman.

Golombok. S., & Tasker F. (1996). Do parents influence the sexual orientation of their children? Findings from a longitudinal study of lesbian families. *Developmental Psychology, 32*, 3–11

Gottesman, I. I., & Carey, G. (1983). Extracting meaning and direction from twin data. *Psychiatric Developments, 1*, 35–50.

Hamer, D. H., Hu, S., Magnuson, V. L., Hu, N., & Pattatucci, A. M. L. (1993). A linkage between DNA markers on the X chromosome and male sexual orientation. *Science, 261*, 321–327.

Herek, G. M., & Glunt, E. K. (1993). Interpersonal contact and heterosexuals' attitudes toward gay men: Results from a national survey. *Journal of Sex Research, 30*, 239–244.

Hirschfeld, M. (1936). Homosexuality. In I. Bloch & M. Hirschfeld (Eds.), *Encyclopaedia Sexualis* (pp. 321–334). New York: Dingwall-Rock.

Johnson, A. M., Wadsworth, J., Wellings, K., Bradshaw, S., & Field, J. (1992). Sexual lifestyles and HIV risk. *Nature, 360*, 410–412.

Kallmann, F. J., (1952). Twin and sibship study of overt male homosexuality. *American Journal of Human Genetics, 4*, 136–146.

Kendler, K. S., & Eaves L. J. (1989). The estimation of probandwise concordance in twins: The effect of unequal ascertainment. *Acta Geneticae et Medicae Gemellologiae, 38,* 253–270.

King, M., & McDonald, E. (1992). Homosexuals who are twins: A study of 46 probands. *British Journal of Psychiatry, 160,* 407–409.

Krauthammer, C. (1993, May 2). Gays and the demand for legitimation. *Chicago Tribune.*

Lauman, E. O., Gagnon, J. H., Michael, R. T., & Michaels, S. (1994). *The social organization of sexuality: Sexual practices in the United States.* Chicago: University of Chicago Press.

LeVay, S. (1996). *Queer science: The use and abuse of research into homosexuality.* Cambridge. MA: MIT Press.

Meyer-Bahlburg, H. F. L. (1993). Psychobiologic research on homosexuality. *Child and Adolescent Psychiatric Clinics of North America, 2,* 489–500.

Molenaar, P. C., Boomsma, D. I., & Dolan, C. V. (1993). A third source of developmental differences. *Behavior Genetics, 23,* 519–524.

Pattatucci, A., & Hamer, D. (1995). Development and familiality of sexual orientation in females. *Behavior Genetics, 25,* 407–420.

Patterson, C. J. (1992). Children of lesbian and gay parents. *Child Development, 63,* 1025–1042.

Pattullo, E. L. (1992, December). Straight talk about gays. *Commentary,* 21–24.

Pillard, R. C. (1990). The Kinsey scale: Is it familial? In D. P. McWhirter, S. A. Sanders, & J. M. Reinisch (Eds.) *Homosexuality/heterosexuality: Concepts of sexual orientation.* New York: Oxford University Press.

Pillard, R. C., & Weinnch, J. D. (1986). Evidence of familial nature of male homosexuality. *Archives of General Psychiatry, 43,* 808–812.

Plomin, R., Defries, J. C., & McClearn, G. E. (1990). *Behavioral genetics: A primer.* 2nd. ed. New York: W. H. Freeman & Company.

Plomin, R., & Daniels, D. (1987). Why are children in the same family so different from one another? *Behavioral and Brain Sciences, 10,* 1–60.

Schmalz, J. (1993, March 5). Poll finds an even split on homosexuality's cause. *New York Times,* p. 11.

Torrey, E. F. (1994). Are identical twins really identical? *Parabola, 19,* 18–21.

Whitam, F. L., Diamond, M., & Martin, J. (1993). Homosexual orientation in twins: A report on 61 pairs and three triplet sets. *Archives of Sexual Behavior, 22,* 187–206.

2

Biopsychosocial Interactions and the Development of Sexual Orientation

Angela M. L. Pattatucci

Recent years have been marked by a resurgence of the century-old argument over whether same-gender sexual orientation is determined in part by genetic or other biological mechanisms and is a transcultural and transhistorical entity (DeCecco & Elia, 1993; Gooren, Fliers, & Courtney, 1990; Pattatucci & Hamer, 1995b). This is commonly referred to as the *nature versus nurture* debate in the development of human behavior patterns, and the central question is, to what degree do human behaviors that exhibit some outward resemblance in pattern have a common background? Proponents of the nature side of the debate often adopt a limited essentialist stance, arguing that same-gender sexual orientation is innate—that people are born lesbian or gay. The nurture side is a social constructionist position, stressing the diversity of same-gender sexual expression among individuals within particular cultural and historical contexts (Vance, 1991; Weeks, 1995). Social constructionists contend that same-gender sexual orientation, as well as most other human behaviors, cannot be definitely understood. From this perspective, some have argued that no investigation into biological contributions can be justified (Hubbard, 1990; Kitcher, 1985). Advocates of the social constructionist stance appear to argue that any genetic factor implicated in the expression of a given behavioral trait in a selected population must be demonstrated to act in an identical manner in *all* manifestations of the trait. Pattatucci and Hamer (1995) respond to this position:

> Too often in these [nature/nurture] debates perspective is lost and extreme views are adopted in their place. For example, hearing references to possible genetic contributions to a complex phenomenon such as sexual orien-

tation, people often adopt the drastic position that those of us working in the field see humans as robot-like automatons, with our behavior strictly determined by genes in a way that is inflexible and immune to social, environmental, and cultural influences. We would argue that a majority of us do not share this view and fully acknowledge that context plays an enormous role in the expression of human behavior. Our goal is not to deny the flexibility and variability of human behavior, but to identify putative genetic factors that are part of an intricate network of psychological mechanisms that facilitate our adaptability in various personal and social contexts. (p. 169)

Abramson and Pinkerton (1995) further elaborate:

> The nature/nurture debate is antithetical to scientific enquiry. Ultimately the phenomena that confront science—and especially social science—are multiply determined. To harangue for priority, be it for nature or nurture, is analogous to claims for divine right, both being self-righteous and unquestionably tautological. . . . Rarely, it seems, is an interactionist position embraced. Such a compromise, asserting that nature and nurture exert separate hut often complementary influences that collectively and interactively determine behavior, is generally perceived as weak, imprecise, or specious. (p. 1)

The question, then, is not "nature *or* nurture," but more properly "nature *and* nurture." To what degree do genetic and environmental factors interact in any given individual to manifest a particular trait of interest—in this case, same-gender sexual orientation?

The concept that genes contribute importantly to complex behavior patterns has a long history in the social and behavioral sciences. For example, the commonly held belief that certain behavioral traits run in families was first formalized into quantitative genetic theory employing family, twin, and adoption studies over a century ago by Francis Galton (Gallon, 1869, 1883, 1889). Elaborating on Galton's pioneering work, R. A. Fisher (1918) forwarded the theory that certain traits may be influenced by the additive effect of multiple genes. Thus, contemporary behavior genetic studies, as well as cultural controversies associated with them, are part of a scholarly and empirical tradition lasting over a century. The major change in recent years is that behavior genetics has moved from a strictly quantitative science, primarily concerned with deriving indirect estimates of genetic contributions to traits from twin and adoption analyses, to a quantitative *and* molecular science, through which specific genes contributing to behavioral variations in populations can be identified by the highly sophisticated techniques of DNA linkage analysis. Although molecular analyses can potentially identify similarities among siblings at the DNA level corresponding to particular behavioral traits, a more elusive question involves the identification of environmental factors that make siblings different. Interestingly, the theoretical perspectives and research methodologies of behavioral genetic research also provide helpful ways to address this question, one central to an understanding of how sexual orientation develops in the context of the family.

Behavior Genetics and the Biopsychosocial Approach

At the heart of behavior genetic research are family studies. Whether it is a twin study, an adoption study, a study of the nuclear family, or an extended family study, the goal of a behavior genetic study is the most parsimonious decomposition of variance within a population into genetic factors and environmental factors. This interaction can be represented by the simple expression below.

$$V_P = V_G + V_E$$

V_P represents the population variance for the behavioral trait under study; V_G represents the genetic contribution to that variance with the environmental component represented as V_E. *Genetic variance* is narrowly defined as molecular events at the DNA level that are vertically transmitted from parents to offspring. A *heritability* estimate is typically derived from twin studies and adoption studies as a first step toward investigating genetic variance for a behavioral trait. The rationale behind this measurement is that if expression of a given trait is in part contributed to by hereditary factors, monozygotic twins, who are identical genetically, will exhibit greater concordance or similarity for the trait than dizygotic or fraternal twins, who have only 50 percent of their segregating genes in common. The heritability estimate is obtained by doubling the difference between the monozygotic and dizygotic twin concordance rates. Adoption studies are typically used to control for an overestimation of heritability. In an adoption study, similarities of genetically *unrelated* individuals reared in the same family should be due primarily to shared environmental factors, while similarities between genetically related individuals adopted into different families should reflect heritable factors. It is important to emphasize that heritability is a descriptive statistic that estimates differences among individuals. It does not refer to group averages, nor can it be applied to specific instances. Furthermore, there are methodological problems that must be considered when using various twin and adoption study designs (Bouchard & Propping, 1993; Neale & Cardon, 1992; Plomin, DeFries, & McClearn, 1990).

Heritability estimates above 50 percent are rare for behavioral traits, suggesting that a significant amount of V_P is due to nongenetic factors. *Environmental variance* is broadly defined as all other biological, familial, social, and cultural factors that contribute to the expression of a trait—in other words, the population variance that cannot be readily explained by heredity. Therefore, *genetic variance* can also be represented by the following expression:

$$V_G = 1 - V_E$$

Environmental variance is further subdivided into two major catego-ries—shared and nonshared environmental factors (Plomin, 1994; Plomin, Chipuer, & Neiderhiser, 1994; Plomin & McClearn, 1993). E_S represents *shared* environmental factors that contribute to family resemblance. Shared environmental variance can be studied by twin and adoption studies. Twin designs estimate the extent to which concordance between identical twins is not attributable to shared heredity. Shared environmental variance is accordingly calculated as the difference between identical twin concor-dance and heritability. Adoption designs provide a more direct measure of E_S. These presume that concordance for a trait between genetically un-related children reared in the same family, known as adoptive siblings, must be a function of shared environmental factors. E_{NS} represents *non-shared* environmental factors within families that are particular to individu-als and do not contribute to family resemblance. Nonshared environmen-tal contributions are calculated by observing concordance rates for a trait among monozygotic twins reared in the same family; differences between twins are assumed to be due to E_{NS}.

Surprisingly, behavior genetic research on personality characteristics, as well as on many common physical traits, reveal that the *nonshared* fac-tors explain much of the environmental influence operating within fami-lies (Grillo & Pogue-Geile, 1991; Loehlin, 1992). This conclusion suggests that important environmental influences operating during development may function to make children in the same family no more similar than children from different families. Such a conclusion, if supported by ongoing research on behavioral development, has enormous importance in under-standing how families influence the course of individual family members' life trajectories.

The analysis of nonshared familial factors has particular importance for the understanding of how sexual orientation develops in family contexts because it questions many assumptions about the influence of the family on lesbian, gay, and bisexual people. Perhaps the most central assumption challenged by these emerging views is the notion that genetically identi-cal (or similar) individuals growing up with the same parents, siblings, and extended family members are psychologically exposed to the same family and environmental influences.

To take into account nonshared environmental factors, the population variance for any trait can be fully represented by this expression:

$$V_P = V_G + (E_S + E_{NS})$$

It is important to note that the interaction between V_G and V_E can occur in both directions. Environmental factors modulate the expression of geneti-cally determined inclinations, and genetic factors influence how individu-als interact with different aspects of their familial, social, and physical environments. Furthermore, because individuals exist within environmental contexts, the expression of a trait known or believed to have a genetic component, regardless of how strong it is alleged to be, must always have an environmental component. Human height, for example, is strongly determined by heritable factors, but nutrition, exercise, and other environmental components are also relevant. However, some personal characteristics, such as last names and religious affiliations, run in families without any genetic contribution. As Plomin (1994) notes:

> Now that genetic influence on behavioural development is becoming widely accepted, it may be useful to emphasize the usefulness—indeed, the necessity—of genetic research for the purpose of identifying environmental influences in development. One simple point along these lines is that genetic research provides the best available evidence for the importance of nongenetic influences in development. A second point is that genetic research suggests where to look for environmental influence. (p. 818)

The most powerful research design for understanding the relative contributions of hereditary and environmental factors in the development of behavioral traits such as same-gender sexual orientation is to study them using complex family research methodologies. Unfortunately, this has historically not been the case; indeed, family-oriented research on lesbian, gay, and bisexual identities is in its infancy. Many researchers studying same-gender sexual orientation have ignored the family entirely; and in those instances where the family has been the focus of analysis, heritable contributions have not been considered. In the remainder of this chapter, I will focus on my research on same-gender sexual orientation in women. This work, done in collaboration with Dean Hamer and others, will be described as an example of the heuristic power of behavior genetics research using family studies to help understand the development of sexual orientation.

Behavior Genetic Studies of Sexual Orientation

Because family studies are such valuable methods for investigating the development and expression of human sexual orientation, it is surprising that more have not been initiated. Over half a century has passed since Magnus Hirschfeld commented on the apparent familiarity of both female and male same-gender sexual orientation (Hirschfeld, 1936). However, systematic behavioral genetic studies designed to examine the sources of this presumed familial aggregation have only recently been attempted. In addition, genetic studies of sexual orientation in women have been particularly sparse. Two nuclear family studies have shown that lesbians have more lesbian sisters than do heterosexual women, supporting the familial aggregation hypothesis for female sexual orientation (Bailey & Benishay, 1993; Pillard, 1990).

The four published twin studies, which address how much genetic influences contribute to familial aggregation of same-gender sexual orientation in women, have yielded contradictory results. Bailey and his colleagues, who analyzed the largest and most systematically collected series of women, estimated heritability to be approximately 0.5 (range .27 to .76) based upon concordance rates of 48 percent for monozygotic twins compared to 16 percent for dizygotic twins raised together (Bailey, Pillard, Neale, & Agyei 1993). Similarly, Whitam, Diamond, and Martin (1993) reported a 75 percent concordance rate for four pairs of female monozygotic twins. In contrast, Eckert, Bouchard, Bohlen, and Heston (1986) described four sets of female identical twins raised apart who were discordant for sexual orientation. King and McDonald (1992) also found low twin concordance rates for same-gender sexual orientation in their combined study of female and male co-twins, but did not present their results by gender. The single published adoption study of female sexual orientation showed that the rate of same-gender sexual orientation was lower in adoptive than biological sisters of lesbian probands (Bailey et al., 1993). Although the results in this study were interpreted in support of genetic influence, the effects of shared environmental factors could not be ruled out because heterosexual probands were not included.

This highlights a crucial difficulty with behavior genetic research on same-gender sexual orientation—namely, the uncertainty about the population incidence of nonheterosexuality in women. Current estimates of same-gender sexual orientation in women range from 0.6 percent to over 10 percent, depending on the criteria and sampling strategy employed (Bailey & Benishay, 1993; Johnson, Wadsworth, Wellings, & Field, 1994; Kinsey, Pomeroy, Martin, & Gebhart, 1953). The variability of current estimates suggests that it is important to establish baseline rates of same-gender sexual orientation in each new empirical investigation, even though this is a difficult task.

A clear prediction for a genetically influenced trait is that it should appear at elevated rates in second-degree and in third-degree lineages as well as within the nuclear family. Behavior genetic terminology refers to *1st degree relatives* as those related to the proband (i.e., index subject in a study) by a factor of 0.5. These relatives randomly share 50 percent of their segregating genes with the proband and include full siblings, children, and biological parents. The term *2nd degree relatives* refers to family members related to the proband by a factor of 0.25, randomly sharing 25 percent of their segregating genes with the proband. These family members include half siblings, nieces and nephews, aunts and uncles who are full siblings of parents, and grandparents. The term *3rd degree relatives* signifies relatedness to the proband by a factor of 0.125. These relatives randomly share 12.5 percent of their segregating genes with the proband and include first cousins, aunts and uncles who are half siblings of parents, great aunts and uncles who are full siblings of grandparents, and great nieces and nephews.

In my work with Dean Hamer, we found that gay males had higher than baseline rates of gay maternal uncles and male cousins through maternal aunts but not of gay paternal relatives (Hamer, Hu, Magnuson, Hu, & Pattatucci, 1993). This result suggested sex-linked transmission in selected families and led to the identification of a linkage between DNA markers on a discrete region of the X-chromosome known as Xq28 and male sexual orientation. Similar extended family and molecular studies of female sexual orientation had not yet been reported and were therefore one of the goals of the investigation (Pattatucci & Hamer, 1995) described below.

Methodological Challenges in Sexual Orientation Research

Ascertainment is a particular problem when studying marginalized and secretive populations such as lesbians, gay men, or bisexual women and men, making it virtually impossible to obtain a truly random sample (Gonsiorek, 1982; Morin, 1977). Rarely addressed, however, is the problem of ascertainment of heterosexual samples. Owing to the social stigma associated with same-gender sexual orientation and bisexuality, one can be reasonably certain that any population of heterosexually identified people will contain individuals who have some degree of same-gender sexual orientation. Furthermore, an asymmetry more than likely exists regarding the amount of time and concentration spent contemplating sexuality and sexual orientation issues between heterosexual people and lesbians, gay men, and bisexual people. For instance, whereas it can be nearly guaranteed that lesbian and bisexual women participating in a study will have devoted considerable time to thinking about their sexual orientation and its expression, this cannot be assumed of a sample of heterosexual women. Although no methodology can completely address this dilemma, my colleagues and I employed a strategy designed to recruit a heterosexual sample through women's studies programs of academic institutions, and a lesbian/bisexual sample through announcements circulated to homophile organizations. Women's studies programs were targeted specifically because the course work regularly confronts gender and sexuality issues. Our hope was that this pool of women would be more comfortable and honest in discussing sexuality-related issues than a general population sample.

A major challenge for any behavioral investigation is to develop a precise definition of the trait under study. This is relatively easy for a trait such as height, but is rather a difficult challenge for a multidimensional characteristic such as sexual orientation. Operational definitions set parameters and thus constrain possibilities. What do the terms *lesbian, bisexual,* and *heterosexual* mean? When two women identify themselves as lesbians, are they referring to the same thing? What criteria do we use for establishing a definition of sexual orientation? Most important, who is excluded by our definition and what important information might be missing?

We have used a study design that assesses sexual orientation using the seven-point Kinsey scale, which ranges from 0 for exclusive opposite-gender orientation to 6 for exclusive same-gender orientation (Kinsey, Pomeroy, & Martin, 1948; Kinsey et al., 1953). Probands rate themselves on four individually administered Kinsey scales assessing self-identification, romantic or sexual attraction, romantic or sexual fantasy, and sexual behavior. We have consistently found these four facets of sexual orientation to be highly intercorrelated, forming a single, statistically cohesive factor. The strong correlations between the different components justify averaging them to yield a composite rating. For convenience, we refer to probands with Kinsey composite ratings of 0 and 1 as *heterosexual*, those with ratings of 2–4 as *bisexual*, and those with ratings of 5 and 6 as *lesbian*.

Bisexuality: A Stable Sexual Orientation in Women?

Using the above criteria, we found that nearly one-third of the 358 women in our study fell into the bisexual range (Pattatucci & Hamer, 1995a). Because our recruiting strategy was highly selective, this pattern cannot be extrapolated to the distribution of sexual orientations among women in the population at large. Nevertheless, this finding is corroborated by other studies, which have similarly reported high rates of bisexuality in female populations (Bailey & Bell, 1993; Bailey & Benishay, 1993; Bailey et al., 1993; Pillard, 1990; Rust, 1992). This variability among women in sexual orientation is distinctly different from results found for men, most of whom rate themselves as either homosexual or heterosexual (e.g., Bailey & Pillard, 1991; Hamer et al., 1993; Whitam, Diamond, & Martin, 1993).

Given the diversity of sexual orientation in the studies of women, we then investigated the stability of their self-identifications over time. If, for example, self-reported sexual orientation in women shows considerable fluctuation over time, then empirical results suggesting that same-gender sexual orientation runs in families would have to be qualified because the results could change if the population was sampled at a different time. Rust (1993) studied 346 lesbians, and reported that 40 percent had self-identified as bisexual in the past, and that one-third of these women had changed their self-identifications between lesbian and bisexual identities several times. The remaining women were in two categories. One group contained women who had self-identified as bisexual prior to, or within the same year as identifying lesbian, never to identify as bisexual again (transitional). The second group were women who had identified as bisexual after coming out as lesbian. The latter group were seen as having bisexual identities that were temporary but not transitional. These retrospective data suggest that there may be considerable fluidity between lesbian and bisexual identities at least as far as self-identification is concerned, but that this rarely extends to the adoption of heterosexual identity.

We directly investigated the self-reported stability for our sample of 358 women by recontacting them twelve to eighteen months after their initial interviews and administering a similar assessment protocol to the one previously described. The results suggest that bisexuality is not necessarily transitory for a large percentage of women, representing a stable sexual orientation. Most of the bisexual women in our recontacted sample did not change in their composite sexual orientation status from one year to the next. Although reassessment within this time frame does not preclude change that might be observed over a longer time period, given the size of our sample and its age range (18 to 68 years), more evidence of bisexuality as transitional to either lesbian or heterosexual orientation would have been evident if it were the case. Clearly, more extensive longitudinal data will needed to be to accurately assess the stability of sexual orientation over time.

An Extended Family Study of Sexual Orientation in Women

A fundamental tenet of behavior genetics is that if a trait is genetically influenced, then it should aggregate in families. Established familiality is a prerequisite for more advanced genetic research. If no familial aggregation of female sexual orientation were observed in any data, then molecular studies aimed at identifying specific genetic loci would be unwarranted.

The clearest evidence linking genetics and sexual orientation in women comes from studies of patients with congenital adrenal hyperplasia (CAH), a group of enzymatic deficiencies in cortisol biosynthesis transmitted by autosomal recessive genes. The most common form, accounting for 95 percent of the cases, is associated with a gene on human chromosome 6 (Higashi, Yoshioka, Yamane, Gotoh, & Fujii-Kuriyama, 1986; Miller, 1988). Insufficient production of cortisol results in the increased accumulation of androgens, causing a masculinization of the genitalia to varying degrees. Influences on the developing brain are also believed to occur, but are not well understood. A "masculine" pattern of gender-role behavior has been reported for CAH patients in several studies (Ehrhardt, 1979; Ehrhardt & Meyer-Bahlburg, 1981; Money & Ehrhardt, 1972; Slijper, 1984). Furthermore, recent studies on adult psychosexual development and sexual orientation indicate that females with CAH report significantly higher rates of same-gender sexual attraction, behavior, and fantasy and lower rates of heterosexual activity compared to their nonaffected sisters (Dittmann, Kappes, & Kappes, 1992; Dittmann, Kappes, Kappes, Borger, Meyer-Bahlburg, Stegner, Willig, & Wallis, 1990; Dittmann, Kappes, Kappes, Borger, Willig, & Wallis, 1990). These results suggest that excess prenatal androgens predispose some women to the development of a same-gender sexual orientation. However, because CAH is a relatively rare condition, and a majority of patients develop a heterosexual orientation, CAH plays a minor role in the overall variability of women's sexual orientation within the general population. Other predisposing genetic and psychosocial factors pertinent to a larger percentage of lesbians and bisexual women have yet to be identified.

As a first step in addressing the possible role of inheritance of sexual orientation in our nonclinical population of women, we conducted a pedigree study. A pedigree study consists of constructing a family tree using the proband (index subject) as the central figure. Information about the sexual orientation of each family member is then obtained from the proband, and is typically corroborated by other family members to yield a comprehensive history for each family. Our goal was to determine if female sexual orientation runs in families, and if so to what degree and in what patterns. The results of this analysis, summarized in Table 2.1, provide clear evidence for a familial component to women's sexual orientation. We observed elevated rates of non–heterosexual orientation in four classes of lesbians' relatives: sisters, daughters, nieces, and cousins through a paternal uncle. Nonheterosexual orientation was defined by composite Kinsey scores from 2 to 6, and the family members of these lesbian women were compared to family members of heterosexual women. Relatives were counted as lesbian or bisexual only if they had shared their sexual orientation privately with the proband, or if they had told another family member who subsequently relayed the information to the proband, or if they had divulged their sexual orientation to others in the family such that it was commonly known. (Using these criteria, we have consistently found nonheterosexual baseline rates of 1.2 percent for women and 2.1 percent for men; see Hamer et al., 1993; Pattatucci & Hamer, 1995a).

Table 2.1   Rates of Nonheterosexual Relatives Among Nonheterosexual (Kinsey 2–6) Probands[a]

RELATIVE	STANDARD APPROACH[b]		COMPLEMENTARY APPROACH[c]	
	NONHET / TOTAL	% NONHET	NONHET / TOTAL	%NONHET
Sisters	26/258	10.1 ($p \le .001$)[d]	22/179	12.3 ($p \le .001$)
Daughters	6/19	31.6 ($p \le .001$)	1/7	14.3 (N.S.)
Nieces	3/48	6.3 ($p \le .05$)	1/13	7.7 (N.S.)
3° Pat. ♀'s[e]	13/186	7.9 ($p \le .001$)	11/130	8.5 ($p \le .001$)
Brothers	20/295	6.8 ($p \le .001$)	12/205	5.9 ($p \le .01$)

[a]Data derived from Pattatucci & Hamer, *Behavior Genetics, 25,* 407–420.

[b]Uses composite Kinsey rating from four individually administered scales assessing romantic/sexual attraction, romantic/sexual fantasy, behavior, and self-identification.

[c]Uses composite Kinsey rating and establishes a sample that is internally consistent for direction and age of onset of their first romantic attraction.

[d]Significance assessed by a one-tailed Fisher's exact test based upon internally established baseline rates of 1.2 percent for females and 2.1 percent for males (N.S. = not statistically significant).

[e]Specifically, female cousins of paternal uncles.

Several investigations have addressed the question of whether the familial transmission patterns of female and male same-gender sexual orientation are etiologically independent or overlapping, but the results to date are ambiguous. The prediction of the model hypothesizing independent patterns is that female and male same-gender sexual orientation will run in different families—that is, that lesbians will have an excess of lesbian sisters but not of gay brothers, and gay men will show the opposite pattern. Pillard (1990) and Bailey and Benishay (1993) found that lesbians have more lesbian sisters than gay brothers, an especially noteworthy finding since the population incidence of same-gender sexual orientation is approximately half as high in women as in men; however, the differences between sisters and brothers were not statistically significant in the samples studied. Similarly, a number of investigators have found that gay men have more gay brothers than lesbian sisters, but again the differences have not been statistically significant (Bailey & Pillard, 1991; Hamer et al., 1993; Pillard & Weinrich, 1986; Whitam et al., 1993). By contrast, Bailey and Bell (1993) reanalyzed data collected by the Kinsey Institute in the 1970s (Bell, Weinberg, & Hammersmith, 1981a,b), and found that both gay men and lesbians had more gay brothers than lesbian sisters.

The prediction of the overlapping model is that elevated rates of same-gender sexual orientation will be found in the opposite-sex siblings of both lesbians and gay men. Significant evidence supporting this prediction has been found (Bailey & Bell, 1993; Bailey & Benishay, 1993; Hamer et al., 1993; Pillard, 1990). Among the male relatives of our probands, increased frequencies of same-gender sexual orientation were observed only in brothers. The rates were significantly above the population incidence, but were lower than in sisters. In our collateral study of gay male probands, the rate of same-gender sexual orientation in sisters was above the internally established baseline level, but lower than in brothers (Hamer et al., 1993). The emerging picture is that factors that underlie the familial aggregation of same-gender sexual orientation are different for women and men, but overlap. The precise set of factors remains unknown.

Given a hypothesis that same-gender sexual orientation among women has genetic and sex-specific components, the observation of elevated rates of same-gender orientation among first-, second-, and third-degree relatives of lesbian and bisexual probands would be suggestive of a genetic component, but not conclusive. The most conclusive evidence would be the discovery and characterization of a gene, which in one form is shown to be associated with a same-gender sexual orientation and in another form is associated with heterosexual orientation. To address the sex-specific provision of the hypothesis, one should observe elevated rates of lesbian compared to gay male relatives of lesbian probands. It would also be predicted that the rate of nonheterosexuality in daughters *should not* exceed the rate in sisters and the rate in sisters *should* exceed the rate in brothers. Because siblings and children are both first-degree relatives, and thus randomly share 50 percent of their segregating genes with the proband, it is expected that sisters and daughters will show similar rates of same-gender sexual orientation. On the other hand, the sex-specific component should cause the rate in sisters to be elevated relative to brothers *despite* their being first-degree relatives.

Contrary to the expectations of a sex-specific genetic component hypothesis for same-gender sexual orientation in women, the observed rate of nonheterosexuality for daughters (shown in Table 2.1) was significantly higher than the rate for sisters ($p < .05$, Fisher exact test). Other studies on the daughters of lesbians have given variable and generally lower rates of same-gender sexual orientation, perhaps owing to differences in sampling and assessment methods (Golombok, Spencer, & Rutter, 1983; Gottman, 1990; Green, 1978; Huggins, 1989; Javaid, 1993; Patterson, 1992, 1995). It should be noted that the sample of informative (≥ 18 years of age) daughters of lesbian probands was less than 7 percent of the size of informative sisters and may in part account for the observed substantial difference in rates. Although the actual number of daughters of lesbian probands in our study was much higher than listed, a majority were too young to be informative for a study on sexual orientation. A larger and more systematic study of the offspring of lesbians, including both their biological and their adoptive children, would be useful. Considering the sex-specific provision of the hypothesis, the absolute rates of nonheterosexuality in sisters and brothers did not differ significantly, although the relative rates (compared to baseline) were higher for sisters compared to brothers ($p < .05$, likelihood ratios test). Thus, neither the daughter vs. sister, nor the sister vs. brother prediction was confirmed in an unambiguous way.

Exploring Environmental Factors

A pattern of familiality that fails to follow expectations precisely does not rule out the existence of genetic components of women's sexual orientation, nor does it imply that genetic components cannot be found. Part of the difficulty may be attributable to our operational definition of same-gender sexual orientation. It is possible that the initial defining criteria treated self-identification, attraction, fantasy, or behavior too generally. For example, Ponse (1978), and later Vance and Green (1984), identified two distinct groups of self-defined lesbians who differ in the ages of their first same-sex experiences. One group, termed *primary lesbians* (Group 1) by Ponse, have engaged in sexual relations with females prior to age 17, are sexually active at an earlier age, view themselves as more stereotypically masculine, and identify as exclusively lesbian despite many having histories of heterosexual experiences. In contrast, *elective lesbians* (Group 2) begin sexual relations with females after age 20, characteristically have been emotionally and sexually involved with men prior to identifying as lesbian, and are more likely to be bisexual in activity. Vance and Green (1984) further elaborate the differences:

> [Group 1 lesbians] also differed developmentally from the other subjects in an array of sexual behaviors and experiences. As a group, they were more likely to have examined their sexual parts during an earlier stage of development, learned of masturbation from their friends, while discovering homosexuality on their own, engaged in sexual intercourse with the opposite sex prior to adolescence, and been discovered by their parents while engaged in either homosexual or heterosexual activity. These differences suggest a pattern of precociousness in the development of sexual behavior for Group 1 women as compared to that experienced by other subjects in this study. It is interesting to compare this finding to documentable differences in the sexual development of males and females: generally, males are more precocious in their sexual activity than are females. (p. 303)

Dancey (1990) investigated differences in menstrual hormonal levels and sex role measures between Group 1 and Group 2 lesbians, but found no significant differences. However, current thought is that the salient hormonal influences on gendered behavior and sexual orientation, if they exist at all, occur prenatally (Meyer-Bahlburg, 1995), and that past sex role research on lesbians may be based upon erroneous assumptions (Faderman, 1991).

The developmental differences reported by Ponse, as well as Vance and Green, for Group 1 and Group 2 lesbians raise some interesting questions. Are self-reports of *current* self-identification, attraction, fantasy, and behavior sufficient to define a population of nonheterosexual women for a study investigating possible genetic contributions to sexual orientation? If a genetic contribution to sexual orientation exists, which women in the nonheterosexual sample have the greatest potential to provide the most information? It is reasonable to predict that the removal of outliers by more specifically assessing one or more of the core variables could potentially result in a sample exhibiting stronger evidence for a genetic contribution to nonheterosexual orientation. Based upon the analyses of Ponse, as well as Vance and Green, one might expect that Group 2 lesbians would be the best candidates for exclusion owing to their active heterosexual histories and late onset of their same-sex behavior. However, Vance and Green (1984) note that a substantial number of Group 1 lesbians also report histories including heterosexual experiences. Subdividing a nonheterosexual sample using Group 1 and 2 criteria may not always be justified. Furthermore, no information is available regarding how these lesbian subgroups compare to a heterosexual sample of women in an internally controlled study. It is also possible that the application of defining criteria could produce an effect opposite of that desired, resulting in the selective elimination of the *most informative* individuals.

In our work, we have focused on the onset of romantic and sexual attraction rather than behavior for our developmental analyses, for two main reasons. First, the mean age of initial attraction to females showed an even greater difference than the onset of same-sex behavior in Vance and Green's (1984) study (9.57 ± 3.59 years for Group 1, versus 18.14 ± 7.46 years for Group 2). Second, experiencing a romantic or sexual attraction is an individual event, whereas sexual behavior (with the exception of masturbation) is a shared experience. Whether a woman engages in a sexual experience with another woman, an activity strongly discouraged in most social environments, is strongly susceptible to outside influences and social expectations. Conversely, a romantic or sexual attraction to a female can be privately experienced and is less likely to be influenced by external factors. Attraction, therefore, may represent a more accurate developmental milestone for investigating intragroup differences among lesbians.

In our studies, women are first asked if they have ever experienced a school-age crush, puppy love, infatuation, or a more serious romantic or sexual attraction directed toward a female; the collateral question regarding romantic and sexual attraction to males is then asked. The two questions yielded reciprocal responses. Fully two-thirds of the heterosexual women reported at least one attraction to another woman, and slightly less than half of the lesbians acknowledged attractions to men. These data are consistent with those of Vance and Green (1984), who reported active heterosexual histories even among their Group 1 sample. However, the findings are a significant departure from similar data for men, where very few heterosexual men reported same-sex attractions and equally few gay men reported opposite-sex attractions (Hamer et al., 1993). As one would expect, however, we found that significantly more bisexual and heterosexual women reported experiencing opposite-gender attractions than did lesbians, and significantly more lesbians and bisexual women reported same-gender attractions than did heterosexual women.

Because the above data suggest considerable overlap, it was of interest to determine differences in the timing for these attractions. Therefore, all women acknowledging same-gender attraction were asked the age at which age they first experienced attraction to a female and/or a male. This more specific question revealed statistically significant differences among the three groups. Same-sex attraction for women was recalled as having occurred first in lesbians (mean age 10.6 years), later in bisexual women (mean age 12.6 years), and last in heterosexual women (mean age 17.8 years). These results indicate that although women in all three groups have recognized same-sex attractions, there are significant differences in the developmental timing of these feelings. With respect to the onset of opposite-sex attraction, this occurred first in bisexual women (mean age 9.5 years), later in heterosexual women (mean age 10.6 years), and last in lesbians (mean age 12.8 years). Thus, these results indicate that although women in all three groups have felt opposite-sex attractions, there were significant differences in the timing of their emergence. Interestingly, mean ages for the onset of attraction to *a particular person* were identical for heterosexual women and lesbians (10.6 years), and slightly earlier for bisexual women (9.5 years). Our analysis therefore suggests that with respect to romantic or sexual attraction, lesbian and heterosexual women develop along parallel paths, but with the object of attraction reversed.

Using Environmental Data to Inform Genetic Interpretations

Given these parallel yet essentially reciprocal paths regarding romantic and sexual attraction, we sought to determine if these environmental data could be used to inform our pedigree analysis. We investigated the degree to which the rates of lesbian, gay, and bisexual relatives in the family pedigrees would be subject to change if a more stringent criterion for nonheterosexuality were applied. Accordingly, the data were reanalyzed to identify lesbians and bisexual women with attraction profiles consistent with the patterns exhibited by our heterosexual sample. These women reported a late onset for their attraction to females, as well as experiencing attractions to males prior to their attractions to women. Probands were eliminated from the nonheterosexual sample if they met either of these two additional criteria, resulting in a group of nonheterosexual women internally consistent with respect to the direction and age of onset of their first attraction.

The application of the developmental data to the genetic analysis had a noticeable effect on the distribution of nonheterosexual relatives in the selected pedigrees, as can be seen by comparing the rates obtained using the standard vs. the complementary approach summarized in Table 2.1. First, the rate for nonheterosexual daughters of probands in this subsample is reduced approximately twofold. A Fisher test for significance reveals that the resulting rate is only marginally significant with respect to the established baseline ($p = .09$). Furthermore, a comparison of the rate in daughters to the rate in sisters indicates no significant difference. An additional effect that the application of the developmental data had on the sample is that it resulted in a significant ($p < .01$, likelihood ratios test) increase in the ratio of nonheterosexual sisters to nonheterosexual brothers. Finally, the subsample also displayed elevations in the rates of sisters and in female cousins of paternal uncles compared to the initial analysis. Thus, by employing a complementary approach that used information obtained from the developmental analysis to inform the pedigree study, we were able to identify a subset of probands in our nonheterosexual sample that exhibit patterns consistent with the notion that sex-specific genetic factors contribute to their sexual orientation.

The above analysis illustrates the power of the complementary approach. Had we concentrated solely on potential genetic sources of variation, either ignoring the environmental sources or only treating them as confounding variables which must be controlled, we would have arrived at the erroneous conclusion that genetic contributions to sexual orientation in women are either non-existent or are so slight that they are overpowered by environmental sources of variability. However, use of the complementary approach enabled the identification of a group of lesbian and bisexual women for whom detectable genetic sources of population variability may exist. This subset includes women who display an early onset of same-sex patterns of attraction, along with either a late onset or absent pattern of attraction to males. These women are similar to Group 1 lesbians described by Vance and Green (1984), suggesting that a strong genetic contribution to same-gender sexual orientation may emerge only for women with particular developmental and psychosexual histories.

Directions for Further Research: Nonshared Environmental Influences on Sexual Orientation

Although investigating genetic sources of variation in sexual orientation is a crucial endeavor for understanding the role of families, perhaps the most exciting frontier for family research lies in studying nonshared environmental sources of variation. Specifically, why are children raised in the same family so different? Why does one child evolve into a lesbian adult while her sibling becomes heterosexual? To approach this question, a methodology that focuses on studying families with more than one child is necessary. Fortunately, behavior genetic techniques are useful even though environmental sources of variation are under study. For example, a nongenetic factor, such as willingness to visit a physician or dentist, can be treated as if it were a genetic trait and investigated employing behavior genetic methodologies. Valuable information about the transmission of this attitude from parent to specific children, as well as concordance rates among siblings, can be obtained. Such an approach has considerable promise in understanding the changing impact of families on different children.

Plomin (1994) has outlined three steps for research on nonshared environmental contributions to identify factors that might account for differences among children in their developmental outcomes. The first is to identify environmental factors specific to each child in a family and subsequently evaluate the degree to which these child-specific measures of the environment are common among siblings in a general population of families. The second step is to assess the magnitude to which particular nonshared environmental components influence behavioral outcomes in individuals. That is, do nonshared environmental factors have any predictive power? Finally, Plomin characterizes the third step as a disentanglement of cause and effect. The direction of effects must be investigated for associations discovered between nonshared environmental factors and behavioral outcomes. For example, is differential parenting the cause or effect of behavioral variations among siblings? Plomin (1994) suggests that longitudinal studies and behavior genetic methodologies can be useful in studying the effects of nonshared environments. Studies of monozygotic twins, who are genetically identical, can be particularly useful. As mentioned previously, nonshared environmental factors account for dissimilarities between monozygotic twins. Therefore, nonshared environmental associations can be directly measured by correlating differences in experience among monozygotic twins with differences in behavioral outcome. It could be very useful to apply this strategy to monozygotic twins discordant for sexual orientation. In this way, we might learn more about why one identical twin is a lesbian and her sister is a heterosexual woman.

On a more fundamental level, it is problematic that the research community has in my opinion never adequately addressed the issue that contemporary investigations into same-gender sexual orientation are typically end-point research. By this, I mean that there is a strong emphasis on studying the lives of individuals after they come out as lesbian, gay, or bisexual, while comparatively little attention is given to how individuals reach that end point. To illustrate, consider the self-descriptions of authors Celia Kitzinger and Sue Wilkinson (1993) presented below:

> [W]e bring, despite our similarities (we are both white, middle class, thirty-something, and British) entirely different experiences of heterosexuality. One of us (CK) has always been lesbian, came out aged 16, has never had or wanted to have sex with men, and developed a feminist awareness through the experience of living as a lesbian under heteropatriarchy. The other (SW) was happily and exuberantly heterosexual, married for 15 years, becoming lesbian only relatively recently through the impact of feminism on her emotional and sexual experience. (pp. 3–4)

Although both women have reached the same lesbian end point, one has to question the validity of homogenizing them into a single research category that treats lesbian identity as a constant and seeks to measure other variables around it. Yet the literature is overflowing with research articles containing the generic phrase: "X number of *self-identified lesbians* were studied."

A primary reason for the pervasiveness of this practice is convenience. It is often difficult to obtain a reasonable-sized sample of lesbians in the first place. Further stratifying the sample can cause major methodological problems in the analysis of data, making such a practice *inconvenient* for researchers. An additional salient factor is that over the years it has become "politically correct" to view sexual orientation as a concrete identity. An unfortunate consequence is that assumptions held for other concrete identities are inappropriately applied to sexual orientation, the most notable being an absence of precipitating events leading to, or serving to solidify, the identity, making the identity itself the *only* point of relevance. For example, one would not think of asking Celia Kitzinger and Sue Wilkinson how they *became* white, female, and British. They just *are* these identities. However, unlike other concrete identities such as race, sex, and nationality, which are commonly bestowed at birth, sexual orientation develops over time. Although it is true that in a majority of instances there is a general presumption of heterosexuality at birth, the degree to which one matches this presumption is a process of self-discovery and, as Sue Wilkinson's description indicates, also a function of time. This is true regardless of whether one views sexual orientation as innate or as a social construction of reality. It is regrettable that more *constructive* attention has not been paid to investigating this self-discovery process for all sexual orientations. How does an initial preteen crush evolve into a concrete sexual orientation? How do social expectations of heterosexuality impact the trajectories of different individuals? These and other similar questions are waiting to be investigated through the study of nonshared environmental influences on development and other family research methodologies.

The identification and characterization of nonshared environmental sources of variability will inform our understanding of genetic contributions to the development of sexual orientation, just as behavior genetic research has provided strong evidence for the importance of environmental contributions to other complex behavioral characteristics. This approach avoids an emphasis on "nature or nurture," but instead correctly emphasizes their complex interaction in producing behavioral outcomes. In addition, whereas traditional disciplinary boundaries once kept researchers investigating sexual orientation apart, the current Zeitgeist emphasizes interdisciplinary studies. As such work continues, a richer appreciation of how families influence the sexual orientations of their members will emerge, and increasingly complex developmental models can be tested.

References

Abramson, P. R., & Pinkerton, S. D. (1995). Nature, nurture and in-between. In P. R. Abramson & S. D. Pinkerton (Eds.), *Sexual nature/sexual culture* (pp. 1–13). Chicago: University of Chicago Press.

Bailey, J. M., & Bell, A. P. (1993). Familiality of female and male homosexuality. *Behavior Genetics, 23*, 313–322.

Bailey, J. M., & Benishay, B. A. (1993). Familial aggregation of female sexual orientation. *American Journal of Psychiatry, 150*, 272–277.

Bailey, J. M., & Pillard, R. C. (1991). A genetic study of male sexual orientation. *Archives of General Psychiatry, 48*, 1089–1096.

Bailey, J. M., Pillard, R. C., Neale, M. C., & Agyei, Y. (1993). Heritable factors influence sexual orientation in women. *Archives of* General *Psychiatry, 50*, 217–223.

Bell, A. P., Weinberg, M. S., & Hammersmith, S. K. (1981a). *Sexual preference: Its development* in *men and women*. Bloomington: Indiana University Press.

Bell, A. P., Weinberg, M. S., & Hammersmith, S. K. (1981b). *Sexual preference: Statistical appendix*. Bloomington: Indiana University Press.

Bouchard, T. J., & Propping, P. (1993). *Twins as a tool of behavioral genetics*. Chichester: John Wiley.

Dancey, C. P. (1990). Sexual orientation in women: An investigation of hormonal and personality variables. *Biological Psychology, 30,* 251–264.

DeCecco, J. P., & Elia, J. P. (1993). A critique and synthesis of biological essentialism and social constructionist views of sexuality and gender. *Journal of Homosexuality, 24,* 1–26.

Dittmann, R. W., Kappes, M. E., & Kappes, M. H. (1992). Sexual behavior in adolescent and adult females with congenital adrenal hyperplasia. *Psychoneuroendocrinology, 17,* 153–170.

Dittmann, R. W., Kappes, M. H., Kappes, M. E.. Börger, D., Meyer-Bahlburg, H. F. L., Stegner, H., Willig, R. H., & Wallis, H. (1990). Congenital adrenal hyperplasia II: Gender-related behavior and attitudes in female salt-wasting and simple-virilizing patients. *Psychoneuroendocrinology, 15,* 421–434.

Dittmann, R. W., Kappes, M. H.. Kappes, M. E., Börger, D., Stegner, H., Willig, R. H., & Wallis, H. (1990). Congenital adrenal hyperplasia I: Gender-related behavior and attitudes in female patients and sisters. *Psychoneuroendocrinology, 15,* 401–420.

Eckert, E. D., Bouchard, T. J., Bohlen, J., & Heston. L. L. (1986). Homosexuality in monozygotic twins reared apart. *British Journal of Psychiatry, 148,* 421–425.

Ehrhardt, A. A. (1979). Psychosocial adjustment in adolescence in patients with congenital abnormalities of their sex organs. In H. L. Vallet & I. H. Porter (Eds.), *Genetic mechanisms of sexual development* (pp. 473–484). New York: Academic Press.

Ehrhardt, A. A., & Meyer-Bahlburg, H. F. L. (1981). Effects of prenatal sex hormones on gender-related behavior. *Science, 211,* 1312–1318.

Faderman, L. (1991). *Odd girls and twilight lovers: A history of lesbian life in twentieth-century America.* New York: Columbia University Press.

Fisher, R. A. (1918). The correlation between relatives on the supposition of Mendelian inheritance. *Transactions of the Royal Society of Edinburgh, 52,* 399–433.

Galton, F. (1869). *Hereditary genius.* London: Macmillan.

Galton, F. (1883). *Inquiries into human faculty and its development.* London: Macmillan.

Galton, F. (1889). *Natural inheritance.* London: Macmillan.

Golombok, S., Spencer, A., & Rutter. M. (1983). Children in lesbian and single-parent households: Psychosexual and psychiatric appraisal. *Journal of Child Psychology and Psychiatry, 24,* 551–572.

Gonsiorek, J. C. (1982). Introduction. In W. Paul, J. D. Weinrich, J. C. Gonsiorek, & M. E. Hotvedt (Eds.), *Homosexuality: Social, psychological, and biological issues* (pp. 57–70). Beverly Hills, CA: Sage Publications.

Gooren, L., Fliers, E., & Courtney, K. (1990). Biological determinants of sexual orientation. *Annual Review of Sex Research, 1,* 175–196.

Gottman, J. S. (1990). Children of gay and lesbian parents. *Journal of Homosexuality, 21,* 177–196.

Green, R. (1978). Sexual identity of thirty-seven children raised by homosexual or transsexual parents. *American Journal of Psychiatry, 135,* 692–697.

Grillo, C. M., & Pogue-Geile, M. F. (1991). The nature of environmental influences on weight and obesity: A behavior genetic analysis. *Psychological Bulletin, 110,* 520–537.

Hamer, D. H., Hu, S., Magnuson, V. L., Hu, N., & Pattatucci, A. M. L. (1993). A linkage between DNA markers on the X chromosome and male sexual orientation. *Science, 261,* 321–327.

Higashi, Y., Yoshioka, H., Yamane, M., Gotoh, O., & Fujii-Kuriyama, Y. (1986). Complete nucleotide sequence of two steroid 21-hydroxylase genes tandemly arranged in human chromosome: a pseudogene and a genuine gene. *Proceedings of the National Academy of Sciences, USA, 83,* 2841–2845.

Hirschfeld, M. (1936). Homosexuality. In I. Bloch & M. Hirschfeld (Eds.), *Encyclopaedia sexualis* (pp. 321–324). New York: Dingwall-Rock.

Hubbard, R. (1990). The political nature of human nature. In D. L. Rhode (Ed.), *Theoretical pespectives on sexual difference* (pp. 63–73). New Haven: Yale University Press.

Huggins, S. (1989). A comparative study of self-esteem of adolescent children of divorced lesbian mothers and divorced heterosexual mothers. In F. Bozett (Ed.), *Homosexuality and the family* (pp. 123–136). Binghamton, NY: Hayworth Press.

Javaid, G. A. (1993). The children of homosexual and heterosexual single mothers. *Child Psychiatry and Human Development, 23,* 235–248.

Johnson, A. M., Wadsworth, J., Wellings, K., & Field, J. (1994). *Sexual attitudes and lifestyles.* London: Blackwell Scientific Publications.

King, M., & McDonald, E. (1992). Homosexuals who are twins: A study of 46 probands. *British Journal of Psychiatry, 160,* 407–409.

Kinsey, A. C., Pomeroy, W. B., & Martin, C. E. (1948). *Sexual behavior in the human male.* Philadelphia: W. B. Saunders.

Kinsey, A. C., Pomeroy, W. B., Martin, C. E., & Gebhard, P. (1953). *Sexual behavior in the human female.* Philadelphia: W. B. Saunders.

Kitcher, P. (1985). *Vaulting ambition: Sociobiology and the quest for human nature.* Cambridge, MA: MIT Press.

Kitzinger, C., & Wilkinson, S. (1993). Theorizing heterosexuality. In S. Wilkinson & C. Kitzinger (Eds.), *Heterosexuality: A Feminism and Psychology reader* (pp. 1–32). London: Sage Publications.

Loehlin, J. C. (1992). *Genes and environment in personality development.* Newbury Park, CA: Sage Publications.

Meyer-Bahlburg, H. F. L. (1995). Psychoneuroendocrinology and sexual pleasure: The aspect of sexual orientation. In P. R. Abramson & S. D. Pinkerton (Eds.), *Sexual nature/sexual culture* (pp. 135–153). Chicago: University of Chicago Press.

Miller, W. L. (1988). Molecular biology of steroid hormone synthesis. *Endocrinology Reviews, 9,* 295–318.

Money, J., & Ehrhardt, A. A. (1972). *Man and woman. Boy and girl.* Baltimore: Johns Hopkins University Press.

Morin, S. F. (1977). Heterosexual bias in psychological research on lesbianism and male homosexuality. *American Psychologist, 32,* 629–637.

Neale, M. C., & Cardon, L. R. (1992). *Methodology for genetic studies of twins and families.* Dordrecht, The Netherlands: Kluwer Academic.

Pattatucci, A. M. L., & Hamer, D. H. (1995a). Development and familiarity of sexual orientation in females. *Behavior Genetics, 25,* 407–420.

Pattatucci, A. M. L., & Hamer, D. H. (1995b). The genetics of sexual orientation: From fruit flies to humans. In P. R. Abramson & S. D. Pinkerton (Eds.), *Sexual nature/sexual culture* (pp. 154–174). Chicago: University of Chicago Press.

Patterson, C. J. (1992). Children of lesbian and gay parents. *Child Development, 63,* 1025–1042.

Patterson, C. J. (1995). Lesbian mothers, gay fathers, and their children. In A. R. D'Augelli & C. J. Patterson (Eds.), *Lesbian, gay, and bisexual identities over the lifespan: Psychological perspectives* (pp. 262–290). New York: Oxford University Press.

Pillard, R. C. (1990). The Kinsey Scale: Is it familial? In D. P. McWhirter, S. A. Sanders, & J. M. Reinisch (Eds.), *Homosexuality/heterosexuality: Concepts of sexual orientation* (pp. 88–100). New York: Oxford University Press.

Pillard, R. C., & Weinrich, J. D. (1986). Evidence of familial nature of male homosexuality. *Archives of General Psychiatry, 43,* 808–812.

Plomin, R. (1994). Genetic research and identification of environmental influences. *Journal of Child Psychology and Psychiatry, 35,* 817–834.

Plomin, R., Chipuer, H. M., & Neiderhiser, J. M. (1994). Behavioral genetic evidence for the importance of nonshared environment. In E. M. Hetherington, D. Reiss, & R. Plomin (Eds.) *Separate social worlds of siblings: Impact of nonshared environment on development* (pp. 1–31). Hillsdale, NJ: Lawrence Erlbaum.

Plomin, R., DeFries, J. C., & McClearn. G. E. (1990). *Behavioral genetics* (2nd ed.) New York: Freeman.

Plomin, R., & McClearn, G. E. (1993). *Nature, nurture, and psychology.* Washington, DC: American Psychological Association.

Ponse, B. (1978). *Identities in the lesbian world: The social construction of self.* Westport, CT: Greenwood Press.

Rust, P. C. (1992). The politics of sexual identity: Sexual attraction and behavior among lesbian and bisexual women. *Social Problems, 39,* 366–386.

Rust, P. C. (1993). "Coming out" in the age of social constructionism: Sexual identity formation among lesbian and bisexual women. *Gender & Society, 7,* 50–77.

Slijper, F. M. E. (1984). Androgens and gender role behaviour in girls with congenital adrenal hyperplasia (CAH). In G. J. DeVries, J. P. C. DeBruin, H. B. M. Uylings, & M. A Corner (Eds.), *Sex differences in the brain. Progress in brain research* (Vol. 61, pp. 417–422). Amsterdam: Elsevier.

Vance, B. K., & Green, V. (1984). Lesbian identities: An examination of sexual behavior and sex role attribution as related to age of initial same-sex sexual encounter. *Psychology of Women Quarterly, 8,* 293–307.

Vance, C. S. (1991). Anthropology redefines sexuality: A theoretical comment. *Social Science and Medicine, 33,* 875–884.

Weeks, J. (1995). History, desire, and identities. In R. G. Parker & J. H. Gagnon, (Eds.), *Conceiving sexuality: Approaches to sex research in a postmodern world* (pp. 33–50). New York: Routledge.

Weinberg, M. S. (1970). Homosexual samples: Differences and similarities. *Journal of Sex Research, 6,* 312–325.

Whitam, F. L., Diamond, M., & Martin, J. (1993). Homosexual orientation in twins: A report on 61 pairs and three triplet sets. *Archives of Sexual Behavior, 22,* 187–206.

3

Family, Ethnic Identity, and Sexual Orientation: African-American Lesbians and Gay Men

Beverly Greene

We have all been socialized in societies in which ethnic, gender, and sexual orientation oppression are pervasive. These interrelated realities and the discriminatory practices that accompany them create a unique range of psychological demands and stressors that those who are targeted by them must learn to address. In addition to the extreme demands of institutional oppression, members of affected groups must manage the routine and mundane developmental tasks and life stressors that are faced by others. Hence, psychological research and clinical training should include an understanding of the salient characteristics of discriminatory systems and institutions. This chapter aims to outline some of the principal issues faced by African-American lesbians and gay men in this regard.

Ethnic and Sexual Identities in Social Interaction

There has been in recent years a significant expansion of the psychological literature that appropriately includes explorations of gay and lesbian sexual orientations and ethnic minority identity from affirmative perspectives, as opposed to the traditional deficit or pathologizing perspectives (e.g., Chan, 1995; Espin, 1984; Greene, 1994a,b; Icard 1986; Loiacano, 1989; Morales, 1989). In both of these areas there are relevant discussions on the effect of membership in institutionally oppressed and disparaged groups on the development of psychological resilience, as well as vulnerability. Despite these gains, lesbians and gay men who are members of ethnic minority groups often do not see themselves or their concerns in the mainstream of psychological inquiry.

The overwhelming majority of the empirical research on or with lesbians and gay men is conducted with a preponderance of white, middle-class respondents (Cabaj & Stein, 1996; D'Augelli & Patterson, 1995; Garnets & Kimmel, 1993). Similarly, research on members of ethnic minority groups rarely acknowledges that all of the group members are not heterosexual (Greene, 1994a). This leaves the field with little exploration of the complex interaction between sexual orientation and ethnic identity development. It also leaves the field with an incomplete view of the realistic social tasks and stressors that are a component of gay and lesbian identity formation for ethnic minority group members. A discussion of the vicissitudes of racism and ethnic identity in same-gender couples and its effect on their relationships is also neglected in the narrow focus on heterosexual relationships found in the literature on psychotherapy with ethnic minority individuals and the equally narrow focus on predominantly white couples in the gay and lesbian literature (Laird & Green, 1996).

Though undoubtedly significant, these biases are rarely stated in titles of papers or in statements explaining the limited generalizability of the findings of such research. This may not only reflect but also reinforce the tendency for ethnic minority families and communities to deny the existence and appropriate visible inclusion of their gay and lesbian members. Similarly it may allow the lesbian and gay communities to avoid examining the diversity, ethnocentrism, and racism within their ranks. In clinical work and in psychological research, these narrow perspectives leave the field with a limited understanding of the diversity within both of these groups. Another more serious consequence of such omissions is that practitioners and researchers alike are left ill-equipped to address, in culturally sensitive and literate ways, the real issues faced by lesbians and gay men of color.

A range of factors should be considered in determining the impact of ethnic identity and its ongoing, dynamic interaction with sexual orientation, or any other aspect of an individual's life. The cultural arrogance of heterocentric thinking leads to a range of inaccurate and unexamined but commonly held assumptions about gay men and lesbians. These assumptions are maintained in varying degrees across ethnic groups, as they are in the dominant culture.

One of the most commonly accepted and most fallacious notions is that to be gay or lesbian is to want to be a member of the other gender, which is socially constructed as the opposite gender. For example, in this distorted framework, men are expected to be sexually attracted to women only, and women to men only. Sexual attraction to the other gender is embedded in the definition of what it means to be a "normal" man or woman. With support from traditional psychological perspectives, this leads to the following interconnected but inaccurate assumptions. The first is the presumption of psychological normalcy of heterosexual or reproductive sexuality. This leads to a second, spurious conclusion that, for example, women who are sexually attracted to other women must wish to be men or at the very least must be considered defective women, and that men who are sexually attracted to other men are similarly defective males (Greene, 1996; Kaschak, 1992).

Another insidious assumption connected to the previous two is that there is a linear connection between sexual orientation and a person's conformity or failure to conform to traditional gender stereotypic roles and physical appearance. The logical but mistaken conclusion in this scheme is that men and women who do not conform to traditional gender-role stereotypes must be gay or lesbian. Its equally mistaken corollary is that those who do conform to such stereotypes must be heterosexual. Hence, an understanding of the meaning and reality of being lesbians and gay men of color requires a careful exploration and understanding of the importance of cultural gender roles, the nature of the culture's traditional gender-role stereotypes, the relative fluidity or rigidity of those roles, their range, and their place in the family hierarchy.

For members of some oppressed groups, specifically African and Native Americans, reproductive sexuality is viewed as the way of continuing the groups' presence in the world. Hence, birth control or sexuality that is not reproductive may be viewed by group members as a deliberate move by the dominant group to limit the growth of these groups or eliminate them altogether. Kanuha (1990) refers to such beliefs as fears of extinction and posits that they are used in the service of scapegoating lesbians and gay men of color, as if they were responsible for threats to the group's survival. It is interesting to note that such fears do not attend to the reality that a lesbian or gay sexual orientation and parenthood are not mutually exclusive, particularly among lesbians of color. This does not mean that fears of extinction are a result of paranoia or that there are no realistic threats to the survival of people of color. Rather, it is the institutional racism of the dominant culture that places the survival of group members at risk, not lesbians, gay men, or heterosexuals who choose not to reproduce. Nonetheless, the internalization of such views, especially when accompanied by the notion that one may be disappointing parents or other family members, can make it more difficult for a gay or lesbian individual to accept his or her sexual orientation while simultaneously maintaining ties to the family of origin (Greene, 1996; Greene & Boyd-Franklin, 1996).

Within the family context, the role and expectations of parents in the lives of adult children are important to consider (Laird & Green, 1996). For example, to what extent do parents or other members of the family of origin control or influence adult family members? This and the importance of the family as a source of tangible and emotional support warrants further exploration and understanding. Other factors to consider include the importance of procreation and the continuation of the family line, continuation of the racial or ethnic group, the degree and intensity of religious values, the importance of ties to the ethnic community, the degree of acculturation or assimilation of the individual, and the history of discrimination or oppression that the particular group has experienced from members of the dominant culture. When examining the history of discrimination of an ethnic group, it is imperative that group members' understandings of their own oppression and their strategies of coping with it be included.

Another important dimension to explore is that of sexuality. Sexuality and its meaning are contextual in nature. For this reason, what it means to be a gay man or lesbian will be related to the meaning of sex and sexuality in the culture. It will be important to explore the range of sexuality that is sanctioned, whether or not or to what degree sexuality can be expressed or must be repressed, whether or not it can be expressed directly or indirectly, and so forth. It will also be important to explore the nature of repercussions for those who deviate from or conform to such norms.

It is clear, of course, that gross descriptions of cultural imperatives of a specific ethnic minority group should never be applied with uniformity to all members of that group. While there is much diversity between ethnic groups and the dominant culture, there is great diversity within those ethnic groups as well. What is proposed is a framework or outline from which to begin looking at lesbians and gay men of color from a more appropriate perspective. Psychotherapists, however, need to explore every individual's cultural background from that person's unique experience. This information can be used to highlight cultural factors bearing significantly on the ways individuals may understand the world, their dilemma, and their range of options.

It is also important to determine the ethnosexual mythology that applies to any person of color and its relationship to his or her understanding of a gay or lesbian sexual orientation (Greene & Boyd-Franklin, 1996). This mythology may be defined as the sexual myths the dominant culture has generated and holds about men and women of color. Such myths often represent a complex combination of racial and sexual stereotypes designed to objectify African Americans, set them apart from their idealized, white counterparts and facilitate their sexual exploitation and control. Thus, their meaning and interaction with the stereotypes held about lesbians and gay men are important areas of inquiry.

Cultural Factors in the Lives of Lesbians and Gay Men of Color

Language

Espin (1984) suggests that for a bilingual woman, her first language may be laden with affective meanings that are not captured in translating the words themselves. As language carries the culture's values, it may contain few or no words for lesbian or gay people that are not negative if the culture views gay and lesbian sexual orientations negatively. She suggests that shifts between first (native) and second languages may represent attempts at distancing and estrangement of certain topics. She observes that the second language may be used to express feelings or impulses that are culturally forbidden and that many women particularly would not dare verbalize in their native tongue. Sexuality is considerably laden with cultural values, and as such, shifts between one language to the other during discussions of this material may be revealing. It is also worth noting that in cultures where English is spoken fluently by the majority of the population, such as in India, some Caribbean islands, and among Native Americans, it is not always processed or understood similarly, nor do the same words have the same meaning as colloquialisms in mainstream America.

Family and Gender Roles

For lesbians and gay men of color, like their heterosexual counterparts, family is regarded as the primary social unit and a major source of emotional and material support (Boyd-Franklin, 1989). Family and ethnic community serve an additional and important function as refuges and buffers against the racism of the dominant culture. Separation and rejection by family and community are felt keenly, and many men and women will not jeopardize these connections for alliances in the broader lesbian and gay community or by divulging their sexual orientation, even acknowledging it to themselves. The boundaries of family for lesbians and gay men of color frequently go beyond the nuclear unit characteristic of Western culture and include persons who are not related by blood or marriage, but who are experienced as though they were. These persons are considered members of an extended family. The complex networks of interdependence and support in these families that include lesbian members may be incorrectly viewed by naive Anglo observers as undifferentiated or symbiotic (Green & Boyd Franklin, 1996).

Strong ties are characteristic of families of lesbians and gay men of color (Gonzalez & Espin, 1996; Mays & Cochran, 1988). Lesbians and gay men of color tend to perceive their ethnic community as not only rejecting their sexual orientations and antagonistic to those who overtly label themselves as lesbian or gay but also being more tenaciously antagonistic than the dominant culture. It is important to note that the latter perception is based on anecdotal reports of lesbians and gay men of color about their respective communities. To my knowledge, no empirical studies to date systematically assess attitudes toward lesbian or gay sexual orientation among varied people of color.

It is also important to distinguish same-gender sexual behavior that may be known and accepted within a culture from a lesbian or gay identity. It is noted that same-gender sexual behavior is known to occur in

Indian, Asian, and Latin cultures between males, but that behavior is not accompanied by self-identification as homosexual. It is noteworthy that in same-gender sexual behavior between Latino men, it is the role of the passive or female-identified recipient that is devalued (Gonzalez & Espin, 1996).

In many cultures, same-gender sexual behavior between women may not be defined or adopted by those who engage in such behavior or relationships as a lesbian sexual orientation. This may be particularly so in cultures where gay men and lesbians are not generally tolerated, and where same-gender sexual behavior is tolerated only if conducted in secret, if not accompanied by the labels "lesbian" or "gay," and if the importance of such relationships is minimized. There may be a sense that there is no need to assume a stigmatized identity by adopting the label, when such relationships or behavior can be engaged in without doing so. Simply engaging in behavior without assuming an identity associated with it, in a culture that will tolerate it in this but no other fashion, may also represent a culturally prescribed way of managing a potential conflict indirectly rather than forcing a confrontation.

Cultural Factors Among African-American Lesbians and Gay Men

Race and sexual orientation are important characteristics of a person's identity that may be either more or less visible. Racial minority status and gay and lesbian sexual orientations are dimensions about which most people socialized in the United States have intense feelings and opinions. Therefore it is important that psychologists learn to explore and understand these issues in appropriate ways. Few topics, however, are more scrupulously avoided in the formal training of psychologists. Just as ethnic minority group members have been harmed by a legacy of racially stigmatizing psychological folklore, gay and lesbian clients are harmed by the negative heterosexist bias that pervades psychotherapy practice. Just as ethnic minority clients can be harmed by unexamined racism in their therapist, gay and lesbian clients can be harmed by unexamined heterosexist bias in their therapists. The ethnic minority gay or lesbian client in therapy is doubly and triply vulnerable to the vicissitudes of the therapist's ignorance of important ways in which routine life stressors may be intensified, and more important stressors made unmanageable, for individuals who are actively discriminated against by the dominant culture and who may find few safe havens on any side (Greene, 1994a,b).

African Americans are a diverse group of persons whose cultural origins, with some Native American and European racial admixture, are in the tribes of western Africa and whose ancestors were unwilling participants in their immigration as primary objects in the slave trade. Their cultural derivatives include strong family ties that encompass nuclear and extended family members in complex networks of obligation and support (Boyd-Franklin, 1989).

Gender roles in African-American families have been somewhat more flexible than their white and many of their ethnic minority counterparts (Greene & Boyd-Franklin, 1996). This flexibility is explained in part as derivative of the values of interdependence and somewhat more egalitarian nature of precolonial African culture. It is also a function of the need to adapt to racism in the United States, which has made it difficult for African-American men to find work and fit the idealized (not realistic) image of the dominant culture's male provider. This circumstance has forced African-American women to assume roles deemed inappropriate for other American women, from the perspective of traditional gender-role stereotypes. It has also been necessary, even when males in families worked, for women to work as well if the family was to survive economically. Hence, rigid gender-role stratification was somewhat impractical. This does not mean that many families did not try to emulate the dominant culture's ideal, nor does it mean that sexism is not a part of contemporary African-American communities. Many African-American men and women experienced themselves as less competent if they were unable to live up to such an ideal, while others understood many of the factors that prevented them from doing so and raised appropriate questions about the wisdom of emulating and internalizing the values of their oppressors (Greene & Boyd-Franklin, 1996).

Motherhood is a highly valued role in African-American communities (Boyd-Franklin, 1989). There are many acceptable ways of "mothering" that do not necessarily involve being a biological parent. This is consistent with the active role of extended family members in child care and child rearing. It is noteworthy that lesbian mothers have always been present in African-American communities and in significant numbers, long before choosing to have children by alternative means became a popular or acceptable topic of discussion among white lesbians (Bell & Weinberg, 1978; Greene & Boyd-Franklin, 1996; Hill, 1987; Mays & Cochran, 1988).

The African-American family has also functioned as a necessary protective barrier and survival tool against the racism of the dominant culture (Boyd-Franklin, 1989). For example, African-American families often mitigate and reinterpret the hostility of the dominant culture such that children do not internalize its demeaning messages. Family and community also function as important havens from the dangers of racism in the dominant culture and the need to be vigilant about them.

The sexual objectification of African Americans during slavery, victim-blaming rationalizations developed to justify the victimization, and subsequent manipulation via popular images have fueled stereotypes of sexual promiscuity and moral looseness (Greene & Boyd-Franklin, 1996). Such images are relevant to the way African-American men and women are viewed, and certainly the way that many view themselves. The legacy of sexual racism plays a role in the response of many African Americans to gay or lesbian family members or people in their community. Generally, the African-American community is viewed by many of its gay and lesbian members as extremely homophobic and rejecting of gay and lesbian persons (Greene, 1994a,b), generating the pressure to remain closeted and hence invisible in such communities.

African-American communities have been viewed by the dominant culture as both more and less homophobic than their white counterparts. Because of the strength of African-American family ties, gay and lesbian family members are not automatically rejected, despite general rejection of gay and lesbian sexual orientations. This may be a reflection of varying levels of tolerance for differences or nonconformity among family members, denial of a person's sexual orientation, or even a distinct way of expressing displeasure with a family member's sexual orientation. African-American families may be more overtly vocal in their disapproval of a gay or lesbian family member, but they would stop short of "disowning" the person. This does not imply that the family member's sexual orientation is accepted, as such "acceptance" may be contingent on his or her silence about being gay or lesbian. Furthermore, acceptance in one's family of origin does not warrant assumption of acceptance within the broader African-American community (Greene & Boyd-Franklin, 1996).

Homophobia among African Americans can be explained as a function of many different determinants (Greene & Boyd-Franklin, 1996). One is the presence of Western Christian religiosity, which is often a part of the strong religious and spiritual orientation of African-American cultures. In this context, selective interpretations of biblical scripture are used to reinforce homophobic attitudes. Clarke (1983) describes heterosexual privilege as another determinant of homophobia, particularly among African-American women. Because of rampant sexism in both dominant and African-American cultures, and because of racism in the dominant culture, African-American women often find themselves on the bottom of the racial and gender ladder. Hence, being heterosexual gives them slightly higher status than being lesbian. And internalized racism may be seen as another determinant of homophobia among African Americans. For those who have internalized the negative stereotypes of African Americans constructed and held by the dominant culture, there is always the notion that one mistake is a negative reflection on African Americans as a group—that they are defined by their weakest rather than their strongest elements.

Sexuality has always been an emotionally charged issue, intensified by the pejorative sexual myths and stereotypes about African-American men and women. One reaction to the negative stereotypes previously mentioned is to avoid any behaviors that may resemble those stereotypes. Hence there may be an exaggerated need to demonstrate "normalcy" and to fit into the dominant culture's depiction of what people are supposed to be—that is, a rejection of any behavior that is not rabidly heterosexual. As a result, acceptance of gay and lesbian sexual orientations may be perceived as a move away from the dominant culture's ideal. Gay men or lesbians may be experienced as an embarrassment to the group, or at least to those who see complete assimilation as the answer to their perceived inferiority.

Such notions may be reflected in the perception of a gay or lesbian sexual orientation as the "white man or woman's disease." Homophobia may also represent a reaction to the perceived shortage of marriageable males in African-American communities, making African-American gay males the object of intense scorn from heterosexual African-American females. The perceived importance of continued propagation of the race can be another issue here. Gay men and lesbians may be construed as contributing to the genocide of African Americans. Conversely, Clarke (1983) notes the history of a quiet tolerance for gay men and lesbians in poor African-American communities, and explains this as "seizing the opportunity to spite the white man" by tolerating members of a group that the dominant culture devalues.

Work by Bell and Weinberg (1978), Bass-Hass (1968), Hill (1987), Mays and Cochran (1988), and Mays, Cochran, and Rhue (1993) are among the few empirical studies that include all or significant numbers of African-American gay and lesbian respondents. Among their findings were that African-American lesbians, when compared to their white counterparts, were seen as more likely to maintain strong involvements with their families, more likely to have children, and more likely to depend on family members or other African-American lesbians for support. They were also observed to have contact with men and with heterosexual peers to a greater extent than their white counterparts. African-American gay men were noted to derive less benefit from the white gay and lesbian communities than their white counterparts. African-American gay men and lesbians were observed to have a greater likelihood of experiencing tension and loneliness, but were deemed less likely to seek professional help. Thus, African-American lesbians and gay men may be more vulnerable than others to negative psychological outcomes.

Despite the acknowledged homophobia in African-American communities, African-American gay men and lesbians claim a strong attachment to their cultural heritage and to their communities, and they cite their identity as African Americans as primary (Greene, 1994a,b; Icard, 1986; Loiacano, 1989). They also cite a sense of conflicting loyalties to the African-American community and the gay and lesbian community, particularly when confronted with homophobia in the African-American community. Still, many report that they are unwilling to jeopardize their ties to the African-American community, despite realistic concerns about rejection by the community if their sexual orientation were known. Furthermore, African-American gay men and lesbians find themselves confronted with racial discrimination in the broader gay and lesbian community in admission to gay and lesbian bars, in employment, and other areas.

Racism, Sexism, Heterosexism, and Conceptions of Families

The importance of families in shaping the identities of individuals on many levels is widely recognized. When we attempt to understand the relationship between a person of color and his or her family, and the family's role in shaping that person's identity, we must ask first about how a person's family should be conceptualized. Who is considered family and what does that mean? What are the expectations for family members, and how do these differ from those for people outside of the family?

Families for African Americans involve an often large and extended group of people or "kin" who may not be blood related and that exists in a complex network of obligation and support. These families tend to be more tribal and group oriented than the dominent culture's model of rugged individualism (Boyd-Franklin, 1989; Greene & Boyd-Franklin, 1996). For many African Americans, the people in the communities that they grew up in are experienced as family. Hence the loss of family or rejection by it can go beyond the loss of nuclear family and have a profound effect on a person's sense of connectedness or belonging. This factor has many important implications for African-American lesbians and gay men.

Ethnosexual stereotypes about African Americans have their roots in images created by a white society struggling to reconcile a range of contradictions. Among them were the use of female slaves for breeding purposes with other slaves and the process of forced sexual relationships with slave masters—what we understand today quite simply as rape. One might also include here the institution of slavery itself, conducted openly and within the law, in a society espousing the principles of democracy. The successful reconciliation of these blatant contradictions was accomplished in part by reconfiguring African Americans as not only less than human but also sexually aggressive victims of their own natural propensities. This reconfiguration of African-American identities served to obscure the reality of a system that allowed African Americans little or no control over their own destinies (Greene, 1994a,b; 1996).

Hooks (1981) described one of the mechanisms for maintaining this distortion. She proposed that the image of women as castrating was promulgated at least in part to stigmatize any woman who wanted to work outside the home or to cross lines established by the gender-role stereotypes of a patriarchal culture. While not created for the purpose of stigmatizing African-American women per se, the effect of such a mechanism on African-Americans' already distorted identities is clear. Given that the status of slave superceded the status of female—and for this reason large numbers of African-American women worked outside the home—African-American women clearly did not fit the traditional stereotypes of women as fragile, weak, and dependent. Indeed, economic conditions have long precluded this status, even for those who would have gladly adopted such roles.

African-American women thus came to be defined as strong, assertive, and independent—everything women were not supposed to be.

Stereotypes of lesbians as masculinized females poignantly intersect with stereotypes of African-American women in this regard (Greene & Boyd-Franklin, 1996). Both are depicted in similar terms, as if they are defective women who want to look or act like men; like men, they are also seen as sexually preoccupied predators. It is important to understand the link between this image of a lesbian, on the one hand, and the institutional racism in the legacy of myths and distortions regarding the sexuality of African-American lesbians, on the other (Greene, 1996).

Racism, sexism, and heterosexism come together in the attempts to present African-American women as the cause of failure in their family structures. Thus emerges the bizarre conclusion that male dominance and female subordination are the real keys to liberating people of African descent. The use of gender hierarchies to minimize the pernicious role of racism in the lives of African Americans is implicated in the stigmatization of African-American lesbians. Men in the culture are encouraged to believe that strong women, not racist institutions, are responsible for their oppression (Greene, 1994a,b; 1996; Greene & Boyd-Franklin, 1996).

For African-American communities, just as for the dominant culture, sexual attraction to the other gender is embedded in what it means to be a "normal" man or woman. Gay men and lesbians are presumed, because they are attracted to members of the same gender, to want to be members of the other gender—and are therefore deemed defective. The threat of being labeled gay or lesbian—the ultimate defect—is used to maintain rigid gender roles, which in turn reinforce gender hierarchies of sexism (Kaschak, 1992). People who do not fit into traditional gender categories are presumed defective, and are subjected to ridicule and humiliation (Kaschak, 1992). A link is established between the coveted achievement of manhood for African-American men, on the one hand, and the subordination of women, on the other. Women who fail to adhere to gender-role stereotypes of subordination—especially lesbians, who refuse in so many ways to exemplify the stereotypic notions—are deemed defective.

Many African-American women, including lesbians, have internalized such myths. When internalized, these myths, distortions, and stereotypic depictions of African-American women's sexuality can intensify the negative psychological effects of sexism, racism, and heterosexism on African-American lesbians. This can further compromise their ability to obtain support from their families, as well as from the larger ethnic communities to which they belong.

Popular ethnosexual myths and images are relevant to the way that African-Americans and lesbians from other ethnic minority groups are viewed, and certainly are relevant to the ways in which many view themselves. The legacy of sexual racism plays a role in how many people of color respond to lesbians in their families or in their communities. These myths and images contribute to the devaluing of African-American lesbians.

In this context, there is the potential for negative effects on the health and psychological well-being of lesbians and gay men of color. Psychologists need to become more aware of the distinct combinations of stressors and psychological demands impinging on members of these groups, particularly the potential for isolation, anger, and frustration. Aside from being culturally literate, the practicing clinical psychologist should develop a sense of the unique experience of the client with respect to his or her ethnic identity, gender, and sexual orientation; and should be aware of the client's need to establish priorities in an often confusing and painful maze of loyalties and estrangements. Effective work with African-American lesbians and gay men must first acknowledge the significance of multiple, overlapping, and conflicting realities and identities that constitute the complexity of their being. Research has much to contribute in this regard. Both as scientists and as practitioners, psychologists are challenged to develop a broader understanding of the complex nature of human beings and the role of varied ethnic, sexual orientation, and other identities as reflections of a healthy range of human diversity.

References

Bass-Hass, R. (1968). The lesbian dyad: Basic issues and value systems. *Journal of Sex Research, 4,* 126.

Bell, A., & Weinberg, M. (1978). *Homosexualities: A study of human diversity among men and women.* New York: Simon & Schuster.

Boyd-Franklin, N. (1989). *Black families: A multisystems approach to family therapy.* New York: Guilford Press.

Cabaj, R. P., & Stein, T. S. (Ed.) (1996). *Textbook of homosexuality and mental health.* Washington, DC: American Psychiatric Press.

Chan, C. S. (1995). Issues of sexual identity in an ethnic minority: The case of Chinese American lesbians, gay men, and bisexual people. In A. R. D'Angelli, & C. J. Patterson, Eds. *Lesbian, gay, and bisexual identities over the lifespan.* NY: Oxford University Press.

Clarke, C. (1983). The failure to transform: Homophobia in the black community. In B. Smith (Ed.) *Home girls: A black feminist anthology* (pp. 197–208). New York: Kitchen Table Women of Color Press.

D'Augelli, A. R., & Patterson, C. J. (Eds.) (1995). *Lesbian gay and bisexual identities over the lifespan: Psychological perspectives.* New York: Oxford University Press.

Espin, O. (1984). Cultural and historical influences on sexuality in Hispanic/Latina women: Implications for psychotherapy. In C. Vance (Ed.), *Pleasure and danger: Exploring female sexuality* (pp. 149–163). London: Routledge & Kegan Paul.

Garnets, L. D., & Kimmel, D. C. (Eds.) (1993). *Psychological perspectives on lesbian and gay male experiences.* New York: Columbia University Press.

Gonzalez, F. J., and Espin, O. M. (1996). Latino men, Latina women, and homosexuality. In R. P. Cabaj & T. S. Stein (Eds.), *Textbook of homosexuality and mental health* (pp. 583–601). Washington, DC: American Psychiatric Press.

Greene, B. (1994a). Lesbian women of color: Triple jeopardy. In L. Comas-Diaz & B. Greene (Eds.), *Women of color: Integrating ethnic and gender identities in psychotherapy* (pp. 389–427). New York: Guilford Press.

Greene, B. (1994b). Lesbian and gay sexual orientations: Implications for clinical training, practice and research. In B. Greene & G. Herek (Eds.), *Psychological perspectives on lesbian and gay issues. Volume 1: Lesbian and gay psychology: Theory, research, and clinical applications* (pp. 1–24). Thousand Oaks, CA: Sage Publications.

Greene, B. (1996). Lesbians and gay men of color: The legacy of ethno-sexual mythologies in heterosexism. In E. Rothblum & L. Bond (Eds.), *Preventing heterosexism and homophobia* (pp. 59–70). Thousand Oaks, CA: Sage Publications.

Greene, B., & Boyd-Franklin, N. (1996). African-American lesbians: Issues in couples therapy. In J. Laird & R.-J. Green (Eds.), *Lesbians and gays in couples and families; A handbook for therapists* (pp. 251–271). San Francisco: Jossey-Bass.

Hill, M. (1987). Child-rearing attitudes of black lesbian mothers. In the Boston Lesbian Psychologies Collective (Ed.), *Lesbian psychologies: Explorations and challenges* (pp. 215–226). Urbana: University of Illinois Press.

hooks, B. (1981). *Ain't I a woman: Black women and feminism*. Boston: South End Press.

Icard, L. (1986). Black gay men and conflicting social identities: Sexual orientation versus racial identity. *Journal of social work and human sexuality*, 4, 83–93.

Jones, B. E., & Hill, M. (1996). African American lesbians, gay men, and bisexuals. In R. P. Cabaj & T. S. Stein (Eds.), *Textbook of homosexuality and mental health* (pp. 549–561). Washington, DC: American Psychiatric Press.

Kanuha, V. (1990). Compounding the triple jeopardy: Battering in lesbian of color relationships. *Women and therapy*, 9, 169–183.

Kaschak, E. (1992). *Engendered lives: A new psychology of women's experience*. New York: Basic Books.

Laird, J., & Green, R.-J. (Eds.) (1996). *Lesbians and gays in couples and families: A handbook for therapists*. San Francisco: Jossey-Bass.

Loiacano, D, K, (1989). Gay identity issues among Black Americans: Racism, homophobia, and the need for validation. *Journal of Counseling and Development*, 68, 21–25.

Mays, V., & Cochran, S. (1988). The Black women's relationship project: A national survey of Black lesbians. In M. Shernoff & W. Scott (Eds.), *The sourcebook on lesbian/gay health* care (2nd ed., pp. 54–62). Washington, DC: National Lesbian and Gay Health Foundation.

Mays, V., Cochran, S., & Rhue, S. (1993). The impact of perceived discrimination on the intimate relationships of black lesbians. *Journal of homosexuality*, 25, 1–14.

Morales, E. (1989). Ethnic minority families and minority gays and lesbians. *Marriage and family review*, 14, 217–239.

4

Social Acceptance of Same-Sex Relationships in Families: Models From Other Cultures

Walter L. Williams

Though the legal recognition of lesbian and gay relationships is under discussion both in North America and Europe, a multicultural anthropological perspective has been largely missing from this discourse. Unknown to most people is the fact that, for most of human history, many cultures have recognized loving relationships between two males or between two females. At least before Western colonialism and Christian missionaries spread homophobic attitudes worldwide, same-sex relationships were socially accepted in many different areas of the world. This essay will briefly present some cross-cultural examples to illustrate various ways societies have incorporated same-sex relationships into family structures. Knowledge of these examples may serve as valuable models for family life in the future, perhaps providing better models than the contemporary Western heterosexual nuclear family. As more bisexuals, transgendered persons, lesbians, and gay men come to construct new forms of family, we need to look to the past in order to envision possibilities for the future.

In the past, some cultures went beyond tolerance and actively encouraged same-sex marriage. In such cultures, same-sex marriages served as an indigenous mechanism of population control. Today, as many peoples around the world strive to revive their indigenous traditions, and as nations struggle to reduce their birthrates, it is important to consider the positive social benefits of same-sex marriages. This is not to say that lesbian and gay marriages should be accepted solely because of their value in population control. Campaigns to legalize same-sex marriage should be based on the merits of justice, equality, and nondiscrimination (Eskridge, 1996). But it is important to recognize that the freedom of people to marry the person of their choice, without discrimination on the basis of sex, is not a new development in human history. If we analyze *all* of human history, and not just Western history of the last millennium, it is clear that social recognition of same-sex relationships was considered a basic part of human liberty in many previous societies.

In contrast, despite hopeful signs in Hawaii, no state in the United States today yet legally recognizes same-sex marriages. Analyzed from a multicultural perspective, this is a flagrant violation of human liberty. This prohibition is as serious a violation of human rights as the previous laws that existed in many states that prohibited persons from marrying someone of a different race. Those so-called miscegenation laws were rightly declared unconstitutional by the Supreme Court in 1967, and it is time that laws prohibiting same-sex marriage be likewise abolished. We have been raised with the concept that government exists to promote "life, liberty, and the pursuit of happiness." What is more basic to the pursuit of happiness than two people who love each other being able to formalize their commitment by marriage? The freedom to choose whom one wants to marry should be seen as a very basic element of human rights (Eskridge, 1996).

Same-Sex Relationships among Youth

As we begin to consider the recognition of same-sex marriages, we can learn much from a cross-cultural perspective. Several patterns emerge from early historical documents written by European explorers in various non-Western cultures. The most widespread comments concerned the sexuality of youths. For example, Spanish explorers among the seventeenth-century Maya of Mexico pointed out that heterosexual marriage was restricted to those older than age 30. This had a major benefit in preventing overpopulation by restricting the number of childbearing years for women and preventing teenage pregnancies. Yet the Maya did not expect people to renounce sexual enjoyment during their youthful decades. On the contrary, Spanish missionaries reported as early as 1619 that Maya told them about the social acceptability of male-to-male sex among youths. The missionaries reported in horror that Maya parents even arranged for the marriage of their teenage son with a younger boy. If anyone approached the boy sexually, that person was punished with the same penalties as those breaking the condition of a heterosexual marriage. This indicates the social acceptance of same-sex relationships among youths (Williams, 1986, see p. 90). The norm for seventeenth-century Maya males is that they would be a boy-wife in their prepubescent years, then in adolescence they would become the "husband" to a younger boy. They remained in this same-sex marriage, following the same rules as partners in a heterosexual marriage, until age 30, when they got married to a woman. Unfortunately, the Spanish explorers did not comment on the sexual activities of females with other females, so we do not know if this pattern applied to young women, but it is clear from these sources that the primary sexual interaction for Maya males below age 30 was with members of their own sex. Inspired by this historical documentation that my archival research uncovered, in 1983 I traveled to the Yucatán to do fieldwork research in Maya villages. To my amazement I found that this pattern of relaxed acceptance of same-sex eroticism among youths has even continued to the present, despite centuries of antihomosexual prejudices foisted upon the Maya by the Spanish conquerors (Williams, 1986: 135–148).

The Maya are not alone in their institutionalization of same-sex marriages. Among the Azande of East Africa, as observed by an anthropologist in the 1930s and 1940s, a young adult warrior was expected to take a male youth as a "temporary wife" before later marrying a woman (Evans-Pritchard, 1970). He even went through the formality of paying a bride-price to the boy's family, just as a man would do for the family of a woman he was marrying. After reaching age 20, the younger partner would himself take a boy-wife as a sexual and affectional partner, and he would fulfill the warrior role himself. Such a practice was the major means by which young males were socialized to their later adult role. It also likely ensured a smoother circumstance during heterosexual marriage later on, since the man had experienced both sides in the husband wife routine (Evans-Pritchard, 1970).

Same-Sex Relationships between Generations

The anthropologist investigating Azande culture reported that even after passing age 30 some Azande men continued to have same-sex relationships with adolescent males, and this was socially acceptable (Evans-Pritchard, 1970). But the most famous example of socially accepted man-boy relationships is ancient Greece. For the Greek educated freeborn class, the adult man involved in such relationships frequently was the principal teacher, vocational trainer, and socialization agent for a youth as he matured into adulthood. Even though there is not enough documentation to know if this pattern was common among the Greek laboring classes, the surviving writings of Greece's greatest female poet Sappho, who administered a girl's school on the island of Lesbos, suggest that this pattern likely applied to educated freeborn females as well (Dover, 1978). Yet historians have typically depicted same-sex relationships among the ancient Greeks as a unique and strange aberration. What is most notable from the emerging cross-cultural scholarship is how common same-sex relationships are for many societies. Such relationships fulfill important roles both in education and training and in care of the elderly.

For example, in Egypt and Asia Minor during the medieval eras, many of the sultanate governments used professional administrators, called

"Mamluk," to run the government (Hardman, 1990). Sultans were highly nervous about challenges to their son's inheritance of rulership, and they did not want to face the danger of a Mamluk conspiring to overthrow their dynasty in order to install the Mamluk's own descendants as a new dynasty. Therefore, the sultans commonly prohibited any Mamluk from having sexual relations with women. If a Mamluk sired a child, he was immediately dismissed from office. For his emotional needs, a Mamluk was instead encouraged to take a pubescent boy as a spouse. This form of same-sex marriage was socially recognized, and also provided a model for others in society who preferred their own sex, but for the Mamluks it had the additional advantage of not producing children to threaten their relations with the dynasty.

In this system, the adult Mamluk would arrange for his marriage with a boy, just as marriages were arranged between families of prospective husbands and wives. The boy's parents were happy to see their son taken into a high position within the royal court. The boy then became not only the Mamluk's lover and partner but also the man's constant companion. The Mamluk would train the apprentice in all his administrative duties, and over the years the boy gradually took over more of the work of his elder partner. By the time the boy matured, the elder man would be ready to retire, and the young man would be appointed as the next Mamluk. He then would take care of the retired elder Mamluk, and would also take a young boy as his own lover-companion-apprentice. The generational process would be repeated as he became the elder teacher. This practice was a crucial element of the way the sultanate governments were administered in the Middle East for over a thousand years. Yet almost nothing has been written about this tradition in modern times, and many people are ignorant of the way past generations of people lived (Hardman, 1990).

Another area of the world where we see a similar arrangement was in pre-modern Japan. Same-sex love was accepted from the highest levels of society. In fact, the respected Shogun Tsunayoshi, who ruled Japan from 1688 to 1703, was so open about his homosexuality that he supported over 150 young male boyfriends in his palace. He provided them with the best education, and the most talented later became artists and dancers in the royal court or leading officials of the government (Watanabe & Iwata, 1989).

With this kind of example from the upper class, same-sex relationships were commonly accepted throughout society, especially among Buddhists, since Buddhism does not consider homosexual behavior a violation of Buddhist religious principles. In this context, a seventeenth-century Jesuit missionary in Japan wrote about homosexuality, "Nobody, neither man nor woman, young or old, regards this sin as abnormal or abominable; this sin is well known among the bonzes [Buddhist monks and nuns], and is even a widespread custom amongst them" (Watanabe & Iwata, 1989: 20). Another missionary wrote about the monks: "The abominable vice against nature is so popular that they practice it without any feelings of shame. They have many young boys with whom they commit wicked deeds"

(Watanabe & Iwata, 1989: 20). Each monk was assigned a boy (age 10–17) as his pupil, and many of these teacher-student pairs became lovers. Monks wrote numerous poems of love expressed toward their student-boyfriend, and this intimate loving relationship underlay the Buddhist system of education.

Intergenerational same-sex relationships were commonly accepted in other areas of Japanese society as well. By the fifteenth and sixteenth centuries, dashing samurai warriors commonly attracted pubescent boys as pages and assistants. Many of these *wakashu* youths and their adult samurai sponsors fell in love and began a relationship. Although the ideal for Japanese men was that they should eventually marry women, many samurai remained in close loving partnerships with their *wakashu* for the rest of their life. Since the samurai trained his younger partner to become a samurai (by about age 23), this homosexual relationship also fulfilled an educative function similar to the teacher-student Buddhist tradition. The younger partner, when he matured, often took a boy as lover, and then supported the retired samurai in his old age. Thus it went, from one generation to the next (Schalow, 1990; Watanabe & Iwata, 1989).

What we can see from these intergenerational patterns is the mechanism by which cultures provided for people who did not reproduce children, by having a younger person (who was intimately connected to them) take care of them when they reached their old age. Rather than conceive of marriage as a union of same-age companions, these types of cultures used intimate same-sex attractions as a basis for connecting the generations together. Both education and job training and care of the elderly have been major concerns of human cultures throughout history, and most cultures have provided for such education and elder care by parent-child relationships. But the alternative arrangements of cultures allowing for nonreproductive relationships provide us with some very interesting things to think about today. Gay, lesbian, bisexual, and transgender thinkers have not adequately addressed the dual issues of education of the upcoming queer generation and care for nonreproductive elders. The creation of a cash economy, with pensions, insurance programs, Social Security, Medicare, and the like, has allowed a person without children to survive much more independently than in past generations. We cannot, however, depend entirely on government safety nets to provide adequately for people in their old age.

Contemporary lesbians, gays, bisexuals, and transgender persons need to think much more seriously about various means of creating stronger and more intimate bonds between generations. From an anthropological perspective, the lack of such intergenerational connections is an astounding and alarming feature of contemporary American society. Ageist laws, which are selectively enforced against homosexuals, prohibit people below age 18 from living with or being in an intimate relationship with an unrelated adult, even if the young person wishes to be with that adult. Gay and lesbian elders are too often emotionally isolated when their friends from their same generation have died, and many languish in heterosexist old-age homes. We need to pioneer new ways of thinking about how to overcome this unusual generational isolation that has developed in the United States and Europe during recent human history.

Same-Sex Relationships in Extended Families

Same-sex marriages between two people of the same age group have also been recognized by different cultures. In China, for example, historians Xiaomingxiong (1984) writing in Chinese, and Bret Hinsch (1990) writing in English, have found that, from the ancient Zhou dynasty to the Wing dynasty in the early 1800s, many egalitarian same-sex relationships were socially recognized. The key to this social acceptance was the same-sex lover's being provided a clear place in the extended family kinship system, usually simply being adopted into the family as a "brother" or "sister" of his or her partner. The person was then introduced to the community as an adoptive adult child of the family. Far from threatening the family, this form of same-sex relationship helped to strengthen the family.

Bisexuality was the most common form of sexual variance in China, but some persons were strictly homosexual. They were not stigmatized, but were socially recognized as being "enthusiasts of same-sex love." Some persons who were married heterosexually also kept lifelong same-sex partners. Other cases were recognized in China in which one of the partners lived in an androgynous gender role, becoming like a wife to a masculine man or a husband to a feminine woman. This is a pattern that is common in many parts of the world (Bullough, 1976; Conner, 1993; Williams, 1986).

Such androgynous persons have often been seen as spiritually gifted religious leaders, and having such a person in the extended family was considered a blessing. Marriage to such a person was highly prestigious, in many cultures from the tropics to the Arctic. For example, Waldemar Borgoras (1907: 449–457), a Russian anthropologist who lived in Siberia among the Chuckehi from 1890 to 1901, reported on feminine male shamans he called "soft men." He wrote that a soft man "seeks to win the good graces of men, and succeeds easily with the aid of the spirits. Thus a soft man has all the young men he could wish for, striving to obtain his favor." The eligible bachelors "beset him with their courtship" even more intently than they wooed unmarried women. When one of these soft men chose a husband, Borgoras recounted:

> The marriage is performed with the usual rites, and I must say that it forms quite a solid union, which often lasts till the death of one of the parties. The couple live much in the same way as do other people. The man tends his reindeer herd and goes hunting and fishing, while the soft man "wife" takes care of the house, performing all domestic pursuits and work. They cohabit

in a perverse way, in the mode of the Greeks, in which the soft man wife always plays the passive sexual role. (Borgoras 1907: 449–457)

Related peoples of eastern Siberia and Alaska were often described by Russian explorers as valuing same-sex marriages. For example, the explorer Davydov reported in 1812 that among Kodiak Island Eskimos and Aleuts, androgynous males called *achnucek* had one and sometimes even two husbands. "These individuals are not only not looked down upon, but instead they are obeyed [as arbitrators] in a settlement and are often wizards" (see Williams, 1986: 254–255). He continued, "A Koniag who has an Achnucek instead of a wife is regarded as lucky. A father or a mother design a son for an Achnucek from his infancy, if he seems to them to resemble a girl" (see Williams, 1986: 45). That is, if parents noticed their son tending toward an effeminate character and preferring to do women's activities, they styled his hair like a woman's and dressed him in women's clothing.

At the age of 10 to 15 years, such a boy would be married to a wealthy man. The husband regarded his boy-wife as a major social accomplishment, and the boy's family benefited from numerous gifts presented by their new son-in-law. There was thus an economic advantage for parents to be favorable toward an androgynous homosexual son. Since the boy was treated with great respect, this practice seemed to provide an effective strategy for easy social mobility among Kodiak families. It is not surprising that early explorers reported the pride of parents in having such a child, and the frequent appearance of same-sex marriages (for additional citations see Williams, 1986: 45–46).

Fewer examples are known of female-female marriages, but that is at least partly the result of less knowledge about women in general (Blackwood, 1985). One example of the social advantage of female-female marriage is evident among the Kaska Indians of western Canada. Kaska families had an economic need for sons because they depended heavily on big-game hunting for their food. Women are not usually depended on for big-game hunting, for the simple reason that if a woman gets pregnant or has to breastfeed a small child, she cannot regularly go out on the hunt. In this situation, a family that has only daughters would be in a perilous situation once the father got too old to hunt.

Kaska custom, however, provides for families without a son to choose one of their daughters to be raised like a son. Parents would choose their most masculine-like female child, and a special transformation ceremony was enacted by a shaman. It was believed to protect her from wanting sex with men, and to give her luck on the hunt. She would be trained by the father to be a hunter. According to an anthropologist's Kaska informants, such a female "often developed great strength and usually became an outstanding hunter" (Honigmann, 1964: 129–130).

Kaskas told the anthropologist that if such a female hunter had sex with a male, her luck with game would be broken. Instead, she would be expected to take a wife just like any male hunter. By institutionalizing such same-sex marriages, Kaska Indians provided for the economic security of the parents in their old age, even if they did not produce male births. They had no incentive to do female infanticide, or to continue having more children in hopes of getting a son. Instead, they used a nonreproductive female to become a hunter. No doubt other societies did the same, but additional research needs to be done to investigate such practices.

The benefits of female-female marriage in inhibiting population growth are due not only to the same-sex marriage itself but also to the reproductive histories of the female's parents. In many patriarchal societies, especially in Asia and the Middle East, having sons is highly valued because only sons support parents in their old age. As a consequence, parents who have only daughters keep on reproducing, in hopes of getting a boy. Because of this practice, large numbers of children are common in such societies. In conducting life-history interviews in Java, I was struck by the number of parents who told me they continued to have more pregnancies because they kept having daughters and wished to have a son (Williams, 1991: 159, 167, 191, 200, 227n2). Having recognized female-female marriages can eliminate the need for parents to keep reproducing.

We desperately need more research on female-female marriages to break through the limits of outdated Western procreative ideologies, yet heterosexist researchers have all too often missed opportunities for gaining an accurate picture of people's lives because they simply did not want to see evidence of same-sex love. Some mention has been made in the ethnographic literature of woman-woman marriage in Africa, usually quickly followed by an anthropologist's denial of any sexual contact between the female spouses. Given the fact that most of these statements are written by heterosexual male anthropologists, I am quite distrustful of their validity. My own field research findings, as an openly gay investigator working in a number of Native American and Asian and Pacific societies, suggests that the many statements of anthropologists that "homosexuality does not exist" in a particular culture are not accurate. The ideal ethnographer to gather the most accurate data on female-female marriages would be a woman who is openly lesbian or bisexual to her informants. Yet continued heterosexist discrimination within the discipline of anthropology all too often inhibits this kind of research (Lewin & Leap, 1996; Society of Lesbian and Gay Anthropologists, 1992; Williams, 1996).

Same-Sex Relationships in Institutions

Besides one-to-one marriages within families, we also find same-sex relationships existing within institutions. Pre-modern China provides institutional models such as the previously discussed Buddhist monasteries that existed throughout Asia, but also in the royal courts and in economic collectives. An example of the latter existed in many areas of southern China up until the twentieth century in the form of all-female silk-weaving economic collectives. In Chinese patrilineal culture, parents in agricultural areas depended on their male sons to provide for them in their old age. Girls were usually married off, becoming part of their husband's family, and did not contribute financially to their parents after marriage. In such an economy, it is not surprising that girls would not be as valued as boys. Accordingly, many poor farm parents did not mind if a silk-weaving collective adopted their daughter, especially if the collective provided a payment to the parents (Sankar, 1986).

Young girls who were brought into the collective were trained to weave silk, and the older women in the collective administered the business, buying the raw silk from farmers and selling the finished cloth in the market. The women all lived together, establishing loving partnerships and friendships. They remained their whole life as a part of this silk-weaving collective, and many of the women seldom left the collective's living and working grounds. The collective took care of them in their old age, and once again we see an economic mechanism for dependable support of elders in a nonreproductive situation. Unmarried women were so associated with silk weaving that they were known by the Chinese name for "spinsters," a term that spread to the English language as well (Sankar, 1986).

These Chinese collectives can provide an important institutional model for the future in the form of employee-owned businesses that could establish working and living complexes on a long-range multigenerational basis. Lesbian and gay community centers and business or professional groups might help to start such collectives, encouraging reinvestment of profits into the growth of the collective rather than into higher payments for the owners and employees. Workers would forgo a higher salary in favor of long-term job and housing stability. Instead of amassing wealth to provide for their children, they would be taken care of in their old age by the collective.

Another institution in China where talented individuals who did not wish to marry and have children could live comfortably was the emperor's royal court. In the court they could easily fit into court society as artists, servants, administrators, or favorites of the emperors. Famous stories of male lovers of certain emperors were passed down through the generations, lending an air of legitimacy to same-sex love (Hinsch, 1990). Such nonreproducers were taken care of in their old age by the court itself, which functioned as a very large adoptive extended family. Rather than being in a one-to-one marriage, such persons established their relationships within the context of the court as their family. We need more research by historians to learn if similar roles for individuals outside the family system might have existed in the royal courts of Europe.

What would life be like, living in such a court system, for a homosexually oriented person? Until now, we have had very little historical evidence from the words of such people. But when I was doing my research in Java, in

1987–88, I was fortunate to meet a highly respected dance teacher in Yogyakarta at the Palace of Sultan Hamengkubuwono IX. His attitudes reveal his comfortable position within the court that must have been common for many homosexually inclined persons in various courts of many cultures. I interviewed this dance teacher and his story appears in my book (Williams, 1991: 105–109). His sexuality was commonly known and quietly accepted by others in the court. Rather than his emotions being focused on one person in a conventional marriage, he had several close male friends within the court who regularly visited him in his apartment in the court's living complex. Continuing with these sexual and affectional arrangements for years, he never experienced repressive reactions from the royal family. In this context, his homosexual behavior was not a major issue for him.

This man's loyalties were clearly to the court itself. Being a respected member of the court's de facto family, he felt accepted and relaxed. The following quotes from his interview give important indicators of the way he fit in to this quasi-kinship system without marriage. While his brothers and sisters did not live in the court, but were married and had children, for himself he said:

> I would rather stay here in the court. It is a nice place to live; it isn't too busy. I don't like a busy life. People must make a living to provide for their needs, but they also have to enjoy their lives. I think many Westerners are so caught up in making money to buy material goods that they forget to do this. Don't work too hard. Do things as you can . . . and you'll live longer.
>
> That is the attitude we follow at the palace. . . . Life is not always measured by wealth. The Javanese philosophy says: "Be rich without treasure, and win without warriors." "It means that we are expected to be wealthy in the sense of our mental attitude; then we will be honored by love and fulfillment. People always want to achieve happiness, but they think wealth is the way to get it. You can more likely become happy by not being demanding. With the right mental attitude, you can achieve victory without fighting.
>
> In my own life, though I have very little money, I feel that I have achieved this. I don't have to worry about the future, and I know that when I am old I will be cared for adequately. Other people worry about having children to take care of them, but children can die or even turn against a parent. I am assured that I will be well attended to at the court. I enjoy my daily activities, and I do not feel under pressure. I enjoy my dance teaching the most of all . . . Thank goodness we still have our traditional way of living . . . at the palace. (Williams, 1991: 106)

This man is the most secure and happy elder person I think I have ever met, and he shows still another alternative for effective social integration of a nonreproductive person throughout his or her life course. The attitudes he expressed are not typical of a person who has children and strives for economic success to provide for them and for his retirement. Because the court provides him a comfortable and dependable life, he does not need either children or economic wealth. How common his experiences have been over the course of human history, we do not really know because so little research has been done on this topic.

What is most lacking, and most needed, is research on societies, past and present, that do not stigmatize same-sex–oriented persons. A number of tantalizing reports on other cultures have been published, but in general most anthropologists and historians seem more intent on documenting lesbian and gay communities in America and Europe than on focusing on the majority of human cultures. Particularly unexplored is research on same-sex eroticism in sub-Saharan African societies. Besides the sources cited elsewhere in this essay, valuable studies about same-sex eroticism in cultures of Latin America, Native America, the Middle East, Asia, and the Pacific include Blackwood (1985 and 1986), Bolton (1994), Bullough (1976), Carrier (1995), Conner (1993), Cory (1956), Duberman, Vicinus, and Chauncey (1989), Dynes (1989), Grahn (1984), Gregersen (1983), Harry & Das (1980), Hart (1968), Heiman & Le (1975), Herdt (1981, 1984, and 1987), Jackson (1989), Lang (1990), Murray (1992a,b and 1995), Parker (1991), Ratti (1993), Robertson (1992), Schmitt & Sofer (1990), Schneebaum (1988), Taylor (1978), Wafer (1991), Whitam & Mathy (1986), and Williams (1990, 1991, 1992a,b, 1996). Based on these studies, we can see that it is not homosexuality that is abnormal in human behavior but homophobic or heterosexist prejudice.

Homophobia, Population Growth, and Imperialism

The social acceptance of same-sex relationships was also evident in early medieval Europe, where same-sex commitment ceremonies were formalized even in the early Christian church (Boswell, 1994). In sharp contrast, the modern West has notably lacked acceptance of same-sex marriages. While more research is needed on this point, I would suggest that a fundamental reason for this antagonism is the rise of modern Western imperialism. Since the initial landings of Columbus's expedition to the Americas in 1492, Europe and its Euro-American offshoots have been exceedingly expansionist. As part of this imperialistic expansion Christian churches sent missionaries around the globe, whose erotophobic teachings insisted repeatedly that the *only* proper purpose of sex is procreation.

With such stringent ideologies promoting population growth Europe would have suffered overpopulation, but it escaped this fate within its own borders by continually exporting generations of soldiers, settlers, and administrators to establish its colonial empires in the New World, Asia, and Africa. Later on, American governments repeated the process by encouraging population growth in order to expand across the continent, conquer the Native Americans, and push farther west to conquer the peoples of the Pacific islands. With such an expansionist ideology, any form of sexuality that was not procreative was stigmatized. Nonreproductive homosexual behavior, as well as masturbation, oral sex, birth control, and abortion, were likewise criminalized. The procreative heterosexual nuclear family was highlighted as the norm for all people, in sharp contrast to societies that do not have such a strong expansionist frenzy and that recognize the diversity of people.

Prompted by the worldwide spread of heterosexist values through Western imperialism, coupled with a dramatic decline in the human infant mortality rate owing to advances in sanitation and medicine, the past century has seen huge population growth. In response to this, in the late twentieth century various nations began efforts to limit population growth. These efforts have been limited in impact because most humans continue to be socialized to procreate. Even in Europe and the United States, despite vast economic and social changes during the twentieth century, ideology propounding the superiority of procreative heterosexuality has only slowly begun to change. The West remains mired in outdated religious teachings and legal arrangements about procreation that are more suited to imperialist empires than to the realities of life in postindustrial modern times. Legal systems continue to privilege marriages that have the potential to be procreative, at a time when the primary need for the future is to reduce the population rather than increase it.

Benefits of Same-Sex Relationships in Reducing Overpopulation and Increasing Adoption of Homeless Children: A Proposal for the Future

Given the current concern for restricting population growth, it would make sense for governments to revive these various traditions of same-sex relationships. Yet such is the continuing impact of Western prejudice that many of the world's contemporary governments still encourage heterosexual marriage for everyone. Those individuals who prefer their own sex still feel the social and political pressures to marry a person of the other sex. Such laws and social pressures negate the benefits to population-control programs that would occur if same-sex marriages were legalized.

As we prepare to enter the twenty-first century, designers of population-control programs, as well as researchers, would do well to become aware of such multicultural models of same-sex relationships. While same-sex marriages do not need to be morally justified by their utility to the goal of limiting population, the reality is that governments may become more motivated by pragmatic considerations than by moral appeals to justice and human rights. The distressing reality is that appeals to justice are simply not very effective in getting many people to reconsider their prejudices. A much stronger motivator for prejudice reduction is recognition that the stigmatized minority group can provide something beneficial for the majority group. In the case of those who want to see limits on population growth, it seems clear that legal and social recognition of same-sex marriages will be helpful in accomplishing this goal.

We need to stress the obsolescence of Western ideologies of compulsory heterosexual procreation for everyone. In the past, it was to a nation's benefit to encourage population growth. That is no longer true: many nations with high population growths today are facing extreme difficulties. In modern societies, governmental legalization and encouragement of same-sex marriages could be one among several effective means of reducing fertility rates. In many countries today, homosexually inclined persons are pressured by their parents to get heterosexually married and have children. This only contributes to overpopulation, as many gay men, bisexuals, transgender persons, and lesbians reproduce in order to hide their same-sex inclinations. How much better it would be if governments would not just tolerate but actively encourage same-sex marriages in order to counter these heterosexist social pressures.

In addition, many births are unplanned and many children are born without parents who are committed to their care. If every *heterosexual* couple had to plan as carefully and as deliberately as lesbian or gay couples do when they want a child, then this would help to ensure that childbearing would not be done so casually. Lesbian and gay child making, in fact, could be a model for a society that is genuinely concerned about the well-being of children. If *every* child born into society was a *wanted* child the future would be very different than the present.

Beyond these social benefits, encouragement of same-sex marriage is needed especially in nations with strict population programs. In China, for example, the government's one-child policy has led parents to have more sons than daughters. If present rates continue, within a few years China will have over 70 million more males than females. If these excess males are going to want to marry, severe social competition for females can be avoided only if China encourages some of these males to pair up into same-sex unions. Combining such encouragement with revival of China's heritage of all-female collectives (especially for girls who have been abandoned by their parents and are now kept in government-run orphanages) could be a policy that would help China out of its dilemma of too many reproductive people. In fact, if same-sex marriages became popular, birth rates might be lowered enough to relax the Draconian one-child policy for those couples who do want to have more than one child.

Another issue facing many nations is increasingly large numbers of orphan children. Native American cultures can be a model, with many of them encouraging childless homosexually inclined persons to become adoptive parents (Williams, 1986). Such persons have the reputation of being very generous people. With this reputation, and being childless, they are seen as the logical persons to become adoptive parents when there is a homeless child. When I was doing research among the Lakota in 1982, I lived in a household headed by a homosexual male who had adopted and raised four boys and three girls in his lifetime. Each of these children's parents had died or become alcoholic, and concerned tribespersons had brought the children to him. The community recognized this openly gay man for being a good parent, devoted to the well-being of his adopted children. The youngest boy was still living with him when I was there, doing well in school as a typical teenager, in the household with his gay male parent, the man's widowed mother, and a number of nephews and nieces, plus an elderly aunt. It was quite an active household, to say the least.

As I participated in this household and observed how the gay person was at the center of this extended family, I noticed how different it was from mainstream American society, where homophobia has caused so many gay men and lesbians to be alienated from their families. In many American communities gay people have much trouble becoming adoptive or foster parents, and lesbian mothers may even have difficulty retaining custody of their biological children. In contrast, traditionalist Native American communities will often effectively utilize such persons to fulfill a useful function for society in preventing the tragedy of a homeless child. When the talents and resources of all people are not utilized, the entire society loses out.

The role of adoption is even more central in nations like Thailand. During my research there in 1987, I found that while bisexuality is accepted, much of the social stigma against gay men, lesbians, and transgender persons is not based on notions of sinfulness or sickness but exists simply because they are seen as being outside the family structure and thus left alone and unprovided for in their old age (Williams, 1990). In this cultural context, it would be helpful for gay men and lesbians to adopt children. Economic reasons are among the major motivators for Thai heterosexuals to have children. In many Third World societies without governmental welfare support systems for the infirm and aged, and without the possibility for most individuals to set aside enough money to support themselves in their old age, people survive by their reliance on kin.

This perspective implies that Third World gay men and lesbians should not necessarily look to a Western-style companionate marriage to one person of the same age for their long-term good, as much as they should strive to fit themselves into an extended family kinship system. Following the model of Native Americans (Williams, 1986), they can do this by providing economic and emotional support for their siblings' children and/or by adoption. Given the massive numbers of homeless children in many Third World countries, gay people could thus help to solve an important problem in their society while also enhancing their own security in old age.

The adoption issue is clearly a crucial one for the future of gay communities in the Third World, if not in America as well. In the United States, as our population ages and there are fewer young people to help support and take care of the elderly, gay men and lesbians might profitably push for adoption rights to orphans and homeless children, both locally and from abroad. Nothing is more effective in creating long-term personal loyalties than raising a child. An anthropological perspective suggests that gay-rights political leaders should therefore push for adoption rights as a prime gay issue (Patterson, 1995).

If governments today would encourage all couples, but especially same-sex couples, to adopt instead of having their own babies, many homeless children could find homes. This would not only help to cut back on population growth but also relieve taxpayers of the burden of supporting so many children in orphanages and foster homes. Not only are such children a great expense to society but, given the adversities they often experience, such young people are at risk for contributing to many different kinds of social problems. If policy makers would adapt Native American ideas of adoption, many homeless children could find good homes and society would be spared great social and financial expense.

Those people who want to have children could be encouraged to instead take jobs working in foster-parent group homes, daycare centers, schools, and other child-care institutions. Gay and lesbian community centers could perform valuable services by coordinating job placement in these areas for unemployed lesbian, bisexual, gay, and transgender persons. Since most such persons do not reproduce and are thus an underutilized resource for providing adoptive homes for children in need, they can be a positive influence. Rather than continuing to ignore the subject, population specialists could be emphasizing to governments the benefits of encouraging some of their people to pair up into same-sex couples. The United Nations could take a leadership role, explaining to governments in detail how they could help to control population growth by legalizing same-sex marriages, encouraging lesbians and gay men to adopt orphaned children, and giving financial incentives to people to adopt children rather than to reproduce. Organizations like the International Gay and Lesbian Association and the National Gay and Lesbian Task Force can be valuable resources, helping governments set up gay-style social groupings, safer-sex education campaigns, rap groups, "coming-out day" plans, media campaigns, and other means of encouraging young lesbians and gay men to build self-esteem rather than to hide in heterosexual marriages.

Most governmental leaders around the world have been convinced of the necessity of population control. What remains to be done is to convince them that this effort will be much easier when procreative ideologies like those propounded by the Christian churches are abandoned. Judeo-Christian attitudes that discourage nonprocreative forms of sex originated at a time when human populations were small and subject to high infant mortality rates. That has all changed in the twentieth century, and procreative religious beliefs must be seen as partly responsible for overpopulation problems today. By pairing gay antidiscrimination campaigns with encouragement of adoption of homeless youth by childless people, government leaders may be persuaded that same-sex eroticism can be an asset in their efforts to reduce population growth. While many lesbian, gay, bisexual, and transgender persons may reproduce in the years before they identify themselves as homosexual, the simple fact is that once persons become involved in same-sex relationships they tend not to procreate as much as those in heterosexual relationships. As soon as population-control specialists and governmental leaders recognize this fact, the programs they sponsor may become more effective. In terms of population programs, therefore, the emergence of an internationally active gay and lesbian movement is a benefit to the future of the earth.

Conclusion

In analyzing lesbian, gay, and bisexual identities relating to families, it is important to break through the limits of the contemporary American heterosexual nuclear family ideology. There are many, many problems facing this truncated version of alienated and isolated nuclear family life. With the breakdown of extended kinship relations and the decline of wide networks of friendships across generational barriers, American culture does not function in an optimal, socially integrated fashion. Many people are isolated and alone, alienated from other generations as well as their peer groups. Others are turned inward, within their small nuclear family of only one or two parents plus their children. That is not the way most people have lived throughout most of human history.

For bisexuals, lesbians, gay men, and transgender persons, focusing solely on gaining same-sex marriage rights, domestic partnerships, and child custody rights within the existing isolated nuclear family format does not go far enough. Beyond developing our own household, we need to augment it with a network of close friendships—what the poet Walt Whitman called "the dear love of comrades." One of the most positive developments in gay and lesbian communities within recent decades is the rise of extensive gay and lesbian friendship networks (Weston, 1991). These close friendships should be ritually recognized, celebrated, and prized because, as humans, we need both family and friends. Kinship and friendship are not opposed to each other but, rather, are complementary forms of intimate relations. Together, friends and family can optimally combine to produce an effective support network for people in society (Williams, 1992b).

Especially for bisexual, transgender, lesbian, and gay people, we should beware of a culturally bound definition of "family" when we think of our various relationships. There are many family forms and functions. If we are going to escape the hegemonic discourse about "traditional family values," we must draw on the wider knowledge of various ways that families operate in a worldwide, multicultural perspective. I hope this essay, by offering examples from a range of cultural variations on intimate relationships, will encourage readers to explore further. In pursuing this study of families, we need to ask not how we can gain the same rights and status of the flawed American heterosexual norm but, instead, how we can provide the very best situation for people, to build networks of families, friends, and communities so that each person can truly reach his or her highest potential. If same-sex–inclined people in different cultures around the world will explore these options, in all our wonderful cultural diversity, we can become a beacon of hope for the future, to create new visions of families and friends for the upcoming century.

References

Blackwood, E. (1984). Lesbian behavior in cross-cultural perspective. M.A. thesis, San Francisco State University.

Blackwood, E. (1985). Breaking the mirror: The construction of lesbianism and the anthropological discourse on homosexuality. *Journal of Homosexuality 11*, 1–18.

Blackwood, E. (Ed.) (1986). *The many faces of homosexuality: Anthropological approaches to homosexual behavior*. New York: Harrington Park Press.

Bolton, R. (1994). Sex, science, and social responsibility Cross-cultural research on same-sex eroticism and sexual intolerance. *Cross-Cultural Research, 28*, 134–190.

Bogoras, W. (1907). *The Chuckchee*, (Vol. 11, part 2), New York: Memoirs of the American Museum of Natural History.

Boswell, J. (1994). *Same-sex unions in pre-modern Europe*. New York: Villard Books.

Bullough, V. (1976). *Sexual variance in society and history*. Chicago: University of Chicago Press.

Carrier, J. (1995). *De los otros: Intimacy and homosexuality among Mexican men*. New York: Columbia University Press.

Conner, R. (1993). *Blossom of bone: Reclaiming the connections between homoeroticism and the sacred*. San Francisco: Harper.

Cory, D. W. (1956). *Homosexuality in a cross-cultural perspective*. New York: Julian.

Dover, K. J. (1978). Greek homosexuality. Cambridge, MA: Harvard University Press.

Duberman, M., Vicinus, M., & Chauncey, G. (Eds.) (1989). *Hidden from history: Reclaiming the gay and lesbian past*. New York: New American Library.

Dynes, W., Johansson, W. J., & Percy, W. A. (Eds.) (1990). *Encyclopedia of homosexuality*. New York: Garland Publishing.

Eskridge, W. N. (1996). *The case for same-sex marriage*. New York: Simon & Schuster.

Evans-Pritchard, E. E. (1970). Sexual inversion among the Azande. *American Anthropologist, 72*, 1428–1434.

Grahn, J. (1984). *Another mother tongue: Gay words, gay worlds*. Boston: Beacon Press.

Gregersen, E. (1983). *Sexual practices: The story of human sexuality*. New York: Franklin Watts.

Hardman, P. (1990). *Homo affectionalism*. San Francisco: One Institute Press.

Harry, J., & Das, M. S. (Eds.) (1980). *Homosexuality in international perspective*. New Delhi, India: Vikas.

Hart, D. (1968). Homosexuality and transvestism in the Philippines. *Behavior Science Notes, 3,* 211–248.

Heiman, E., & Le, C. V. (1975). Transsexualism in Vietnam. *Archives of Sexual Behavior, 4,* 89–95.

Herdt, G. (1981). *Guardians of the flutes: Idioms of masculinity.* New York: McGraw-Hill.

Herdt, G. (1984). *Ritualized homosexuality in Melanesia.* Berkeley: University of California Press.

Herdt, G. (1987). *The Sambia: Ritual and gender in New Guinea.* New York: Holt, Rinehart and Winston.

Hinsch, B. (1990). *Passions of the cut sleeve: The male homosexual tradition in China.* Berkeley: University of California Press.

Honigmann, J. J. (1964). *The Kaska Indians.* New Haven: Yale University Press.

Jackson, P. (1989) *Male homosexuality in Thailand.* Elmhurst, NY: Global Academic Publishers.

Lang, S . (1990). *Manner als frauen—frauen als manner: Geschlechtsrollenwechsel bet den Indl'anern Nordamerikas.* Hamburg: Wayasbah-Verlag.

Lewin, E., & Leap, W. L. (Eds.) (1996). *Out in the field: Reflections of lesbian and gay anthropologists.* Urbana: University of Illinois Press.

Morris, R. J. (1990). Aikane: Accounts of Hawaiian same-sex relationships in the journals of captain Cook's third voyage (1776–80). *Journal of Homosexuality, 19,* 21–54.

Murray, S. O. (1992a). *Oceanic homosexualities.* New York: Garland Publishing.

Murray, S. O. (1992b). The 'underdevelopment' of gay homosexuality in Mexico, Guatemala, Peru and Thailand. In K. Plummer (Ed.), *Modern homosexualities* (pp. 29–38). London: Routledge.

Murray, S. O. (Ed.) (1995). *Latin American male homosexualities.* Albuquerque: University of New Mexico Press.

Murray, S. O., & Roscoe, W. (Eds.) (1996). *Islamic homosexualities.* New York: New York University Press

Murray, S. O., & Roscoe, W. (Eds.) (1997). *African homosexualities.* New York: New York University Press.

Parker, R. (1991). *Bodies, pleasures and passions: Sexual culture in contemporary Brazil.* Boston: Beacon Press.

Patterson, C. J. (1995). Adoption of minor children by lesbian and gay adults: A social science perspective. *Duke Journal of Gender Law and Policy, 2,* 191–205.

Ratti, R. (Ed.) (1993). A *lotus of another color: The unfolding of the South Asian gay and lesbian experience.* Boston: Alyson Press.

Robertson, J. (1992). The politics of androgyny in Japan: Sexuality and subversion in the theater and beyond. *American Ethnologist, 19,* 419–442.

Sankar, A. (1986). Sisters and brothers, lovers and enemies: Marriage resistance in southern Dwangtung. In E. Blackwood (Ed.), *The many faces of homosexuality: Anthropological approaches to homosexual behavior* (pp. 69–81). New York: Harrington Park Press.

Schalow, P. (1990). Introduction. In I. Saikaku (Ed.), *The great mirror of male love* (Schalow trans., pp. 1–46). Stanford, CA: Stanford University Press.

Schmitt, A., & Sofer, J. (Eds.) (1990). *Homosexuality and Islam.* New York: Haworth Press.

Schneebaum, T. (1988). *Where the spirits dwell: An odyssey in the New Guinea jungle.* New York: Grove Press.

Society of Lesbian and Gay Anthropologists. (1992). Proposal to the American Anthropological Association for the creation of a task force on discrimination against lesbians and gay men in anthropology. Report for the American Anthropological Association.

Taylor, C. L. (1978). El ambiente: Homosexuality in Mexico. Ph.D. dissertation, University of California, Berkeley.

Wafer, J. (1991). *The taste of blood: Spirit possession in Brazilian candomble'.* Philadelphia: University of Pennsylvania Press.

Watanabe, T., & Iwata, J. (1989). *The love of the samurai: A thousand years of Japanese homosexuality.* (D. R. Roberts, trans.). London: GMP Publisher.

Weston, K. (1991). *Families we choose: Lesbians, gays, kinship.* New York: Columbia University Press.

Weston, K. (1993). Lesbian/gay studies in the house of anthropology. *Annual Review of Anthropology, 22,* 339–367.

Whitam, F., & Mathy, A. (1986). *Homosexuality in four societies.* New York: Praeger.

Williams, W. L. (1986). *The spirit and the flesh: Sexual diversity in American Indian culture.* Boston Beacon Press.

Williams, W. L. (1990). Male homosexuality in Thailand. *Journal of Homosexuality, 19,* 126–138.

Williams, W. L. (1991). *Javanese lives: Women and men in modern Indonesian society.* New Brunswick, NJ: Rutgers University Press.

Williams, W. L. (1992a). Benefits for nonhomophobic societies: An anthropological perspective. In W. Blumenfeld (Ed.), *Homophobia: How we all pay the price* (pp. 258–274). Boston: Beacon Press.

Williams, W. L. (1992b). A cross-cultural perspective on the relationship between male-male friendship and male-female marriage: American Indian and Asian examples. In P. Nardi (Ed.), *Men's friendships* (pp. 186–200). Newbury Park CA: Sage Publications.

Williams, W. L. (1996). Being gay and doing fieldwork. In E. Lewin & W. L. Leap (Eds.), *Out in the field: Reflections of lesbian and gay anthropologists* (pp. 70–85). Urbana: University of Illinois Press.

Xiaomingxiong. (1984). *Zhongguo Tongxingai Shilu.* Hong Kong: Pink Triangle Press.

II

Aspects of Family Relationships

5

Lesbian, Gay, and Bisexual Youths' Relationships with Their Parents

Ritch C. Savin-Williams

Much of the popular literature on lesbian, gay, and bisexual youths and their parents focuses on the difficult prospects they face when the child declares her or his same-sex attractions to parents. The youth must decide whether and, if so, when and how to disclose the nature of her or his sexuality to parents. Less popular than the personal "coming out" stories of youths (e.g., Heron, 1994) are writings that narrate the reactions of parents once they discover that their child will not be fulfilling their heterosexual expectations (e.g.. Borhek, 1993; Fairchild & Hayward, 1989). The emphasis in these compelling personal accounts and advice-giving tracts centers on the necessary trauma youths encounter if they decide to disclose to parents, or the consequences of not disclosing, and the stages that parents experience in coping with this unsettling news. These youths and their parents are described by therapists, counselors, educators, and others as necessarily facing unique developmental issues not encountered by families in which all immediate members are heterosexual (e.g., Coleman & Remafedi, 1989; Strommen, 1989).

The popular tracts promote the view that after the self-acknowledgment and self-labeling processes are essentially completed, the most difficult task confronting bisexual, gay, and lesbian youths is disclosing same-sex desires to parents. No task is perceived as more intricate, treacherous, or omnipresent as disclosing to parents (MacDonald, 1983). Many youths cite in their personal narratives that they had few expectations that their parents would react in a positive, supportive fashion to the news that they have a lesbian, bisexual, or gay child. Youths fear being disowned, rejected, thrown out of the home, or emotionally or physically harassed.

Once parents become aware of their child's nonheterosexual orientation they often react with emotions and actions that cause considerable fear among the youths. The spectrum of parental reactions has been characterized by a number of writers as similar to those experienced by those undergoing grief and mourning (Anderson, 1987; DeVine, 1984; Robinson, Walters, & Skeen, 1989). In these models parents progress through a series of stages before they are able to accept their child's sexual orientation. As described by Anderson (1987), the initial stages include shock, in which societal-based fears and prejudices surface and the child is in the greatest danger of being disowned, assaulted, or ejected from the home, and denial, in which a parent may refuse to acknowledge that anything is different or may pray for change, send the child to a therapist, or discount the revelation as just an adolescent phase. Then follow anger and guilt, in which a parent feels anger toward the supposed external "causes" of the child's homosexuality or feels guilty that she or he may have caused the "disorder" through bad parenting. Acknowledgment of feelings and concerns without necessarily accepting the child's condition as moral, normal, or long lasting follows the anger and guilt. Finally, integration may come gradually through quiet acceptance followed by increased levels of understanding that eventually lead to the establishment of deep levels of intimacy, a comprehensive understanding of what it means to be gay in our culture, and political activism in gay causes. At the very least, at this point the child's sexual orientation and identity are seldom the focus of attention and conflict within the family.

Some parents never reach the latter stages. Under such circumstances sexual minority youths may regret having ever disclosed to parents; relations with parents become strained and perhaps irreversibly damaged. MacDonald (1983) observed that a youth may become a:

> half-member of the family unit: afraid and alienated, unable ever to be totally open and spontaneous, to trust or be trusted, to develop a fully socialized sense of self affirmation. This sad stunting of human potential breeds stress for gay people and their families alike—stress characterized by secrecy, ignorance, helplessness, and distance. . . . Gay people may be, in fact, the only minority in America whose families consistently reject them. (p. 1)

Whether the youth's fears of disclosure are real or imagined and whether parental reactions follow the grieving or mourning stages are difficult to ascertain because relatively few empirical studies have examined the nature of lesbian, gay, and bisexual youths' relations with their parents. Perhaps unwittingly, the personal narratives literature has often contributed to the view that the processes of youth disclosures and parental reactions are nearly identical for most lesbian, gay, and bisexual youths and their parents. Although few writers expressly defend the view that all youths have identical lives and that their parents experience identical symptoms and recoveries, their tracts sometimes make this assumption implicit. Many educators, clinicians, health-care providers, and other professionals embrace almost without question these models, which can influence their perspectives and subsequent treatment of bisexual, lesbian, and gay youths and their parents.

Recent reviews assess that which is known regarding whether, when, how, and why youths disclose to parents (Savin-Williams, in press) and the reactions of parents to the disclosure (Savin-Williams & Dube, in press). In this chapter the nature of the parent-youth relationship is examined, including that which is known regarding the importance of parents for lesbian, bisexual, and gay youths; reasons not to disclose to parents; whether lesbian, gay, and bisexual youths disclose to parents; and the association between disclosure to parents and the youths' psychological health. Finally, literature is reviewed that examines the overall relations that sexual minority youths have with their parents, with particular attention given to ethnic minority families. It is not my intent to discount the perspectives advanced by the personal stories of bisexual, lesbian, and gay youths and their parents, but to present data from empirical research that address issues raised by these narratives.

Importance of Parents

Relations with parents are clearly a source of concern among many gay, bisexual, and lesbian youths. For example, Martin and Hetrick (1988) noted that the second most common presenting problem among those who sought assistance from their New York City social and educational agency for sexual minority youths (Hetrick-Martin Institute) was family relations. These ranged "from feelings of isolation and alienation that result from fear that the family will discover the adolescent's homosexuality, to actual violence and expulsion from the home" (p. 174). Knowing the parents' heterosexual expectations of them and the expressed reality of their homosexuality led many youths to feel a "sense of contradiction and failure" that in turn resulted in "guilt, shame, anger, and a not unfounded fear of rejection" (p. 174).

The limited empirical research conducted thus far has focused on the fact that disclosure to parents is seldom easy because of the significance of parents in the youths' lives. For example, 93 percent of a college sample of gay men (D'Augelli, 1991) reported that a "problem" that was "somewhat" to "extremely troubling" to them was telling parents about their sexual orientation. This percentage dropped to 69 percent among gay and 61 percent among lesbian youth group members (D'Augelli & Hershberger, 1993), perhaps because a larger percentage of these youths had already disclosed to parents. Although nearly one-quarter of support group youths reported that disclosing to parents was "extremely troubling," ranking second to worries about AIDS, college gay men ranked it first, just ahead of terminating a close relationship. The fact that half of the college men characterized disclosing to parents as *"extremely* troubling" supports the view that until this event has occurred it remains a central concern in the lives of gay youths.

From a perspective of parental impact on current aspects of a youth's self-concept, the significance of parents fares poorly compared to the importance of other people and influences in the lives of college youths. Among college gay men, only 15 percent rated their parents as currently the most important people in their life, considerably less than gay male friends (54 percent) and heterosexual friends who were aware of their sexual identity (25 percent) (D'Augelli, 1991). In another sample composed primarily of college students, lesbians ranked relationships with parents fifth and gay men ranked them eighth of twelve in a list of items important for one's sense of self-worth, ahead of possessions, frequent sex, having children, and religion (Savin-Williams, 1990). Rating as more important for both sexes were same-sex friends, career, academic success, and romantic relationship; gay men also included physical looks and a social life as more important. Despite the seeming irrelevance of relationships with parents, over half of the college students had at least weekly contact with their mother; comparable percentages with father were 33 percent (daughters) and 42 percent (sons).

The mixed findings by research scholars regarding the significance of parents in the lives of sexual minority youths are further illustrated by Hershberger and D'Augelli (1995). They found that high family support and high victimization correlated, suggesting that youths actively sought the support of their family when they experienced victimization, or perhaps the family extended support when the child was injured or distressed. Family support appeared to buffer an adolescent against the harmful effects of victimization on her or his mental health, but only if the family support was high and the victimization that the adolescent faced was low.

Reasons Not to Disclose to Parents

The relationship between importance of parents and youth disclosing to them has seldom been investigated. Perhaps because parents are of great or of slight importance to them, some youths elect to postpone, possibly indefinitely, telling parents about their sexuality. Youths may not expect them to react positively to the announcement that they have a lesbian, bisexual, or gay child or, in more extreme cases, fear "that they would be rejected, punished, perhaps physically assaulted, or expelled from the family" (Anderson, 1987: 165). Whether these fears are in danger of being implemented or are merely imagined is difficult to ascertain except on a case-by-case family basis.

Individual life histories, revealed in personal narrative accounts, document many of the most severe reactions that youths receive from parents once they disclose. Empirical research conducted with youths from the Hetrick-Martin Institute supports these reports of dire consequences that some youths encounter after disclosure. Their parents were often unable to move beyond their initial shock and rage, erupting in a barrage of verbal or physical assaults. The majority of violent physical attacks experienced by 500 primarily African-American and Latino New York City sexual minority youths occurred in the family (Hunter, 1990). The range of abuse these youths experienced included ridicule, battering, and rape; as a result some attempted suicide. A recent review of the literature on the verbal and physical abuse that sexual minority youths, especially male prostitutes, runaways, and homeless youths, suffer confirms the high incidence of violence they receive in the home (Savin-Williams, 1994).

These consequences of disclosure were also documented by Pilkington and D'Augelli (1995) in a sample of community support group youths. Slightly over 60 percent had experienced some degree of verbal or physical harassment from a family member, ranging from verbal insults (36 percent) to physical assaults (10 percent). Significantly more girls than boys were physically assaulted. Mothers (22 percent) were the most frequent abusers, followed by brothers (15 percent), fathers (14 percent), and sisters (9 percent). For one-quarter of the youths, fear of verbal and physical abuse reduced the possibility of greater openness about their same-sex attractions.

Another motivation for not disclosing to parents emerges in personal narratives and "coming out" stories, one that is altruistic in intent. Youths desire neither to disappoint nor to hurt parents or to place them in an awkward position with relatives and neighbors. They also fear the long-term effects that such disclosure would have on their relationships and status within the immediate and extended family. Yet many youths report that by not telling they feel isolated and alienated from the family and fearful of what parents would do if they were to discover the youth's sexual orientation.

Brown (1988) described tactics that some youths use to survive this "cognitive dissonance" of wanting yet fearing disclosure to family members. One is to maintain an emotional or geographic distance from the family, becoming "independent" with little physical or verbal contact with family members. Another adolescent tactic was suggested by Herdt and Boxer (1993): avoidance of any discussion of personal issues by establishing a "demilitarized zone" of off-limits topics. Parents may respect these boundaries because they fear that they may come to "know" a truth they do not want to hear. A third ploy is to disclose to the parent or sibling who will most likely be supportive and assist in the masquerade of heterosexuality.

The prevalence of these horror stories in the lives of sexual minority youths is difficult to assess because remarkably few empirical studies have examined the relations lesbian, gay, and bisexual youths have with their parents. More specifically, reasons for not disclosing to parents have seldom been systematically investigated. The greatest deterrents to more openness between youths and their parents appear to be the youths' fear of rejection and verbal or physical abuse. For example, D'Augelli (1991) noted that fear of rejection characterized those in his sample of sixty-one college men who had not yet disclosed to parents. Indeed. youths who lived at home and had disclosed to family members were more likely to be victimized by them than those who had not disclosed (D'Augelli, Hershberger, & Pilkington, in press). Although one-quarter of a sample of urban support group youths reported that they feared verbal abuse from their parents, relatively few (7 percent) expressed fear that they would suffer physical harm from parents if they were to be more open about their sexuality (D'Augelli & Hershberger, 1993; Pilkington & D'Augelli, 1995). In a similar sample of Chicago youths, seven (3 percent) reported that they had been thrown out of the home and were living in shelters or with friends (Herdt & Boxer, 1993). The fear of rejection, especially from the father, haunted many of those who were debating disclosing, although few expected the dire consequences faced by their seven peers or that they would be physically assaulted.

In several studies, however, youths who had not disclosed to parents often expected a more negative parental reaction than that which youths who had disclosed reported that they received. For example, in D'Augelli and Hershberger's (1993) study of 194 youths from various urban support groups, 52 percent of nondisclosers expected their mother to be intolerant or rejecting; 64 percent expected the same reactions from their father. Few (10 percent) of the nondisclosers expected their fathers to be accepting. These percentages contrast markedly from those who had disclosed to their parents: Only 20 percent of the mothers and 28 percent of the fathers were intolerant or rejecting. In all cases reported thus far, greater fear surrounds youths disclosing to fathers than to mothers, whether the fear is justified or not (Cramer & Roach, 1988).

Disclosers and nondisclosers may represent two very different populations. For example, perhaps disclosers have a fairly accurate perception that their parents would respond positively to having a gay child. This could reflect the parents' liberal, accepting nature or the parents' already strong suspicions that they have a gay child. Perhaps disclosers are more sex atypical than nondisclosers (see Pilkington & D'Augelli, 1995) and thus less able to hide their same-sex attractions, forcing them out of the closet earlier—by their own inclinations or by being pushed out by peers. Nondisclosers may very well be accurate in their expectations that parental reactions will be harsh and abusive. Unknown are the expectations of disclosers before they tell their parents about their same-sex attractions.

Conclusion

Although aware of their same-sex attractions prior to puberty and disclosing this information to a trusted peer, many adolescents conceal their sexuality from parents until late adolescence or early adulthood, when they are more emotionally and financially independent (Savin-Williams & Diamond, in press). For some youths, parents are among the last to learn about their homoerotic attractions, in large part because the youths want to avoid being verbally or physically assaulted or emotionally rejected by parents, although relatively few believe that they would be as summarily rejected or abused as were the Hetrick-Martin Institute youths. The greatest fear of youths may not be one of rejection but of hurting or disappointing their parents (Cramer & Roach, 1988). The possibility that this desire to avoid disappointing parents is the primary motivator not to disclose has not been systematically explored by researchers of sexual minority youths.

The decision to delay disclosure may initially protect youths from feared parental reactions, but it may also create an irreplaceable fissure in the parent-child relationship. As stressful as disclosing their sexuality to parents can be, not disclosing to parents can be an even greater stressor in the lives of lesbian, bisexual, and gay youths (Rotheram-Borus, Rosario, & Koopman, 1991). When the physical and emotional danger of disclosing is real, however, the only viable alternative for a youth may be misleading and lying to parents. The other possibility, that the anticipated family crisis may not be as traumatic in reality as it appears in fantasy, must also be seriously considered when debating the consequences of disclosing.

Disclosure to Parents

In recent surveys of over 5,000 readers of *The Advocate,* a national gay and lesbian newsmagazine for a highly educated affluent, and politically aware population, two-thirds of bisexual, lesbian, and gay adults reported that they had disclosed their sexual identity to their mother and nearly half had told their father (Lever, 1994, 1995). The lesbian or bisexual women (mean age, 34) disclosed to parents at the average age of 24 years; for the gay or bisexual men (mean age, 38), 20 years. Many of the respondents who had not directly disclosed to parents believed that their parents had deduced reality. These results, consistent with previous research with adults reported in the 1970s (e.g., Bell & Weinberg, 1978), indicated that more had disclosed to mother than to father, but they are inconsistent with all but the most recent studies in that such a large number of individuals had openly discussed their sexuality with their parents.

One explanation of this recent cultural shift in the percentage of same-sex–oriented individuals who have disclosed to parents is the increased visibility and acceptance of sexual minorities and their communities during the last decade (*USA Today*, 1996). For example, lesbian, gay, and bisexual characters are almost routinely included in television shows and in movies (Duin, 1996). Even religious conservatives, who emphasize "family values," have dramatically increased the visibility of homosexuality through antigay campaigns. These cultural events have resulted in an openness about same-sex attractions that has likely filtered down to interactions among family members. Thus, it is not surprising that current cohorts of bisexual, gay, and lesbian youths are recognizing, acknowledging, and publicly proclaiming their same-sex attractions to friends, family, talk show hosts, the information highway, and anyone else who will listen at increasingly earlier ages (Cohen & Savin-Williams 1996; Savin-Williams, 1996; Savin-Williams & Diamond, in press).

Research on sexual minority youths and their struggles deciding whether they should disclose to family members has been relatively rare until the last five years. One of the first was Anderson's (1987) qualitative study of ninety gay, lesbian, and bisexual Seattle youths between the ages of 15 and 19 years who dropped by his "rap group" for gay youth (75 percent male) during a fifteen-month period. "Relatively few" had disclosed to parents, which is consistent with the adult studies of that era.

Recent research with sexual minority youths attending similar urban support groups and college campus groups documents the considerable variability in reports regarding the percentage of youths who have disclosed to at least one parent (see Table 5.1). In most studies, over 60 percent of the youths were white, with the notable exception of the Chicago-based Horizons youth group (Herdt & Boxer, 1993). The remaining youths were usually African Americans, with only single-digit percentages of Latino, Asian, and Native American youths. In most samples the youths were in their late teens or early twenties when completing the questionnaire or interview. All studies included gay or bisexual males, but half excluded lesbian or bisexual females. Even in the five inclusive studies, however, the female youths never constituted over one-third of the total sample. Characteristics other than sex and age, such as physical attributes, cognitive abilities, personality traits, social class, and political ideologies, are seldom provided.

In studies of adolescents who attended urban youth serving support groups, roughly 60 to 80 percent had disclosed to their mothers (Table 5.1). Far fewer, 30 to 60 percent were out to their fathers. Percentage of disclosure differed depending in part on when data were collected. The first three studies, which registered twenty points lower than the others, were conducted in the 1980s. The youths thus represent a slightly earlier cohort of sexual minority youths and this may well account for the smaller numbers who had disclosed to parents. In general, the more recent the study, the larger the percentage of youths who had disclosed to parents. Also noteworthy is that sex differences in whether adolescents had disclosed to either parent rarely appear to be large or significant. Finally, if racial varia-

Table 5.1. Percentage of Youths Who Have Disclosed to Parents

	Number of Subjects		Avg. Age	Mother		Father		A Parent	
	Gay	Lesbian		Gay	Lesbian	Gay	Lesbian	Gay	Lesbian
Support Groups									
Remafedi (1987)	29	—	18.3	62%		34%			
Sears (1991)	24	12	23					54%	58%
Herdt & Boxer (1993)	141	61	18.3	54%	63%	28%	37%		
D'Augelli & Hershberger (1993)	142	52	18.9					75%	75%
Telljohann & Price (1993)	89	31	19					74%	84%
Savin-Williams & Wright (1995)	51	23	18.3	67%	83%	58%	65%		
College Groups									
Savin-Williams (1990)	214	103	20.3	53%	59%	37%	25%		
D'Augelli (1991)	61	—	21	39%		27%			
Rhoads (1994)	40	—	22.5	61%		48%			
Savin-Williams (1995)	97	—	22.5	65%		47%			

tions in disclosure levels existed in the multiethnic sample studies, they were not reported.

A second population source used by investigators to assess developmental milestones of gay, bisexual, and lesbian youths is college campus groups. These youths are on average several years older and more highly educated, more likely to have two parents in the home and to come from higher social class families, and less likely to be an ethnic minority, as well as many other variables that have not been assessed (e.g., outlook on life, temperament). Table 5.1 indicates that on average 20 percent *fewer* college students than support group members reported that they had disclosed their same-sex attractions to parents. Many of the undisclosed college men believed, however, that their parents knew or were suspicious. Similar to the youth group samples, college students of both sexes were less "out" to their fathers than to their mothers. Average age of disclosure to mother and father ranged from 16.6 years to 20.1 years, some three months to over one year after a friend was told (D'Augelli & Hershberger, 1993; Savin-Williams, 1995; Sears, 1991).

Reasons for the lower percentage of disclosure among college students have not been offered, perhaps because investigators have not previously noted this population difference. If they had, the most likely explanations would center on the distinct possibility that the support group and college samples may have been drawn from different populations. Youths who attend support groups may do so because they have told their parents and need peer support, housing, medical services, and counseling; or the youth group may have encouraged them to "come out" fully. College students may feel that they can be out on campus, participate in anonymous research, and remain closeted to their parents who reside in a distant community. Disclosing to parents may be perceived as too risky, including being cut off financially, which they may believe would terminate their career and professional aspirations. Or the population variation may merely be an urban-rural difference. The support groups are located almost exclusively in urban areas where resources are more readily available and visibility of sexual minority communities is higher; by contrast, the college groups investigated draw heavily from small towns and cities in upstate New York, Pennsylvania, Iowa, and Minnesota. D'Augelli and Hart (1987) observed that in rural and small towns, youths who dare to question their sexuality often face isolation, anonymity, and few resources or positive role models. Such youths are thus less likely to be out to their family and small-town community where interest is sometimes taken by others in everyone else's life.

Conclusion

Based on research reviewed in this section, it is not possible to estimate the exact percentage of youths who have disclosed to parents their same-sex attractions. Information regarding when they disclosed this information and how they shared this secret about themselves is even more sparse (Savin-Williams, in preparation). A parent may be the first to know or the last, told directly, perhaps within the context of a family meeting, or become suspicious because of a son's or daughter's sex atypical behavior or interests.

Parents are seldom the first person a youth tells about her or his same-sex attractions and mothers are usually told before fathers. A greater percentage of mothers than fathers know about their child's same-sex attractions. In current research surveys, 40 to 75 percent of sons have disclosed to their mothers and 30 to 55 percent have disclosed to their fathers. Less is known about daughters, but the proportions appear about the same, with perhaps slightly more daughters having openly discussed the issue with their mothers.

The most consistent conclusion that can be drawn from the empirical data is the existence of a cohort effect. Since the 1990s began a greater percentage of youths are disclosing to their parents; the irreversibility of this trend is not yet certain given the political climate that many sexual minority youths must now encounter. The effects that either early or late disclosure has on a youth's self-evaluation, however, are considerably less certain than the knowledge that disclosure is occurring earlier.

Disclosure and Youths' Self-Evaluation

One question that has been investigated by several researchers is how disclosure to parents of one's same-sex attractions affects a young person's mental health. Research has thus far failed to unequivocally demonstrate that disclosure to parents is a healthy decision. Three seemingly contradictory findings regarding the relationship between disclosure and mental health have been supported by research data.

One finding is that those who disclose to parents are *more unhealthy*. For example, in a study of 138 primarily African-American and Hispanic gay and bisexual males seeking assistance from the Hetrick-Martin Institute (mean age, 16.8 years), suicide attempters were more likely than nonattempters to have disclosed to parents or to have been discovered to be gay (Rotheram-Borus, Hunter, & Rosario, 1994). Similarly, youths from other urban support groups who had previous suicide attempts were more likely to have disclosed to a nonparent family member earlier, to have positive relations with parents, and to have parents aware of their child's sexual orientation (D'Augelli & Hershberger, 1993). They did not differ from nonattempters in parental reactions to disclosure or in the distress they faced in discussing their sexual orientation with parents. D'Augelli and Hershberger (1993) suggested that suicide attempters were more out to parents because the youths were aware of same-sex attractions from an early age, which gave them a longer period of time in which to disclose, or because of the youth's past suicide attempts, which sensitized parents to the realization that their child was suffering from issues directly related to his or her sexual identity.

Other research suggests that disclosure to parents is *unrelated* to psychological health. Life satisfaction was unrelated to general openness about being gay in a study of college men (D'Augelli, 1991). Similarly, among a younger cohort of youths, self-esteem and all clinical scale scores on the Brief Symptom Inventory were unrelated to whether one was out to parents (D'Augelli & Hershberger, 1993). In a third study, consisting of 137 males (82 percent white and 13 percent African American) recruited through advertisements in gay publications, bars, social support groups, and university groups, gay youths (mean age, 19.6 years) who attempted suicide were no more likely than those who did not to have disclosed to parents (Remafedi, Farrow, & Deisher, 1991). Finally, among 103 bisexual and lesbian women ages 16 to 23 years, parental knowledge and acceptance of the daughter's same-sex attractions were unrelated to her self-esteem level (Savin-Williams, 1990).

The third alternative, that those who disclose to parents score *better* on psychological functioning measures, is based on the finding that youths use parents, especially mothers for gay boys, as protectors of being victimized by others (Pilkington & D'Augelli, 1995). Indeed, college men open about their same-sex attractions less often feared verbal and physical harassment or worried about telling their parents (D'Augelli, 1991). One of the best predictors of a male youth's self-esteem in another study was the mother's (but not the father's) knowledge of his same-sex attractions (Savin-Williams, 1990). Finally, a third indication of greater psychological health is the finding that youths who were least likely to think of suicide were those whose mother and father knew their sexual orientation (D'Augelli & Hershberger, 1993).

Conclusion

It has been suggested that if the consequences are affirming and supportive, disclosure to parents enhances a youth's self-esteem (Borhek 1993). Although parents are often a significant factor in their child's developing sense of self-worth and sexual identity, especially in terms of youths feeling comfortable with their sexuality and disclosing that information to others (Savin-Williams, 1990), the effects that disclosure to parents has on the self-evaluations of sexual minority youths have not been systematically or definitively explored.

The three alternatives reviewed above as to whether disclosure and mental health are related are worthy hypotheses for further investigations. Current research findings are generally correlational in nature and thus are not necessarily informative regarding the causal pathway between disclosure and psychological health. For example, if one assumes that disclosure and psychological health are related, one could just as cogently argue that those who are already functioning in a healthy manner are most likely to risk disclosing to family members as to contend that by outing oneself to parents one gains a measure of psychological health. That is, a satisfying relationship with parents may encourage youths to disclose to them or, perhaps equally likely, their relationship is satisfying because youths have disclosed to them. Perhaps both are true. A third possibility is that disclosure and mental health are connected through a third variable. Youths may be psychologically healthy because they grew up in a family context that celebrated being true to one's nature, including disclosing one's sexual self to family members.

The three alternatives join a long list of needed items on a research agenda that explores the psychological effects on adolescents who decide to disclose to parents, to postpone telling until a more opportune time in their life, or to never disclose the nature of their sexuality. They also reflect a more basic shortcoming: relatively little is known regarding the youth-parent relationship in its most general terms.

The Youth-Parent Relationship

Although few researchers have addressed the relationships that sexual minority youths have with their parents other than the initial disclosure reactions or a global rating of how important the parents are to the child, limited empirical evidence suggests that the relationships are positive and satisfying, especially with the mother. This conclusion is incongruent with many of the personal narratives of youths and parents presented in the popular literature.

In general, relationships with the mother, regardless of whether the child has disclosed her or his sexual identity to her, have been reported to be considerably better than with the father. This is apparent in studies of adult children (Ben-Ari, 1996; Cramer & Roach, 1988) and youths (Herdt & Boxer, 1993; Savin-Williams, 1990). For example, Cramer and Roach (1988) reported that relationships with fathers were less positive for adult sons than with mothers for those who had disclosed, those who wanted to disclose but had not, and those who did not want to disclose. Almost 60 percent of boys and 50 percent of girls who came to the youth serving agency Horizons in Chicago had positive or very positive relationships with their mothers, but only 30 percent of boys and 24 percent of girls had similar positive relationships with their fathers (Herdt & Boxer, 1993).

Another study supporting the more positive relationship with the mother than the father was reported with a sample of gay, bisexual, and lesbian youths ages 14 to 23 years (Savin-Williams, 1989). Satisfaction with the relationship and contact with parents were greater for mothers than for fathers for both sons and daughters. Nearly 40 percent of the youths reported very bad relationships with their fathers; with mothers the number of bad relationships was far less, 15 percent. On a nine-point (low-high) scale, over half of lesbian and bisexual women (55 percent) and gay and bisexual men (51 percent) rated their maternal relationship as a 7 or better (Savin-Williams, 1989). Comparable percentages for the paternal relationship were 35 percent and 29 percent. The overall mean was on the positive side for mothers but on the slightly negative side for fathers. Another measure of the parental relationship was assessed, contact with parents. Nearly 60 percent of the youths had at least weekly contact by phone, mail, or visit with their mother. Weekly contact with fathers was reported by 40 percent of the gay men and 33 percent of the lesbian women. The gay and bisexual male youths maintained more contact with both parents than did the lesbian and bisexual women. Thirteen percent of the men and 8 percent of the women had at least daily contact with mother; 11 percent of the men and 5 percent of the women had the same frequency of contact with fathers. Although no comparable data were collected with heterosexual youths, it appears that the vast majority of these 317 youths had positive, satisfying relations with their parents.

Research with youths and their parents has seldom addressed the longitudinal nature of the parent-child relationship, including prior to disclosure, immediately after disclosure, and during various markers after the youth's announcement. In one study of adult men (Cramer & Roach, 1988), one-third felt that disclosure had no negative impact. Based on interviews with 202 youths, Herdt and Boxer (1993) assessed time changes. They were impressed that the overall quality of the mother-child relationship did not appear to be affected, regardless of the mother's initial response to the news of her child's gay or lesbian identity. Father awareness was associated with more *positive* relationships, although whether the changes in their relationship after disclosure would be positive or negative could not be predicted by the data they collected.

Only one investigation has attempted to predict the nature of the youth-parent relationship based on characteristics of the youths, parents, and their relationships (Savin-Williams, 1989). Based on anonymous questionnaires from 103 lesbian and bisexual women, the study found that women who reported satisfying relationships with their parents and who had relatively young parents were most likely to have disclosed to them (see also Kahn, 1991). Daughters who were most satisfied with their maternal relationships had the most contact with their mothers, a satisfying relationship with their fathers, mothers who knew their same-sex orientation, and high self-esteem. Those most satisfied with their paternal relationships had the most contact with their fathers (although contact did not significantly predict the fathers' knowledge of their daughters' sexual orientation), a satisfying relationship with their mothers, married parents, and fathers who knew their same-sex attractions.

Among the 214 gay and bisexual male youths in the same study (Savin-Williams, 1989), sons who were most satisfied with their maternal relationships had young mothers and fathers, considerable contact with their mothers, satisfying paternal relationships, and high self-esteem. Those most satisfied with their paternal relationships had the most contact with their fathers, satisfying maternal relationships, fathers who knew their sexual orientation, and high self-esteem.

As noted earlier, several studies have reported that gay sons had better relations with parents than did lesbian daughters. Muller (1987) found additional support for this. While 72 percent of gay males reported positive relationships with their parents over time, only 46 percent of lesbians achieved this state. The lower level of acceptance experienced by lesbian daughters from their parents was attributed by Muller to the mother's heightened disappointment that the daughter would not be fulfilling the mother's expectations for grandchildren. Another study, however, attributed the lower level of daughter-parent relations to the daughter's relationship with father (Herdt & Boxer, 1993). More daughters than sons reported negative changes in their relationships with their fathers after disclosure. However, the greater negative changes in the daughters' than the sons' relationships with fathers were independent of whether the fathers knew about their daughters' sexual identity. That is, over time relations between father and daughter decreased regardless of disclosure.

An alternative explanation is that while lesbians may be closer to both parents during childhood and early adolescence, this closeness is jeopardized by disclosure of lesbian status. In contrast, because gay men have worse parental relationships prior to disclosing their homosexuality, they improve relations with their parents after disclosure. In particular, the sex difference may be most apparent in the father-son relationship, which is often so impaired prior to the revelation that any minor improvement in honesty, communication, and trust would be considered a positive development for the relationship (Cramer & Roach, 1988; Herdt & Boxer, 1993). Thus, over 20 percent of men in one sample (Cramer & Roach, 1988) reported an improvement in their relationship with their fathers after disclosure. This was considerably higher than with mothers—7 percent. Additional support for this view comes from the gay and bisexual males interviewed by Savin-Williams (1995), who reported that they never felt particularly close to their fathers because they did not enjoy the activities that they wanted to do, such as playing sports and fixing mechanical things. To them, their fathers appeared embarrassed or disappointed in their sons' atypical behaviors and interests; the gay and bisexual sons more typically enjoyed reading, artistic efforts, and housework. Once they disclosed to their fathers the relationships improved, perhaps, some speculated, because the fathers felt absolved of any blame for the sons' feminine interests and behaviors (i.e., it now made sense). Herdt and Boxer (1993) noted that, "For some fathers it may be a relief to understand their children in a new way; to be aware of an aspect of their lives previously hidden or even confusing to them" (p. 218). It should be noted, however, that despite this improvement, gay and bisexual sons were still more satisfied with maternal than paternal relations (Savin-Williams, 1989).

Largely left unexplored, however, is the father-daughter relationship. Perhaps the relationship moves in the opposite direction—toward a deterioration—regardless of the daughter's disclosure of same-sex attractions solely because of her approaching sexual maturity and the dynamics that ensue. In the case of a daughter who does not aspire to loving men, the father may be particularly disappointed in her because he perceives she has rejected wanting men, which he may feel is a rejection of the masculinity that he represents. Or if she has engaged in sex atypical behavior ("tomboy") throughout her life, which probably included playing sports and rough-and-tumble activities with her father, the father may feel guilty that he has "caused" his daughter to become a lesbian. These are matters purely of speculation because few researchers explore the uniqueness of the lesbian daughter-father relationship.

Conclusion

Perhaps the significance of the mother in the lives of lesbian, gay, and bisexual youths lies in her unique role as "mother" and the seemingly more distant and less satisfying relationship that such youths have with the father. This finding is congruent with adult studies (see review in Bell, Weinberg, & Hammersmith, 1981) and for many adolescents in our society regardless of sexual orientation who view mothers as considerably more supportive, warm, and emotional than they do fathers. Apparently this support is most likely to come from a young mother when the issue is her daughter's sexual identity. These daughters were most likely to have disclosed to their young mothers and to have positive self-esteem. A young mother was also important for gay and bisexual sons; those who reported the highest levels of satisfaction with the maternal relationship had young mothers. The significance of the mother's youthfulness may be a cohort effect; she would have had a greater probability of being raised in a culture in which the visibility of homosexuality may have encouraged her to be more knowledgeable, open, and tolerant, if not accepting, of same-sex attractions in her child.

Although Herdt and Boxer (1993) indicated that disclosure had a minimal effect on the youth-parent relationship, which is also contrary to much of the popular literature, the long-term effects of disclosure on the relationships youths have with their parents are unknown. The closer a lesbian, gay, or bisexual youth is to the parent being confided in, the greater the parent's reaction will impact the youth. In part this may be a moot issue because few youths tell parents at a sufficiently young age to have post-disclosure long-term relations with parents until they are adults. Perhaps indicative of these future relations, the adult men in one study who had disclosed to their parents reported that their relations with their parents deteriorated initially following disclosure (significant for both mother and father) and significantly improved after disclosure (Cramer & Roach, 1988).

Ethnic Sexual Minority Youths and Their Families

Morales (1989) observed that most lesbian, bisexual, and gay ethnic minority youths live in three often competing and sometimes mutually exclusive communities—gay, ethnic, and white:

> While each community provides fundamental needs, serious consequences emerge if such communities were to be visibly integrated and merged. . . . It requires a constant effort to maintain oneself in three different worlds, each of which fails to support significant aspects of a person's life. (p. 219)

One major difference that many writers note between white and ethnic family constellations is the greater integration of the extended family within the ethnic support system. The constellation of the traditional, extended family was described by Morales (1983) as a support system that resembles a "tribe" with multiple, often biologically related family groups. For ethnic minority youths, the family often "constitutes a symbol of their basic roots and the focal point of their ethnic identity" (p. 9) and can consequently be a source of great pride and strength. Thus, when youths declare their same-sex attractions to parents, they risk not only intrafamily relationships but also their strong association, identification, and support within their extended community.

Given the emotional centrality of the extended family, youths with same-sex attractions may feel that they must inevitably choose between their familial or ethnic affiliation and their personal sexual identity. Many believe that they can never publicly disclose their same-sex attractions because they do not want to humiliate or bring shame to their close-knit, multigenerational extended family (Tremble, Schneider, & Appathurai, 1989). As a result, "relatively low rates of disclosure to families have been reported among Asian, African-American, and Latino gay men and lesbians" (Garnets & Kimmel, 1993: 333). If they decide to disclose their sexual orientation, ethnic minority youths risk losing the support of their extended family and hence their ethnic community (Garnets & Kimmel, 1993; Greene, 1994). Morales (1989) noted that "to live as a minority within a minority leads to heightened feelings of isolation, depression and anger centered around the fear of being separated from all support systems, including the family" (p. 219).

Several authors have noted that Asian-American youths risk disgracing themselves, their immediate family, and all past generations, living and dead, if they publicly declare their same-sex attractions (Carrier, Nguyen, & Su, 1992; Chan, 1989, 1995). Chan (1989) reported in her study of Chinese, Japanese, and Korean young adults who had disclosed to most of their friends, that almost 80 percent had told a family member, usually a sister; only one-quarter had disclosed to parents. To disclose tarnishes the family's honor in the eyes of the ethnic community; it is not the children who have failed but the parents. Thus, many remain quietly closeted. Loiacano's (1989) informants also described difficulties finding support, acceptance, and expression within the black community once they disclosed to others. Parents who suspect that their child has same-sex attractions may be co-conspirators in this silence, hesitant to publicly acknowledge their bisexual, lesbian, or gay child to avoid embarrassing relatives and the ethnic community. If a youth progresses to the point of self-recognition of her or his sexual status, familial and cultural proscriptions against disclosing this publicly may block further self-development. Thus, a wall of silence is likely to form around a family with a lesbian daughter, gay son, or bisexual child.

This portrait of ethnic families, however, may be too severe. Espin (1987) noted that a Latina lesbian/bisexual youth may face rejection from her ethnic community but seldom from her family:

> Latin families tend to treat their lesbian daughters or sisters with silent tolerance: Their lesbianism will not be openly acknowledged and accepted, but they are not denied a place in the family, either. Very seldom is there overt rejection of their lesbian members on the part of Hispanic families. (p. 40)

This does not imply, however, that a Latina youth is free from anxiety and the psychological burden of keeping her sexual attractions secretive. Pressure to lead a double life and thus protect the family from "embarrassment," and herself from possible stigmatization and rejection from the Hispanic community, places the Latina youth in a compromising position, pitting her needs, family of origin, ethnic community, and lesbian communities against each other.

Conclusion

Regardless of ethnicity, many youths share common dilemmas in deciding whether to disclose their sexual attractions to their family of origin. The extent of these similarities has often been assumed and seldom investigated by white researchers. The inverse, that disclosure to parents has singular attributes unique to ethnic minority youths, has been the predominant assumption in the literature on ethnic minorities. However, data on ethnic minority youths who are lesbian, bisexual, or gay are primarily based on reflections of interviewed informants and mental health professionals and not on empirical research.

One deterrent to sorting through these issues is that relatively few studies on sexual minority youths have sufficient numbers of ethnic minority individuals to conduct separate analyses. The low numbers may be because lesbian, gay, and bisexual ethnic minority youths do not feel comfortable disclosing their sexual orientation to white researchers or investigators did not adequately recruit ethnic minorities, either because they were not well represented in the available population or for reasons that are not stated or unknown. Several studies with sufficient numbers of ethnic minority youths with same-sex attractions did not include ethnicity as a discriminating independent variable, perhaps because investigators assumed ethnic status did not matter or they overlooked it. In either case, the net effect has compounded the silence about ethnicity and sexual orientation among lesbian, gay, and bisexual youths and has perhaps precluded other ethnic minority individuals from disclosing their sexual orientation and participating in research projects. Thus, because an extremely limited empirical base of support underlies much of the discourse on ethnicity and sexual orientation, caution must be emphasized in accepting without further investigation any generalizations about the uniqueness or sameness of ethnic minority gay, lesbian, and bisexual youths and their families.

Another important consideration is that in describing the experiences of ethnic minority youths disclosing to parents, issues of variability must not be ignored. Not all ethnic groups are similar to each other and distinct from the majority culture in the same way. For example, when contrasted with white families, on average both Chinese Americans and Native American families place greater value on contact with extended family members and the wisdom of older generations. However, within each ethnic group families have distinct functions and structures because of their "pre-American" histories and their encounter with the American experience. Social class, religious values, and degree of enculturation (immigration status) may also exert diversifying effects *within* an ethnic group. Unfortunately, examples of these effects are quite limited in the literature on sexual minority development.

The dual identities, multiple roles, emotional conflicts, and psychological adjustments that lesbian, bisexual, and gay ethnic minority youths encounter when they disclose to their parents need extensive empirical investigation. The family may not offer them safety from sexual prejudice, which may thus threaten the youths' ethnic identity. In the face of multiple oppressions, bisexual, gay, and bisexual ethnic youths face a difficult task as they attempt to integrate their personal and group identities (Cross, 1991). The recent formation of support groups for youths of color give them a reference group for support and validation.

Conclusion

It is difficult to recommend a research agenda when the paucity of research is as significant as it is regarding the relations lesbian, bisexual, and gay youths have with their parents. At this point in the development of research, few issues exist that are not in need of considerable investigation. The published personal narratives and self-help tracts for youths and their parents provide fertile ground for developing testable hypotheses that can guide future research.

Although this literature documents the negative disruptions and sometimes chaos that follow initial disclosure, the crisis mentality of many of these writings may have been overdrawn. Few of the most disruptive, pathological scenarios caricatured by personal chronicles have received widespread confirmation from the empirical research conducted thus far. The personal narratives from both sexual minority youths and their parents do, however, accurately portray the significance of the other in their life. Parents are often figures of authority and respect and youths desire their support and approval. Regardless of their sexual desires and identity, bisexual, gay, and lesbian youths are still recognized by most parents as their children.

To maintain their sense of self-integrity and their desire to be honest with parents, many youths are disclosing to their parents at increasingly earlier ages. The age of disclosure may be dependent on the population from which a youth sample is drawn. Those who attend college appear more reluctant than youths from urban support groups to disclose, perhaps because they more often fear the power of parents to sever them from financial and emotional support. Because they frequently live away from home most of the year, college students are often able to lead a new, private life as lesbian, gay, or bisexual persons without disclosing to parents until a "safe" time arrives. Thus, many are out on campus and closeted at home. Because they live at home, however, many urban youths may have great difficulty keeping their sexual identity secret.

Mothers are more likely to be told than are fathers, in large part because youths have better relations with their mothers and they expect their fathers to react more negatively than their mothers. Few youths, however, expect either parent to respond with outright rejection or a physical assault. Some evidence suggests that more important than fear of rejection as a motivator not to disclose is the desire not to hurt or disappoint parents. Youths do not want to harm their status within the family and the positive relations that most have with their parents.

Few investigators have explored the reasons youths choose not to disclose their same-sex orientation to parents. Also obscure from a research point of view is whether parents know their child's sexual proclivities not because the child disclosed to them but because they became suspicious of his or her behavior or mannerisms, friends she or he selected, and/or the absence of heterosexual activities. Worth distinguishing are the families in which the youth's same-sex attractions have been openly disclosed, have not been discussed but everyone knows that everyone else knows, are a source of parental suspicion, and are not known. Family dynamics under these various conditions need to be investigated.

As indicated above, research reviewed in this chapter has been largely derived from the perspectives of lesbian, bisexual, and gay youths and not from their parents. Researchers have neglected asking parents their views regarding having a gay member in the family, largely because few parents are willing to discuss having a gay child and because few youths are willing to volunteer their parents to researchers (see further discussion in Savin-Williams and Dube, in press). To better understand the life-course interactions of sexual minority youths and their parents, prospective, longitudinal studies are needed that assess the relations that youths *and* their parents have prior to disclosure, shortly after disclosure, and then at regular intervals thereafter. Researchers must recognize, as Herdt and Boxer (1993) argued, that a youth's disclosure takes place within the context of the family and that this act subsequently affects all family members. A longitudinal, interactional research design would allow investigators to study the cause-and-effect relationship of disclosure and family dynamics in a more detailed fashion.

Given the current reality that most data on youth-parent relations originate from the youth, of vital importance to researchers is to clarify the nature of the youth population sampled and to reign in overly dramatized characterizations about "gay youths." Each sample needs to be elaborately described, especially in terms of how youths were recruited and the youths' sociodemographic and psychosocial characteristics, such that other investigators are better able to compare findings among various populations. Similarities across many populations might then warrant generalizations about sexual minority youth; differences could then be attributable to population variations or characteristics. That which is currently believed about the youth-parent relations among sexual minority youths may not reflect the lives of the vast majority of bisexual, gay, and lesbian youths who do not volunteer for research, perhaps because they are not prepared to acknowledge their same-sex orientation to others, such as researchers. Also left untapped by research recruitment strategies are those who vow never to volunteer for political or personal reasons (e.g., those who resent psychologists "studying us"). Until alternative methods with a large number of localized, unique samples of sexual minority youths are implemented or representative samples of lesbian, gay, and bisexual youths can be recruited (currently an impossibility), extreme caution must be observed regarding any attempt to generalize or extrapolate from existing empirical studies.

Finally, the influence of the youths' and parents' ethnicity and family backgrounds has been largely ignored by researchers. To better understand the unique conditions that sexual minority youths who are also ethnic minorities in North American culture have in relating to their parents, researchers must make special efforts and invent new strategies to recruit the full spectrum of ethnic youths in future research projects. Although ethnic minority youths may face special circumstances when attempting to blend their sexuality and their ethnic identity, they may also have distinctive sources of strength that need to be recognized.

References

Anderson, D. (1987). Family and peer relations of gay adolescents. *Adolescent Psychiatry, 15,* 163–178.

Bell, A. P., & Weinberg, M. S. (1978). *Homosexualities: A study of diversity among men and women.* New York: Simon & Schuster.

Bell, A. P. Weinberg, M. S., & Hammersmith, S. K. (1981). *Sexual preference: Its development in men and women.* Bloomington, IN: Indiana University Press.

Ben-Ari, A. (1996). The discovery that an offspring is gay: Parents', gay men's, and lesbians' perspectives. *Journal of Homosexuality, 30,* 89–112.

Borhek, M. V. (1993). *Coming out to parents: A two-way survival guide for lesbians and gay men and their parents,* 2nd ed. Cleveland, OH: Pilgrim.

Brown, S. (1988). Lesbians, gay men and their families. *Journal of Gay & Lesbian Psychotherapy, 1,* 65–77.

Carrier, J. M., Nguyen, B., & Su. S. (1992). Vietnamese American sexual behaviors and HIV infection. *Journal of Sex Research, 29,* 547–560.

Chan, C. S. (1989). Issues of identity development among Asian American lesbians and gay men. *Journal of Counseling and Development, 68,* 16–20.

Chan, C. S. (1995). Issues of sexual identity in an ethnic minority: The case of Chinese American lesbians, gay men, and bisexual people. In A. R. D'Augelli & C. J. Patterson (Eds.), *Lesbian, gay, and bisexual identities over the lifespan: Psychological perspectives* (pp. 87–101). New York: Oxford University Press.

Cohen, K. M., & Savin-Williams, R. C. (1996). Developmental perspectives on coming out to self and others. In R. C. Savin-Williams & K. M. Cohen (Eds.), *The lives of lesbians, gays, and bisexuals: Children to adults* (pp. 113–151). Fort Worth, TX: Harcourt Brace.

Coleman, E., & Remafedi, G. (1989). Gay, lesbian, and bisexual adolescents: A critical challenge to counselors. *Journal of Counseling and Development, 68,* 36–40.

Cramer, D. W., & Roach, A. J. (1988). Coming out to mom and dad: A study of gay males and their relationships with their parents. *Journal of Homosexuality, 15,* 79–91.

Cross, W. E. (1991). *Shades of Black: Diversity in African-American identity.* Philadelphia: Temple University Press.

D'Augelli, A. R. (1991). Gay men in college: Identity processes and adaptations. *Journal of College Student Development, 32,* 140–146.

D'Augelli, A. R., & Hart, M. M. (1987). Gay women, men, and families in rural settings: Toward the development of helping communities. *American Journal of Community Psychology, 15,* 79–93.

D'Augelli, A. R., & Hershberger, S. L. (1993). Lesbian, gay, and bisexual youth in community settings: Personal challenges and mental health problems. *American Journal of Community Psychology, 21,* 421–448.

D'Augelli, A. R., Hershberger, S. L., & Pilkington, N. W. (in press). Lesbian, gay, and bisexual youths and their families: Disclosure of sexual orientation and its consequences. *American Journal of Orthopsychiatry.*

DeVine, J. L. (1984). A systemic inspection of affectional preference orientation and the family of origin. *Journal of Social Work and Human Sexuality, 2,* 9–17.

Duin, J. (1996, January 25). Homosexuality is "in" on prime time television. *Washington Times*, p. 1.

Espin, O. M. (1987). Issues of identity in the psychology of Latina lesbians. In Boston Lesbian Psychologies Collective (Eds.), *Lesbian psychologies: Explorations and challenges* (pp. 35–55). Urbana. IL: University of Illinois Press.

Fairchild, B., & Hayward, N. (1989). *Now that you know: What every parent should know about homosexuality* (updated ed.). San Diego, CA: Harcourt Brace Jovanovich.

Garnets, L. D., & Kimmel, D. C. (1993). Lesbian and gay male dimensions in the psychological study of human diversity. In L. D. Garnets & D. C. Kimmel (Eds.), *Psychological perspectives on lesbian and gay male experiences* (pp. 1–51). New York: Columbia University Press.

Greene, B. (1994). Ethnic minority lesbians and gay men: Mental health and treatment issues. *Journal of Consulting and Clinical Psychology, 62,* 243–251.

Herdt, G., & Boxer, A. (1993). *Children of Horizons: How gay and lesbian teens are leading a new way out of the closet.* Boston: Beacon Press.

Heron, A. (Ed.) (1994). *Two teenagers in twenty: Writings by gay and lesbian youth.* Boston: Alyson.

Hershberger, S. L., & D'Augelli, A. R. (1995). The impact of victimization on the mental health and suicidality of lesbian, gay, and bisexual youths. *Developmental Psychology, 31,* 65–74.

Hunter, J. (1990). Violence against lesbian and gay male youths. *Journal of Interpersonal Violence, 5,* 295–300.

Kahn, M. J. (1991). Factors affecting the coming out process for lesbians. *Journal of Homosexuality, 21,* 47–70.

Lever, J. (1994, August 23). Sexual revelations. *The Advocate,* pp. 17–24.

Lever, J. (1995, August 22). Lesbian sex survey. *The Advocate,* pp. 22–30.

Loiacano, D. K. (1989). Gay identity issues among black Americans: Racism, homophobia, and the need for validation. *Journal of Counseling and Development, 68,* 21–25.

MacDonald, G. B. (1983, December). Exploring sexual identity: Gay people and their families. *Sex Education Coalition News, 5,* pp. 1 & 4.

Martin, A. D., & Hetrick, E. S. (1988). The stigmatization of the gay and lesbian adolescent. *Journal of Homosexuality, 15,* 163–183.

Morales, E. S. (1983, August). Third world gays and lesbians: A process of multiple identities. Paper presented at the 91st Annual Convention of the American Psychological Association, Anaheim, CA.

Morales, E. S. (1989). Ethnic minority families and minority gays and lesbians. *Marriage and Family Review, 14,* 217–239.

Muller, A. (1987). *Parents matter.* New York: Naiad Press.

Pilkington, N. W., & D'Augelli, A. R. (1995). Victimization of lesbian, gay, and bisexual youths in community settings. *Journal of Community Psychology, 23.* 33–56.

Remafedi, G. (1987). Male homosexuality: The adolescent's perspective. *Pediatrics, 79,* 326–330.

Remafedi, G., Farrow, J. A., & Deisher, R. W. (1991). Risk factors for attempted suicide in gay and bisexual youth. *Pediatrics, 87,* 869–875.

Rhoads, R. A. (1994). *Coming out in college: The struggle for a queer identity.* Westport, CT: Bergin & Garvey.

Robinson, B. E., Walters, L. H., & Skeen, P. (1989). Response of parents to learning that their child is homosexual and concern over AIDS: A national study. *Journal of Homosexuality, 18,* 59–80.

Rotheram-Borus, M. J., Hunter, J., & Rosario, M. (1994). Suicidal behavior and gay-related stress among gay and bisexual male adolescents. *Journal of Adolescent Research, 9,* 498–508.

Rotheram-Borus, M. J., Rosario, M., & Koopman, C. (1991). Minority youths at high risk: Gay males and runaways. In M. E. Colten & S. Gore (Eds.), *Adolescent stress: Causes and consequences* (pp. 181–200). New York: Aldine DeGruyter.

Savin-Williams, R. C. (1989). Coming out to parents and self-esteem among gay and lesbian youths. *Journal of Homosexuality, 18,* 1–35.

Savin-Williams, R. C. (1990). *Gay and lesbian youth: Expressions of identity.* New York: Hemisphere.

Savin-Williams, R. C. (1994). Verbal and physical abuse as stressors in the lives of lesbian, gay male, and bisexual youths: Associations with school problems, running away, substance abuse, prostitution, and suicide. *Journal of Consulting and Clinical Psychology, 62,* 261–269.

Savin-Williams, R. C. (1995, June). Parents' reactions to the discovery of child's sexual orientation. Paper presented at the Lesbian, Gay, and Bisexual Identities and the Family: Psychological Perspectives Conference, Pennsylvania State University, University Park, PA.

Savin-Williams, R. C. (1996). Self-labeling and disclosure among gay, lesbian, and bisexual youths. In P. J. Green & J. Laird (Eds.), *Lesbian and gay couple and family relationships.* San Francisco: Jossey-Bass.

Savin-Williams, R. C. (in press). The disclosure of same-sex attractions by lesbian, gay, and bisexual youths to their families. *Journal of Research on Adolescence.*

Savin-Williams, R. C., & Diamond L. M. (in press). Sexual orientation as a developmental context for lesbian, gay, and bisexual children and adolescents. In W. K. Silverman & T. H. Ollendick (Eds.), *Developmental issues in the clinical treatment of children and adolescents.* Boston: Allyn & Bacon.

Savin-Williams, R. C., & Dube. E. M. (in press). Parental reactions to the disclosure of their child's same-sex attractions. *Family Relations.*

Savin-Williams, R. C., & Wright, K. (1995). A longitudinal study assessing urban sexual minority adolescents for HIV infection and psychological health. Unpublished data, Cornell University and Children's Hospital of Michigan.

Sears, J. T. (1991). *Growing up gay in the South: Race, gender, and journeys of the spirit.* New York: Harrington Park Press.

Strommen, E. F. (1989). "You're a what?": Family member reactions to the disclosure of homosexuality. *Journal of Homosexuality, 18,* 37–58.

Telljohann, S. K., & Price, J. P. (1993). A qualitative examination of adolescent homosexuals' life experiences: Ramifications for secondary school personnel. *Journal of Homosexuality, 26,* 41–56.

Tremble, B., Schneider, M., & Appathurai, C. (1989). Growing up gay or lesbian in a multicultural context. *Journal of Homosexuality, 17,* 253–267.

USA Today (1996, March 19). More folks say gay is O.K., p. 1.

6

Gay and Lesbian Relationships in a Changing Social Context

Steven E. James
Bianca Cody Murphy

In the last thirty years, the social and political landscape for gay and lesbian couples has undergone radical shifts. Changes in laws and social policies, new definitions of what constitutes "family," the AIDS epidemic, the queer movement, and the antigay backlash—all affect gay and bisexual men, lesbian and bisexual women. As clinicians, we hold a systemic and ecological view; we recognize that there are biological, psychological, social, political, economic, spiritual, and environmental influences on what might appear to be individual human behaviors or isolated couple interactions. We believe that each gay and lesbian couple must be understood within a broad matrix of interlocking and interdependent contexts (Roth & Murphy, 1986). In this chapter, we will explore these interlocking contexts and the ways that changing social and political attitudes affect the establishment and maintenance of lesbian and gay couples.

Gay and Lesbian Relationships in Context

We have identified a number of contexts that influence the circumstances and affect the dynamics in gay and lesbian couples. We discuss these contexts as if they were separate and discrete, although we recognize that they are not.

1. Gay and lesbian couples must be understood within the prevailing sociopolitical climate—within the norms and mores of the historical period and the dominant culture in which they exist. In the United States at

the end of the twentieth century, gay and lesbian couples exist in a society that is heterosexist. Greg Herek (1986), a social psychologist who has done extensive work on heterosexism and homophobia, defines heterosexism as "a world-view, a value system that prizes heterosexuality, assumes it is the only appropriate manifestation of love and sexuality, and devalues homosexuality and all that is not heterosexual" (p. 925). The dominant culture is not only heterosexist but also homophobic. Herek (1986) has defined *homophobia* as the prejudice, discrimination, and hostility directed at gay men and lesbian women because of their sexual orientation. Members of the couple are affected by living in a society that makes them and their relationships invisible, in a society that actively discriminates against them, and in a society where there is widespread violence against gay men and lesbians because of their sexual orientation.

2. Gay and lesbian couples must be understood in the context of both partners in a gay male couple being men and both partners in a lesbian couple being women. Whether one takes a sociobiological approach that suggests men and women act the way they do because of biological forces (Wilson, 1975) or one contends that it is socialization that creates what we perceive to be gender differences (Chodorow, 1978; Dinnerstein, 1976; Gilligan, 1982), it has been frequently noted that sex roles, communication, negotiation styles, work ethics, attitudes toward sex and relational attitudes or capacities are all affected by sex and gender (Reinisch, Rosenblum, & Sanders, 1987). Biology and the differential gender socialization of men and women in our society present lesbian couples with issues that are different from those of gay male couples (Browning, Reynolds, & Dworkin, 1991; Eldridge, 1987; McCandlish, 1982; Murphy, 1992, 1994; Roth, 1989; Vargo, 1987).

3. Gay and lesbian couples must be understood within the multiple cultures that are relevant to them. Even within a particular dominant culture, racial and ethnic minority membership of the partners in the couple influences their relationship, as well as their attitudes toward being gay or lesbian. The attitudes and gender socialization of one's own cultural group may be very different from that of the dominant culture. The individuals in the couple may share a cultural background or come from differing cultural groups. A number of clinicians have suggested that the cultural expectations of Asian, African-American, Latino or Latina, and Jewish gay men and lesbian women present them (and the couples in which they are members) with unique stresses (Beck, 1982; Chan, 1992; Espin, 1987; Greene, 1994; Leong, 1996; Loiacano, 1989; Mays, 1986; Mays, Cochran & Rhue, 1993; Morales, 1992; Murray, 1995; Peterson, 1992; Tafoya & Rowell, 1988). Ethnic and racial minority gay men and lesbian women live in at least three communities: the gay and lesbian community, the racial or ethnic community, and the dominant mainstream society. Although each community offers some support, each has its own expectations and demands, which often conflict with each other. The tension of living in these multiple communities, in all

of which one feels marginalized, adds to identity difficulties, which can be particularly difficult if there are racial and cultural differences between the partners (Garcia, Kennedy, Pearlman, & Perez, 1987).

4. The "demographic" characteristics of the couple are yet another relevant context. Gay and lesbian couples vary considerably on other items, such as socioeconomic status, race or ethnicity, rural or urban. As with all couples, heterosexual or homosexual, the members of the couple may differ from each other in important ways. They may be of different ages (Steinman, 1990), from different religious traditions (Mendola, 1980), from different socioeconomic classes (Conner, Davis, & Dowsett, 1993), from different racial or ethnic groups (Garcia et al, 1987; Lockman, 1984; Mays et al., 1993). Gay and lesbian couples in which one or both partners have a chronic illness or disability are also faced with additional challenges and dual minority membership (Rolland, 1994). Those living in a rural area may be more isolated than those in urban centers (Silverstein, 1981). Furthermore, gay and lesbian couples at different ages have different issues. Older gay men and lesbians are, in general, less likely to disclose their sexual orientation to others (Tully, 1989), perhaps because many remember the oppression of their youth (Kimmel, 1977).

5. Gay and lesbian couples must be understood within the context of their specific families of origin. In the popular literature there are numerous references to the impact of family on couple relations, reflected, for example, in the humorous saying "I married you and not your family." As many family theorists have noted, however, this is not really a joke (Boszormeyni-Nagy & Spark, 1973). McGoldrick (1980) concluded that there are not two but six (each partner and each partner's two parents) in the marital bed, and Haley (1973) claimed that what distinguishes humans from other animals is the fact of having in-laws. Other animals mature, separate, and mate on their own. Only humans carry their whole family into the bargain. Gay and lesbian couples, like their heterosexual counterparts, are not only affected by their development within a particular family of origin but also their families continue to affect their relationship in the present (Berger, 1990a; Murphy, 1989; Serovich, Skeen, Walters, & Robinson, 1993).

6. Every couple must be understood as composed of two unique individuals, each with his or her own idiographic characteristics. With a lesbian couple, for example, the assumption that the two women are similar in certain relational capacities because of their socialization as women may obscure individual differences. Although it is important to acknowledge and to explore the effects of their shared experience of being both female and lesbian in a sexist, homophobic culture, we must not lose sight of the distinctness and the unique impacts of their individual issues (Murphy, 1994).

7. Finally, gay and lesbian couples must be understood within the gay and lesbian community context. Prior to the 1880s, there was no homosexual identity (Katz, 1995). Although homosexual behavior is universal throughout history (Bullough, 1976), and has been found in diverse human

cultures and other animal species (Ford & Beach, 1951), the concept of "the homosexual"—the "gay man" or "lesbian woman"—is relatively new. It was only in the later half of the nineteenth century in Western cultures that the social and personal identities of the homosexual were established in contemporary terms (Chauncey, Duberman, & Vicinus, 1989). Prior to that, sexual behavior or sexual orientation was not seen as defining a person and his or her way of life in the way that homosexuality is considered an identity in Western society today. In the past, homosexuality was something you did. Since the end of the nineteenth century in the Western world, however, being a gay man or lesbian woman is something you are.

Although there was what we might today label as a hidden "homosexual culture" prior to the Stonewall revolution in 1969, few gay men or lesbian women were willing to publicly affirm their identities. The emergence of a vocal gay rights movement out of the civil rights and women's liberation struggles created a context in which a thriving gay and lesbian community developed—at least in large urban areas. There is no unified gay or lesbian culture, any more than there is a unified American culture. Cultural norms and behaviors are mediated by such factors as class, ethnicity, and rural versus urban residence. Yet when attempting to understand gay and lesbian couples, one must do so keeping in mind how they interact with and are affected by the context of gay and lesbian cultures in which they live, including the emerging "queer culture."

Defining Gay and Lesbian Couples

What is a "gay "or "lesbian" couple? When thinking about issues of sexual orientation, it is important to note that there is a distinction between behavior and identity. To engage in a homosexual act is one thing, to label oneself gay or lesbian is another. Assuming the identity of gay man or lesbian woman is what is commonly referred to as "coming out." It is possible for a woman to have engaged in sexual relationships only with men and yet label herself lesbian, bisexual, or heterosexual. Sexual behavior isn't even necessary to have a sexual identity. For example, most adolescents who have not had any sexual relationships assume the identity of heterosexual. On the other hand, one may enter into a primary sexual and/or emotional relationship (behavior) with a member of the same gender and not identify oneself as lesbian or gay. It is possible for a man who identifies himself as straight and a man with a bisexual identity to be in a gay relationship. Similarly, it is possible for two women, one with a lesbian identity and one with a bisexual identity, to be involved in a lesbian relationship. What makes the relationship gay or lesbian is that the partners in the relationship are of the same *biological sex*.

The definitions of what constitutes a gay or lesbian "couple" vary from couple to couple in terms of their commitment to each other and the structure of their relationship. This is true for heterosexual couples as well as for same-sex couples. Gay male and lesbian couples may consider themselves a family or they may not; they may live together or apart; they may be monogamous or have an open sexual relationship; they may have had a public "marriage," a private commitment ceremony, wear rings or have other ways of marking their commitment to each other, or none at all; and while the relationship is usually between two people (hence the word *couple*), it may include more than two partners. What makes them a couple is their definition of themselves as such.

Given the above discussion, our definition of gay and lesbian couples that will serve as groundwork for this chapter is relatively simple. Gay male and lesbian couples are composed of individuals of the same *biological sex* who have *chosen each other as sexual and/or emotional partners*.

Effects of Changing Social Contexts on Gay and Lesbian Couples

Getting Together

It was not so long ago that the *only* place for gay men and lesbian women to meet each other was the gay or lesbian bar. Gay and lesbian bars often were not well advertised and were located in out-of-the-way places. To find the local gay bar often meant that one had to know where to look or whom to ask. To maintain the patrons' anonymity, the bars were often dark places located in remote or dangerous neighborhoods. These bars, such as New York City's Stonewall bar, were often the only public places that gay men and lesbian women, as well as transvestites and transsexuals, could congregate. Many gay bars had back rooms where men (gay-identified and others) would go for anonymous sexual encounters.

However, the bar scene was (and still is) available to only some gay men and lesbian women. In small towns there may not be a gay or lesbian bar, much less any other gay or lesbian community or social center. Owing to drinking-age requirements, gay and lesbian youth are not able to go to bars and are left with no places for socialization. However, for those to whom the bar is available, it may become a place, and sometimes the only place, where gay men and lesbian women feel free to be themselves.

The bars present gay men and lesbian women with a number of challenges. First, bars are places where people drink. Bar socialization, together with stresses of living in a society that is hostile to them, has been found to contribute to a high rate of alcoholism among gay men and lesbian women (Glaus, 1989; Shannon & Woods, 1991; Weinberg, 1986). Second, for gay men particularly, the bar has been a mecca for sex. American men have been socialized to see sex as a game of conquest and challenge. The combination of alcohol and the availability of sexual partners led to the widespread occurrence of multiple partners and anonymous sexual encounters. In *And the Band Played On*, Randy Shilts (1987) suggests that rampant gay male sex in

San Francisco bars in the late 1970s and early '80s was a reaction against the repression of homosexual sex by the larger culture. Gay men flocked to gay bars, where they basked in the accepting and sexually permissive culture; what was previously denied and hidden (sex) was now available and celebrated. Finally, the bar atmosphere is generally not conducive to the social interaction usually associated with the development of long-term couples. Yet in a number of studies, gay men reported that the most frequent place for meeting a partner was the gay bar (Berger, 1990b; Jay and Young, 1979: Mendola, 1980). Lesbian women frequently reported meeting their partners at feminist or lesbian activities that were part of the women's movement (Jay & Young, 1979; Peplau, Cochran, Rook, & Padesky, 1978).

The changing sociopolitical climate has a strong effect on the ways gay men and lesbian women have of learning about relationships and of meeting potential partners. Although in some communities the bar still remains the primary place for socialization for both gay men and lesbian women, today there are a burgeoning number of other places for gay men and lesbian women to meet. With the emergence of visible gay and lesbian communities in the last twenty years, there has also appeared a growing number of gay and lesbian social and political activities. These include gay and lesbian outdoor clubs, teen groups, singles' cruises, golf teams, organized sports, and computer clubs. In addition, gay and lesbian rights organizations (such as the National Gay and Lesbian Task Force, the Human Rights Campaign Fund, and the National Center for Lesbian Rights), as well as gay political groups associated with traditional political parties (such as the Log Cabin Republicans), have emerged. Here gay men and lesbian women may meet others who share their interests or intellectual activities. They may find that they have more in common than simply being gay or lesbian. The development of these nonbar venues for socialization has been both one of the most visible results of the lesbian and gay rights movement and, in turn, one of the greatest sources for continued momentum of that movement. To the extent that the gay and lesbian movement has enabled more people to come out, the gay rights movement can be considered a force in increasing the opportunities for lesbian women and gay men to find relationship partners.

More and more colleges and universities, and even some high schools (e.g., participating schools in the Massachusetts Gay/Straight Alliances Program), have active lesbian, gay, and bisexual groups. These groups help adolescents counter the effects of what Friedman (1991) has called "universal heterosociality." Additionally there are community groups sponsored by churches or concerned citizens that support gay and lesbian youth (e.g., Boston Area Gay and Lesbian Youth, or BAGLY). Gay and lesbian youth can learn to be friends with and date each other in much the same way that heterosexual adolescents do. This preparatory dating can help gay and lesbian youth learn about relationships in preparation for entering into long-term, committed arrangements.

Not having had such an opportunity for adolescent dating can lead to serious difficulties in couple formation. Martin and Hetrick (1988) have noted that social isolation or hiding from family, friends, or religious organizations, may play a part in adolescent promiscuity and prostitution. In communities where there are no resources for gay and lesbian youth, the only place a gay person (and here they were just talking about gay adolescent males in particular) can make "contacts" is in certain neighborhoods, parks, or bookstores, and that contact is unfortunately usually only sexual in nature. As Martin and Hetrick state, "For a few furtive moments the adolescent can achieve some relief from the overpowering tension of hiding. His obsessive concern with his sexual orientation which results from his fear of disclosure is transformed into an obsessive concern for sexual behavior (p. 171).

Many gay and lesbian adults did not benefit from a lesbian and gay youth culture. However, today it may be easier for them to meet gay and lesbian partners. The rise of gay and lesbian social groups at large progressive companies such as Digital Equipment Company, John Hancock Insurance Company, and Lotus Corporation enhance the possibility that is always present for heterosexuals—that they will meet a potential partner through work. Lesbian and gay professional organizations (e.g., lawyers, physicians, travel agents, psychologists) have blossomed in the past several years. Many colleges and universities, including the military academies, now have gay and lesbian alumni groups. All of these contribute to the increasing richness and variety of opportunities for gay men and lesbian women to meet and socialize with potential partners.

Furthermore, as gay men and lesbian women become more visible, they may be introduced to potential partners through the informal dating services of friends and families who attempt to "fix up" their gay or lesbian friends. There are also more formal dating services similar to those for heterosexual singles, as well as organized singles' social groups and dances. In the back of many gay and lesbian newspapers and magazines one can place ads comparable to the singles pages found in many mainstream papers (Laner & Kamel, 1988; Lumby, 1988).

Once they begin dating, where do gay and lesbian couples go for socialization? Gay men and lesbian women once feared that if others noticed their relationship, they might be taunted, harassed, or assaulted. In the old days, then, the bar was the only public place that gay and lesbian couples could go for socialization. However, since the bar was also a place of flirtations and pickups, gay and lesbian couples worried that their mates wouldn't be recognized as such—everyone was a potential threat. Many gay and lesbian couples stayed at home and became isolated.

Now there are lots of places for gay and lesbian couples, not only to meet but also to socialize. There are gay and lesbian neighborhood organizations such as Gays and Lesbians of Watertown (GLOW), where gay and lesbian neighbors come together for potluck suppers or other social events. There are lesbian bridge clubs and gay men's dinner groups. In response to the recognition of alcoholism, many gay and lesbian communities offer alcohol-free events, and there are gay and lesbian AA meetings. Each year there are large social events, such as Women's Week in Provincetown, Massachusetts, during which over 6,000 women gathered for social, athletic, and cultural events (Thousands pack, 1995); the Gay Games, an international competition like the Olympics but for lesbian and gay athletes; and annual Gay Pride marches held in many cities and towns around the country.

Despite these improvements in the social landscape for lesbian women and gay men, in most communities there is still cause for caution. Gay and lesbian women yet need to be careful about public displays of affection. Gay men and lesbian women who are simply open about their sexuality may be considered to be "flaunting" their sexuality. Incidents of violence against gay men and lesbian women continue to rise in America. That's why communities like Provincetown, Key West, and San Francisco have become great meccas for gay men and lesbian women, who feel safer in these havens for gay men and lesbian women.

Making a Commitment

A number of years ago the only recognition of a gay or lesbian couple's commitment to each other was a change of address—if they decided to live together. (It should be noted that many gay and lesbian couples do not live together.) Today there are many ways couples have of communicating their commitment to each other and to their friends, families, and communities. But in most parts of America, such declarations of commitment and love can put gay and lesbian couples at risk.

A large majority of gay men and lesbian women keep their sexual orientation secret from some family and friends (Bell & Weinberg, 1978; Bernstein, 1990; Chafetz, Sampson, Beck, & West, 1974; Jay & Young, 1979). Human rights laws protect gay men and lesbian women in only nine American states. In the other forty-one states and in most cities and towns, gay men and lesbian women have no legal recourse when they are fired from their jobs, evicted from their homes, or lose custody of their children simply because of sexual orientation. In fact, in almost half of the states they would be considered criminals. In a 1986 Supreme Court decision (*Bowers vs. Hardwick*, 1986), the Court upheld the right of states to prosecute adults for engaging in consensual sexual acts with each other in the privacy of their own home. It is no wonder that many gay and lesbian couples keep their relationships secret.

The desire to keep their sexual orientation hidden puts strains on that relationship and may negatively influence communication and intimacy between the partners, as well as with others (Murphy, 1989). Furthermore, secrecy may result in an invasion of the couple's boundaries by unknowing others. For example, partners may be asked to events individually or fixed up on dates because others mistakenly see them as single. Couples can become isolated, fearing that if they let other people close to them, their sexual orientation may be discovered. This can lead to a phenomenon that Krestan and Bepko (1980) have termed *fusion* in lesbian couples.

While many couples still keep their relationships secret, more and more couples are sharing the fact of their relationship with friends and families. Today, a growing number of gay and lesbian couples choose to create a ceremony to validate and celebrate their commitment to each other. Butler (1990), Sherman (1992), and Ulrig (1984) have compiled books of ceremonies for use by gay and lesbian couples. These gay and lesbian commitment ceremonies range from a private exchange of rings to a public celebration with family and friends. Some gay or lesbian couples register for shower and wedding presents as well. Increasing numbers of religious denominations celebrate the commitment of lesbian and gay couples through "services of union" or "commitment ceremonies." These rituals provide emotional and social support, religious blessing, and a sanctioning of the union. Some couples change their names, choosing a new common name or hyphenating their last names, as a sign of their shared lives. For some, the name change is preparatory to the creation of a larger family through birth or adoption. By the time this book is published, Steve James will have become Steve James-Herrmann, in preparation for the adoption with his partner, Todd Herrmann, of the couple's first child.

However, as Ellis and Murphy (1994) note, laws and regulations continue to "maintain heterosexuality as the only sanctioned mode of intimate relationships" (p. 50). Persons of the same sex cannot legally marry. Insurance companies do not provide benefits to "nonfamily" members, often ruling out partners of the same sex. Rights that automatically accrue to a legally designated spouse (e.g., inheritance, bereavement leave, property ownership, hospital visitation rights) have to be specially requested and granted, and are often denied to a nonheterosexual (and therefore nonlegal) partner.

In many states, attempts are being made to obtain the legal right to marriage for gay and lesbian couples (Wolfson, 1996). In response to this movement, some state legislatures have created preemptive laws that will renounce the legality of lesbian and gay marriages that may be created in other states—Utah passed such a law in 1995. Although most lesbian and gay couples would like to have their relationships validated, legally recognized, and supported, the majority would not choose to be "married" even if they had that as a legal option (Berger, 1990b; Mendola, 1980). Many same-sex couples, particularly lesbian-feminist couples, reject what they perceive to be the "patriarchal institution" of marriage, with its overtones of ownership of the partner. Therefore, it is important to ask the couple to define the nature of its relationship without imposing heterosexist terms like "marriage" on the relationship unless the couple does.

Couples are exploring other ways of protecting and supporting their relationships. Gay and lesbian couples can attempt to protect each other through wills, power-of-attorney agreements, health-care proxies, and relationship contracts (Curry & Clifford, 1992), but these avenues of protection are beyond the financial means of many couples. In order to create these protections, the couple may have to reveal themselves as lesbian or gay to an attorney or in court—a step that might not be in their best interests in some communities or in certain professions. What should a lesbian police officer in a small, homophobic town do to protect her partner's right to visit her in the hospital if that officer is wounded in the line of duty? What risks might a gay teacher run by presenting a health-care proxy to a physician who is caring for the man's partner? Remembering to bring a notarized copy of the proxy to the hospital may not be the first thing on one's mind when the news of a catastrophic accident or illness involving a life partner is received. This kind of legal discrimination adds another set of burdens to the validity of the lesbian and gay relationship.

Staying Together

Once a couple gets together, there are a number of factors that affect the relationship over time. How the couple handles coming out, the social supports for their relationship, the way the couple handles roles and boundaries, the nature of their sexual relationship—all affect how the relationship is maintained and sustained.

COMING OUT

The literature on coming out indicates that disclosing one's sexual orientation fosters the development of a cohesive self-identity. Having an open identity as a gay man or lesbian woman across life contexts improves one's self-esteem (Cass, 1979, Dank, 1971, Hencken & O'Dowd, 1977; Moses, 1978; Ponse, 1978) and enhances overall psychological adjustment (Coleman, 1981/82; Gonsiorek, 1982). A study that one of us conducted on lesbian couples and their parents showed that lesbian women who disclosed their sexual orientation to their parents reported that they were happy that they had done so, even if their parents disapproved of their lesbianism. The adverse consequences of parental disapproval were overshadowed by the benefits the women attributed to their decision to affirm their lesbian identity (Murphy, 1989).

The gay and lesbian liberation movement has helped many gay and lesbian couples feel more comfortable in affirming their same-sex relationships. Although many parents still disapprove of their adult children's homosexuality, there are groups like Parents and Friends of Lesbians and Gays (P-Flag), which provide support both to lesbian and gay couples and to their families and friends. Like mixed-gender couples, lesbian and gay couples are probably more successful in their relationships when they have supportive families or substitute families (Murphy, 1989, 1994).

ROLES AND MODELS

Until the 1970s, there were few models of gay or lesbian couples. Even today, the overwhelming number of models of intimate relationships in our society are heterosexual couples. Those are the couples we see on TV, read about in books, and are discussed in advice columns. The partners in these heterosexual couples assume roles in relation to each other that are frequently based on sex roles. Furthermore, negotiation traditions in families of origin may provide role models for mixed-gender couples, but to the extent that these models are based on social constructions grounded in the differing genders, they may not serve as useful models to same-gender couples (James, 1991).

In reviewing popular American films, Murphy (1991a) discovered that there were few images of lesbian couples in the movies and that those images that did exist reflected common stereotypes: older women seducing younger women, girls schools as hotbeds of lesbianism, relationship triangles (usually with men), and relationships that end in death, suicide, despair, or depression. With the emergence of gay and lesbian film producers and gay film festivals, there are now more positive models. Some films with gay and lesbian themes (e.g., *Lianna, Philadelphia, Clare of the Moon, Parting Glances*) even make it into mainstream theaters, giving gay and lesbian couples (and the society at large) a more positive view of same-sex relationships. There are still few models, especially for racial or ethnic minority couples, but films like *The Incredible Story of Two Girls in Love* or *My Beautiful Laundrette* are beginning to appear.

McWhirter and Mattison (1984) and Brown (1989) have suggested that the lack of role models for gay and lesbian couples can be helpful because it affords an opportunity to create new kinds of relationships freed from the constraints of social expectations. However, many gay and lesbian couples particularly in the 1950s and '60s constructed their relationships around a sex-role division of labor (Davis & Kennedy, 1989; Nestle, 1981).

Although some couples still assume butch-femme roles in relation to each other, studies of lesbian couples show that the butch-femme pattern is extremely rare (Maracek, Finn, & Cardell, 1988; Lynch & Reilly, 1985/86). Same-sex couples are more likely than heterosexual couples to have a relationship pattern based on role flexibility and equality, as well as shared decision making (Blumstein & Schwartz, 1983; Harry, 1983; Kurdek, 1995). However, gender stereotypes continue to influence perceptions of task negotiation and authority (Ashmore, Del Boca, & Wahlers, 1986; Huston, 1986). To the extent that two males in a relationship each believe that they are to dominate the decision-making process, then they may be set up for conflict as they try to allocate resources. Lesbian couples in which both partners are socialized as women to be nurturant, care taking, and relationship oriented are more likely to emphasize power equality, intimacy, closeness, and communication in their relationships (Eldridge & Gilbert, 1990; Peplau et al., 1978; Reilly & Lynch, 1990). And, not surprisingly, what lesbian women value in relationships is more similar to what heterosexual women value than it is to what gay men value (Peplau, 1981; Peplau & Gordon, 1982).

NEGOTIATION STYLES

The use of resources in any relationship is a complicated pattern of negotiation that may, over time, follow familiar pathways. Such paths are, in part, a reflection of the partners' roles in their relationship. These roles affect the couple's use of resources in a variety of ways. In negotiating, there may be authority given to one or the other partner based on the issue at hand—for example, in a discussion about the car, the "more mechanical" of the two may lead. In a negotiation about how to spend free time during the coming weekend, the partner who has been feeling particularly stressed at work may hold sway. In lesbian and gay couples, as with heterosexual couples, these patterns and roles can be complicated by the socialization that the partners have received about how men and women are supposed to negotiate and how one's gender is related to authority in certain areas.

Negotiation styles of gay and lesbian couples may also be influenced by their marginal role in the dominant culture. People who identify as nonheterosexual in America learn to repress any outward demonstrations of their feelings; they learn to pass as something they are not, and they may develop a flexibility in their interactional styles. To the extent that these skills become a pattern of the lesbian, gay, or bisexual person's interpersonal style, then it would not be surprising to find that gay and lesbian couples are more flexible in their means of problem solving and negotiation. James (1991) found such flexibility in the negotiation styles of gay male couples, who scored higher than average on standard measures of dyadic satisfaction, consensus, and trust.

SEX IN THE AGE OF AIDS

Sexual activity and sexual satisfaction are important in the maintainence of gay and lesbian relationships. Lesbian couples have less sex than heterosexual or gay male couples throughout their relationship, however they experience more nongenital sexual contact—hugging, holding, kissing, and cuddling (Loulan, 1987). Research conducted prior to the AIDS epidemic showed that gay men have more frequent sex, have more sexual variety, and are less sexually exclusive than heterosexual men and either heterosexual or lesbian women (Bell & Weinberg, 1978; Blumstein & Schwartz, 1983). (See Murphy, 1994, for a more thorough discussion of the differences between gay male and lesbian sexual expression.)

Given the sexual traditions in the gay male community, it is not surprising, in retrospect, that the AIDS virus that initially required repeated sexual

exposure and / or access to its host's blood stream would have such a dev-
astating impact on gay men. But part of gay male sexuality has been a creative attitude toward sex, and this aspect of the marginalization of gay men
has proved an advantage in their response not only to HIV but also to the
dominant culture's indifference to the epidemic.

Just at the time that HIV/AIDS began to be recognized as an epidemic
within the gay community, it became clear that government and social
agencies were not responding to what was initially called the "gay plague"
(Shilts, 1987). This indifference became a challenge to the gay community
to care for its own, and support for gay men and lesbians has increased
within the AIDS-impacted community. For example, Omoto and Crain
(1995) have shown that the AIDS epidemic increased gay and lesbian volunteer social networks and their involvement in the gay community. As
AIDS service organizations blossomed in communities around the country, staffed by gay men and lesbian women primarily, these groups became
settings for social interactions between volunteers. Many relationships have
been born out of a shared sense of duty to community among volunteers.

The AIDS epidemic has affected sexual relationships among all couples,
but none more so than gay male couples. One of the effects of the AIDS
epidemic is that some gay male couples are becoming monogamous, and
the range of sexual activity is changing (Berger, 1990a; Connell, Crawford,
Kippac, & Dowsett, 1989). However, many gay male couples, particularly
younger gay men, are not practicing safer sex.

The AIDS prevention movement in the gay male community has resulted
in gay male sexuality moving from the darkened back room out into the
light. Today gay male couples find that they talk more about sex, are more
creative in their activities, and are more experimental than gay male couples
were twenty years ago. Sex education has involved safer sex videos, parties, and seminars that celebrate gay male sexuality and encourage open
communication between partners. Lesbian sexuality and sexual expression
have also been affected. There are safer-sex education programs and videos directed primarily at lesbian women, encouraging more open and frank
discussion about what two women do sexually with each other.

As a result of both the safer-sex movement and the women's and gay
movement, there have been a number of self-help books about sex specifically for gay men and lesbian women (Loulan, 1984, 1987; Sisley & Harris,
1977). Rothblum and Breheny (1993) edited a volume on what have been
called "Boston marriages," in which they discuss the phenomenon of lesbian relationships in which there is little if any sexual behavior. This work
has brought asexual romantic relationships out of the closet, so to speak,
in the lesbian community.

Social Supports

As we noted earlier, the gay and lesbian liberation movement has given
rise to numerous social supports for gay and lesbian couples. Since stud-

ies of normative gay and lesbian couples have shown that gay and lesbian couples often turn to friendship groups for support, rather than biological families, these social networks have become essential providers of a supportive environment for gay and lesbian couples in good times and in bad (Weston, 1991).

While in the past organized religions have generally been very hostile to homosexuality, there are many organizations for gay, lesbian, and bisexual people—Dignity for Roman Catholics, Am Tikva for Jews, Integrity for Episcopals, Welcoming Congregations for Unitarians. While some of these organizations do not receive official sanction from their religious leaders, they do provide gay and lesbian couples with spiritual communities that recognize, validate, and support their couple relationships. Not only have these organizations created support for gay and lesbian couples within their respective denominations, but they have also begun to work beyond the bounds of their congregations, creating community support (McNeill, 1995; Reich, 1994).

The health-care needs of gay men and lesbian women are receiving more attention. Heterosexist assumptions by health-care workers are yet one more challenge to gay and lesbian relationships. Questions such as "Are you sexually active?" are immediately followed by "Do you use birth control?" These questions can be uncomfortable for the woman who has another woman as her sexual partner. Many people who are in gay or lesbian relationships feel uncomfortable disclosing that information to their health-care providers. But a number of gay and lesbian health centers have developed around the country in response to both the AIDS epidemic and the desire of gay and lesbian patients to have health-care that is respectful of their lifestyle and sensitive to their health-care needs. The mainstream health-care industry is becoming more sensitive to the needs of gay and lesbian couples, too. As more and more health-care organizations, from HMOs to employee assistance programs, recognize gay and lesbian partnerships, there may be less need for lesbian- or gay-specific health centers.

The gay and lesbian movement has created social supports for gay and lesbian couples throughout the lifespan, from adolescence through old age. Whereas in the past the gay and lesbian community has been a youth culture, groups like OLOC (Old Lesbians Organizing Committee) and SAGE (Senior Action in a Gay Environment) provide opportunities for gay and lesbian individuals and couples to network and gain support from their peers. Recognizing that as couples age many need the services of nursing homes and supportive living environments, many organizations have begun planning gay and lesbian retirement communities, hospices, and nursing homes where gay and lesbian individuals can feel comfortable and safe, and couples can be assured that their relationships will be supported as one or both partners requires health, medical, or social services (Catalano, 1990).

SUPPORT FROM MENTAL HEALTH PROFESSIONALS

When couples feel the need for more professional support, they can turn to clinicians, increasing numbers of whom have some training to work with gay and lesbian clients (Murphy, 1991b). The first wave of gay and lesbian psychology was focused primarily on disproving the theory that gay men and lesbian women were mentally ill or unhealthy (Bell & Weinberg, 1978; Hooker, 1957; Morin, 1977; Weinberg, 1973). As the field of lesbian and gay psychology developed, psychologists, social workers, and other mental health professionals began to look at the issues facing gay men and lesbian women because of their sexual orientation (Browning, Reynolds & Dworkin, 1991; Gonsiorek, 1982; Riddle & Sang, 1978; Shannon & Woods, 1991). Others began to study issues relevant to gay and lesbian couples (Berger, 1990b; Blumstein & Schwartz, 1983; Burch, 1993; Clunis & Green, 1988; DeCecco & Freedman, 1975; DeCecco, 1988; Eldridge & Gilbert, 1990: Krestan & Bepko; 1980; Laner, 1977; McWhirter & Mattison, 1984; Peplau, 1981; Roth & Murphy, 1986; Roth, 1989; Silverstein, 1981; Tanner, 1978). Researcher Larry Kurdek, for example, has conducted comparison studies for a number of years of gay, lesbian, and cohabiting couples (Kurdek, 1991; 1995; Kurdek & Schmitt, 1986, 1987).

The work of researchers and clinicians has led to a rise in the number of self-help and relationship enhancement books written specifically for gay and lesbian couples (Berzon, 1988; Clunis & Green, 1988; Driggs & Finn, 1991; Marcus, 1992; Tessina, 1989). In addition there are couples workshops and relationship enhancement groups.

If gay and lesbian couples desire relationship counseling, they can find a therapist who has training in lesbian and gay issues. Most of the professional organizations for mental health providers—the American Psychological Association (APA), the American Counseling Association (ACA), the National Association of Social Workers (NASW), the American Orthopsychiatric Association (Ortho), the American for Family Therapy Association (AFTA)—have sections or interest groups for clinicians working with gay and lesbian issues. In the American Psychological Association, for example, there is a specific division—Division 44, The Society for the Study of Lesbian and Gay Issues—as well as the Committee for Lesbian and Gay Concerns in the Practice Directorate. Gay and lesbian couples can contact these professional organizations for referrals to couples therapists.

Mental health clinicians now offer therapy groups about lesbian partner abuse (Leeder, 1988; Morrow & Hawxhurst, 1989), for partners of HIV-infected gay men (Bor, Prior, & Miller 1990; Geis, Fuller, & Rish, 1986), and for lesbian partners of women who have been sexually abused. Couples thinking about children have numerous resources (Barrett & Robinson, 1990; Bozett & Sussman, 1990; Martin, 1993; Patterson, 1995).

As researchers and family therapists have begun to explore gay and lesbian relationships (mostly lesbian and gay therapists), they have developed new normative theories of the life cycle of lesbian and gay couples. McWhirter and Mattison (1984) studied couples who had been together anywhere from one to thirty-seven years, and they developed a six-stage model of gay male couple development. While their original study was based on gay male couples prior to the AIDS epidemic, they subsequently interviewed gay male couples where one or both partners had AIDS. Clunis and Green (1988), using McWhirter and Mattison's model, developed a similar model for lesbian couples. Roth and Murphy (1986) emphasized a systemic approach to therapeutic work with lesbian couples, and Slater (1995) suggested a life-cycle perspective for lesbian families.

Queer Culture

The gay and lesbian rights movement in the United States flowed naturally from the civil rights and women's movements, and in turn has given birth to queer culture. "Queer" refers to the nonheterosexual; it is an all-encompassing term to include bisexual men and women, gay men and lesbian women, and "the Ts"—transsexuals, transvestites, and transgenderists. Through the literature of these constituencies, their songs, films, parties, organizations, and increasing media representations, more and more people are openly connecting to the movement.

As a new generation adds its ranks to queer culture, their perspectives, experiences, and expectations are shaping the movement. This new generation has an affiliation with the mass media that was previously unknown. A vast cultural exposure, through television and computer networks, has brought a familiarity with the terms and concepts related to gender, sexual behavior, and sexual orientation identity that previous generations did not have at comparable stages in their development. In turn, these important differences will undoubtedly affect the new generation's views of relationships. Androgyny appears to be a more comfortable choice, in both dress and behavior. Bisexual experimentation is more openly discussed, as are other sexual issues. "Gender-bending" behaviors may well impact on this new generation's expectations of sex and gender roles in relationships.

The virulence of public debate about lesbian and gay issues, as the religious right attacks what it calls "perversions," and the increasing violence against gay men, lesbian women, and other "queer" folks, together with a more confrontational political style in the queer community, encourages activism and protest. Such activism contributes to the drive toward full legal and social equality for gay and lesbian relationships. While the queer community is not unified around any one model for relationships—for example, legal marriages that mimic cross-gender marriages—the most basic organizing theme in the queer movement is the struggle against discrimination.

Conclusion

As the traditional family structures of America in the twentieth century become part of an ever more distant history, there exists the possibility that lesbian, gay, bisexual, and transgendered couples will offer lessons to mixed-gendered couples. These lessons may show ways of coping in relationships with an absence of productive role models, ways of negotiating resource allocations in nonpatriarchal family structures, and ways of creating family networks of choice rather than continued dependence on biological links.

The changing social mores and political landscape have radically altered the environment for some lesbian and gay couples. However, it is important to recognize that we have much further to go, in both the larger dominant culture and within gay and lesbian communities themselves, to create an environment that validates and supports the diversity of gay and lesbian relationships.

In the United States at present, no lesbian or gay male couple can marry or be assured of the same legal, economic, or social support for their relationship that automatically accrues to heterosexual couples who do marry. Furthermore, the positive changes in the larger culture that we have discussed in this chapter do not extend to all gay and lesbian couples. Many couples are still limited in their places for meeting and socialization, have no legal protection of civil rights, and have no support from family or friends. Finally, there is an emerging backlash against the advances of the gay and lesbian civil rights movement. Groups like the Coalition for Family Values have attacked the basic concept of civil rights for gay men and lesbian women. These verbal attacks are not unrelated to increasing reports of verbal and physical violence against lesbian and gay men.

Within the lesbian and gay communities themselves, much still needs to be done. Lesbian women and gay men need to be more sensitive to racial, ethnic, and class differences. Transsexual, transgender, and queer activists also challenge the traditional gay and lesbian community to open itself and become more tolerant of cross-gender behaviors. The gay and lesbian community, although victim of one form oppression from the dominant culture, must remember that its members can be perpetrators of other forms of oppression.

As a society, we need to work toward optimizing opportunities for gay and lesbian relationships to thrive and grow. We must continue to push for social change, to create a new vision for society in which all loving relationships are nurtured and supported. With whatever role models they follow, with whatever personal "baggage" from previous relationships they bring, with whatever perceptions of social pressures they carry, people will continue to create gay and lesbian relationships. The complex systems of interacting influences and multiple contexts that we have begun to explore in this chapter are merely intellectual wrappings on the gift of love that such partners give to one another.

References

Ashmore, R. D., Del Boca, F. K., & Wahlers, A. J. (1986). Gender stereotypes. In R. D. Ashmore & F. K. Del Boca (Eds.), *The social psychology of female-male relations: A critical analysis of central concepts* (pp. 69–119). New York: Academic Press.

Barrett, R. L., & Robinson, B. E. (1990). *Gay fathers*. Lexington, MA: Lexington Books.

Beck, E. T. (1982). *Nice Jewish girls: A lesbian anthology*. Watertown, MA: Persephone.

Bell, A. P., & Weinberg, M. S. (1978). *Homosexualities: A study of diversity among men and women*. New York: Simon & Schuster.

Berger, R. M. (1990a). Passing: Impact of the quality of same-sex couple relationships. *Social Work, 35*(4), 328–332.

Berger, R. M. (1990b). Men together: Understanding the gay couple. *Journal of Homosexuality, 19*(3), 31–49.

Bernstein, B. E. (1990). Attitudes and issues of parents of gay men and lesbians and implications for therapy. *Journal of Gay and Lesbian Psychotherapy, 1*(3), 37–53.

Berzon, B. (1988). *Permanent partners: Building gay and lesbian relationships that last*. New York: Dutton.

Blumstein, P., & Schwartz, P. (1983). *American couples: Money. work and sex*. New York: Pocket Books.

Bor, R., Prior, N., & Miller, R. (1990). Complementarity in relationships of couples affected by HIV. *Counseling Psychology Quarterly, 3*(2), 217–220.

Boszormeyni-Nagy, I., & Spark, G. (1973). *Invisible loyalties: Reciprocity in intergenerational family therapy*. New York: Harper & Row.

Bowers v. Hardwick, 478 U.S. 186 (1986).

Bozett, F. W., & Sussman, M. B. (Eds.) (1990). *Homosexuality and family relations*. New York: Harrington Park Press.

Brown, L. (1989). New voices, new vision: Toward a lesbian/gay paradigm for psychology. *Psychology of Women Quarterly, 13*, 445–458.

Browning, C., Reynolds, A., & Dworkin, S. (1991). Affirmative psychotherapy for lesbian women. *The Counseling Psychologist, 19*, 177–196.

Bullough, V. (1976). *Sexual variance in society and history*. New York: John Wiley.

Burch, B. (1993). *On intimate terms: The psychology of difference in lesbian relationships*. Urbana: University of Illinois.

Butler, B. (1990). *Ceremonies of the heart*. Seattle: Seal Press.

Cass, V. (1979). Homosexual identity formation: A theoretical model. *Journal of Homosexuality, 4*, 219–235.

Catalano, D. (1990). The emerging gay and lesbian hospice movement. In R. J. Kus (Ed.), *Keys to caring: Assisting your gay and lesbian clients* (pp. 321–329). Boston: Alyson.

Chafetz, J., Sampson, P., Beck, P., & West, J. (1974). A study of homosexual women. *Social Work, 19*, 714–723.

Chan, C. S. (1992). Cultural considerations in counseling Asian American lesbians and gay men. In S. H. Dworkin & F. J. Gutierrez (Eds.), *Counseling gay men and lesbians: Journey to the end of the rainbow* (pp. 115–124). Alexandria, VA: American Association for Counseling and Development.

Chauncey, G., Duberman, M., and Vicinus, M. (1989). Introduction. In M. Duberman, M. Vicinus, & G. Chauncey, Jr. (Eds.), *Hiddden from history: Reclaiming the gay and lesbian past* (pp. 1–13). New York: Penguin.

Chodorow, N. (1978). *The reproduction of mothering: Psychoanalysis and the sociology of gender.* Berkeley: University of California Press.

Clunis, D. M., & Green, G. D. (1988). *Lesbian couples.* Seattle: Seal Press.

Coleman, E. (1981/82). Developmental stages of the coming out process. *Journal of Homosexuality, 7*(2/3), 31–43

Connell, R. W., Crawford, J., Kippac, S., & Dowsett, G. W. (1989). Facing the epidemic: Changes in the sexual lives of gay and bisexual men in Australia and their implications for AIDS prevention strategies. *Social Problems, 36*(4), 384–402.

Connell, R. W., Davis, M. D., & Dowsett, G. W. (1993). A bastard of a life: Homosexual desire and practice among men in working class milieux. *Australian and New Zealand Journal of Sociology, 29*(1), 112–135.

Curry, H., & Clifford, A. (1992). *A legal guide for lesbian and gay couples.* Berkeley, CA: Nolo Press.

Dank, B. (1971). Coming out in the gay world. *Psychiatry, 34*(2), 180–197.

Davis, M., & Kennedy, E. L. (1989). Oral history and the study of sexuality in the lesbian community: Buffalo, New York, 1940–1960. In M. Duberman, M. Vicinus, & G. Chauncey, Jr. (Eds.), *Hidden from history: Reclaiming the gay and lesbian past* (pp. 426–440). New York: Penguin.

DeCecco, J. (Ed.) (1988). *Gay relationships.* New York: Harrington Park.

DeCecco, J., & Freedman, M. (1975). A study of interpersonal conflict in homosexual relations. *Homosexual Counseling Journal, 2*(4), 147–149.

Decker, B. (1984). Counseling gay and lesbian couples. In R. Schoenberb, R. S. Goldberg, & D. Shore (Eds.), *Homosexuality and social work* (pp. 39–52). New York: Haworth.

Dinnerstein, D. (1976). *The mermaid and the minotaur: Sexual arrangements and human malaise.* New York: Harper & Row.

Driggs, J. H., & Finn, S. (1991). *Intimacy between men: How to find and keep gay love relationships.* New York: Routledge.

Eldridge, N. S. (1987). Gender issues in counseling same-sex couples. *Professional Psychology: Research and Practice, 18,* 567–572.

Eldridge, N. S., & Gilbert, L. A. (1990). Correlates of relationship satisfaction in lesbian couples. *Psychology of Women Quarterly, 14,* 43–62.

Ellis, P., & Murphy, B. C. (1994). The impact of misogyny and homophobia on therapy with women. In M. Mirkin (Ed.), *Women in context: Toward a feminist reconstruction of psychotherapy* (pp. 48–73). New York: Guilford.

Espin, O. (1987). Latina lesbian women. In Boston Lesbian Psychologies Collective (Ed.), *Lesbian psychologies* (pp. 35–55). Chicago: University of Illinois Press.

Ford, C., & Beach, F. (1951). *Patterns of sexual behavior.* New York: Harper & Row.

Friedman, R. (1991). Couple therapy with gay couples. *Psychiatric Annals, 21,* 485–490.

Garcia, N., Kennedy, C., Pearlman, S., & Perez, J. (1987). The impact of race and cultural differences: Challenges to lesbian relationships. In Boston Lesbian Psychologies Collective (Ed.), *Lesbian psychologies* (pp. 142–160). Chicago: University of Illinois Press.

Geis, S. B., Fuller, R. L., & Rish, J. (1986). Lovers of AIDS victims: Psychosocial stresses and counseling needs. *Death Studies, 10,* 43–53.

Gilligan, C. (1982). *In a different voice.* Cambridge, MA: Harvard University Press.

Glaus, K. O. (1989). Alcoholism, chemical dependency and the lesbian client. *Women and Therapy, 8*(1/2), 131–144.

Gonsiorek, J. C. (1982). An introduction to mental health issues and homosexuality. *American Behavioral Scientist, 25*(4), 367–384.

Greene, B. (1994). Ethnic-minority lesbians and gay men: Mental health and treatment issues. *Journal of Counseling and Clinical Psychology, 62*(2), 243–251.

Haley, J. (1973). *Uncommon therapy: The psychiatric techniques of Milton H. Erickson, M.D.* New York: Norton.

Harry, J. (1983). Gay male and lesbian relationships. In E. Macklin & R. Rubin (Eds.), *Contemporary families and alternative lifestyles* (pp. 216–234). Beverly Hills, CA: Sage Publications.

Hencken, J. D., & O'Dowd, W. T. (1977). Coming out as an aspect of identity formation. *Gai Saber, 1,* 18–22.

Herek, G. (1986). The social psychology of homophobia: Toward a practical theory. *Review of Law and Social Change, 14*(4), 923–934.

Herek, G. (1989). Hate crimes against lesbians and gay men. *American Psychologist, 44,* 948–955.

Hooker, E. (1957). The adjustment of the male overt homosexual. *Journal of Projective Techniques, 21,* 18–31.

Huston, A. (1985). The development of sex typing: Themes from recent research. *Developmental Review, 5,* 1–17.

James, S. (1991). The male couple dynamic: Resource allocations, negotiation styles, and perceptions of satisfaction contributing to success and longevity in gay male relationships. *Dissertations Abstracts International, B, 52*(1), 519.

Jay, K., & Young, A. (1979). *The gay report.* New York: Summit Books.

Katz, J. (1995). *The invention of heterosexuality.* New York: Dutton.

Kimmel, D. (1977). Psychotherapy and the older gay male. *Psychotherapy: Theory, Research, and Practice, 14,* 386–393.

Krestan, J., & Bepko, C. (1980). The problem of fusion in the lesbian relationship. *Family Process, 19,* 277–289.

Kurdek, L. A. (1991). The dissolution of gay and lesbian couples. *Journal of Social and Personal Relationships, 8,* 265–278.

Kurdek, L. (1995). Developmental changes in relationship quality in gay and lesbian cohabitating couples. *Developmental Psychology, 31*(1), 86–94.

Kurdek, L. A., & Schmitt, J. P. (1986). Relationship quality of partners in heterosexual married, heterosexual cohabitating, and gay and lesbian relationships. *Journal of Personality and Social Psychology, 51,* 711–720.

Kurdek, L. A., & Schmitt, J. P. (1987). Perceived emotional support from family and friends in members of homosexual, married, heterosexual cohabitating couples. *Journal of Homosexuality, 14* (3/4), 57–68.

Laner, M. K. (1977). Permant partner priorities: Gay and straight. *Journal of Homosexuality, 3*(1), 21–39.

Laner, M. R., & Kamel, G. W. (1988). Media mating 1: Newspaper "personals" ads of homosexual men. In J. DeCecco (Ed.), *Gay relationships* (pp. 73–89). New York: Harrington Park.

Leeder, E. (1988). Enmeshed in pain: Counseling the lesbian battering couple. *Women & Therapy, 7*(1), 81–99.

Leong, R. (Ed.) (1996). *Asian American sexualities.* New York: Routlege.

Lockman, P. (1984). Ebony and ivory: The interracial gay male couple. *Lifestyles, 7*(1), 44–55.

Loiacano, D. K. (1989). Gay identity issues among Black Americans: Racism, homophobia, and the need for validation. *Journal of Counseling and Development, 68*, 21–25.

Loulan, J. (1984). *Lesbian sex.* San Francisco: Spinsters.

Loulan, J. (1987). *Lesbian passion.* San Francisco: Spinsters.

Lumby, M. E. (1988). Men who advertise for sex. In J. DeCecco (Ed.), *Gay relationships* (pp. 61–72). New York: Harrington Park.

Lynch, J. M., & Reilly, M. E. (1985/86). Role relationships: Lesbian perspectives. *Journal of Homosexuality, 12*(2), 53–69.

Marcus, E. (1992). *The male couple's guide: Finding a man, making a home, building a life.* New York: HarperCollins.

Marecek, J., Finn, S., & Cardell, M. (1988). Gender roles in the relationships of lesbians and gay men. In J. DeCecco (Ed.), *Gay relationships.* New York: Harrington Park.

Martin, A. (1993). *The lesbian and gay parenting handbook.* New York: HarperCollins.

Martin, A. D., & Hetrick, E. S. (1988). The stigmatization of the gay and lesbian adolescent. *Journal of Homosexuality, 15*(1/2), 163–184.

Mays, V. M. (1986, August). *The black women's relationship project: A national survey of black lesbians.* Paper presented at the annual meeting of the American Psychological Association, Washington, DC.

Mays, V. M., Cochran, S. D., & Rhue, S. (1993). The impact of perceived discrimination on the intimate relationships of black lesbians. *Journal of Homosexuality, 25*(4), 1–14.

McCandlish, B. (1982). Therapeutic issues with lesbian couples. In J. C. Gonsiorek (Ed.), *Homosexuality and psychotherapy* (pp. 71–78). New York: Haworth.

McGoldrick, M. (1980). The joining of families through marriage: The new couples. In E. Carter & M. McGoldrick (Eds.), *The family lifecycle* (pp. 93–119). New York: Gardner.

McNeill, J. (1995). *Freedom glorious freedom.* Boston: Beacon.

McWhirter, D. P., & Mattison, A. M. (1984). *The male couple: How relationships develop.* Englewood Cliffs, NJ: Prentice-Hall.

Mendola, M. (1980). *The Mendola report.* New York: Crown.

Morales, E. S. (1992). Counseling Latino gays and Latina lesbians. In S. H. Dworkin & F. J. Gutierrez (Eds.), *Counseling gay men and lesbians: Journey to the end of the rainbow* (pp. 125–140). Alexandria, VA: American Association for Counseling and Development.

Morin, S. (1977). Heterosexual bias in psychological research on lesbianism and male homosexuality. *American Psychologist, 32*, 629–637.

Morrow, S. L., & Hawxhurst, D. M. (1989). Lesbian partner abuse: Implications for therapists. *Journal of Counseling and Development, 68*(1), 58–62.

Moses, A. E. (1978). *Identity management in lesbian women.* New York: Praeger.

Murphy, B. C. (1989). Lesbian couples and their parents. *Journal of Counseling and Development, 68*, 46–51.

Murphy, B. C. (1991a, August). *The portrayal of lesbians in film: Reflections of lesbian relationships*. Paper presented at the annual meeting of the American Psychological Association, San Francisco, CA.

Murphy, B. C. (1991b). Educating mental health professionals about gay and lesbian issues. *Journal of Homosexuality, 22*(3/4), 229–246.

Murphy, B. C. (1992). Counseling lesbian couples: Sexism, heterosexism and homophobia. In S. H. Dworkin & F. Gutierrez (Eds.), *Counseling gay men and lesbians: Journey to the end of the rainbow* (pp. 63–79). Alexandria, VA: American Association for Counseling and Development.

Murphy, B. C. (1994). Difference and diversity: Gay and lesbian couples. *Journal of Gay and Lesbian Social Services, 1*(2), 5–31.

Murray, S. O. (1995). *Latin American male homosexualities*. Albuquerque: University of New Mexico.

Nestle, J. (1981). Butch-femme relationships: Sexual courage in the 1950s, *Heresies, 12*, 21–24.

Omoto, A., & Crain, A. (1995). AIDS volunteerism: Lesbian and gay community-based responses to HIV. In G. Herek & B. Greene (Eds), *AIDS, Identity and Community: The HIV epidemic and lesbians and gay men: Vol 2: Perspectives on lesbian and gay issues* (pp. 187–209). Thousand Oaks, CA: Sage Publications.

Patterson, C. (1995). Lesbian mothers, gay fathers and their children. In A. R. D'Augelli & C. J. Patterson (Eds.), *Lesbian, gay, and bisexual identities over the lifespan* (pp. 262–290). New York: Oxford University Press.

Peplau, L. A. (1981). What homosexuals want in relationships. *Psychology Today, 15*, 28–38.

Peplau, L. A., Cochran, S., Rook, K., & Padesky, C. (1978). Loving women: Attachment and autonomy in lesbian relationships. *Journal of Social Issues, 34*(3), 7–27.

Peplau, L. A., & Gordon, S. L. (1982). The intimate relationships of lesbians and gay men. In E. R. Allgeier & M. B. McCormick (Eds.), *Gender roles and sexual behavior* (pp. 226–244). Palo Alto, CA: Mayfield.

Peterson, J. (1992). Black men and the same-sex desires and behaviors. In G. Herdt (Ed.), *Gay cultures in America: Essays from the field* (pp. 147–164). Boston: Beacon.

Ponse, B. (1978). *Identities in the lesbian world*. Westport, CN: Greenwood.

Reich, D. (1994). Fighting the right on civil rights for lesbians, gays, and bisexuals. *World: Journal of the Unitarian Universalist Association, 8*(4), 12–16.

Reilly, M. E., & Lynch, J. M. (1990). Power-sharing in lesbian partnerships. *Journal of Homosexuality, 19*(3), 1–30.

Reinisch, J. M., Rosenblum, L. A., & Sanders, S. A. (1987). *Masculinity/femininity: Basic perspectives*. New York: Oxford University Press.

Riddle, D., & Sang, B. (1978). Psychotherapy with lesbians. *Journal of Social Issues, 34*(3), 84–100.

Rolland, J. S. (1994). In sickness and in health: The impact of illness on couples' relationships. *Journal of Marital and Family Therapy, 20*(4), 327–347.

Roth, S. (1989). Psychotherapy with lesbian couples: Individual issues, female socialization and the social context. In M. McGoldrick, C. Anderson, &

F. Walsh (Eds.), *Women in families: A framework for family therapy* (pp. 286–307). New York: Norton.

Roth, S., & Murphy, B.C. (1986). Therapeutic work with lesbian clients: A systemic therapy view. In M. Ault-Riche (Ed.), *Women and family therapy* (pp. 78–89). Rockville, MD: Aspen Press.

Rothblum, E., & Brehony, K. A. (1993). *Boston marriages: Romantic but asexual relationships among contemporary lesbians*. Amherst, MA: University of Massachusetts Press.

Serovich, J. M., Skeen, P., Walters, L. H., & Robinson, B. E. (1993). In-law relationships when a child is homosexual. *Journal of Homosexuality, 26*(1), 57–76.

Shannon, J. W., & Woods, W. J. (1991). Affirmative psychotherapy for gay men. *Counseling Psychologist, 19*, 197–215.

Sherman, S. (1992). *Lesbian and gay marriage: Private commitments, public ceremonies*. Philadelphia: Temple University.

Shilts, R. (1987). *And the band played on: Politics, people and the AIDS epidemic*. New York: St. Martin.

Silverstein, C. (1981). *Man to man: Gay couples in America*. New York: Quill.

Sisley, E., & Harris, B. (1977). *The joy of lesbian sex*. New York: Simon & Schuster.

Slater, S. (1995). *The lesbian family lifecycle*. New York: Free Press.

Steinman, R. (1990). Social exchanges between older and younger gay male partners. *Journal of Homosexuality, 20*(3/4), 179–206.

Tafoya, T., & Rowell, R. (1988). Counseling gay and lesbian Native Americans. In M. Shernoff & W. A. Scott (Eds.), *The sourcebook on lesbian/gay health care* (pp. 63–67). Washington, DC: National Lesbian/Gay Health Foundation.

Tanner, D. M. (1978). *The lesbian couple*. Lexington, MA: Lexington Books.

Tessina, T. (1989). *Gay relationships for men and women: How to find them, how to make them last*. New York: Putnam.

Thousands Pack Provincetown for Women's Week (1995, October 19). *Provincetown Advocate*, p. 11.

Tully, C. T. (1989). Caregiving: What do midlife lesbians view as important? *Journal of Gay and Lesbian Psychotherapy, 1*, 87–104.

Ulrig, L. (1984). *The two of us: Affirming, celebrating and symbolizing gay and lesbian relationships*. Boston: Alyson.

Vargo, S. (1987). The effects of women's socialization on lesbian couples. In Boston Lesbian Psychologies Collective (Eds.), *Lesbian psychologies* (pp. 161–73). Urbana, IL: University of Illinois Press.

Weinberg, G. (1973). *Society and the healthy homosexual*. New York: Anchor.

Weinberg, T. S. (1986). Love relationships and drinking among gay men. *Journal of Drug Issues, 4*, 637–648.

Weston, K. (1991). *Families we choose: Lesbian and gay kinship*. New York: Columbia University Press.

Wilson, E. O. (1975). *Sociobiology: The new synthesis*. Cambridge, MA: Harvard University Press.

Wolfson, E. (1996). Why we should fight for the freedom to marry: The challenges and opportunities that will follow a win in Hawaii. *Journal of Gay, Lesbian, and Bisexual Identity, 1*(1), 79–80.

7

Lesbian, Gay, Bisexual, and Transgender Friendships in Adulthood

Jacqueline S. Weinstock

Friends as family, families of friends, families of creation, chosen families: it is likely that these are familiar phrases to many self-identified lesbians, gay men, bisexual women and men, and/or transgender persons (LGBTs). They represent concepts that have appeared in a diversity of personal (e.g., Hochman, 1994; Preston, 1995; Weinstock & Rothblum, 1996a) and professional (e.g., Becker, 1988, 1991; Nardi, 1992b; Stanley, 1996; Weinstock & Rothblum, 1996b; Weston, 1991) writings that explore LGBTs' lives and communities. Other, related ideas include the notions that LGBTs' friendships are important to healthy functioning and that they are, in certain respects, unique or unusual in their significance, form, and/or function (see, e.g., Kurdek, 1988; Nardi & Sherrod, 1994; Stanley, 1996; Weston, 1991).

Despite seemingly widely held beliefs in the importance and uniqueness of LGBTs' friendships, empirical research on LGBTs' conceptions of, desires for, and experiences in friendships is quite rare. This is especially evident relative to the attention paid to heterosexual friendships and to other aspects of LGBTs' lives. Furthermore, most of the empirical knowledge about lesbians' and gay men's friendships has been gleaned from studies aimed at exploring the nature and composition of social support networks more generally and, in particular, the role of friends in supporting—or interfering with—LGBTs' romantic partner relationships (see also Weinstock, in press). Yet even these studies are limited in number. As Berger and Mallon (1993: 168) have noted with regard to gay men's social networks, "Much that is known to date about the social networks of gay men derives from unsystematic observation and professional opinion." This statement is relevant to lesbians, bisexuals, and transgender persons as well.

The major purpose of this chapter is to review the available research on the forms, functions, and meanings of friendships for adult lesbians, gay men, bisexual women and men, and transgender persons. Yet because most of the limited research conducted to date has focused on lesbians' and gay men's friendships, this review of necessity concentrates on these two groups. A second goal for this chapter is to critically examine the extent and kind of empirical attention LGBTs' friendships have garnered relative both to that paid to other aspects of LGBTs' lives and to heterosexual friendships.

As with other realms of research and theorizing about LGBT lives, relationships, and communities, work on friendships is at a transition point. Initially, research questions emerged from a pathologizing perspective. Efforts then shifted to focusing on documenting the lives of lesbians and gay men, with an emphasis on demonstrating that, contrary to popular (and, in earlier days, pathologizing) beliefs, "we are just like them," a normalizing approach. As part of this approach, bisexual and transgender identities were typically ignored, rejected, or further pathologized (Bornstein, 1994; Feinberg, 1996; Firestein, 1996b). But in recent years, a more affirmative research agenda has begun to emerge, one that is less concerned with the possible negative uses of LGBT research (e.g., as evidence of pathology). Instead, the focus is on examining LGBT lives in all their complexity and diversity, and on highlighting ways that LGBT lives and experiences might help to expand—rather than simply fit within—conventional ways of knowing and relating (Bornstein, 1994; Devor, 1989; Feinberg, 1996; Firestein, 1996b; Nardi, 1992b; Weinstock & Rothblum, 1996b). This third phase of research is in its infancy, a fact particularly evident in the research and theorizing on LGBT friendships. The final goal of this chapter, then, is to offer directions for future research and theorizing that both emerge from and build upon the diverse and complex experiences and perspectives of LGBT persons, as well as the various contexts of LGBT lives.

The chapter begins with a review of the available research on lesbians' and gay men's friendships in adulthood, organized according to the following themes: (1) the characteristics of friendships; (2) the functions of friendships; (3) sex, gender, and sexuality issues in friendships; and (4) friends as lovers, and lovers and ex-lovers as friends. Most of the available research has focused on the first two of these themes. Following this review, an analysis of the current limitations and politics of LGBT friendship research is presented, along with suggestions for further research and for additional approaches to the study of LGBT friendships.

Before proceeding with the chapter, a few caveats must be noted. Most of what is known about LGBT friendships emerges from studies of white, middle- to upper-class, well-educated, able-bodied, nontransgendered lesbian and gay samples. Additionally, research respondents have not typically been drawn from random samples; indeed, for reasons of access and visibility, most samples have been drawn from among those who are participants in established gay and lesbian activities and organizations. Furthermore, most studies have been based on relatively small samples; thus most researchers have been unable to examine friendships as they vary with respect to, for example, age, current romantic relationship context, or parental role. Consequently, this review is largely limited not only to lesbians' and gay men's friendships but also to white, middle-class cultures in the United States. Furthermore, it is shaped by the author's greater familiarity with and embeddedness in these same cultures, as well as in a lesbian feminist literature and culture. While efforts have been made to consider other perspectives where information was available, this review remains limited and does not speak to the full diversity of LGBT friendship experiences.

Finally, sex and gender have typically been confounded in the existing literature. Before the rise of the current bisexual and transgender movements, and as part of the feminist movements, a distinction was made between *sex* and *gender*, such that *sex* was to be used to refer to biological maleness and femaleness, while *gender* was to be used to refer to the psychological, social, and cultural characteristics and personality traits associated with biological maleness and femaleness. Feminists have argued about this, however, with some preferring to use the terms *sex* and *gender* interchangeably to highlight the likely interaction between biological and social aspects of sex (Golombok & Fivush, 1994). Regardless of usage, however, most studies concerned with the role of gender in friendships have not assessed gender identity and gender-related role behavior independently of sex identity, but rather have relied upon the latter to indicate the former. Today, there is increasing recognition of the complexity of both sex determination and gender identity, and of the limited reliability of using one as an indicator of the other (Bornstein, 1994; Feinberg, 1996; Nataf, 1996). Researchers, however, have not yet adopted an adequate system for speaking about or assessing these two distinct constructs. This limitation is reflected in the current review.

The Characteristics of Friendships of Lesbians and Gay Men

Across the available studies of lesbian and gay social support networks, and the few specifically aimed at examining friendships, lesbians and gay men report having and valuing both casual and close friends. Indeed, friends are a typical part of lesbians' and gay men's social networks. For example, based on the questions about community and social life in the National Lesbian Health Care survey (Bradford & Ryan, 1988, 1991: Bradford, Ryan, & Rothblum, 1994; Ryan & Bradford, 1993), only a very few of the almost 2,000, mostly white, middle-income lesbians between the ages of 25 and 44 reported having no one they could count on to talk to about personal problems (1 percent) or for a ride when needed (4 percent). While most respondents were currently involved in relationships with another woman, and specific numbers of friends were not reported, it was clear that the women were socially connected and had friends. In another, smaller scale study, D'Augelli and his colleagues (D'Augelli, 1989a, 1989b; D'Augelli, Collins, & Hart, 1987) found that their sample of young adult, largely professional, and (presumed) white lesbians living in a rural community and participating in a lesbian social group reported an average of ten close friends.

Berger and Mallon (1993) conducted a questionnaire study of gay men's perceived social support and satisfaction with support networks. The 166, mostly white, gay men aged 23 to 78 who returned completed questionnaires reported an average of 8.5 people in their social networks, with four of these being identified as close friends. Berger's (1996) small-scale interview study and an earlier study of 112 self-identified gay men also indicated that these men had friends and participated, at least occasionally, in gay community activities. Most participants were white and all were between the ages of 40 and 72; among the survey respondents, most identified as either exclusively (86.5 percent) or primarily (11.6 percent) homosexual. Another study, conducted in the United Kingdom by Hart, Fitzpatrick, McLean, Dawson, and Boulton (1990) on access to social support and care, also reported active social lives. This study involved 502 participants, ages 16 to 67, with a criterion for inclusion of having had sex with another man some time in the last five years; no other demographics were reported. These men reported that they were part of a close social network and had people to turn to for practical help if needed. Furthermore, 69 percent reported feeling part of a close circle of friends that kept in frequent contact, and 84 percent reported having someone to confide in on a regular basis. In another study of the support networks of persons with AIDS (PWAs), particularly gay men, Hays, Chauncey, and Tobey (1990) found that the men's inner circle or network ranged in size from nine to thirty-two, with a mean of fourteen. Of the ten closest network members (the focus of the researchers' inquiries), a little over half were friends and one-third were relatives. Furthermore, 66 percent of the closest network members were male and 54 percent were identified as gay or lesbian. Additionally, one fellow PWA was typically included in the list of the closest ten network members.

In a questionnaire study designed specifically to explore gay men's and lesbians' friendships (Nardi & Sherrod, 1994), 161 self-identified gay men and 122 lesbians answered questions about their casual, close, and best friends. Most of these respondents were white, college educated, middle and upper-middle class, urban, and in their 30s and 40s. Both the lesbians and gay men reported an average of sixteen to seventeen casual friends and 7.5 close friends. These numbers appear similar to those typically reported by heterosexual respondents (see Sherrod, 1987). In an early study by Bell and Weinberg (1978), lesbians and gay men actually reported more friends than did heterosexual respondents.

Studies that have centered on the experiences of lesbian and gay couples are also informative with regard to the presence and characteristics of friends. Among McWhirter and Mattison's (1984) predominantly white, young, and middle adult sample of 156 gay male couples, most had formed extended families that included gay couples and close friends, as well other family members. All respondents reported having gay male friends, and almost all said they spent most or almost all of their free time with these friends. In a questionnaire study with a similar sample of 69 gay and 50 lesbian cohabiting couples, Kurdek (1988) found that friends constituted 43 percent of respondents' total support network, while family members constituted only 13.5 percent. Taken all together, these studies indicate that lesbians and gay men are indeed embedded in social networks of friends.

These and other studies also suggest that lesbians and gay men tend to have friendships with others who are similar to them in terms of both sex and sexual identities. That is, lesbians and gay men typically have more lesbian and gay male friends, respectively, than any other type of friend. Sixty-four percent of the women respondents to the National Lesbian Health Care Survey (Bradford & Ryan, 1988; Ryan & Bradford, 1993) reported that their women friends were only or mostly other lesbians, while another 30 percent reported an equal number of lesbian and heterosexual women friends; the remaining women reported that most of their women friends were heterosexual (5 percent) or that they did not have any women friends (1 percent). Similarly, D'Augelli and his colleagues (D'Augelli, 1989a, 1989b; D'Augelli et al., 1987) found that the lesbians in their rural sample also tended to have social networks that mostly contained other lesbians. Of an average of ten close friends, almost six were lesbian (and three of these, on average, were members of the social group from which the sample was drawn). Indeed, 35 percent of the women reported having few or no heterosexual friends, and almost half of them reported no involvement in nongay social circles. Of the women who had both gay and nongay friends, 70 percent reported that these groups did not socialize together.

These same patterns appear in gay men's friendships. Almost all the gay couple respondents in McWhirter and Mattison's (1984) study reported spending most or almost all of their free time with gay male friends. Similarly, two-thirds (66 percent) of the respondents in Hart et al.'s (1990) study reported that one-half or more of their friends were gay men, while 75 percent noted that half or more of their social life was spent with gay men. Relatedly, approximately two-thirds of those identified as part of the gay men's social networks in Berger and Mallon's (1993) study were other men; their sexual identities, however, were not reported.

Finally, based on the one questionnaire study designed specifically to explore both gay men's and lesbians' friendships, 82 percent of the gay male respondents reported that their best friend was gay or bisexual; less than 10 percent had a best friend who was a heterosexual woman (Nardi, 1992a). Among the lesbian respondents, 76 percent reported having a lesbian or bisexual best friend (Nardi, 1992b). No further information was provided regarding the specific proportion of respondents with bisexuals as best friends. Furthermore, the sex and sexual identities of the remaining respondents' best friends were not reported. Still, these percentages indicate that, contrary to popular myths that "gay guys are a girl's best friend" (Rauch & Fessler, 1995), both gay men and lesbians typically form their close friendships with other gay men and lesbians, respectively.

Yet other kinds of friendships do exist, as reflected in collections of personal stories (Daly, 1996b; Nestle & Preston, 1994; Preston, 1995; Weinstock & Rothblum, 1996a) and the research already described. For example, the men in Berger and Mallon's (1993) sample noted approximately three women out of an average network size of 8.5, and almost all the men in Hart et al.'s (1990) study reported having close heterosexual friends. Most (89 percent) of these men also reported that their friends were aware of their sexual orientation. Additionally, of the 84 percent that felt they had a person they could confide in regularly, this confidant was usually a male friend (63 percent) or partner (52 percent), with family members (38 percent) and female friends (32 percent) noted much less frequently—but still noted.

Similarly, while 99 percent of the lesbian respondents in the National Lesbian Health Care Survey reported having women friends, only 10 percent reported that all their women friends were lesbians. Furthermore, 78 percent reported having some close male friends, and only 9 percent of these women reported that all their male friends were gay (Bradford & Ryan, 1988; Ryan & Bradford, 1993). The women surveyed by D'Augelli and colleagues were most likely to turn to other lesbians for help, but they also reported that they tended to socialize with and receive some support from heterosexual friends, especially heterosexual women friends. Gay men, too, were a part of some of the women's support networks, particularly when the women had large networks.

A rare exception to the omission of attention to bisexual women's and men's friendships, and to lesbians' and gay men's friendships with bisexual women and men, is Rust's (1995) questionnaire study with 332 lesbians and 45 bisexual women across a wide age range; most were, however, well educated and Euro-American. Rust asked these respondents about their preferences for friends and lovers, and found that more than half the lesbians—and especially the politically active lesbians—said they prefer other lesbians as friends and avoid bisexual women as friends. Furthermore, over one-fourth of the bisexual respondents also reported a preference for lesbians as friends. As Rust noted, negative attitudes toward bisexuals appear to interfere with the development of friendships with bisexual women.

In addition to the above patterns with regard to sex and sexual identity, relationship status and age appear to be shared by lesbian and gay male friends. Among the gay men 40 years of age or older that Berger (1996) studied, most preferred same-age peers. And in an interview study with 20 white lesbians 50 years of age and older (Raphael & Robinson, 1984), all reported seeking out friends who were age peers; those who were single also reported having more lesbian friends than did coupled lesbians. Similarly, almost three-quarters of the gay male couples in Berger's (1990) study reported that most of their close friends were also in couple relationships, while Bell and Weinberg (1978) found that, as with heterosexuals, lesbian and gay respondents who were in couple relationships reported spending less time with friends and less time out of the house than did single lesbians and gay men.

Shared parenting activities may also be a factor in the formation and development of LGBT friendships, one that may become increasingly important as more out LGBTs raise children (Stein, 1997; Weinstock, in press). Lewin (1993) interviewed 73 lesbian and 62 heterosexual mothers, most of whom were white, college educated, and in their mid-thirties. All had at least half-time physical custody of at least one child under the age of 18 (all had either one or two children in total). Additionally, while there was some diversity in socioeconomic status, and in the manner in which they became mothers, all were considered single in that they were not, at the time of the interviews, married to the fathers of their children. Lewin found that both the lesbians and the heterosexual women tended to turn more to friends who were like themselves with respect to child rearing. Specifically, lesbian mothers preferred other mothers as friends, regardless of sexual identity. They especially preferred those mothers raising children in similar circumstances (e.g., as single mothers); indeed, their friendships with nonmothers became more distant with time. Furthermore, in contrast to the primacy of friends noted in other studies, Lewin (1993) found that the lesbian single mothers were just as likely as the heterosexual single mothers to view family members—especially their own parents—as the most reliable sources of support in child rearing. That is, the lesbian mothers did not appear to substitute friendship for kinship relationships in their social support networks.

In addition to shared sex, sexuality, age, relationship status, and parental role, another variable that has been explored is the extent to which friends are likely to share problem behaviors such as alcohol or drug abuse. Kus (1991) interviewed 20 Protestant, college-educated gay men with above-average incomes who had been sober for at least one year, to study how sobriety affects friendship circles. Before sobriety, these men believed that they had many friends, although they also lost friends owing to their drinking. Indeed, the friends they lost often complained they drank too much, told them they were being irresponsible, or that they had a problem. The friends that remained were those who also drank. It was in sobriety that the men realized these friends had been only "drinking buddies," and not really friends. As a consequence of their sobriety, their social networks did initially decrease, but eventually these men began to expand their friendship circles in ways that included primarily other gay men in Alcoholics Anonymous, or nondrinkers. Similar studies also suggest that friends tend to be similar with respect to drinking attitudes and behaviors (Nardi, 1982; Shernoff, 1984).

Other aspects of identity and experience, such as socioeconomic class, race, ethnicity, physical ability, and religion, are also likely shared, although these issues—as with heterosexual friendship research—have not been the focus of much study. In the National Lesbian Health Care Study (Bradford & Ryan, 1988), one of the few studies to both gather and report the race and ethnic composition of lesbians' friendship networks, 61 percent of the respondents reported that their friends were only or mostly of the same ethnicity, 23 percent reported that their friends were equally likely to share their ethnicity as to have a different ethnicity, and 13 percent reported that most of their friends had different ethnic backgrounds from their own (the remaining 1 percent reported having no friends). Recognizing both the sparsity of friendships across racial differences and the limited attention to the role of race and ethnicity in friendship formation and development, Hall and Rose (1996) conducted an in-depth interview study with 6 African-American lesbians and 6 white lesbians who each had at least one other-race friendship (specifically a friendship between an African American and a white lesbian). Their findings indicate that despite the presumably free choice involved in friendships and the absence of any formal structures to shape or restrict them, racism and racial politics pervaded these lesbians' preliminary ponderings about whether to pursue a friendship with a lesbian of another race. In a similar, small-scale, interview-based study, Mays, Cochran, and Rhue (1993) interviewed 8 self-identified African-American lesbians in part to examine the effects of perceived racial or ethnic and sexual orientation discrimination on friendships. They found that for these women, racism was highlighted as affecting their friendships with whites, rather than heterosexism affecting their friendships with heterosexuals. More specifically, all the lesbians noted that they avoided friendships with openly racist people, and that they were cautious with whites—including white lesbians—because of anticipated racism. These findings, coupled with the existing literature that identifies the presence of multiple forms of oppression within LGBT communities (Allen, 1990; Allison, 1994; Beemyn & Eliason, 1996; Hemphill, 1991), suggest that as with their heterosexual counterparts (Blieszner & Adams, 1992; Franklin, 1992; O'Connor, 1992; Rawlins, 1994), LGBT friendship "choices" are not random, but are likely shaped toward similarity by existing sociopolitical attitudes and structures.

The Functions of Friendships of Lesbians and Gay Men

Social service professionals have argued that friendships are central to the process of developing and maintaining positive lesbian and gay identities, and to responding to the stressors associated with these identities in a heterosexist society (Kus, 1991; Nardi, 1982, 1992b; Shernoff, 1984). Some (Berger, 1984; Bums & Rofes, 1988; D'Augelli & Hart, 1987) have also argued for including gay and lesbian social support networks in their work with clients and for helping clients locate social networks in the local lesbian and gay community as a means of fostering their psychosocial adjustment. Some empirical support for these arguments can be gleaned from research on lesbians' and gay men's social support networks in general, as well as from the few existing studies on friendships themselves.

Research and theorizing on the role of social support in gay and lesbian communities was initially limited by a view of homosexuals as disturbed individuals removed from social life (Berger & Mallon, 1993). But by World War II and after, researchers were exploring, as Evelyn Hooker put it, homosexuals' "loosely knit extended series of overlapping networks of friends'" (Hooker, in Berger & Mallon, 1993: 156). From the 1960s and onward, lesbian and gay communities have increasingly been recognized as providing support for gay men and lesbians in claiming positive sexual identities, serving as role models, and being a source for social interactions and relationship and sexual opportunities (D'Augelli & Gamets, 1995). Three of the four studies concerned with the role of social support in the adjustment of gay and lesbian adults that Berger and Mallon (1993) identified in their review found a positive relationship between social support and individual adjustment. More recently, in their friendship study, Nardi and Sherrod (1994) found that lesbians and gay men "placed an equally high value on friendship; spent about the same amount of time with their friends in a typical week; believed themselves to be equally 'open, trusting, and truly themselves' in the company of their friends; and felt equally satisfied with the quality of their friendships" (p. 192). In addition to the general valuation of friendships, ratings of the importance of having friends increased significantly for casual, close, and best friends. Ratings of the importance of four different types of social support (labeled "Tangible," "Belonging," "Appraisal," and "Self-Esteem" Support) also increased significantly for each friendship type, with each form of support rated at least somewhat important across types.

Friends as Family

In examining the relationship between social support and psychological health, and the role of friends as supports, some attention has focused on assessing and comparing the relative importance of friends, family, and others for lesbians, gay men, and heterosexuals. A diversity of theorists, researchers, and social service providers have suggested that the context of heterosexism makes it likely that lesbians and gay men, compared to heterosexuals, will receive less support from their families of origin and from society in general, for both themselves and for their romantic partnerships. Given this, a context is created in which friendships take on a special meaning and function. Specifically, friends become family for lesbians and gay men because it is with friends that they are more likely to be able to be themselves and find support for their stigmatized identities and relationships (Friend, 1996; Kimmel, 1992; Nardi, 1982, 1992b; Paul, Hays, & Coates, 1995; Weinstock, in press; Weinstock & Rothblum, 1996a, 1996b; Weston, 1991). As Nardi (1992b: 110) put it, "friendship takes on the roles typically provided by heterosexual families."

As noted in the introduction to this chapter, the concept of "friends as family" is reflected in a variety of personal stories of friendships (Hochman, 1994; Preston, 1995; Weinstock & Rothblum, 1996a) as well as in professional writings (Becker, 1988, 1991; Nardi, 1992b; Stanley, 1996; Weinstock & Rothblum, 1996b; Weston, 1991). Yet empirical research is quite limited (for an important exception, see Weston, 1991). Little is known, for example, about the extent of—and specific, contextual reasons for—conceptualizing and creating friends as family, nor the particular meanings and enactments of friends as family. Indeed, as argued elsewhere (Weinstock, in press), "friends as family' may take on one of several different meanings. One meaning has already been introduced—that of friends as substitute family members. That is, friends serve as replacements for the loss of access to or support from traditional families of origin, and/or limited opportunities and supports for creating families with partners and children. Although Weston (1991) reported that only a minority of her 80 lesbian and gay male interviewees expressed this meaning, it is the one most frequently reflected in the literature.

Most of Weston's interviewees spoke of building families of friends as a political challenge to the family as traditionally conceptualized—especially with regard to the privileging of heterosexuality and of biological ties. Weinstock (in press) noted that this challenge to the traditional structure of the family that excludes nonromantic, nonkin relationships (Nardi, 1992b; Raymond, 1986) may take two forms. In one, "friends as family" may reflect a critique of and challenge to the centering of romantic partners and blood kin in lesbians' and gay men's lives, in favor of placing friendships—based on shared political as well as personal commitments—at the center (Card, 1995; Jo, 1996; Kitzinger, 1996; Kitzinger & Perkins, 1993; Strega, 1996; Weston, 1991). In the other form, there may be a centering of friends along with a romantic partner, children, and/or families of origin; here, "friends as family" may serve as a metaphor and a strategy for recognizing and prioritizing friends, as well as more traditional forms of kin. Implications of these diverse meanings of friends as family, and of the use of this metaphor itself, are considered in the discussion section. Here, two particular areas of research where friends may indeed function as family are reviewed.

HIV/AIDS and Friendship

Several studies have focused on friendships in the context of the HIV/AIDS epidemic, which has called upon gay men's social support networks and friendships to respond to individual needs, as well as community and societal demands raised by this crisis. Because social support—especially informal support—has been found to be important to the coping, adaptation, and recovery processes involved with serious illnesses, it seems especially important to study social support for gay men with AIDS. As noted earlier, Hart et al. (1990) examined the effects of HIV and AIDS on gay men's access to needed support and care. Almost all of the men in that study felt they had people to whom they could turn for practical help, and most identified friends as among their closest supports. Hays et al. (1990) examined the unique challenges posed by AIDS for gay men's friendships and social support networks. For example, not all network members may have known of or talked about the individual's sexual orientation prior to the AIDS diagnosis. Second, social support networks may have been compartmentalized, with family, heterosexual friends, and gay male friends in distinct groups. Third, because AIDS remains a stigmatized condition, members of an individual's support network may feel fearful, ashamed, or uncomfortable, and thus limit their support. Gay men may be less likely to react this way; they may also be likely to have had experience with death and dying over the course of the AIDS crisis, and thus have the skills for dealing with this illness. On the other hand, having seen so many sicknesses and deaths, gay men may feel "bereavement overload," making it difficult for them to provide support. A similar tension may arise for people with AIDS providing support to others who are similarly afflicted. While they may be very important sources of support because of their familiarity with the progression of the disease and of emotional reactions to it, at the same time, people with AIDS in advanced stages of the illness may be too threatening to those in less advanced stages. Furthermore, as Paul et al. (1995) point out, AIDS has already depleted many members of urban gay men's social support networks.

HIV/AIDS may also affect the individual person with AIDS in ways that in turn influence his support networks. For example, internalized homophobia may be aroused, which may influence one's willingness to be honest with friends or to sustain connections with other gay men. Hays et al. (1990) sought to identify aspects of support networks associated with the well-being of gay men with AIDS by focusing on the ten closest network members. They found that those men whose closest networks included a higher proportion of friends evidenced greater psychological well-being than men whose closest networks included a higher proportion of relatives. Similarly, those with a high proportion of gay people and those with another person with AIDS in their networks evidenced less anxiety than those with fewer gay people and those without another person with AIDS as part of their networks. Hay et al. (1990) also found that emotional support and practical information were most strongly associated with well-being, with the degree to which the person with AIDS felt he reciprocated in providing support also related to well-being. Furthermore, those friendships that were close prior to the AIDS diagnosis became stronger following diagnosis, while preexisting casual friendships became less valued.

Another study (Hays, McKusick, Pollack, Hilliard, Hoff, & Coates, 1993) examined gay men's self-disclosure of HIV status to friends, lovers, relatives, and colleagues. Because gay men rely more on gay peers than on relatives for support, the researchers hypothesized that HIV+ men would be more likely to disclose to gay friends than to relatives or coworkers. They also expected participants to perceive gay friends' responses as more helpful. The sample consisted of 163 HIV+ men in San Francisco, most of whom were white, professional, and had at least some college education. Nearly all had disclosed their HIV status to their partner (98 percent) and to their closest gay friend (95 percent), while 77 percent had disclosed to their closest heterosexual friend; there was no difference in these rates for stage of HIV infection (asymptomatic, symptomatic, AIDS diagnosis). Disclosure rates for coworkers, employers, and family members, on the other hand, did vary by stage of HIV infection; whereas overall, 60 percent disclosed to coworkers, 47 percent to employers, and 60 percent to a family member (most often a sister, and least often a father), asymptomatic men were less likely to disclose their status to relatives and colleagues than were symptomatic men or men with an AIDS diagnosis. Additionally, respondents' closest gay and heterosexual friends were perceived as more helpful than relatives and colleagues; there were no differences by stage of infection, nor were there any differences in ratings of partners by partner HIV status. It appears that gay friends and lovers provide the first line of support to gay men diagnosed as HIV+; the gay men in the sample did not wait to become symptomatic before disclosing to gay friends and partners, while they did wait to do so with relatives and colleagues. It was also gay friends and partners who were perceived as most helpful.

The importance of friends was also identified in another AIDS-related study by Kelly et al. (1995), this time with respect to their role in setting peer norms for safer sex and, thus, preventing the transmission of the HIV virus. Their study involved almost 6,000 males who entered gay bars in sixteen small cities and completed a survey on their sexual behavior. Men who engaged in more safe-sex practices were found to be more likely to perceive their peer group as advocating safer sex, suggesting that friendships may play a very important role in shaping social norms that promote safer sex behavior.

Romantic Partners, Parenting, and Friendships

The role of friends in supporting gay and lesbian partner relationships and parenting activities has also been considered. Kurdek (1988; Kurdek & Schmitt, 1987) found that gay men and lesbians in couples experienced friends and partners as their primary supports, with friends named slightly more frequently than partners and clearly more frequently than family members and coworkers. There was as well a positive relationship between social support and psychological adjustment that held for support provided by friends and partners, but not for support from family members. Furthermore, when comparing gay, lesbian, and heterosexual couples, Kurdek and Schmitt (1987) found that the gay and lesbian couples' friends were perceived as providing more emotional as well as social support than were family of origin members, while the heterosexual couples reported receiving similar social support from friends and family, and more emotional support from family than friends.

Berger (1990) also examined the role of friends in supporting gay male couples, and found that friends' as well as family members' attitudes were important to relationship maintenance. But as a diversity of social service professionals and some researchers have noted, friends may also pose challenges to couples (Clunis & Greene, 1988; Slater, 1994, 1995), and vice versa as Stanley (1996) notes. Friends may present competing demands for partners' time and commitment, and partners may differ in their ways of engaging in friendships. Indeed, 12 percent of the couples in Berger's (1990) study reported relationship conflicts regarding partners' friends. Friends also may become sexually involved with each other. Perhaps, as Berger suggests, the tendency for gay couples to form friendships with other couples is aimed at reducing this possibility. Overall, however, while friends may pose some challenges to couple relationships, the support of friends appears to be central; the available research indicates that lesbians and gay men do have and value friendships and that these friendships play important and supportive functions not only in the lives of individual lesbians and gay men but also in their couple relationships.

Sex, Gender, and Sexuality Issues in Lesbians' and Gay Men's Friendships

The study of lesbians' and gay men's friendships has the potential to shed much light on the issues of sex, gender, and sexuality in friendships, issues that have been of great interest to researchers of heterosexuals' friendships (Fehr, 1996; Monsour, 1992; Sherrod, 1989; Werking, 1994a, 1994b, 1997b; Winstead, Derlega, & Rose, 1997; Wright, 1989). Unfortunately, heterosexual researchers have tended to define sexuality in terms of sexual attraction rather than sexual identity. Furthermore, while focusing on differences in women's and men's same-sex friendships, and sexual attraction in other-sex friendships, these researchers have typically ignored not only sexual identity itself but also sexual attraction in same-sex friendships. In these ways, it has reflected both heterocentric and heterosexist biases (Werking, 1997b). Lesbian and gay friendship researchers have paid more attention to these factors, but both groups have paid limited attention to the independent and interactive roles of gender identity, gender role-related behavior, sex identity, sexual identity, and sexual attraction across a diversity of friendship dyads. Indeed, these variables have rarely all been independently assessed and considered in analyses.

Lesbians' and Gay Men's Same-Sex Friendships

Nardi and Sherrod (1994) are the only researchers identified to date who set out to specifically compare lesbians' and gay men's same-sex friendships. Aware of the prevalence of studies that revealed both similarities and differences in heterosexual women's and men's same-sex friendships (see Fehr, 1996, for a review), and of the great attention paid to sexual attraction in heterosexuals' other-sex friendships (see Werking, 1997b, for a review), these researchers were interested in examining the manner in which lesbians' and gay men's same-sex friendships are similar to and different from heterosexuals' same- and other-sex friendships. Their results indicated not only that friendships were salient for both gay men and lesbians but also that their friendships were similar in a variety of ways, including, on average, the number of friends they had, time spent with friends, satisfaction with the quality of their friendships, and the high value they placed on their friendships. The authors note that these similarities have also been found for heterosexual women and men.

But lesbians and gay men also appeared to be equally disclosing, instrumental, and expressive in their same-sex friendships, in contrast to the greater expressiveness and greater instrumental focus in heterosexual women's and men's same-sex friendships, respectively. Nardi and Sherrod (1994) suggest that gay men's same-sex friendships may be more expressive than heterosexual men's same-sex friendships, while lesbians' same-sex friendships may be more instrumental than heterosexual women's same-sex friendships. Thus, in these ways, gay men and lesbians may be gender atypical (Nardi, 1992b). They go on to suggest that sexual orientation may mediate the influence of gender, at least on some dimensions of friendship. More research is warranted, however, before drawing this or any other conclusion; especially critical are studies that actually assess and examine gender identity and gender-related role behavior as well as sex and sexual identities.

Nardi and Sherrod (1994)'s survey also included questions about sexual activity and sexual attraction in same-sex friendships. Nardi (1992b) reported that of those lesbians and gay men whose best friend was also a lesbian or gay man, respectively, 79 percent of the gay men and 77 percent of the lesbians reported having been—at some past point—at least minimally sexually attracted to their best friend; 52 percent of the men and 31 percent of the women reported a current attraction. Furthermore, Nardi (1992b) noted that 59 percent of both the men and the women reported having had sex with their best friend in the past, and 20 percent of the men and 19 percent of the women reported currently having sex with their best friend. With respect to being at least somewhat in love with their friends, 57 percent of the men and 54 percent of the women reported having had these feelings in the past, while 48 percent of the men and 28 percent of the women reported currently having these feelings.

Two significant differences found between lesbians and gay men are important to note. Lesbians and gay men reported similar amounts of conflict, but lesbians reported being bothered more by major conflicts with friends than did gay men, and being more likely to express their emotions when conflicts occurred. With respect to sexual behavior, gay men were more likely to have had sex with casual and close friends, while lesbians were more likely to have had sex with best friends. Nardi and Sherrod (1994) point out, however, that lesbians were twice as likely than gay men to report that their best friend was a former lover, and significantly more likely to describe their best friend as their current lover. Based on these findings, Nardi and Sherrod (1994) suggest that gay men and lesbians may be gender typical when it comes to sex and conflict. Nardi (1992a, 1992b) also posits that gay men may achieve intimacy through sex; thus they may engage in sex in the early stages of a relationship, and then decide whether the relationship is to continue as a romantic one, end completely, or become a friendship. The latter is more likely if closeness has been established before the sexual activity ends.

Caution is warranted, however, and more research needed, before drawing any conclusions from Nardi and Sherrod's (1994) study about sexual attraction and behavior in lesbians' and gay men's same-sex friendships. In addition to concern regarding the different percentages recorded across published reports (Nardi, 1992a, 1992b; Nardi & Sherrod, 1994), it is possible that some respondents reported on their current lover relationship—even though they were asked to select someone other than a current lover as their best friend for the relevant friendship questions (Nardi, 1992a). It is also possible that much of the past sexual behavior, sexual attractions, and/or feelings of love that were reported actually occurred in the context of a lover relationship rather than a friendship; this may be especially likely for the lesbian respondents, almost half of whom reported on a best friend who was a former lover. The former lover relationship may also explain some of the continued feelings of love and attraction, as well as sexual behavior. Furthermore, because the survey took place at a particular point in time, it is not possible to determine the number of respondents who actually reported on friendships that were following the friendship script (Rose, 1996; Rose, Zand, & Cini, 1993; Vetere, 1982) to the development of a romantic, lover relationship.

What Nardi and Sherrod's work does suggest is that the study of sexual attraction and behavior in friendships should not be confined to heterosexuals' other-sex friendships, and that further study of lesbians' and gay men's same-sex friendships may help inform both research and theory regarding friendships in general and the place, meaning, experience, and negotiation of sexual identity, sexual attraction, sex identity, gender identity, and gender-related roles in the context of friendships. The study of lesbians' and gay men's friendships with each other, with heterosexual and bisexual women and men, and with transgender persons is also likely to further such understandings.

Lesbians' and Gay Men's Friendships with Each Other

A major challenge typically noted in heterosexuals' other-sex friendships—sexual attraction (O'Meara, 1989, 1994; Swain, 1992; Werking, 1994b, 1997a, 1997b)—is less likely to be as central an issue in lesbians' and gay men's friendships with each other; the same-sex friendships of lesbians and gay men present greater challenges in this regard. Indeed, if lesbians' and gay men's friendship patterns paralleled those of heterosexual women and men with regard to the challenge of sexual attraction, lesbians and gay men ought to have more other-sex friendships than same-sex friendships. This does not, however, appear to be the case, suggesting that there is more than sexual attraction influencing the formation of friendships between women and men. Unfortunately, friendships between lesbians and gay men have not been the focus of much study, although some published personal narratives (Hochman, 1994; Nestle & Preston, 1994) suggest the presence and importance of these friendships.

Lesbians' and Gay Men's Friendships with Heterosexual Women and Men

A diversity of personal reflections and some research was found on friendships between lesbians and gay men, and heterosexual women and men (Bond & Weinstock, 1997; Preston, 1995; Weinstock & Rothblum, 1995a). Some of this writing has been generated by heterosexuals themselves interested in exploring why they are more attracted to queer culture than to the mainstream heterosexual world and/or how differing sexualities may influence a particular friendship or friendships in general (Boyd, 1995; Conner & Cohan, 1996; Cornogg, 1995; Daly, 1996a; Neustatter, 1996; Powers, 1996). As with the literature on heterosexuals' other-sex friendships (Werking, 1997b), the presence or possibility of sexual attraction, as well as reactions to it, has received considerable attention (Anzaldúa, 1996; Bond & Weinstock, 1997; Bright, 1996; O'Boyle & Thomas, 1996). Palladino and Stephenson (1990), for example, examined the role of the sexual self in the development of friendships between lesbians and heterosexual women. They argued that, given the connectedness of many female-female relationships, it is likely that erotic feelings will emerge as an issue in friendships between lesbians and heterosexual women. The authors present case illustrations from their clinical work that indicate some of the ways the sexual self may be "circumvented and/or distorted in the development of lesbian-heterosexual relationships" (p. 249). They conclude that lesbians and heterosexual women need to define and accept their own sexual selves if they are to become friends. To reach this point, they advocate open discussion of each woman's sexual self so as to break free of patriarchal constructions of female sexuality and presumptions of heterosexuality.

Kolodner (1992) was also interested in sexual orientation as a factor in women's friendships. She analyzed the responses of 13 heterosexual women and 18 lesbians who filled out an intimacy measure with regard to friendships with both heterosexual women and lesbians. All but one of the lesbians in the study could report on friendships with heterosexual women and lesbians, whereas only about 55 percent of the heterosexual women could. Kolodner noted that the heterosexual women reported different experiences in their friendships with other heterosexual women and with lesbians. Specifically, there was more romantic love, total intimacy, supportiveness, and acceptance in their same-sexuality friendships than in their other-sexuality friendships.

Based on separate focus group interviews, O'Boyle and Thomas (1996) identified several barriers to close friendships between lesbians and heterosexual women, including concern by the lesbians that heterosexual women might be wary of any physical intimacy they express or of conversations about their sexual relationships. The lesbians in this study noted that they tended to restrict such behaviors in their friendships with heterosexual women. Similarly, the heterosexual women who had lesbian friends reported engaging in less personal disclosure and discussion of their sexual relationships with lesbians than they did with their heterosexual women friends. But the most significant barrier O'Boyle and Thomas (1996) identified was that of lesbians' oppression, which tended to inhibit discussions between lesbians and heterosexual women. This, in turn, allowed negative stereotypes to persist. O'Boyle and Thomas (1996) argue that both lesbians and heterosexual women have to overcome a profound sense of difference, and that to do so, heterosexual women must confront their own heterosexism, while lesbians have to focus on aspects of their heterosexual friends' identities and interests that are shared.

Lesbians' and Gay Men's Friendships with Bisexual and Transgender Persons

The ability to further understanding of the ways that gender identity, gender role behavior, sex identity, sexual attraction, and sexual identity may be experienced and negotiated in friendships would be greatly enhanced by the study of the friendships of bisexual and transgender persons. Unfortunately, as this review indicates, there has been limited research and theoretical attention given to such friendships. Yet recent writings on bisexual and transgender lives, communities, and political organizing (Feinberg, 1993, 1996; Firestein, 1996b; Kennedy & Davis, 1993; Rust, 1995) suggest a powerful potential of such friendships for supporting both the personal and public fight for survival and social justice in an oppressive society. Furthermore, the ability to understand the independent and interactive roles of sex, gender identity, gender-role behavior, gender socialization, sexual attraction, and sexual identity in friendships may actually hinge on studying friendships across all combinations of these factors, and in particular among those who identify as bisexual and/or transgendered.

Reflections on Sex, Sexuality, Gender, Gender Role, and Gender Role Socialization

Gender has been an important variable in the study of heterosexuals' friendships (Blieszner & Adams, 1992; Fehr, 1996; Werking, 1997b; Winstead et al., 1997; Wright, 1988, 1989); it is also important to consider when reflecting upon the forms, functions, and qualities of LGBT friendships across a diversity of dyads. Yet gender identity and the adoption of traditional gender socialization patterns have frequently been inferred rather than assessed. But as Wright (1988) argued, differences identified as gender differences may be due not to gender but to factors associated with gender, such as gender role—the extent to which one reflects societal expectations of masculinity and femininity. Some heterosexual friendship studies have included measures of gender role, but they have, to date, produced mixed results (Fehr, 1996). LGBT friendship researchers have not, however, assessed gender role (but see McRoy, 1990, described below, for an important exception), and neither literature includes studies that independently assess and examine gender identity, gender role, sex identity, and sexuality. Such studies are necessary, especially in the study of LGBT friendships, given that lesbians and gay men may differ in their patterns of gender atypicality (Diamond, 1997) and given the conflicting hypotheses and findings to date regarding the gender-related patterns of lesbians' and gay men's friendships (Nardi, 1992a, 1992b; Nardi & Sherrod, 1994).

One exception to the absence of attention to gender role is McRoy's (1990) research on the role of traditional male sex-role socialization in both gay and heterosexual men's friendships. Noting that homophobia and antifemininity are part of traditional male sex-role socialization and yet are also likely to be barriers to intimacy in friendships with men (and lover relationships with either women or men), McRoy examined the relationship between intimacy in men's friendships, homophobia, and antifemininity in a sample of 82 gay men and 90 heterosexual men, most of whom were Caucasian university students and/or members of gay-affiliated groups. The men ranged in age from 17 to 60, although the gay men, averaging 35, were significantly older than the heterosexual men, whose mean age was 29. Results based on completion of a variety of measures indicated that, not surprisingly, the heterosexual men were significantly more homophobic than the gay men. They were also significantly more antifeminine, and they reported significantly less intimacy with their closest male friend. Specifically, heterosexual men reported less sharing of personal information and concerns in their friendships, less verbal and physical expression, less provision of understanding and support, and less open expression of their feelings in their closest male friendships than did gay men. It is important to note, as McRoy does, that these findings are correlational; it is possible that intimacy in same-sex friendships reduces antifemininity. Still, the findings suggest that homophobia and antifemininity may actually inhibit closeness among men (Fehr, 1996). Indeed, as Allan (in Franklin, 1992: 211) put it, men are traditionally socialized to be "non-intimate, non-self-disclosing, homophobic, non-nurturing, and competitive." No wonder, then, that friendships among men who reflect traditional gender roles tend to replicate both sexism and heterosexism (Messner, 1992). Given this, the current controversy in the heterosexual friendship literature over the definition and measurement of intimacy and, in particular, the appropriateness of relying upon verbal intimacy as a central measure of the closeness and quality of a friendship (Parks & Floyd, 1996; Tavris, 1992; Werking, 1994a; Wood & Inman, 1993) appears in a new light. It may be that by applying a "feminine ruler" to the study of intimacy in friendship (Wood & Inman, 1993), men's friendships are judged against an unfair standard (Swain, 1989; Werking, 1994a). At the same time, care must be taken not to ignore the ways that traditionally "male friendship patterns fit into an overall system of power," nor how men's traditionally defined and experienced friendships themselves "construct men's attitudes and relationships with women" (Messner, 1992: 217) in ways that reflect and reinforce both sexism and heterosexism.

Lesbians' and Gay Men's Friends as Lovers, and Lovers and Ex-Lovers as Friends

Much has been made of, but little empirical attention has been given to, the blurring of the lines between friends and lovers among lesbians and gay men. For example, the tendencies for many lesbians to consider their lovers to be their best friends and to remain friends with ex-lovers have been frequently highlighted (Clunis & Greene, 1988; Peplau, 1991) and occasionally researched (Becker, 1988; Nardi & Sherrod, 1994; Stanley, 1996). As already noted, 71 percent of the gay men and 84 percent of the lesbians in Nardi and Sherrod's (1994) study considered their partner to be their best friend. Furthermore, despite the confounds already noted, findings from this study suggest that most lesbians and gay men are at least minimally sexually attracted to and in love with their friends at some point in time (Nardi, 1992b); the findings also suggest that some lesbians and gay men can be sexually involved with their friends and still remain friends (Preston, 1995; Weinstock & Rothblum, 1996a). Gay men and lesbians may, however, move from friends to lovers and lovers to friends in different ways. As noted earlier, Nardi (1992a) suggested that sexual involvement may precede the development of a friendship for gay men, while for lesbians it may follow from it.

Vetere's (1982) research provides some support for the pattern for lesbians noted above. She interviewed 23 white, middle-class, self-identified lesbians (or, for one, a woman-identified bisexual) between the ages of 19 and 33, most of whom were involved with women at the time of the study. Eighteen of the 23 women's first love relationship grew out of a friendship, as did their current lover relationship. Overall, 21 (91 percent) of the women experienced having a friend become a lover; almost all also experienced being attracted to a woman friend. Furthermore, the women tended to conceptualize lover relationships as friendships, with 19 women perceiving this friendship with their lover to have special effects on the relationship. While 12 of these women felt only positive effects, 7 felt there were both negative and positive effects. Among the negative effects were the experience of conflict between the role of friend and lover, feeling that the friendship outstripped the lover relationship at times, and the need for more personal space or autonomy. Among the positive effects were mutual closeness, a sense of security, and individual growth. Additional positive effects included experiencing the relationship as more than a sexual one and having the friendship help carry the relationship through rough times. Vetere (1982: 61) concluded that friendship appears to be "a prime developmental and maintenance factor in the respondents' lesbian love relationships." The women she studied also tended to see a continuum between lovers and friends.

But what about ex-lovers as friends? Autobiographical stories of transitions from lovers to friends exist for both lesbians and gay men (Preston, 1995; Weinstock & Rothblum, 1996a), although the available research has focused on lesbians. While not all ex-lovers remain close friends, it does appear that many lesbians and gay men hope to—and do—stay connected to ex-lovers as friends and family (Becker, 1988; Slater, 1995; Slater & Mencher, 1991; Nardi & Sherrod, 1994). Indeed, Slater (1995) noted that sustaining friendships with ex-lovers is normative in lesbian communities. Stanley (1996) appears to concur, based on the two focus-group interviews she conducted with mostly white, well-educated young adult lesbians to discuss the role of friendships in their lives, as well as secondary analyses on data from another, demographically similar sample of 550 lesbians (275 couples). Across all three samples, lesbians appeared to place great value on friendships with ex-lovers, although they also recognized the challenges that such friendships often create for the friends' current lover relationships. Similarly, Kimmel and Sang (1995) reported on an unpublished 1994 study by Fertitta in which 50 percent of the lesbians sampled—compared to 25 percent of the heterosexual women—reported being close to their ex-lovers.

Becker's (1988) exploration of the ex-lover transition is the most extensive to date. She collected 98 ex-lover transition stories from interviews with 40 lesbians between the ages of 24 and 66; 75 percent of the sample was white, and half had working-class backgrounds. The stories reflected a diversity of possible experiences within and outcomes of the ex-lover transition, including ex-lover relationships that ran the gamut from hostility to closeness. While not all the women developed friendships with their ex-lovers, and of those who did, a diversity of friendships were constructed, some of the women did establish close and even best friendships with their ex-lovers. In exploring the motivating factors for lesbians to remain friends after a breakup, Becker highlighted the bond of oppression among lesbians, who likely experienced stigma associated with their relationships and limited recognition or support for the relationships and the relationship breakups. Having shared this stigma and developed together some sense of pride in their identities as lesbians, they may be motivated to set aside their differences to try to sustain some form of connection and care. Indeed, this is one way the women can continue to work against the negative stereotypes of lesbians and lesbian relationships portrayed in the larger culture, as well as validate the lover relationship they shared. Other factors that may contribute to the development and maintenance of ex-lovers as friends and family include the relatively small size of lesbian and gay communities and, at least to date, the smaller proportion of lesbian and gay couples, compared to heterosexual couples, engaged in raising children.

Current and Future Directions for LGBT Friendship Research and Theorizing

In this final section, limitations of the existing approach to the study of LGBT friendships are highlighted, and suggestions for further research and theorizing are offered.

Limited Samples and Research Designs

As noted at the beginning of this chapter, studies of friendship have typically been conducted with young, white, middle-class, self-identified, presumably able-bodied lesbians and gay men who are at least somewhat socially and/or politically connected to public lesbian and gay activities. It is critical that research be expanded to include bisexual and transgender persons, as well as the full diversity of ages, races, ethnicities, and physical abilities that comprise LGBT communities. Furthermore, cohort and historical context need to be considered, along with other factors that shape LGBT experiences, including age at time of coming out, history of sexual identity development and of other sexual identities, and relationship circumstances—including current and prior experiences with families of origin, partners, and children.

In addition to expanding sample diversity, research on LGBT friendships would benefit from reliance upon an expansion of methods. To date, surveys and interviews collected at one point in time from one member of a friendship have been relied upon. Much might be learned from longitudi-

nal studies, from studies that collect data from all participants in a friendship dyad or network, and from observations and participant observations
of friendship dyads and networks (Duck, West, & Acitelli, 1997). These
methods may enable researchers to deepen as well as move beyond the
focus on perceptions of friendship to examining both the actual practices
and material conditions of particular friendships. In all of these approaches,
researchers ought to specify the type of friendship being explored (best,
close, or casual) as well as the length of the friendship.

Limited Attention to LGBTs' Friendships

While the above noted limitations are important, of greater concern is the
limited empirical attention paid to LGBT friendships in general. Much more
research and theoretical attention has been paid to LGBT experiences with
romantic partners, children, and families of origin. This focus is similar to
that which has dominated the personal relationship literature on heterosexuals—studies of heterosexual dating and marital relationships. In other
words, despite personal, professional, and theoretical reflections to the
contrary, friendships appear to hold as unprivileged a place in LGBT relationship literature as they do in heterosexual relationship research. The
privileging of partners is particularly evident when researchers, practitioners, and theorists concentrate on the roles that friends may play in supporting—or interfering with—LGBT lover relationships, and few ask this
question in reverse. Furthermore, although many LGBT researchers and
theorists have adopted the language of friends as family as a means of
valuing friendships, this language itself may confer greater importance and
status to the family. This point is further addressed shortly.

The Focus of Existing Friendship Research

Most of the available research on LGBT friendships has been directed at
identifying who LGBTs tend to be friends with and the role of friends as
personal and social supports. While the information garnered from this
research is important, there are several limitations and issues to consider.

EXPANDING THE STUDY OF WHO LGBTs TEND TO BEFRIEND

Most of the research aimed at identifying LGBT friends has focused on the
sex and sexual identities of the friends. It seems critical that this focus be
expanded to consider more particular aspects of individuals that draw
friends together. By gathering information only about the identity markers of sex and sexuality, it is difficult to determine the extent to which shared
sexuality and sex identity are themselves relevant to LGBT friendship
choices, rather than other characteristics associated with these identities—
for example, shared politics and personal commitments in the world of
work and/or play (Card, 1995; see also Franklin, 1992; Hemphill, 1991;

Raymond, 1986). Furthermore, such studies, conducted at one point in time, reinforce the view of sexuality as stable and unidimensional.

EXPANDING THE STUDY OF THE ROLES OF FRIENDS

Research is also needed that more closely examines the positive and negative, and the actual and anticipated functions that friends play in LGBT lives, as well as how these may all vary across time and diverse contexts, including diverse identity, cultural, familial, and life-course contexts. For example, it is likely that friends play different roles in LGBT lives depending on each person's involvement in and satisfaction with romantic partnerships, children, and families of origin; friends may also play different roles for LGBT persons in young, middle, and late adulthood, all of which may vary, as well with changing social and legal contexts. Researchers might ask, for example, whether LGBT persons, like their heterosexual counterparts, reduce the time and attention paid to friendships as they move through adulthood and become more involved in families and careers. They may also consider whether there are cohort and/or age differences in the likelihood of remaining friends with ex-lovers and/or in the use and meaning of the phrase "friends as family."

In addition to age, cohort, and relational contexts of LGBT lives, more attention to the roles friends play in the development and support of LGBT communities and politics seems critical. To date, this focus appears more in published personal reflections and theorizing than in research. Empirical attention to the roles friends play in supporting—and diverting—the aims of diverse LGBT political agendas and in bridging—as well as reinforcing—differences across sexual identity, race, class, and culture, is clearly warranted. At the same time, researchers need to more fully consider the contexts of oppression that shape the formation, structure, and experience of LGBT friendships. Available studies suggest that lesbians and gay men tend to be friends with other lesbians and gay men. The formation of such friendships may help provide the means for living more honestly and fully as LGBT persons; indeed, the context of oppression may actually create a greater need for—and thus importance of—friendships in LGBT lives. Yet the prevalence of shared sexuality friendships may also reflect and perhaps reinforce heterosexism. Those who have studied heterosexual friendships note that people tend to like those who like them, and who they tend to come in contact with; people also tend to become friends with those they meet through already formed social networks. Furthermore, equality has been identified as a defining element in friendships (Fehr, 1996). If the same factors influence the formation of LGBT friendships, it is no wonder that in a context of heterosexism, both LGBT and heterosexual persons tend to develop friendships within rather than across these boundaries. Yet while the importance of LGBT friendships with each other should not be underestimated, it is necessary as well to consider the possibilities for reducing negative attitudes toward LGBT persons that friendships between heterosexuals and LGBTs may provide. Indeed, as Patterson (1996) has noted, the contact hypothesis developed by Allport suggests that equal-status contact may be associated with the reduction of negative attitudes toward lesbians and gay men. Further study of those friendships that are formed between LGBTs and heterosexuals, and of the factors that contribute to their formation and continuation, may provide much insight into both the meaning and the impact of heterosexism, and suggest possibilities for combating it. Additionally, studying the friendships of LGBT persons who are also members of other oppressed groups, and comparisons of these friendships with both privileged LGBTs and non-LGBT persons from other oppressed groups, may be particularly useful for gaining a deeper understanding of the impact of oppression on friendships.

Confounding of Sex, Gender, and Sexuality

As has already been noted, both heterosexual and LGBT researchers have frequently ignored or confounded sex, gender, and sexuality when studying friendships. Heterosexual friendship researchers are becoming increasingly aware of their heterosexist bias (Rawlins, 1994; Werking, 1997b), and both groups are beginning to recognize the need for independently assessing and examining sex, gender, and sexual identity, as well as sexual attraction, sexual behavior, gender-role socialization, and gender-related behaviors, in all friendship studies. The study of friendships among those who vary in the extent to which they accept and enact traditional gender-related patterns of behavior, as well as the extent to which they are able—and choose—to pass as a member of one of the more traditionally accepted categories of sex, gender, and sexuality, may be particularly useful in understanding how these factors are experienced and negotiated in friendships. Furthermore, at the same time as more attention is paid to measuring the variables identified above, it is important to recognize their fluid, complex, and constructed meanings (Bornstein, 1994; Butler, 1993; Demo & Allen, 1996; Klein, 1990; Rust, 1995). It is not clear how researchers might best address these complexities, yet it is clear that they must be addressed.

The Politics of LGBT Friendship Research

It has already been noted that LGBT friendship researchers ought to pay more attention to the contexts of LGBT lives and the ways that heterosexism itself may impact upon the role and importance of friendships. Rejection by conventional society has historically encouraged efforts by LGBT persons to develop self-help, support, and mutual-aid groups. As D'Augelli (1989b) noted, the formation of such groups helps to create a feeling of power, accomplishment, and pride, as well as an informal helping community. Informal supports are particularly important to LGBTs who typically receive few formal supports for their identities and relationships in the society at large. Indeed, it may be just this context that fosters the construction of friends as family in some lesbians' and gay men's lives.

FRIENDS AS FAMILY

A diversity of researchers and theorists have noted the tendency for lesbians and gay men to refer to friends as family, but as already noted, "friends as family" can hold different meanings (see also Weinstock, in press), including friends as substitute family relationships, friends as central organizing relationships instead of romantic partners and kin, and friends as central along with partners and kin.

Each meaning of "friends as family" suggests quite different images of and possibilities for LGBT friendships. For example, if "friends as family" refers largely to the notion of friends as substitute family members, the need for such friendship families may decrease as access to traditional family supports and forms increases. On the other hand, if "friends as family" represents a challenge to the prioritization of romantic partners and kin over friends, then efforts to construct such friendship families ought to be less affected by increased access to traditional family forms. To date, researchers and theorists have been more likely to recognize and draw upon the language of "friends as family" than to examine its meanings, roots, and forms for particular LGBT persons. Such examinations are critical, along with consideration of the ways that changing historical and personal life contexts may impact LGBT desires for and commitments to friendships, families, and friends as family.

It is also necessary to examine the implications of relying upon the terminology of "friends as family" itself across all these intended meanings. Weston (1991) argued that by speaking of friends as family, lesbians and gay men are in many ways reinforcing the traditional social organizational framework that places family and kin at its center. This language may also reflect the adoption of mainstream assumptions about the privileged role of family in relation to friends. Similarly, when LGBT researchers and theorists draw upon the language of "friends as family" to describe the functions of LGBT friendships, attention is focused on the private realm of family life rather than on the potential of friends for fostering LGBT political and community actions (Weinstock, in press). Thus, researchers and theorists should use caution in their reliance upon this language, for the effort to recognize the importance of friends in LGBT persons' lives by referring to "friends as family" may itself confer greater importance and status to family over friendships.

Conclusion

There is much about LGBT friendships that remains to be explored, but what is available suggests both the importance of friendships in LGBT lives and the need for researchers and theorists to turn their attention more directly to these friendships. Furthermore, the development of a theoretical approach to the study of friendships that itself centers on friendship seems warranted. The LGBT friendship literature to date, like the heterosexual friendship literature, appears to have emerged from—and to reflect—both a heterosexist view of relationships and a privileging of romantic relationships. Yet the relative prioritization of partners and friends remains an open empirical question. It is also an open political question for LGBT persons themselves.

References

Allen, J. (Ed.) (1990). *Lesbian philosophies and cultures.* Albany: State University of New York Press.

Allison, D. (1994). *Skin: Talking about sex, class and literature.* Ithaca, NY: Firebrand Books.

Anzaldúa, G. (1996). Lifeline. In M. Daly (Ed.), *Surface tension: Love, sex, and politics between lesbians and straight women* (pp. 64–69). New York: Simon & Schuster.

Becker, C. S. (1988). *Unbroken ties: Lesbian ex-lovers.* Boston: Alyson Publications.

Becker, C. S. (1991). A phenomenology of friendship families. *The Humanistic Psychologist, 19,* 170–184.

Beemyn, B., & Eliason, M. (Eds.) (1996). *Queer studies: A lesbian, gay, bisexual, and transgender anthology.* New York: New York University Press.

Bell, A. P., & Weinberg, M. S. (1978). *Homosexualities: A study of diversity among men and women.* New York: Simon & Schuster.

Berger, R. M. (1984). Realities of gay and lesbian aging. *Social Work, 29,* 57–62.

Berger, R. M. (1990). Men together: Understanding the gay couple. *Journal of Homosexuality, 19*(3), 31–49.

Berger, R. M. (1996). *Gay and gray: The older homosexual man,* 2nd ed. New York: Haworth Press.

Berger, R. M., & Mallon, D. (1993). Social support networks of gay men. *Journal of Sociology and Social Welfare, 20,* 155–174.

Blieszner, R., & Adams, R. G. (1992). *Adult friendship.* Newbury Park, CA: Sage Publications.

Bond, L. A., & Weinstock, J. S. (1997, March). The challenge of differing sexual identities to women's friendships. In J. S. Weinstock (Chair), *Lesbian friendship and social change.* Symposium conducted at the annual meetings of the Association for Women in Psychology, Pittsburgh, PA.

Bomstein, K. (1994). *Gender outlaw: On men, women and the rest of us.* New York: Routledge.

Boyd, R. (1995). A whole new world. In J. Preston, with M. Lowenthal (Eds.), *Friends and lovers: Gay men write about the families they create* (pp. 225–236). New York: Penguin Books.

Bradford, J., & Ryan, C. (1988). *The National Lesbian Health Care Survey: Final report.* National Lesbian and Gay Health Foundation, Virginia Commonwealth University.

Bradford, J., & Ryan, C. (1991). Who we are: Health concerns of middle-aged lesbians. In B. Sang, J. Warshow, & A. J. Smith (Eds.), *Lesbians at midlife: The creative transition* (pp. 147–163). San Francisco: Spinsters Ink.

Bradford, J., Ryan, C., & Rothblum, E. D. (1994). National Lesbian Health Care Survey: Implications for mental health care. *Journal of Consulting and Clinical Psychology, 62*, 228–242.

Bright, S. (1996). What is it about straight women? In M. Daly (Ed.), *Surface tension: Love, sex, and polities between lesbians and straight women* (pp. 95–98). New York: Simon & Schuster.

Bums, R., & Rofes, E. (1988). Gay liberation comes home: The development of community centers within our movement. In M. Shernoff & W. A. Scott (Eds.), *The sourcebook on lesbian/gay health care*, 2nd ed. (pp. 24–29). Washington, DC: National Lesbian and Gay Health Foundation.

Butler, J. (1993). Imitation and gender insubordination. In H. Abelove, M. A. Barale, & D. M. Halperin (Eds.), *The lesbian and gay studies reader* (pp. 307–320). New York: Routledge.

Card, C. (1995). *Lesbian choices.* New York: Columbia University Press.

Clunis, D. M., & Green, G. D. (1988). *Lesbian couples: Creating healthy relationships for the '90s.* Seattle: Seal Press.

Conner, K., & Cohan, M. (1996). Negotiating difference: The friendship of a lesbian-identified woman and a heterosexual man. In J. S. Weinstock & E. D. Rothblum (Eds.), *Lesbians and friendship: For ourselves and each other* (pp. 205–222). New York: New York University Press.

Cornogg, C. C. (1995). Letting it in. In J. Preston, with M. Lowenthal (Eds.), *Friends and lovers: Gay men write about the families they create* (pp. 205–215). New York: Penguin Books.

Daly, M. (1996a). Interview with Jessica Hagedom. In M. Daly (Ed.), *Surface tension: Love, sex, and politics between lesbians and straight women* (pp. 197–201). New York: Simon & Schuster.

Daly, M. (1996b) (Ed.). *Surface tension: Love, sex, and politics between lesbians and straight women.* New York: Simon & Schuster.

D'Augelli, A. R. (1989a). Lesbian women in a rural helping network: Exploring informal helping resources. *Women and Therapy, 8*(1/2), 119–130.

D'Augelli, A. R. (1989b). The development of a helping community for lesbians and gay men: A case study of community psychology. *Journal of Community Psychology, 17*, 18–29.

D'Augelli, A. R., Collins, C., & Hart, M. M. (1987). Social support patterns of lesbian women in a rural helping network. *Journal of Rural Community Psychology, 8*(11), 12–22.

D'Augelli, A. R., & Garnets, L. D. (1995). Lesbian, gay, and bisexual communities. In A. R. D'Augelli & C. J. Patterson (Eds.), *Lesbian, gay, and bisexual identities over the lifespan: Psychological perspectives* (pp. 293–320). New York: Oxford University Press.

D'Augelli, A. R., & Hart, M. M. (1987). Gay women, men, and families in rural settings: Toward the development of helping communities. *American Journal of Community Psychology, 15*, 79–93.

Demo, D. H., & Allen, K. R. (1996). Diversity within lesbian and gay families: Challenges and implications for family theory and research. *Journal of Social and Personal Relationships, 13*, 415–434.

Devor, H. (1989). *Gender blending: Confronting the limits of duality.* Bloomington: Indiana University Press.

Diamond, L. M. (1997). *Discontinuous development of sexual orientation in young lesbian, bisexual, and questioning women.* Unpublished master's thesis, Cornell University, Ithaca, NY.

Duck, S., West, L., & Acitelli, L. K. (1997). Sewing the field: The tapestry of relationships in life and research. In S. Duck (Ed.), *Handbook of personal relationships: Theory, research and interventions* (pp. 1–23). New York: John Wiley & Sons.

Fehr, B. (1996). *Friendship processes.* Thousand Oaks, CA: Sage Publications.

Feinberg, L. (1993). *Stone butch blues.* Ithaca, NY: Firebrand Books.

Feinberg, L. (1996). *Transgender warriors: Making history from Joan of Arc to RuPaul.* Boston: Beacon Press.

Firestein, B. A. (1996a). Bisexuality as paradigm shift: Transforming our disciplines. In B. A. Firestein (Ed.), *Bisexuality: The psychology and politics of an invisible minority* (pp. 263–291). Thousand Oaks, CA: Sage Publications.

Firestein, B. A. (Ed.) (1996b). *Bisexuality: The psychology and politics of an invisible minority.* Thousand Oaks, CA: Sage Publications.

Franklin, C. W. II. (1992). "Hey, Home—Yo, Bro": Friendship among Black men. In P. M. Nardi (Ed.), *Men's friendships* (pp. 201–214). Newbury Park, CA: Sage Publications.

Friend, R. A. (1996). Older lesbian and gay people: A theory of successful aging. In R. M. Berger (Ed.), Gay *and gray: The older homosexual man,* 2nd ed. (pp. 277–297). New York: Haworth Press.

Garnets, L. D., & Kimmel, D. C. (1993). Introduction: Lesbian and gay male dimensions in the psychological study of human diversity. In L. D. Garnets & D. C. Kimmel (Eds.), *Psychological perspectives on lesbian and gay male experiences* (pp. 1–51). New York: Columbia University Press.

Golombok, S., & Fivush, R. (1994). *Gender development.* New York: Cambridge University Press.

Hall, R., & Rose, S. (1996). Friendships between African-American and White lesbians. In J. S. Weinstock & E. D. Rothblum (Eds.), *Lesbians and friendship: For ourselves and each other* (pp. 165–191). New York: New York University Press.

Hart, G., Fitzpatrick, R., McLean, J., Dawson, J., & Boulton, M. (1990). Gay men, social support and HIV disease: A study of social integration in the gay community. *AIDS Care, 2.* 163–170.

Hays, R. B., Chauncey, S., & Tobey, L. A. (1990). The social support networks of gay men with AIDS. *Journal of Community Psychology, 18.* 374–385.

Hays, R. B., McKusick, L., Pollack, L., Hilliard, R., Hoff, C., & Coates, T. J. (1993). Disclosing HIV seropositivity to significant others. *AIDS, 7,* 425–431.

Hemphill, E., with Beam, J. (Eds.) (1991). *Brother to brother: New writings by black gay men.* Boston: Alyson Publications.

Hochman, A. (1994). *Everyday acts and small subversions: Women reinventing family, community, and home.* Portland, OR: Eighth Mountain Press.

Jeffreys, S. (1993). *The lesbian heresy: A feminist perspective on the lesbian sexual revolution.* North Melbourne, Vic, Australia: Spinifex Press.

Jo, B. (1996). Lesbian friendships create lesbian community. In J. S. Weinstock & E. D. Rothblum (Eds.), *Lesbian friendships: For ourselves and each other* (pp. 288–291). New York: New York University Press.

Kelly, J. A., Sikkema, K. J., Winett, R. A., Solomon, L. J., Roffman, R. A., Heckman, T. G., Stevenson, L. Y., Perry, M. J., Norman, A. D., & Desiderato, L. J. (1995). Factors predicting continued high-risk behavior among gay men in small cities: Psychological, behavioral, and demographic characteristics related to unsafe sex. *Journal of Consulting and Clinical Psychology, 63,* 101–107.

Kennedy, L. L., & Davis, M. (1993). *Boots of leather, slippers of gold: The history of a lesbian community.* New York: Routledge.

Kimmel, D. C. (1992). The families of older gay men and lesbians. *Generations, 17*(3), 37–38.

Kimmel, D. C., & Sang, B. E. (1995). Lesbians and gay men in midlife. In A. R. D'Augelli & C. J. Patterson (Eds.), *Lesbian, gay, and bisexual identities over the lifespan: Psychological perspectives* (pp. 190–214). New York: Oxford University Press.

Kitzinger, C. (1996). Toward a politics of lesbian friendship. In J. S. Weinstock & E. D. Rothblum (Eds.), *Lesbian friendships: For ourselves and each other* (pp. 295–299). New York: New York University Press.

Kitzinger, C., & Perkins, R. (1993). *Changing our minds: Lesbian feminism and psychology.* New York: New York University Press.

Klein, F. (1990). The need to view sexual orientation as a multivariable dynamic process: A theoretical perspective. In D. P. McWhirter, S. A. Saunders, & J. M. Reinisch (Eds.), *Homosexuality/heterosexuality* (pp. 277–282). New York: Oxford University Press.

Kolodner, E. M. (1992). Sexual orientation as a factor in women's friendships: An empirical exploration of intimacy. Unpublished paper, Yale University, New Haven, CN.

Kurdek, L. A. (1988). Perceived social support in gays and lesbians in cohabiting relationships. *Journal of Personality and Social Psychology, 54,* 504–509.

Kurdek, L. A., & Schmitt, J. P. (1987). Perceived support from family and friends in members of homosexual, married, and heterosexual cohabiting couples. *Journal of Homosexuality, 14,* 57–68.

Kus, R. J. (1991). Sobriety, friends, and gay men. *Archives of Psychiatric Nursing, 5,* 171–177.

Lewin, E. (1993). *Lesbian mothers: Accounts of gender in American culture.* Ithaca, NY: Cornell University Press.

Lorde, A. (1984). *Sister outsider: Essays and speeches.* Freedom, CA: Crossing Press.

Mays, V. M., Cochran, S. D., & Rhue, S. (1993). The impact of perceived discrimination on the intimate relationships of black lesbians. *Journal of Homosexuality, 25*(4), 1–14.

McRoy, D. T. (1990). *Gay and heterosexual men's friendships: The relationships between homophobia, antifemininity and intimacy.* Unpublished doctoral dissertation, California School of Professional Psychology, Los Angeles.

McWhirter, D. P., & Mattison, A. M. (1984). *The male couple: How relationships develop.* Englewood Cliffs, NJ: Prentice-Hall.

Messner, M. A. (1992). Like family: Power, intimacy, and sexuality in male athletes' friendships. In P. M. Nardi (Ed.), *Men's friendships* (pp. 215–237). Thousand Oaks, CA: Sage Publications.

Monsour, M. (1992). Meanings of intimacy in cross- and same-sex friendships. *Journal of Social and Personal Relationships, 9,* 277–295.

Nardi, P. M. (1982). Alcohol treatment and the non-traditional "family" structures of gays and lesbians. *Journal of Alcohol and Drug Education, 27*(2), 83–89.

Nardi, P. M. (1992a). Sex, friendship, and gender roles among gay men. In P. M. Nardi (Ed.), *Men's friendships* (pp. 173–185). Newbury Park, CA: Sage Publications.

Nardi, P. M. (1992b). That's what friends are for: Friends as family in the gay and lesbian community. In K. Plummer (Ed.), *Modem homosexualities: Fragments of lesbian and gay experience* (pp. 108–120). New York: Routledge.

Nardi, P. M., & Sherrod, D. (1994). Friendships in the lives of gay men and lesbians. *Journal of Social and Personal Relationships, 11*, 185–199.

Nataf, Z. I. (1996). *Lesbians talk transgender.* London: Scarlet Press.

Nestle, J., & Preston, J. (Eds.) (1994). *Sister and brother: Lesbians and gay men write about their lives together.* New York: HarperCollins.

Neustatter, A. (1996). "How we met": An interview with Gloria Steinem and Robin Morgan. In M. Daly (Ed.), *Surface tension: Love, sex, and politics between lesbians and straight women* (pp. 29–33). New York: Simon & Schuster.

O'Boyle, C. G., & Thomas, M. D. (1996). Friendships between lesbian and heterosexual women. In J. S. Weinstock & E. D. Rothblum (Eds.), *Lesbian friendships: For ourselves and each other* (pp. 240–248). New York: New York University Press.

O'Connor, P. (1992). *Friendships between women: A critical review.* New York: Guilford Press.

O'Meara, D. (1989). Cross-sex friendship: Four basic challenges of an ignored relationship. *Sex Roles, 21*, 525–543.

O'Meara, J. D. (1994). Cross-sex friendship's opportunity challenge: Uncharted terrain for exploration. *Personal Relationships Issues, 2*(1), 4–7.

Palladino, D., & Stephenson, Y. (1990). Perceptions of the sexual self: Their impact on relationships between lesbian and heterosexual women. *Women and Therapy, 9*, 231–253.

Parks, M. R., & Floyd, K. (1996). Meanings for closeness and intimacy in friendship. *Journal of Social and Personal Relationships, 13*, 85–108.

Patterson, C. J. (1996). Contributions of lesbian and gay parents and their children to the prevention of heterosexism. In E. D. Rothblum & L. A. Bond (Eds.), *Preventing heterosexism and homophobia* (pp. 184–201). Thousand Oaks: Sage Publications.

Paul, J. P., Hays, R. B., & Coates, T. J. (1995). The impact of the HIV epidemic on U. S. gay male communities. In A. R D'Augelli & C. J. Patterson (Eds.) *Lesbian, gay, and bisexual identities over the lifespan: Psychological perspectives* (pp. 347–397). New York: Oxford University Press.

Peplau, L. A. (1991). Lesbian and gay relationships. In J. C. Gonsiorek & J. D. Weinrich (Eds.), *Homosexuality: Research implications for public policy* (pp. 177–196). Newbury Park, CA: Sage Publications.

Powers, A. (1996). Queer in the streets, straight in the sheets: Notes on passing. In M. Daly (Ed.), *Surface tension: Love, sex, and politics between lesbians and strgaiht women* (pp. 133–141). New York: Simon & Schuster.

Preston, J., with Lowenthal, M. (1995). *Friends and lovers: Gay men write about the families they create.* New York: Dutton.

Raphael, S., & Robinson, M. (1984). The older lesbian: Love relationships and friendship patterns. In T. Darty & S. Potter (Eds.), *Women-identified women* (pp. 67–82). Palo Alto: Mayfield.

Rauch, K., & Fessler, J. (1995). *Why gay guys are a girl's best friend.* New York: Fireside.

Rawlins, W. K. (1994). Reflecting on (cross-sex) friendship: De-scripting the drama. *Personal Relationship Issues, 2*(1), 1–3.

Raymond, J. G. (1986). *A passion for friends: Towards a philosophy of female affection.* Boston: Beacon Press.

Rose, S. (1996). Lesbian and gay love scripts. In E. D. Rothblum & L. A. Bond (Eds.), *Preventing heterosexism and homophobia* (pp. 151–173). Thousand Oaks: Sage Publications.

Rose, S., Zand, D., & Cini, M. A. (1993). Lesbian courtship scripts. In E. D. Rothblum & K. A. Brehony (Eds.), *Boston marriages: Romantic but asexual relationships among contemporary lesbians* (pp. 70–85). Amherst: University of Massachusetts Press.

Rothblum, E. D. (1994). Transforming lesbian sexuality. *Psychology of Women Quarterly, 18,* 627–641.

Rothblum, E. D., & Brehony, K. A. (1993). *Boston marriages: Romantic but asexual relationships among contemporary lesbians.* Amherst: University of Massachusetts Press.

Rubin, L. B. (1985). *Just friends: The role of friendship in our lives.* New York: Harper & Row.

Rust, P. C. (1995). *The challenge of bisexuality to lesbian politics: Sex, loyalty, and revolution.* New York: New York University Press.

Ryan, C., & Bradford, J. (1993). The National Lesbian Health Care Survey: An overview. In L. D. Garnets & D. C. Kimmel (Eds.). *Psychological perspectives on lesbian and gay male experiences* (pp. 541–556). New York: Columbia University Press.

Shernoff, M. J. (1984). Family therapy for lesbian and gay clients. *Social Work, 29,* 393–396.

Sherrod, D. (1987). The bonds of men: Problems and possibilities in close male relationships. In H. Brod (Ed.), *The making of masculinities: The new Men's Studies* (pp. 213–239). Boston: Allen & Unwin.

Sherrod, D. (1989). The influence of gender on same-sex friendships. In C. Hendrick (Ed.), *Review of personality and social psychology. Vol. 10: Close relationships* (pp. 164–186). Newbury Park, CA: Sage Publications.

Slater, S. (1994). Approaching and avoiding the work of the middle years: Affairs in committed lesbian relationships. *Women and Therapy, 15*(2), 19–34.

Slater, S. (1995). *The lesbian family life cycle.* New York: Free Press.

Slater, S., & Mencher, J. (1991). The lesbian family life cycle: A contextual approach. *American Journal of Orthopsychiatry, 61,* 372–382.

Stanley, J. L. (1996). The lesbian's experience of friendship. In J. S. Weinstock & E. D. Rothblum (Eds.), *Lesbian friendships: For ourselves and each other* (pp. 39–59). New York: New York University Press.

Stein, A. (1997). *Sex and sensibility: Stories of a lesbian generation.* Berkeley: University of California Press.

Strega, L. (1996). A lesbian love story. In J. S. Weinstock & E. D. Rothblum (Eds.), *Lesbian friendships: For ourselves and each other* (pp. 277–287). New York: New York University Press.

Stuart, E. (1995). *Just good friends: Towards a lesbian and gay theology of relationships.* New York: Mowbray.

Swain, S. (1989). Covert intimacy: Closeness in men's friendships. In B. J. Risman & P. Schwartz (Eds.), *Gender in intimate relationships: A microstructural approach* (pp. 71–86). Belmont, CA: Wadsworth.

Swain, S. O. (1992). Men's friendships with women: Intimacy, sexual boundaries, and the informant role. In P. Nardi (Ed.), *Men's friendships* (pp. 153–171). Newbury Park: Sage Publications.

Tavris, C. (1992). *The mismeasure of woman.* New York: Simon & Schuster.

Vetere, V. A. (1982). The role of friendship in the development and maintenance of lesbian love relationships. *Journal of Homosexuality, 8*(2), 51–65.

Weinstock, J. S. (in press). Lesbians' friendships at midlife. *Journal of Gay and Lesbian Social Services.*

Weinstock, J. S., & Rothblum, E. D. (Eds.) (1996a). *Lesbians and friendship: For ourselves and each other.* New York: New York University Press.

Weinstock, J. S., & Rothblum, E. D. (1996b). What we can be together: Contemplating lesbians' friendships. In J. S. Weinstock & E. D. Rothblum (Eds.), *Lesbians and friendship: For ourselves and each other* (pp. 3–30). New York: New York University Press.

Werking, K. (1994a). Hidden assumptions: A critique of existing cross-sex friendship research. *Personal Relationships Issues, 2*(1), 8–11.

Werking, K. (1994b) (Ed.). Special Issue: Cross-sex friendships. *Personal Relationships Issues, 2*(1).

Werking, K. (1997a). Cross-sex friendship research as ideological practice. In S. Duck (Ed.), *Handbook of personal relationships: Theory, research and interventions,* 2nd ed. (pp. 391–410). New York: John Wiley & Sons.

Werking, K. (1997b). *We're just good friends: Women and men in nonromantic relationships.* New York: Guilford.

Weston, K. (1991). *Families we choose: Lesbians, gays, kinship.* New York: Columbia University Press.

Winstead, B. A., Derlega, V. J., & Rose, S. (1997). *Gender and close relationships.* Thousand Oaks, CA: Sage Publications.

Wood, J. T., & Inman, C. C. (1993). In a different mode: Masculine styles of communicating closeness. *Journal of Applied Communication Research, 21,* 279–295.

Wright, P. H. (1988). Interpreting research on gender differences in friendship: A case for moderation and a plea for caution. *Journal of Social and Personal Relationships, 5,* 367–373.

Wright, P. H. (1989). Gender differences in adults' same- and cross-gender friendships. In R. G. Adams & R. Blieszner (Eds.), *Older adult friendship: Structure and process* (pp. 197–221). Newbury Park, CA: Sage Publications.

8

The Family Lives of Children Born to Lesbian Mothers

Charlotte J. Patterson

Conceptions of families have traditionally been heavily laden with heterosexist and patriarchal assumptions. Not only are parents, children, and other family members expected to exemplify heterosexuality, but they are also expected to respect patriarchal values and customs. Families in which children are raised by women who identify themselves as lesbian represent a challenge to such expectations, and this challenge can lead to concerns about the nature of family lives, as well as about the progress of child development within such families. To the degree that lesbian-headed families exemplify neither heterosexual nor patriarchal values, questions may arise as to how kinship is constructed and with what impact upon children (Allen & Demo, 1995; Patterson, 1992, 1995a; Weston, 1991).

There is considerable diversity among the group of women who regard themselves as lesbian mothers (Falk, 1989; Green & Bozett, 1991; Lewin, 1993; Martin, 1993; Ricketts & Achtenberg, 1990). One important source of such diversity is the context in which women became mothers. The largest and most visible group of lesbian mothers are women who gave birth to children in the context of heterosexual relationships, after which they assumed lesbian identities. Another group of women gave birth or adopted children only after they had identified as lesbian. A considerable research literature has developed relevant to the first group, and it has generally revealed that children of divorced lesbian mothers grow up in ways that are very similar to children of divorced heterosexual mothers. This literature has been reviewed elsewhere (e.g., Falk, 1989; Green & Bozett, 1991; Patterson, 1992, 1995b; Tasker & Golombok, 1991, 1997), and will not be discussed at length here.

In the present chapter, the focus will be on the second group of families, whose children were born after their mothers came out as lesbians. Because these kinds of families seem to be growing in numbers, they have often been called families of the "lesbian baby boom" (Patterson, 1994a, 1995a; Weston, 1991). Research with these families is as yet quite new, but a number of findings similar to those reported for families of divorced lesbian mothers have been reported. I present first the research on lesbian mothers themselves and then consider findings about children born to or adopted early in life by lesbian mothers. After discussing research findings to date, I suggest some directions for further study and examine the existing research for evidence with regard to one issue of particular interest—the extent to which biological linkages are related to the structure of family lives in the families of the lesbian baby boom. The chapter then concludes with a general discussion of what has been learned and what directions seem promising for further work.

Lesbians Choosing to Become Mothers

Although for many years lesbian mothers were generally assumed to have become parents only in the context of previous heterosexual relationships, women are increasingly choosing to undertake parenthood in the context of pre-existing lesbian identities (Brewaeys, Ponjaert, Van Hall, & Golombok, 1997; Chan, Brooks, Raboy, & Patterson, 1997; Chan, Raboy, & Patterson, 1998; Crawford, 1987; Mitchell, 1996; Patterson, 1992, 1994a, 1994b, 1995a, 1995c, 1996; Pies, 1985, 1990). A substantial body of research addresses the transition to parenthood among heterosexual men and women (e.g., Cowan & Cowan, 1992; Cowan, Cowan & Kerig, 1993), examining ways in which decisions to have children are made, normative changes during the transition to parenthood, and factors related to individual differences in adjustment to parenthood.

While many issues that arise for heterosexuals also face lesbians and gay men (e.g., concerns about how children will affect couple relationships, economic concerns about supporting children), lesbians and gay men must cope with many additional issues because of their situation as members of stigmatized minorities (Patterson, 1994b). These issues are best understood by viewing them against the backdrop of pervasive societal heterosexism and antigay or antilesbian prejudice (Herek, 1995). For instance, antigay and antilesbian prejudice is evident in institutions involved with health care, education, and employment that often fail to support and, in many cases, are openly hostile to lesbian and gay parents and their children (Casper, Schultz, & Wickens, 1992; Polikoff, 1990; Pollack & Vaughn, 1987). Prospective lesbian and gay parents may encounter antigay prejudice and bigotry even from their families of origin (Pollack & Vaughn, 1987; Weston, 1991). Many if not most of the special concerns of prospective lesbian and gay parents arise from problems created by such hostility (Patterson, 1994b).

A number of interrelated issues are often faced by prospective lesbian and gay parents (Patterson, 1994b). Lesbians and gay men who want to become parents need accurate, up-to-date information on how they can become parents, how their children are likely to develop, and what supports are available to assist gay- and lesbian-parented families. In addition to these educational needs, lesbians and gay men who are seeking biological parenthood are likely to encounter various health concerns, ranging from medical screening of prospective birth-parents to assistance with donor insemination (DI) techniques, prenatal care, and preparation for birth. As plans progress, a number of legal concerns about the rights and responsibilities of all parties emerge (Polikoff, 1990). There are also financial issues; in addition to the support of a child, special costs of medical and legal assistance can be considerable. Finally, social and emotional concerns of many different kinds are likely to emerge. For instance, prospective parents may experience disappointment if family members and friends are not supportive of their desire to become parents (Crawford, 1987; Martin, 1993; Pies, 1985, 1990; Patterson, 1994b).

As this outline of issues suggests, numerous research questions are posed by the emergence of prospective lesbian and gay parents. What factors influence lesbians' and gay men's inclinations to make parenthood a part of their lives, and through what processes do they operate? What impact does parenting have on lesbians or gay men who undertake it, and how do these effects compare with those experienced by heterosexual people? How well do special services such as support groups serve the needs of lesbian and gay parents and prospective parents? What are the elements of social climates that are supportive for gay and lesbian parents and their children? As yet, little research has addressed such questions.

Although few studies have explored the transition to parenthood among lesbian or gay adults, there has been some research on lesbian mothers themselves. The earliest studies of childbearing among lesbian couples were reported by McCandlish (1987) and by Steckel (1985, 1987). Both investigators reported research based on small samples of lesbian couples who had given birth to children by means of DI. Their focus was primarily on the children in such families (see below), and neither investigator attempted systematic assessment of mothers. McCandlish (1987: 28) however, noted that, regardless of their degree of interest in parenting prior to birth of the first child, the nonbiological mothers in each couple unanimously reported an "unexpected and immediate attachment" to the child. Although both mothers took part in parenting, they reported shifting patterns of caretaking responsibilities over time, with the biological mother taking primary responsibility during the earliest months, and the nonbiological mother's role increasing in importance after the child was

12 or more months of age. Couples also reported changes in their own relationships following the birth of the child, notably a reduction or cessation in sexual intimacy. Results of these pioneering studies thus raised many intriguing issues and questions for further research.

Hand (1991) examined the ways in which lesbian and heterosexual couples with children under 2 years of age shared child care, household duties, and occupational roles. One of Hand's notable findings was that lesbian mothers shared parenting more equally with their partners than did heterosexual mothers and fathers. Lesbian nonbiological mothers were significantly more involved in child care and regarded their parental role as significantly more salient than did heterosexual fathers. Lesbian biological mothers viewed their maternal role as more salient than did any of the other mothers, whether lesbian or heterosexual. Fathers viewed their occupational roles as more salient than did any of the mothers, whether lesbian or heterosexual.

Another study (Osterweil, 1991) involved 30 lesbian couples with at least one child between 18 and 36 months of age. Consistent with Hand's results for parents of younger children, Osterweil reported that biological mothers viewed their maternal role as more salient than did nonbiological mothers. In addition, although household maintenance activities were shared about equally, biological mothers reported somewhat more influence in family decisions and somewhat more involvement in child care. Osterweil also reported that the couples in her study scored at about the mean for normative samples of heterosexual couples in overall relationship satisfaction.

Patterson (1995a, 1996b) studied families headed by lesbian couples who had children between 4 and 9 years of age living at home. Consistent with results of other investigators (Koepke, Hare, & Moran, 1991; Osterweil, 1991), Patterson found that lesbian parents' relationship satisfaction was generally high relative to norms for relationship satisfaction among heterosexual couples. Although they reported sharing household tasks and decision making equally, the couples reported that biological mothers were somewhat more involved in child care and that nonbiological mothers spent somewhat longer hours in paid employment. Within this context, they also reported greater satisfaction with division of labor when child care was shared more equally between them.

Flaks, Ficher, Masterparque, & Joseph (1995) studied 15 lesbian parenting couples, and compared them with 15 heterosexual parenting couples. Results indicated that lesbian and heterosexual parents were similar in their levels of satisfaction with couple relationships. Lesbian couples showed more awareness of skills needed for effective parenting than did heterosexual couples, but this may have been attributable to gender rather than to sexual orientation as such, in that all mothers (whether lesbian or heterosexual) scored higher than fathers.

Chan and his colleagues (Chan et al., 1998; Chan et al., in press) studied 55 lesbian-headed families and 25 heterosexual-headed families with school-age children who had been conceived using donor insemination (DI). Families who participated in this study were recruited from among the clients of a single sperm bank that worked with health-care providers across the United States; thus, families resided in many parts of the country. Results showed that, even though lesbian and heterosexual couples reported similar arrangements in terms of paid employment, lesbian parents reported sharing unpaid child-care tasks more equally than did their heterosexual counterparts. Consistent with earlier reports (e.g., Hand, 1991), heterosexual fathers were less willing than nonbiological lesbian mothers to assume equal responsibility for the care of their children. Similar findings were reported by Mitchell (1996).

From Europe, two major studies have been reported recently (Brewaeys et al., 1997 and Golombok, Tasker, & Murray, 1997). Brewaeys and her colleagues studied 30 lesbian mothers who conceived children using DI, and compared them with 38 heterosexual mothers who conceived using DI, and with 30 heterosexual mothers who conceived children in the conventional way. Parents in all three types of families were relatively satisfied in their couple relationships and there were no differences among family types in this regard. In terms of parenting, lesbian nonbiological mothers were reported to have more positive interactions with their children than were heterosexual fathers regardless of the mode of conception. Lesbian nonbiological mothers also participated in more child-care activities and were more active in disciplining children than were heterosexual fathers; but fathers of children who were conceived via DI showed a higher level of participation in child care than did fathers who had conceived children in the conventional way.

Golombok and her colleagues (1997) studied a group of lesbian mothers (15 single lesbian mother and 15 lesbian couples), a group of single heterosexual mothers, and compared them with a group of heterosexual couples. Three major findings emerged: (1) single heterosexual mothers and lesbian mothers were reported to show more warmth and more positive interaction with their children than coupled heterosexual mothers; (2) lesbian mothers were also rated as having more positive interactions with their children than were single heterosexual mothers; and, (3) single heterosexual mothers and lesbian mothers reported more serious (though not more frequent) disputes with their children than coupled heterosexual mothers.

Overall, then, the results from initial research on these lesbian mothers are clear. In independent studies from the United States and Europe, lesbian mothers have been found to express satisfaction with their couple relationships. Lesbian couples, by and large, reported being able to negotiate their division of labor equitably. In addition, lesbian nonbiological mothers were consistently described as more involved than heterosexual fathers with their children.

Research on Children Born to or Adopted by Lesbian Mothers

Although many writers have recently noted an increase in childbearing among lesbians, research with children in these families is as yet relatively new (Mitchell, 1996; Patterson, 1992, 1994a, 1995a; Patterson, Hurt, & Mason, in press; Polikoff, 1990; Riley, 1988; Tasker & Golombok, 1991; Weston, 1991). In this section, research to date on children born to or adopted by lesbian mothers is summarized.

In one of the first systematic studies of children born to lesbians, Steckel (1985, 1987) compared the progress of separation-individuation among preschool children born via DI to lesbian couples with that among same-aged children of heterosexual couples. Using a variety of techniques, Steckel compared independence, ego functions, and object relations among children in the two types of families. Her main results documented impressive similarity in development among children in the two groups. Similar findings, based on extensive interviews with five lesbian mother families, were also reported by McCandlish (1987).

The first study to examine psychosocial development among preschool and school-aged children born to or adopted by lesbian mothers was conducted by Patterson (1994a). She studied 4- to 9-year-old children, using a variety of standardized measures, and found that children scored in the normal range for all measures. On the Achenbach and Edelbrock (1983) Child Behavior Checklist, for example, scores for children of lesbian mothers' on social competence, internalizing behavior problems, and externalizing behavior problems differed significantly from those for a large clinical sample of (troubled) children used in norming the test, but did not differ from the scores for a large representative sample of normal children also used in norming the test (Achenbach & Edelbrock, 1983). Likewise, children of lesbian mothers reported sex-role preferences within the expected range for children of this age. On most subscales of the self-concept measure (Eder, 1990), answers given by children of lesbian mothers did not differ from those given by same-aged children of heterosexual mothers studied in the standardization sample.

On two subscales of the self-concept measure, however, children of lesbian mothers reported feeling more reactions to stress (e.g., feeling angry, scared, or upset), but also a greater sense of well-being (e.g., feeling joyful, content, and comfortable with themselves) than did same-aged children of heterosexual mothers in the standardization sample (Eder, 1990). One possible interpretation of this finding is that children of lesbian mothers reported greater reactivity to stress because, in fact, they experienced greater stress in their daily lives than did other children. Another possibility is that, regardless of actual stress levels, children of lesbian mothers were better able to acknowledge both positive and negative aspects of their emotional experience. Although this latter interpretation is perhaps more consistent with the differences in both stress reactions and well-being, clarification of these and other interpretations must await further research.

While results of Patterson's (1994a, 1996) study (described above) addressed normative questions, a more recent report based on the same sample focused on individual differences. In particular, Patterson (1995a) studied the families in her sample that were headed by a lesbian couple and assessed division of labor, satisfaction with division of labor, and satisfaction with couple relationships as predictors of children's adjustment. Results revealed that parents' satisfaction with their relationships, though generally high, was not associated with children's adjustment. Parents were, however, more satisfied and children were better adjusted when labor involved in child care was more evenly distributed between the parents. These results suggest that family process variables may be as crucial as predictors of child adjustment in lesbian families as they are in heterosexual families (Patterson, 1992).

Chan and his colleagues (1998, in press) studied a group of 80 families formed by lesbian and heterosexual parents via DI, and reported that children's overall adjustment was unrelated to parents' sexual orientation. Regardless of parents' sexual orientation or relationship status, parents who were experiencing higher levels of parenting stress, higher levels of interparental conflict, and lower levels of love for each other had children who exhibited more behavior problems. Among lesbian couples, nonbiological mothers' satisfaction with the division of labor, especially in family decision making, was related to better couple adjustment, which was in turn related to children's positive psychological adjustment (Chan et al., 1997), a result that is consistent with research on heterosexual families (Cowan et al., 1993). Flaks and his colleagues (1995) also compared children from lesbian mother families with heterosexual families, and found no differences in the children's level of psychological adjustment owing to the mother's sexual orientation.

In the Brewaeys et al. study (1997), psychosocial adjustment among a group of 4- to 8-year-old children who were conceived via DI by lesbian mother headed families ($N = 30$) and heterosexual parents ($N = 38$) was compared with that among a group of children who were conceived by heterosexual parents in the conventional way ($N = 30$). When children were asked about their perceptions of parent-child relationships, all children reported positive feelings about their parents and there were no differences in children's reports as a function of family types. Children's behavior and emotional adjustment were also assessed and results indicated that, overall, children who were conceived via DI in heterosexual families exhibited more behavior problems than children who were naturally conceived. In particular, girls who were conceived via DI in heterosexual families exhibited more behavioral problems than girls from other family types. Brewaeys and her colleagues suggested that these differences observed in the heterosexual DI families may be attributable to issues of confidentiality regarding the child's origins. They found that this type of concern did not occur in lesbian-parented families, who generally disclosed information about DI. Further research on the role of secrecy regarding the origin of children conceived via DI could advance our understanding family functioning among these families.

In another European study, Golombok and her colleagues (1997) reported on the psychological well-being of children raised since birth by lesbian mothers, and by heterosexual single mothers. These children were compared with children raised in two-parent heterosexual families. Results indicated that children of lesbian mothers did not show unusual emotional or behavior problems (as reported by parents or by teachers); there were no differences as a function of family type. In terms of children's attachment relationships to their parents, children from mother-only families (lesbian mothers and heterosexual single mothers) scored higher on an attachment-related assessment than did children reared by heterosexual couples, suggesting the possibility that children from mother-only families had more secure attachment relationships with their mothers. With respect to children's perceived competence, children from mother-only families reported lower perceived cognitive and physical competence than those children from father-present families. Thus, key findings in this study seemed to depend on the parents' gender rather than their sexual orientation.

In sum, much has been learned about the mothers and the children of the lesbian baby boom. The mental health of both groups appears to be robust. At the same time, most research has addressed the concerns of individuals or couples—whether children or mothers or parenting couples—rather than of families as units. Even though many intriguing questions could be posed about other family members or about family lives as such, little work has focused at this level. In the next section, I outline a set of issues relevant to the lives of families of the lesbian baby boom—vis-à-vis the degree to which biological linkages affect family life—and draw on some initial findings from my own Bay Area Families Study to address these issues.

Biological Linkages and the Structure of Family Lives

In conceptualizing parenthood, it is helpful to distinguish three facets of the status or role—the biological, the social, and the legal. Traditionally, all three facets of parenthood have been expected to correspond to one another. When a heterosexual couple fell in love, got married, and had children, there was no separation among the biological, social, and legal aspects of parent-child relations. Biological mothers and fathers were expected to perform the social duties of parenthood by feeding, clothing, housing, and caring for their children. The law was expected to recognize and protect the relationships between biological parents and their children.

When a child said, "This is my mother," it was expected that legal, biological, and social aspects of parenthood were embodied in the one particular woman to whom the child pointed.

In the contemporary world, however, these three aspects of parenthood are often disconnected. With many births taking place outside of marriage, and with frequent divorces and remarriages, children are increasingly unlikely to be cared for by both biological parents throughout their childhood and adolescence, and increasingly likely to live with adults (such as stepparents) who are not their legal parents. In the contemporary United States, the expected correspondence among legal, biological, and psychosocial aspects of parenthood is less common than it once was.

The separation of biological, legal, and psychosocial aspects of family life is nowhere more evident than in lesbian and gay communities. Some writers have, in fact, described lesbian and gay families as "families of choice." For instance, Weston (1991: 27) has suggested that "organized through ideologies of love, choice and creation, gay families have been defined through a contrast with what many gay men and lesbians . . . called 'straight,' 'biological,' or 'blood family.'" In creating psychological and social connections among lesbians and gay men, then, Weston suggests that choice may well be more important than biological linkages, and certainly that it is more important than connections established by law.

Families that are created when lesbians have children often bring such issues out in high relief. Consider, for example, a lesbian couple attempting to conceive a child using the resources of a sperm bank. There are three adults involved—the two women and a male sperm donor. If a child is conceived, there will be two biological parents—a biological mother and a biological father—who generally have not met. In most states, there will likely be only one legal parent—namely, the biological mother. While there will be two social parents, one of them will be a legal stranger to the child, as she is biologically unrelated. Even though the sperm donor and the lesbian couple have never met, it is interesting to note that all three generally agree that he will *not* participate in the social or legal aspects of parenthood. Thus, children brought up in this family will find that the expected correspondences of social, biological, and legal aspects of parent-child relations do not hold true for them (Patterson, 1996; Riley, 1988; Weston, 1991).

What are the implications of this kind of separation among the aspects of parent-child relations for family life among lesbian couples, single lesbian mothers, and their children? In what follows, I examine some preliminary results from the Bay Area Families Study that address this question. This is an exploratory effort, intended more to open up than to resolve questions. First, I will describe the Bay Area Families Study itself. Then, I will describe ways in which biological links among family members were found to be related to conceptualizations of the families themselves, to day-to-day life in the household, and to children's contacts with members of their extended families.

Overview of the Bay Area Families Study

The data were collected as part of the Bay Area Families Study (Patterson, 1994, 1995a, 1996; Patterson et al., in press). Families were eligible to participate if they met each of three criteria. First, at least one child between 4 and 9 years of age had to be present in the home. Second, the child had to have been born to or adopted by a lesbian mother or mothers. Third, only families that lived within the greater San Francisco Bay Area (e.g., San Francisco, Oakland, and San Jose) were considered eligible.

Recruitment began when the author contacted her friends, acquaintances, and colleagues who might be likely to know eligible lesbian-mother families. She described the proposed research and solicited help in locating families. From names gathered in this way, the author telephoned each family to describe the study and to ask for participation. In all, contact was made with 39 eligible families, of whom 37 participated in the study, for a response rate of over 90 percent. Participation involved a single home visit during which all data reported here were collected.

Twenty-six of the 37 participating families (70 percent) were headed by a lesbian couple. Seven families (19 percent) were headed by a single mother living with her child. In four families (11 percent), the child had been born to a lesbian couple who had since separated, and the child was in de facto joint custody (i.e., living part of the time with one mother and part of the time with the other mother).

Sixty-six lesbian mothers took part in the study. Their ages ranged from 28 to 53 years, with a mean age of 39 years of age. Sixty-one (92 percent) described themselves as white or non-Hispanic Caucasian, two (3 percent) as African-American or black, and three (4 percent) as coming from other racial or ethnic backgrounds. Most were well educated; 74 percent, had received college degrees and 48 percent had received graduate degrees. The great majority of mothers (94 percent) were employed on a regular basis outside the home, and about half said that they worked forty hours or more per week. More than half were in professional occupations (e.g., law, nursing), but others were in technical or mechanical occupations such as car repair (9 percent), business or sales such as real estate (9 percent), or in other occupations such as artist (14 percent). Only 4 mothers were not employed outside the home. Thirty-four families reported family incomes over $30,000 per year, and 17 families reported incomes over $60,000 per year.

The mean age of participating children was 6 years and 2 months; there were 19 girls and 18 boys. Thirty-four of the children were born to lesbian mothers, and 3 had been adopted. Thirty of the children were described by their mothers as white or non-Hispanic Caucasian; 3 as Hispanic; and, 4 as of some other racial or ethnic heritage.

Some additional descriptive information was also collected. Mothers were asked to explain the circumstances surrounding the child's conception, birth, and/or adoption. Mothers were also asked about the child's biological father or sperm donor, the degree to which the mothers had knowledge of or contact with him, and the degree to which the focal child had knowledge of his identity and/or contact with him. In addition, mothers were asked to give the child's last name and to explain how the name had been selected.

The mothers' accounts of the conception, birth, and/or adoption of their children made clear that, in general, the focal children were very much wanted. In fact, bringing children into their lives had required considerable planning and—often—investment of significant amounts of time and money. The average amount of time that it took for biological mothers to conceive focal children after they began to attempt to become pregnant was ten months. Adoptive mothers reported that, on average, the adoption process took approximately twelve months. In the great majority of cases, then, these lesbian mothers had devoted substantial time and effort to making the birth or adoption of their children possible.

There was tremendous variability in the amount of information that families had about the donor or biological father of the focal child. In nearly half of the families (46 percent), the child had been conceived via DI with sperm from an anonymous donor (e.g., sperm that had been provided by a sperm bank or clinic). In these cases, families had only very limited information (e.g., race, height, weight, hair color) about the donor, and none knew the donor's name. In about a quarter of the families (27 percent), the child was conceived via DI, with sperm provided by a known donor (e.g., a family friend). In 4 families (11 percent), children were conceived through heterosexual intercourse. In 3 families (8 percent), the child was adopted. In the 3 remaining families, some other set of circumstances applied or the parents acknowledged that the child had been born to one of the mothers, but preferred not to disclose any additional information about their child's conception.

Even among those who knew the child's biological father or donor, mothers reported relatively little contact with these men. More than half (62 percent) of the families reported no contact at all with the biological father or donor during the previous year. Only 10 families (27 percent) had had two or more contacts of any kind with the biological father or sperm donor during the previous year.

Given that many families did not know the identity of the child's sperm donor or biological father and that most currently had little or no contact with him, it is not surprising that the donor or biological father's role with the child was seen by mothers as being quite limited. In more than half of the families (60 percent), mothers reported that the donor or biological father had no special role in the child's life; this figure includes families in which the sperm donor had been anonymous. In about one-third of the families (35 percent), the biological father's identity was known to parents and children, but he enacted the role of family friend rather than that of father. There were only two families in which the biological father was acknowledged as such, and in which he was described as assuming a (noncustodial) father's role.

Conceptualizations of Families

When lesbian couples have children, they often reflect upon the nature of their families in ways that would be unusual among heterosexual couples. Central to these reflections is usually the question about what role the couple wants to allow biological linkages to play in their thoughts about family structure and functioning. To what extent should biological linkages determine family identities and roles? And if not on the basis of biological links, then on what grounds will such decisions be made?

One concrete way in which this set of issues arose for families who participated in the Bay Area Families Study was in the selection of children's names. In traditional heterosexual families, children are generally expected to bear their father's surname. Having no such person in their household, lesbian mothers in this sample were faced with questions about this issue. Should a child be given the surname of the woman who bore him or her, or of the other woman in the parenting couple, or should the child be given some other name altogether? For instance, if there was a known donor, should the child be given the donor's surname? And upon what grounds should such decisions be based?

Mothers in the Bay Area Families Study took a number of different approaches to these issues. By far the most common solution was to give children the surname of the biological mother. In these instances, the family consisted, for example, of Ms. Smith, her biological child or children who had the last name of Smith, Ms. Jones, and her biological child or children who had the last name of Jones (all of the names used here are pseudonyms). Despite the fact that they did not all share the same surname, none of the family members was at all unclear about their identity as a family; all of these women and their children clearly regarded one another as family members. When asked about why they selected this approach, women often said that it seemed the "natural" thing to do, or that they had not really considered giving children any other surname.

The next most popular approach was to give the child a hyphenated surname, created from the surnames of both mothers. In these instances, the family might consist of Ms. Smith, Ms. Jones, and their child or children, whose surname was Smith-Jones. An alternative arrangement in some families was for all members of the family to take the hyphenated surname. Women who had selected this approach generally remarked on the degree to which this method of naming enhanced their feeling of family identity—of all being members of the same family.

There were also some other resolutions of the issues involved in assigning surnames. For instance, in one family, the child was given the nonbiological mother's surname, in an effort to emphasize the contributions of the nonbiological as well as the biological mother to family life. In another family, the two women wanted to hyphenate their last names, but felt that the resulting name would be too long and cumbersome. After considerable thought, they decided upon a new last name—a word from another language that was meaningful to them—and gave it as the child's surname. In addition, they hyphenated their own last names to this new name. The family thus became Ms. Smith-Cousteau, Ms. Jones-Cousteau, and the child, whose last name was Cousteau. This unusual arrangement allowed them to enhance the sense of all belonging to the same family, while still allowing the child to have a brief, nonhyphenated surname.

In summary, although many other arrangements are possible, and although a few were in fact selected by one or two families, most children were given the surnames of their biological mothers. Thus, even in these "families of choice," biological connections were seen as significant in the process of selecting names for children.

Despite their reliance on biology for naming, however, lesbian families headed by couples were nearly unanimous in regarding both women as mothers. The only exceptions to this rule were "lesbian stepfamilies," in which children had been born before the relationship between the two women had been initiated. In these cases, the mother's partner might be called by her first name, and not regarded as a "real" or "full" parent; indeed, the extent to which she should be regarded as a parent, and for what purposes, might be under active discussion in the family. Apart from these few cases, all of the children and their mothers agreed on the women's identities as parents.

In light of the emphasis on biological linkages involved in women's choices of surnames for their children, it was interesting that only one family regarded the child's sperm donor or biological father to be a parent. Even though the man's biological links with the child were generally acknowledged by all, he was not usually viewed by either mother as a parent, or as acting in a parental role with the child. Not one family had given their child a surname that came from the biological father or from his family.

Thus, lesbian mother families who participated in the Bay Area Families Study both were and were not guided by their understandings of biological linkages in creating their conceptualizations of family ties. On the one hand, the boundaries of the "nuclear family" were clearly drawn to include both biological and nonbiological mothers and their adoptive as well as biological children, but not sperm donors or biological fathers. From this perspective, one might say that concepts of family were created without regard for biological ties. On the other hand, children's surnames were generally selected so as to emphasize children's ties with their biological mothers, while minimizing or rendering less visible ties between children and their nonbiological mothers. From this perspective, one might say that understandings of family ties were very much influenced by biological linkages. One possible way to comprehend these two findings under a single rubric would be to say that biological connections were not regarded as central to family formation or to creation of family boundaries, but were seen as important in structuring relationships within the family, once constituted. If this generalization is correct, then biological connections should be important also in structuring everyday activities within the family.

Division of Labor in Lesbian Mother Households

In the Bay Area Families Study, the principal assessments of couple functioning used an adaptation of Cowan and Cowan's (1990) Who Does What?, which assesses division of labor across a number of domains, and an adaptation of Locke and Wallace's (1959) Marital Adjustment Test, which assesses the quality of couple relationships. Although 37 families participated in the study, some were headed by single lesbian mothers. Results are presented here for the 26 families that were headed by a lesbian couple. For further details, see Patterson (1995a, 1996).

The actual and ideal participation reported by biological and nonbiological mothers in each of three domains of family work were compared. Results showed that biological and nonbiological mothers did not differ in their evaluations of ideal distributions of labor in the three domains; most believed that tasks should be shared relatively evenly in all domains. In terms of the actual division of labor, biological and nonbiological mothers did not differ in their reported participation in household labor or family decision making. In the area of child care, however, biological mothers reported themselves as responsible for more of the work than nonbiological mothers. Thus, although lesbian mothers agreed that ideally child care should be evenly shared, they reported that in their families, the biological mother was actually more responsible than the nonbiological mother for child care.

To assess satisfaction with division of labor, comparisons between actual and ideal divisions of labor were made. Results showed that biological mothers reported that they would prefer to do fewer household tasks and to be responsible for less child care. Nonbiological mothers did not report feeling that they should be significantly more involved in household tasks, but did agree that an ideal allocation of labor would result in their doing more child care. There were no effects for family decision making. Thus, although they were satisfied with division of labor in other domains, both mothers felt that an ideal allocation of labor would involve a more equal sharing of child-care tasks.

Each respondent also had been asked to provide a global rating of each mother's overall involvement in child-care activities. Biological mothers reported on this measure that they were more involved than nonbiological mothers. Reports of the nonbiological mothers were in the same direction, but did not reach statistical significance. Global judgments thus confirmed the more detailed reports described above in showing that, if anyone, it is the biological mother who takes more responsibility for child care.

In interviews, parents were asked to give estimates of the average number of hours both biological and nonbiological mothers spent in paid employment each week. Results showed that biological mothers were less likely than nonbiological mothers to be working forty hours per week or more in paid employment. Thus, whereas biological mothers reported greater responsibility for child care, nonbiological mothers reported spending more time in paid employment.

There were no differences between relationship satisfaction reported by biological and nonbiological mothers. Consistent with expectations based on earlier findings with lesbian mothers (Koepke et al., 1992), lesbian mothers reported feeling very satisfied in their couple relationships. Similarly, overall satisfaction with division of family labor was relatively high, and there were no significant differences between biological and nonbiological mothers in this regard.

The study also assessed the strength of overall association among the three measures of child adjustment on the one hand and the four measures of parents' division of labor and satisfaction with division of labor on the other. Results showed a significant association between the two sets of variables. Parent reports of division of labor, satisfaction with division of labor, and the measures of child adjustment were significantly associated with one another. When biological mothers did less child care and when nonbiological mothers did more and were more satisfied, children's adjustment was rated as being more favorable.

In this study, then, both children and mothers reported more positive adjustment in families in which the nonbiological mother was described as a relatively equal participant in child care and in which the biological mother was not described as bearing an unequal burden of child-care duties. In other words, the most positive outcomes for children occurred in families that reported sharing child-care tasks relatively evenly between parents.

Overall, then, how did biological linkages structure everyday life in these lesbian mother households, if at all? Results from the Bay Area Families Study suggest that, although "gendered" divisions of labor were not as prominent in lesbian as in heterosexual families, there were nevertheless some differences between the roles of biological and nonbiological mothers. Biological mothers reported spending somewhat more time overall in child care and somewhat less time overall in paid employment than did nonbiological mothers. Even within the relatively narrow range represented in this sample, lesbian mothers who reported sharing more equally were more satisfied and described their children as better adjusted. Thus, more equal sharing was associated with positive outcomes among both lesbian mothers and their children. Lesbian mothers described themselves and their children as better off when the parental division of labor was not structured by biological linkages between parents and children, even while acknowledging that some tasks (especially child care) were at least partially structured along biological lines.

Contacts with Members of Extended Families

Given that biological linkages were related to a number of aspects of life within lesbian mother households, one can also ask whether biological ties structure contacts with members of extended families who live outside the child's household. In families headed by lesbian couples, the issue of relationships with members of extended families can be complicated by antilesbian prejudice. Among the relatives of a mother who is not biologically related to her child, there may also be some hesitancy about acknowledging kinship with children to whom they are not biologically linked (Laird, this volume; Patterson, 1996). Whether concerns focus on the absence of biological connections or on the lack of legal protections for family relationships, negotiation of such issues is often a concern among the families of nonbiological lesbian mothers (Patterson, 1996). A question of interest, then, is: To what extent are children of lesbian mothers in contact with members of biological versus nonbiological mothers' extended families?

Another important question concerns the possible associations of children's contacts with grandparents and other adults, on the one hand, and children's adjustment, on the other. Research on heterosexually parented children has revealed that contacts with grandparents and other supportive adults outside the home are associated with positive outcomes for children (Cherlin & Furstenberg, 1992; Tinsley & Parke, 1984, 1987). Another aim of the Bay Area Families Study, then, was to assess the extent to which this was also the case for the children of lesbian mothers. Thus, the study explored the extent to which children maintained contact with grandparents and other adults outside their immediate households, and on the possible associations of any such contacts with children's mental health (Patterson et al., in press).

As part of a family interview, lesbian mothers were asked to provide information about their children's contacts with grandparents and with any other adults outside the immediate household who were seen by the mothers as being important to the child. For each person named, mothers were asked to give the person's relationship to the child and an estimate of the person's frequency of contact with the child, including visits, telephone calls, cards, and letters. In the context of this interview, mothers were asked whether or not each "potential grandparent" (including biological mother's parents, nonbiological mother's parents, and biological father or sperm donor's parents, if known) were still living or had died. This allowed exploration of the degree to which families were in touch with living members of their extended families.

As expected on the basis of anecdotal reports (Laird, 1993, this volume; Lewin, 1993), most children were described by their mothers as being in regular (i.e., at least monthly) contact with grandparents and other adults outside their immediate households. More than 9 out of 10 children had regular contact with at least one grandparent; most also had regular contact with adult friends of their mothers, and many had frequent contact with aunts, uncles, and other members of the mothers' extended families. Stereotypic views of lesbian mother families as isolated from kinship networks were certainly not borne out by these data.

In contrast to the general picture of social engagement with friends and relatives outside the household that emerged from these data, very few children were described as having contact with parents or other relatives of their sperm donor or biological father. Given that, in many cases, the identity of the sperm donor was not known to children or their mothers (i.e., the child had been conceived via anonymous donor insemination), this outcome was not surprising. Only 4 children were reported to have annual or more frequent contact with the mother of their biological father, and only 1 child was reported to have annual or more frequent contact with the father of their biological father. None of these contacts were described as taking place as often as monthly. These results are consistent with mothers' reports that biological fathers or sperm donors and their relatives did not play significant roles in the lives of these children.

In families headed by two mothers, children were more likely to be in contact with parents of their biological as compared with parents of their nonbiological mothers. After correcting for cases in which a grandparent had died, most (74 percent) had annual or more frequent contact with their nonbiological mother's mother, but nearly all (97 percent) had annual or more frequent contact with their biological mother's mother. Results for grandfathers were similar, with two-thirds (67 percent) reported as having at least annual contact with the nonbiological mother's father, but almost all (92 percent) reporting annual or more frequent contact with the biological mother's father. The same pattern held for other relatives, with annual or more frequent contact more likely between the child and the adult relatives of the biological rather than the nonbiological mother.

When more stringent criteria for contact were applied, the pattern of greater contact with relatives of biological as compared with nonbiological mothers was even more pronounced. For instance, while most children were described as being in at least monthly contact with both mother and father of the biological mother, the majority were not said to be in such active contact with the parents of the nonbiological mother. In fact, more than twice as many children were said to be in regular (i.e., monthly or more frequent) contact with the parents of their biological than their nonbiological mother. Similarly, children were described as much more likely to be in regular contact with the other relatives of their biological than their nonbiological mothers. Thus, whether contact is defined as sporadic cards, letters, or visits, on the one hand, or as regular and repeated contacts, on the other, children were described as being more in touch with the relatives of their biological mothers. In this sense, biological linkages seemed to be strongly associated with the creation of kinship networks outside the child's household.

Even though biological links were related to contacts with relatives outside the household, many children also had regular contact with adults to whom they were not related. In addition to contacts with adult friends of their mothers, and with the parents of their same-aged friends, many children had regular contacts with adult women who had been former romantic partners of their mothers. Almost 1 in 3 (32 percent) of the children was reported to have at least annual contact with such a person, and 1 in 5 (22 percent) was described as having regular contact. Even without ties of blood or marriage, then, many children were described as having important and continuing relationships with mothers' former romantic partners.

Summary of Research on Biological Linkages and Family Lives

Findings from the Bay Area Families Study suggest that, in the families of the lesbian baby boom, daily lives were structured in ways that were related to biological linkages between family members, but not always in expected ways. In each of the three domains studied here, some expected linkages emerged and some did not.

Conceptualizations of family boundaries were not dictated by biological linkages in this sample. Biological fathers or sperm donors were generally not regarded as members of the nuclear or extended families of lesbian mothers or their children, even though their biological connections were acknowledged. At the same time, nonbiological lesbian mothers were regarded by all as members of children's nuclear families, despite acknowledgement of the absence of biological connections between these mothers and their children. Thus, conceptualizations of family boundaries were created without regard for biological linkages.

The selection of surnames for children, on the other hand, was likely to be guided to some degree by biological linkages among family members. Children were much more likely to be given the surname of their biological mother than that of their nonbiological mother. Since biological fathers or sperm donors (whose identities were unknown in some families) were not regarded as family members, their surnames were almost never given to children. Within the family, however, children's names that were derived from biological linkages were more common than any others.

Division of family labor was also structured, to some degree, by biological linkages within the families who participated in the Bay Area Families Study. Given that biological fathers or sperm donors did not live in the family household, and were not regarded as family members, it was not surprising that they did not figure in the division of family labor. Within two-mother families, household tasks and family decision making were shared evenly between the mothers. Biological mothers reported somewhat greater involvement in child-care activities and nonbiological mothers reported somewhat greater involvement in paid employment. Although there was thus some structuring of family work patterns along biological lines, the differences were small, and mothers sought to minimize this whenever possible.

Finally, there were links between biological ties and children's contacts with members of their parents' extended families. Since biological fathers or sperm donors were not usually regarded as family members, it was not surprising that children were generally not in contact with any of the relatives of these men. In this sense, biological ties were irrelevant to children's experiences of kinship. Within the family, however, children were more likely to be in regular contact with grandparents and other relatives of their biological as compared with those of their nonbiological mothers. In this sense, biological ties were related to children's contacts with extended family members outside their households.

What generalizations might embrace such diverse results? In general, it appears that the conceptualization of family boundaries was less influenced by biological ties than was the day-to-day functioning of families, once constituted. In other words, biological ties did not define family membership itself, but—once a family had identified itself as such—they did seem to structure many important family activities. The extent to which such findings will hold true for other lesbian-headed families is a topic for future research.

General Discussion

Families in which children have been born to women who identify as lesbians pose a number of interesting challenges for psychological research and theory (Flaks, 1994; Laird, 1993; Patterson, 1995a; Riley, 1988). Because they fit neither patriarchal nor heterosexist models of family life, lesbian mothers and their children provide an opportunity to evaluate the importance of received ideas in both areas. Research to date, though still limited in quantity, suggests that both lesbian mothers and their children are well adjusted and functioning normally. This finding, if borne out in subsequent studies, suggests that scholars may need to reconsider traditional notions about the importance of heterosexual male and female parents in human development.

Although research on lesbian childbearing is relatively new, the existing literature has a number of notable strengths. Well-designed studies have been conducted, both in the United States and in Europe, by a number of different investigators, using varied methods, and—in many cases—involving well-matched samples of comparison families in which parents identify as heterosexual. Despite various differences among the studies, all report essentially the same conclusions with regard to the development of children with lesbian mothers, and this adds to confidence in the conclusions of such research.

Even acknowledging recent advances, however, there remains much to learn about lesbian mothers and their children. Little information is yet available about the processes through which lesbian women decide whether or not to make parenthood part of their lives, and almost nothing is known about the degree to which the transition to parenthood among lesbians is similar to or different from that among heterosexual men and women. Detailed observational studies of parent-child interactions and relationships could add greatly to knowledge about aspects of parenting that are related to children's adjustment in these nontraditional families. Longitudinal studies that follow families over time could enhance understanding of development during infancy, childhood, and adolescence. A more comprehensive understanding of the significant factors in human development seems likely to result from future research in this area.

Such new understandings are likely to be useful from a number of different perspectives. Like cross-cultural research, studies of lesbian-mother families can open up new perspectives on the process of social change and can point the way to living arrangements that are different from accepted norms in contemporary American culture. Unlike heterosexual couples, for example, lesbian couples seem to have succeeded in sharing most of the labor involved in family life in a relatively even manner. Despite early indications that there may be benefits for children who grow up in such environments (Okin, 1989; Patterson, 1995a), the costs and benefits of these arrangements have yet to be fully documented. Further study of such phenomena will certainly enhance appreciation of the possible alternatives to ways of living that are currently more common.

From the standpoint of theory, empirical evaluation of long-held views may lead to reconsideration of some cherished beliefs (Patterson, 1992, 1995a). For instance, received notions about the importance of parental heterosexuality for child development would seem to have received a vigorous challenge from results of research to date (Chan et al., 1998; Flaks et al., 1995). Some of the research findings discussed above can also be seen as challenging the significance of patriarchal traditions (Mitchell, 1996; Riley, 1988). To the extent that trends in research to date are borne out in future work, some reconstruction of developmental theories may be necessary.

From the standpoint of law and social policy, the results of research on lesbian mothers and their children are also of great interest (Falk, 1989; Patterson, 1992, 1995c; Patterson & Redding, 1996; Polikoff, 1990). Certainly the research findings considered here provide no justification for discriminatory laws or policies that curtail or otherwise limit parental rights as a function of sexual orientation. Issues relevant to biological, social, and legal aspects of parenting that are under study with lesbian-mother families are also likely to be relevant to many other families in which there is some separation of the various aspects of parenting, and in this way to be relevant to law and policy across a broad spectrum.

References

Achenbach, T. M., & Edelbrock, C. (1983). *Manual for the Child Behavior Checklist and Revised Child Behavior Profile*. Burlington: University of Vermont, Department of Psychiatry.

Allen, K. R., & Demo, D. H. (1995). The families of lesbians and gay men: A new frontier in family research. *Journal of Marriage and the Family, 57*, 111–127.

Brewaeys, A., Ponjaert, I., Van Hall, E. V., & Golombok, S. (1997, April). Donor insemination: Child development and family functioning in lesbian mother families with 4 to 8 year old children. Paper presented at the 1997 Biennial Meeting of the Society for Research in Child Development, Washington, DC.

Casper, V., Schultz, S., & Wickens, E. (1992). Breaking the silences: Lesbian and gay parents and the schools. *Teachers College Record, 94*, 109–137.

Chan, R. W., Brooks, R. C., Raboy, B., & Patterson, C. J. (in press). Division of labor among lesbian and heterosexual parents: Associations with children's adjustment. *Journal of Family Psychology*.

Chan, R. W., Raboy, B., & Patterson, C. J. (1998). Psychosocial adjustment among children conceived via donor insemination by lesbian and heterosexual mothers. *Child Development, 69*, 443–457.

Cherlin, A. J., & Furstenberg, F. F., Jr. (1992). *The new American grandparent*. Cambridge, MA: Harvard University Press.

Cowan, C. P., & Cowan, P. A. (1990). Who does what? In J. Touliatos, B. F. Perlmutter, & M. A. Straus (Eds.), *Handbook of family measurement techniques* (pp. 447–448). Newbury Park, CA: Sage Publications.

Cowan, C. P., & Cowan, P. A. (1992). *When partners become parents: The big life change for couples*. New York: Basic Books.

Cowan, P. A., Cowan, C. P., & Kerig, P. K. (1993). Mothers, fathers, sons, and daughters: Gender differences in family formation and parenting style. In P. A. Cowan, D. Field, D. Hansen, A. Skolnick, & G. Swanson (Eds.), *Family, self and society: Toward a new agenda for family research* (pp. 165–195). Hillsdale, NJ: Erlbaum.

Crawford, S. (1987). Lesbian families: Psychosocial stress and the family-building process. In Boston Lesbian Psychologies Collective (Eds.), *Lesbian psychologies: Explorations and challenges* (pp. 195–214). Urbana: University of Illinois Press.

Eder, R. A. (1990). Uncovering young children's psychological selves: Individual and developmental differences. *Child Development, 61*, 849–863.

Falk, P. J. (1989). Lesbian mothers: Psychosocial assumptions in family law. *American Psychologist, 44*, 941–947.

Flaks, D. (1994). Gay and lesbian families: Judicial assumptions, scientific realities. *William and Mary Bill of Rights Journal, 3,* 345–372.

Flaks, D., Ficher, I., Masterpasqua, F., & Joseph, G. (1995). Lesbians choosing motherhood: A comparative study of lesbian and heterosexual parents and their children. *Developmental Psychology, 31,* 104–114.

Golombok, S., Tasker, F. L., & Murray, C. (1997). Children raised in fatherless families from infancy: Family relationships and the socioemotional development of children of lesbian and single heterosexual mothers. *Journal of Child Psychology & Psychiatry, 38,* 783–791.

Green, G. D., & Bozett, F. W. (1991). Lesbian mothers and gay fathers. In J. C. Gonsiorek & J. D. Weinrich (Eds.), *Homosexuality: Research implications for public policy* (pp. 197–214). Newbury Park, CA: Sage Publications.

Hand, S. I. (1991). *The lesbian parenting couple.* Unpublished doctoral dessertation, Professional School of Psychology, San Francisco.

Herek, G. M. (1995). Psychological heterosexism in the United States. In A. R. D'Augelli & C. J. Patterson (Eds.), *Lesbian. gay and bisexual identities over the lifespan: Psychological perspectives* (pp. 321–346). New York: Oxford University Press.

Koepke, L., Hare, J., & Moran, P. B. (1992). Relationship quality in a sample of lesbian couples with children and child-free lesbian couples. *Family Relations, 41,* 224–229.

Laird, J. (1993). Lesbian and gay families. In F. Walsh (Ed.), *Normal family processes,* 2nd ed. (pp. 282–328). New York: Guilford.

Lewin, E. (1993). *Lesbian mothers: Accounts of gender in American culture.* Ithaca, NY: Cornell University Press.

Locke, H., & Wallace, K. (1959). Short marital adjustment and prediction tests: Their reliability and validity. *Marriage and Family Living, 21,* 251–255.

Martin, A. (1993). *The lesbian and gay parenting handbook.* New York: HarperCollins.

McCandlish, B. (1987). Against all odds: Lesbian mother family dynamics. In F. W. Bozett (Ed.). *Gay and lesbian parents* (pp. 23–38). New York: Praeger.

Mitchell, V. (1996). Two moms: Contribution of the planned lesbian family to the deconstruction of gendered parenting. In J. Laird & R. J. Green (Eds.), *Lesbians and gays in couples and families: A handbook for therapists* (pp. 343–357). San Francisco: Jossey-Bass.

Okin, S. M. (1989). *Justice, gender and the family.* New York: Basic Books.

Osterweil, D. A. (1991). *Correlates of relationship satisfaction in lesbian couples who are parenting their first child together.* Unpublished doctoral dissertation, California School of Professional Psychology, Berkeley/Alameda.

Patterson, C. J. (1992). Children of lesbian and gay parents. *Child Development, 63,* 1025–1042.

Patterson, C. J. (1994a). Children of the lesbian baby boom: Behavioral adjustment, self-concepts, and sex role identity. In B. Greene & G. M. Herek (Eds.), *Lesbian and gay psychology: Theory, research, and clinical applications* (pp. 156–175). Newbury Park, CA: Sage Publications.

Patterson, C. J. (1994b). Lesbian and gay couples considering parenthood: An agenda for research, service, and advocacy. *Journal of Gay and Lesbian Social Services, 1,* 33–55.

Patterson, C. J. (1995a). Families of the lesbian baby boom: Parents' division of labor and children's adjustment. *Developmental Psychology, 31,* 115–123.

Patterson, C. J. (1995b). Lesbian mothers, gay fathers, and their children. In A. R. D'Augelli & C. J. Patterson (Eds.), *Lesbian, gay and bisexual identities over the lifespan: Psychological perspectives* (pp. 262–290). New York: Oxford University Press.

Patterson, C. J. (1995c). Adoption of minor children by lesbian and gay adults: A social science perspective. *Duke Journal of Gender, Law, and Policy, 2*, 191–205.

Patterson, C. J. (1996). Lesbian mothers and their children: Findings from the Bay Area Families Study. In J. Laird & R. J. Green (Eds.), *Lesbians and gays in couples and families: A handbook for therapists* (pp. 420–438). San Francisco: Jossey-Bass.

Patterson, C. J., Hurt, S., & Mason, C. (in press). Families of the lesbian baby boom: Children's contacts with grandparents and other adults. *American Journal of Orthopsychiatry*.

Patterson, C. J., & Redding, R. E. (1996). Lesbian and gay families with children: Implications of social science research for policy. *Journal of Social Issues, 52*, 29–50.

Pies, C. (1985). *Considering parenthood*. San Francisco: Spinsters/Aunt Lute.

Pies, C. (1990). Lesbians and the choice to parent. In F. W. Bozett & M. B. Sussman, (Eds.), *Homosexuality and family relations* (pp. 137–154). New York: Harrington Park Press.

Polikoff, N. (1990). This child does have two mothers: Redefining parenthood to meet the needs of children in lesbian mother and other nontraditional families. *Georgetown Law Review, 78*, 459–575.

Pollack, S., & Vaughn, J. (Eds.) (1987). *Politics of the heart: A lesbian parenting anthology*. Ithaca, NY: Firebrand Books.

Ricketts, W., & Achtenberg, R. (1990). Adoption and foster parenting for lesbians and gay men: Creating new traditions in family. In F. W. Bozett & M. B. Sussman (Eds.), *Homosexuality and family relations* (pp. 83–118). New York: Harrington Park Press.

Riley, C. (1988). American kinship: A lesbian account. *Feminist Issues, 8*, 75–94.

Steckel, A. (1985). *Separation-individuation in children of lesbian and heterosexual couples*. Unpublished doctoral dissertation, Wright Institute Graduate School, Berkeley, CA.

Steckel, A. (1987). Psychosocial development of children of lesbian mothers. In F. W. Bozett, (Ed.), *Gay and lesbian parents* (pp. 75–85). New York: Praeger.

Tasker, F. L., & Golombok, S. (1991). Children raised by lesbian mothers: The empirical evidence. *Family Law, 21*, 184–187.

Tasker, F. L., & Golombok, S. (1997). *Growing up in a lesbian family: Effects on child development*. New York: Guilford Press.

Tinsley, B. J., & Parke, R. D. (1984). Grandparents as support and socialization agents. In M. Lewis (Ed.), *Beyond the dyad* (pp. 161–194). New York: Plenum.

Tinsley, B. J., & Parke, R. D. (1987). Grandparents as interactive and social support agents for families with young infants. *International Journal of Aging and Human Development, 25*, 259–277.

Weston, K. (1991). *Families we choose: Lesbians, gays, kinship*. New York: Columbia University Press.

9

Older Gay Men and Lesbians in Families

Gilbert Herdt and Jeff Beeler

F. Scott Fitzgerald once said that "there are no second acts in American lives." The famous novelist meant to capture the sense in which Americans grow up with a linear time perspective on the life course, perhaps deriving from a frontier society that always looks forward and never back. Americans grow up expecting "to make something of themselves" on the stage of our society. We receive little reward for "failing" the first time around—whether in career, marriage, friendship, or love—failure is not one of the admired American attributes. But it is our contention that "you don't get a second chance" works differently if one is gay or lesbian at this point in American history. To quote the proverbial Aunt Matilda who scolded her aging Cousin Harry: "You are over 50 and still haven't married! How can you be such a successful banker and such a lousy catch!" Cousin Harry offers no resistance to this admonishment, being a closeted homosexual of the old school, who prefers the family duplicity of silence in the face of heteronormal admonishments. But he notices that his family appreciates the many things he does for them. Harry's openly gay friends encourage him to "finally do it"—to come out to his family. It's not too late for a second chance, his friends urge. This is why we have drawn the title of this chapter from the dramatic metaphor of Fitzgerald. Today, the story of many lesbians and gay men is undergoing great cultural change in our society, owing to social progress, political and economic change, and the decline of homophobia. The notion that people don't get a second chance in life is being increasingly challenged by older lesbians and gay men who are finding a new voice in a society that is more positive about their presence, even when they have to fight to be acknowledged. Indeed, we are finding that for a whole generation of older gay people, it is only when they near retirement and face the later part of their lives that they feel the freedom and desire to be out.

By older we mean over age 55. This is the approximate point in the life course when the heterosexual typically looks forward to retirement and enjoys grandchildren. The stereotype of older lesbian and gay men, however, is that this is the point in their lives where they begin to become increasingly lonely, isolated and "left out." Although the older literature suggests that this is not the case (Reid, 1995; Berger, 1982), it may be even less the case today when historical circumstances and cultural change have opened up new possibilities for a "second act." We especially need to consider in this chapter the family context of such changes.

Older lesbians and gay men constitute a diverse group, most of whom, although born in a period when homosexuality was almost always concealed, nonetheless came of age during a time of transition in which the homophile movement became increasingly visible and vocal (D'Emilio & Freedman, 1988). Starting with the Mattachine Society and the Daughters of Bilitis in the fifties—consisting of a handful of individuals willing to speak out about their sexual orientation and to reach out to others—and moving to Stonewall and the gay rights movement it sparked at the end of the sixties, many historic transformations in gay lives began to unfold. These included the formation of the "gay and lesbian community" and the expression of the "gay lifestyle" in the seventies, the response to the AIDS crisis and the "maturing" of the gay community in the eighties, to the nearly ubiquitous place of gay people in our society today, marching in Gay Pride parades, with hundreds of thousands of participants (Herdt, 1992; Herdt & Boxer, 1996; Herrell, 1992). It is no longer surprising to see gay and lesbian characters in books, movies, and even on television, or gay and lesbian advocacy groups within corporations, communities, schools, and the government. The widespread legislative and judicial battles for gay rights, involving the legalization of gay marriages and nondiscrimination laws, will surely continue to evolve in the twenty-first century. If someone in our culture today is totally unaware of gay issues at all, one might wonder just what closet *they've* been in!

But these dramatic and rapid social changes touched individual lives very differently. Some people may have been active and involved from the very beginning. Others may have lived much of their lives closeted and then came out in varying degrees later in life. Older men and women may have been selective in the degree to which they were open about their sexuality. For still others, much of this upheaval may have been peripheral to their lives, whether they were living as gay men and lesbian women, closeted or not, or whether they were passing as heterosexual; it was something happening somewhere else with other people. And still others may have been completely unaffected, possibly to an extent even unaware of many of the changes and events occurring around them. As a result, older gay and lesbian adults today are an extremely heterogenous group, and they are not easy to generalize or categorize. The openly and actively gay older adult may have previously lived as closeted in varying degrees; his friends may still be closeted; and some still pursue a heterosexual lifestyle, contending with homosexual desires and feelings through a combination of secrecy, denial, expression, and repression.

It seems fair to say that the degree of disclosure within an individual's life is significant to his or her subsequent social development and to the quality and character of life. This is not to suggest that for all individuals disclosure necessarily leads to a qualitatively *better* life, nor necessarily to better psychological adjustment or development, but that it certainly leads to a *different* life and a *different* psychological development and adjustment. In general, however, it has long been known that being engaged in a gay and lesbian community contributes to feelings of positive well-being (Williams & Weinberg, 1974). In the past, stage-model theorists believed that a normative developmental sequence for gay men and lesbians was necessary for positive identity formation and subsequent emotional and psychological health (Troiden, 1989; Cass, 1979, Coleman, 1982). Within these models, disclosure was posited as an important developmental step. Recent studies, however, have shown the limitations of these models and questioned the extent to which they apply to all people at all times (Herdt & Boxer, 1996). Surely, disclosure is likely to affect the way in which one *enacts* one's identity in relation to others.

For those gay men and lesbian women who have not disclosed to their family, the dramatic change in the cultural climate may provide an impetus to reevaluate their relationships with family members. They may reconsider whether to disclose or not based upon their ability to envision quite different scenarios of response than they might have imagined ten, twenty, or thirty years prior. Along with the possibility of contemplating disclosure, which was unthinkable earlier, there are the possibilities of developing new roles for themselves within the family, of changing the quality and nature of their relationships, and of forging a new sense of self and place in the world.

Much remains hidden, however. We know little to nothing about how older gay men and lesbians typically interact with their families, whether out or closeted, single or partnered. Nor are we aware of how cultural changes affect long-held patterns of adjustment among older gay men and lesbians. For example, it remains unclear to what degree older gay men and lesbians *have already* disclosed to family members, remained in duplicitous passing, or continue to be closeted. Most telling, we certainly have little understanding of what happens when older gay men and lesbians *do* disclose to their families. Will Aunt Matilda still accept Cousin Harry?

A recent series of focus groups in Chicago, based within a project exploring the needs of older gay men and lesbians, suggests that there may be increasing numbers of older gay men and lesbians who *do* come out in later life. One focus group in particular consisted of gay men over age 45 who had recently ended long-term heterosexual marriages and came out as gay. Many of these men cited the importance of the visibility of the gay community not only in helping them to decide to come out but also, in some cases, in helping them to figure out that they were gay in the first place. As one man remarked, "at age 21, my Dad told me to get married and I did." Later he realized that he would not be able to stifle his homoerotic desires. Many of these men report initially feeling as if they were "the only ones in their situation," only to find with time that others like them were "everywhere [they] turned." Isolation and secrecy are keys to understanding their prior development.

This chapter explores these issues by reviewing and discussing the relevant literature and making suggestions for future research. The only substantial body of literature focuses on the reactions of families and parents to a family member's disclosure of homosexuality. Unfortunately, most prior studies addressed younger adults' disclosure to their parents and parental reactions (Boxer, Cook, & Herdt, 1991). The question, then, is to what degree these findings apply to older gay men and lesbian women and to what extent the process differentiates them from younger cohorts.

Why Disclose?

The beginning point in most of the literature addresses the basic question, Why disclose? To be more precise, however, the relative question is whether to disclose or *not* to disclose. A variety of scholars have studied disclosure and the many reasons for disclosure (Ben-Ari, 1995b). These include the desire for honesty—"to stop living a lie"; to open communication, to strengthen family bonds, deepen love, provide opportunities for mutual support and caring (Jourard, 1971); to develop the sense of a "we-feeling" (Levinger & Shoek, 1972); the validation of one's self-concept (Kelvin, 1977); to increase intimacy (Ben Ari, 1995a; Cramer & Roach, 1988; Mattison & McWhirter, 1995); to increase the ability to exercise self-expression and social control (Derlega & Grzelak, 1979); to avoid loneliness, to decrease the "price of passing," which may often involve feeling "invisible," or distancing oneself from other family members, and a feeling of guilt or sadness due to loss of intimacy (Isay, 1996). Reasons for nondisclosure, according to some scholars (Ben Ari, 1995b; Cramer & Roach, 1988), include the fear of rejection—emotional as well as material rejection (i.e., adolescents thrown out of house) (Herdt & Boxer, 1996); the fear of hurting or disappointing parents or causing them emotional pain (Boxer et al., 1991); concern over parents' sense of guilt, or the gay or lesbian person's sense of guilt; fear of being forced to get treatment; protection of the family from crisis; uncertainty about one's identity; fear of criticism, ridicule, and loss of power (Komarovsky, 1976);

increased vulnerability (Kelvin, 1977); and risk of jeopardizing the relationship (Rosenfeld, 1979; Kooden et al., 1979).

Although in many respects these issues identified may be relevant to older gay and lesbian individuals as well as to the younger generation, there are a number of differences arising from being in a different point in development that may bring other issues to the fore (Boxer & Cohler, 1989). Moreover, even when an issue may be common to older and younger gay men, and lesbians, it may be experienced with a different valence, as clinical studies have repeatedly shown (Silverman, 1996).

The most obvious difference separating older and younger gay men and lesbians is dependence. Younger adults tend to be much more dependent upon their parents, financially and emotionally. They may still receive, in varying degrees, financial support from their parents, as well as housing, at least intermittently, until they leave home. They may also receive emotional support and guidance. In general, older adults are more independent and have more resources available to them, both materially and psychologically, which provides greater agency. In fact, they may very well *be providing* care to aging parents. As a result, fear of financial loss and rejection may have much more practical salience for a younger than older gay or lesbian person. Moreover, younger gay men and lesbians may have little to no connection to a network of gay friends or the gay community, making them dependent upon their family for support. By contrast, older gay or lesbian people, on the other hand, may very well have a "family of choice."

What does family mean in this context? Driskill (1994) identifies five family functions that merit reflection: (1) to directly protect its children from harm or danger, (2) to teach its children how to socialize appropriately in the culture, (3) to promote self-esteem and a sense of value and worth in its children, (4) to help its children develop a sense of identity, and (5) to teach survival skills to cope in the larger world. Adolescent and young adult gay men and lesbians are still developing; their families are *in process*. Without the gay community and a network of friends, they may depend upon their actual biological family to provide all these functions. Older gay men and lesbians, however, may be developmentally more independent and secure, having a support network in the community to which they can turn.

Another significant difference lies in the risk that disclosure may entail in terms of current social status and opportunity, where opportunity is conceptualized as access to means of increasing one's social status. At different points in development—represented by relative age and generational position—the relative weight of these concerns may shift. Herdt and Boxer (1996) found that adolescents tended to postpone disclosure while still living with and dependent upon their parents. Once they are independent, however, one might conjecture that when weighing the risks of disclosure, loss of social status (of which a young adult has relatively little) is a minimal concern in relation to potential loss of opportunity resulting from discrimination. As a young adult progresses through early and middle adulthood, however, we might surmise that this equation would shift. As an individual becomes more established and commands more resources, opportunity loss may become less of a concern. However, the risk of losing established status may increase. The implications of this point are unclear. What is clear, however, is that the social risk of stigma and homophobia associated with disclosure may be experienced very differently by older versus younger adults, in terms of both the type of potential loss and the resources available with which to cope with these risks.

Partnership defines a third critical difference between older and younger gay men and lesbians. Murphy (1989) investigated the effect of disclosure to parents on lesbian *couples*. She noted that many of the couples complained that maintaining secrecy of their lesbianism and their relationship caused them to be distant, anxious, and awkward in communications with their family. This led to decreased contact with family members and resulted in either a sense of isolation or "pseudocloseness." Additionally, a smaller percentage listed in-law problems as a source of conflict within their relationship. If we add to our opening vignette that Cousin Harry has had the same male roommate for the last twenty years—Aunt Matilda refers to them as the "two bachelors"—it is not difficult to see that this relationship would provide an entirely different set of problems from those of younger, unpartnered gay men. Cousin Harry is not only "invisible" to his family, but his family and his significant relationship are mutually exclusive. At Thanksgiving, does Harry stay with his partner of twenty years or travel to his natal family, which might be the last occasion to celebrate with his 81-year-old mother? The closeted homosexual couple may feel they must maintain the facade of heterosexuality. When relatives come to visit and appearances have to be maintained, they must sleep in separate bedrooms. In short, for older gay men and lesbians who are partnered, there are complicated and practical issues of maintaining a balance between commitments to family and the love and bond to a partner, which may create tensions that motivate disclosure.

Finally, the length of time in which patterns of relating have been maintained may well constitute a major threshold and barrier to familial relationships. It may constitute a significant difference between older and younger gay men and lesbians. Mahoney (1994) has identified three "patterns for juggling the closet." These include creating geographical and emotional distance; collusion ("I know you know and you know I know you know but we don't need to say anything about it"); and a selectivity of knowing, in which some family members know and others do not know, creating a pattern of knowing or not knowing that prefigures all interactions between family members. Creating and maintaining emotional distance from one's parents at age 20 may require considerable psychological energy that eventually fails, resulting in disclosure—or a lifelong resignation to secrecy. But what happens after thirty to forty years of maintaining these patterns? It is not difficult to imagine that relief for a 20-year-old may be experienced as a threat to a 50-year-old in a similar situation. The older person may not be able to handle the sudden increase in intimacy. Most important, *acceptance* by a parent at this age may be just as painful as rejection—perhaps more so, as the guilt and sadness resulting from the loss of *decades* of intimacy and growth may be quite overwhelming.

Duplicity and collusion take on new meaning in this regard. The purpose of collusion may, over the years, subtly shift. Collusion may initially express itself as not being able to talk about one's mutually understood but unspoken sexual orientation, to avoid the crisis of confronting it directly. Over the years, however, each party in the collusion may come to terms with the silence; and the silence may infect other areas of emotional relatedness. As a result, twenty years later, conflict over homosexuality may not be the primary purpose or effect of collusion. That is, an announcement of "I'm gay" would almost certainly be met with, "I know, I've accepted that." The purpose behind collusion over time may be to avoid painful discussions about the emotional relationship between the two individuals. That is, "I'm gay," "I know" might lead to "Why didn't you tell me before?" which might lead to "I didn't want to hurt you," leading to the feeling, "Why couldn't you trust me?" and so on. Older gay men's and lesbians' patterns of adjustment are significant above and beyond their direct psychological and relational impact. We would suggest that over time these relational duplicities may well become more significant, *in and of themselves*, than the fact of homosexuality. Put another way, younger gay men or lesbians have the fact of homosexuality to disclose and integrate into their relationships with their families. Upon disclosure, older gay men and lesbians have an entire *life* to integrate into their relationships with their families from *a new perspective*.

Finally, key sibling relations may be more significant for older adults than for younger people. Cicirelli (1995) has investigated sibling relationships (a much understudied topic) and found that a high percentage of adults do, in fact, maintain contact with siblings, especially their favored siblings. Moreover, siblings seem most often to serve as confidantes, with a substantial portion of adults who maintain contact expressing feeling close to their brothers or sisters. With older adults, these relationships appear to serve a unique function in that these adults report that much of their contact with siblings involves life review and reminiscence. Siblings are, generally speaking, able to reminiscence with each other about a much broader period of the life span, ranging from childhood to older age. This is critical, as investigators in aging have posited that reminiscence serves the important function of enhancing ego integrity (Tobin, 1991).

The research literature on disclosure points out that often adolescents and young adults disclose to siblings prior to disclosing to parents (Boxer et al., 1991; Herdt & Boxer, 1996). However, this may be viewed as generally serving an instrumental function, such as gathering support prior to informing their parents, or as a "testing the waters," in order to discuss with the sibling the pros and cons of disclosure to parents and family. With younger adults it is clearly the parental reaction that is of primary importance, for reasons discussed above as well as for the role parents continue to play in the development of adolescents and young adults. With increasing years, however, relationships with siblings may indeed become more salient, in the light of Cicerelli's findings. This would especially be true as parents begin to age and actually become dependent upon their children, reversing roles and dependent relationships. Aside from the emotional and psychological function siblings may play in the lives of older adults, it is not difficult to imagine some practical consequences of nondisclosure as well. For example, returning to Cousin Harry, one can imagine his sister saying, "Why don't you move out of your apartment with Bill—he'll do fine on his own—and move in with Mom? She needs help now and the rest of us have families to take care of. Besides, you'll save some money." No imaginary answer to this real-life situation could overestimate the pathos that might emerge for Harry.

To summarize thus far, although there are similarities between older and younger gay men and lesbians surrounding the decision to disclose or not to disclose, there are also significant differences. Even similarities may be experienced with a different emotional valence. Older gay men and lesbians typically have greater stability and resources—both financially, socially, and emotionally—and probably experience less anxiety over possible deleterious consequences of disclosure, with the exception of the risk of increased vulnerability of social status owing to stigma, although that is culturally mediated and appears to be less significant now than previously. The role of the family in meeting the needs of the gay or lesbian individual is significantly different between younger and older gay men and lesbians and, moreover, older gay men and lesbians may have developed alternative "families of choice" with which to meet their particular needs (Weston, 1993). For older gay men or lesbians who are partnered, problems of negotiating critical decisions between one's family of origin and one's life partner may trigger disclosure, while among younger adults this may not occur until a later time. For younger adults, homosexuality itself may be the primary issue to be addressed, while with older adults decades of relating with their families in duplicitous ways may be more of a burden than the homosexuality itself. And finally, siblings may be more important in the lives of older adults versus younger ones. These observations would suggest pitfalls and risks of simply extrapolating findings from research on younger gay men and lesbians and applying these results to older gay men and lesbians. We think this is likely to lead to inaccurate formulations and a poor understanding of their lives and needs.

Reaction and Adjustment

The next element discussed in the literature on disclosure is the family's—particularly parents'—reactions to disclosure and the subsequent process of adjustment. There are a number of key differences between the lives of older and younger gay men and lesbians that come to mind. A good start might be the findings of many researchers that show how parents are already aware of or suspicious regarding their offsprings' sexual orientation prior to disclosure (Ben-Ari, 1995a; Boxer et al., 1991). DeVine (1984) terms this understanding "subliminal awareness" and identifies it as the first "stage" in the disclosure process.

We think it is often the case that the family of an older gay or lesbian person is either more *or* less "subliminally aware" of the sexual orientation of the undisclosed gay or lesbian family member. What may be innocuous during adolescence and young adulthood may become increasingly suspicious as time passes and the closeted homosexual fails to pursue a "normal heterosexual" life course. To not have a girlfriend in high school is one thing; to be 50 and a bachelor living with a roommate of fifteen years is quite another. Such "off-time" and "off-course" markers have been well discussed by Boxer and Cohler (1989). Correspondingly, as reasons for suspicion increases, acceptable social excuses decrease. In high school, a son may "be shy"; in college, "occupied with his studies"; beginning a career, "focused on his work." Eventually, though, the voice of Aunt Matilda grows stronger and stronger: How can you be such a lousy catch? On the other hand, the literature points out that all parents begin with a heterosexual assumption, one which lesbians and gay men, despite their orientation, may confirm. That is, many gay men, and even more lesbians, marry and have families, embarking on a heterosexual life course[1] (Chodorow, 1992). If parents had any suspicions originally, their children's subsequent life course would seem to argue against them. As a result, parents or family members of older lesbians and gay men seem either likely to have developed *very* strong suspicions and "subliminal awareness" or, on the contrary, to have little to no subliminal awareness or suspicions.

The reactions of families are notable in this process. First, most of the literature describes an initial stage of shock or surprise in familial reaction. In some cases, however, parents express relief (Mattison & McWhirter, 1995) about the revelation of same-gender desires or relations. Ben Ari (1995b) has pointed out that when parents have suspicions, often they do not feel free to talk with anyone about their suspicions and consequently they end up keeping a secret analogous to the secret being kept by the gay

---

1. In a recent study we completed in Chicago, we found that 50 percent of our female participants had been married, in contrast to 35 percent of male participants (Herdt, Beeler, & Rawls, in press).

or lesbian individual (see Muller, 1987). Some of these parents may experience relief being able to discuss the issue in much the same way a gay or lesbian person may feel relief not having to keep the secret anymore. For those parents of older lesbians and gay men for whom the suspicions have shifted to being "obvious but ignored," one might expect little in the way of shock or surprise. For these parents, it is possible that relief may be a much more salient dimension. Conversely, the parents or families of gay men and lesbians who have married, had children, and generally pursued a heterosexual life course would likely experience shock and surprise even more than parents of young adults. Moreover, the degree of adjustment required by the disclosure of an older adult is likely to tend toward either extreme. In the case of the bachelor, the revelation fits in with the pattern of life everyone has become accustomed to and is unlikely to cause the shock waves a similar disclosure might cause by a young college student. On the other hand, disclosure, followed by divorce and the breakup of a family that has been together for the last twenty years, is likely to cause considerable consternation all around.

Perhaps the most dramatic difference between younger and older gay men and lesbians is the context in which parents frame their reactions to disclosure. Parents of adolescents and young adults are likely to reflect upon and react to disclosure within the context of their offspring's *future*. Parents of older lesbians and gay men, in contrast, are likely to experience the disclosure within the context of their offspring's *past*. A family's response may take on considerably different characteristics for older as opposed to younger gay men and lesbians, which evokes several key points in the family cycle.

First and foremost, much of the literature on disclosure focuses on parents' "grief" reaction subsequent to disclosure. Our reading of these studies suggests a cautionary point. Grieving is viewed as arising from a sudden, perhaps wrenching, disappointment in the hopes and dreams parents have had for their children—a normative life path of marriage and family—as well as for themselves, or grandchildren (Robinson, Walters, & Skeen, 1989). In a sense, some parents lose an important and anticipated chapter of their own envisioned future: becoming grandparents. With an older gay or lesbian person, however, these dreams may have long ago been abandoned and refashioned. Simply put, at 52, no one expects Cousin Harry, at his age, to suddenly begin producing a brood of grandchildren. Moreover, with each passing year out of young adulthood to Harry's present age, the hope that Harry will have children and fulfill reproductive norms undoubtedly declines with a corresponding increase in finding other things about Harry to value. In short, disappointment in terms of future plans and expectations is often cited as one of the central aspects of adjusting to disclosure of homosexuality by family members; in older adults, this dimension is generally likely to be much less salient. Disclosure assumes the role of *explaining* the past rather than *shaping* the future. The exception may be gay men and lesbians who *have* married and have had children. Although they are not disappointing parental hopes per se, parents may be upset that the "ideal" family was broken up by their son's or daughter's declaration of homosexuality. In such a scenario, concern about the grandchildren's future may engender a future- rather than past-oriented perspective.

Along similar lines, fearfulness regarding the future well-being of their offspring is also common among parents who have just learned of their son's or daughter's homoerotic sexual orientation. They are often fearful that their children may be at risk for acquiring AIDS (Robinson, Walters, & Skeen, 1989), experiencing stigma and discrimination, or being subjected to violence (gay bashing). The family may be fearful that their child or sibling will never be able to find and keep a partner. Moreover, with a surplus inventory of negative stereotypes, they may envision their offspring rapidly changing in the near future and begin behaving in accordance with the stereotypes. In short, parents experience uncertainty regarding the future of their child. With older lesbians or gay men, however, the anxiety about the offspring's future is likely to be dramatically less acute. Although many of these concerns may be equally valid for older gay men and lesbians, generally speaking parents have a large sample of thirty to forty years by which to estimate what their offspring's future will be like. Again, disclosure on the part of older gay men and lesbians is likely to be integrated into an understanding of the past more than a prediction of the future.

DeVine (1984) suggests that one of the reasons disclosure creates a crisis in the family is that there are no existing roles in the typical family for a gay or lesbian individual. Put another way, there is no preestablished bundle of expectations to guide and shape one's behavior. This is, in a sense, again future oriented—how will this person, *from here on out*, fit in? Older gay men and lesbians, by contrast, have over the course of the years adjusted and developed roles within their family, however imperfect. Again, with older gay men and lesbians this issue is past oriented: they will fit in the way they have, de facto, fit in over the past thirty years. Finally, related to this, Strommen (1989), citing Weinberg (1972), suggests that there are typically two conflicting themes when parents come to terms with a son's or daughter's homosexuality: the theme of love and acceptance on one hand and the theme of conventionality on the other. It would seem, in a general sense, that conventionality might become less and less conflictual over time as nonconventionality in the life course has become increasingly a fact—over the years—with or without disclosure. Thus, Cousin Harry is viewed as an odd duck at this point, whether he is gay or not. In fact, in the current cultural climate it might even be viewed as *more* conventional (meaning that we have a cultural model accounting for his behavior) for him to be gay as opposed to simply a bachelor. If the gay or lesbian individual were heterosexually married and had children when they disclosed, conventionality may become even *more* critical as it affects a number of people, including the children.

In contrasting the reactions of families of older versus younger adults, there may be significant differences in the way disclosure affects the family's view of the past. Cramer and Roach (1988) point out that disclosure may result in the parent's or family member's viewing the past relationship with the gay or lesbian person as fraudulent. For adolescents and young adults, this sense of previous interaction having an inauthentic or fraudulent character is likely to pale in significance compared to future-oriented concerns. For the parent or sibling of an older gay or lesbian person, however, a sense that the past *thirty or forty years* have been fraudulent is highly significant. One might imagine that this is acutely true in cases where the gay or lesbian individual is disclosing to a heterosexual *spouse,* in-laws, or children.

Again, we think it would be hazardous to extrapolate from studies of parents and their adolescent or young adult offspring in attempting to characterize parent and sibling reactions and subsequent adjustment to disclosure by an older adult. Although one might presume many similarities between these two groups, including the important observation that prior relationships are the best predictor of response (Savin-Williams, 1989; Borhek, 1983; Weinberg, 1972), there are likely many differences as well. Further study focusing specifically on older adults and their families is necessary before generalizations can reasonably be made.

Effects of Disclosure

Finally, the third major element of disclosure discussed in the literature is its effects, both on the disclosing individual and on parents and siblings. We will only briefly review and comment on some of the themes found in the literature on this topic.

The current literature on disclosure assumes that disclosure will create a crisis. DeVine (1984), in his influential article on the process of parental adjustment to disclosure, opens with the sentence "affectional preference orientation becomes a major crisis for the family system because. . . . " He proceeds to list five reasons without considering the possibility that in some instances there may not be a crisis at all. Perhaps a generational difference enters here. This perspective is pervasive, although there are some exceptions beginning to emerge (Ben-Ari, 1995a,b; Mahoney, 1994). Although it is quite easy to imagine how disclosure on the part of an older adult may lead to crisis, particularly if he or she is involved in a heterosexual marriage with children, it is also relatively easy to imagine that Cousin Harry's revelation might elicit no more than a shrug and a feeling of "I figured as much." The point is that in research with older gay men and lesbians who disclose to family members, it should not be taken for granted that this event will create a crisis. In some cases it may produce a positive effect.

Then there is the match between anticipation and event. Cramer and Roach (1988) report that within their study, a much higher percentage of their subjects *expected* deterioration in their relationships following disclosure than actually *experienced* deterioration. Relationships were often strained at first but improved over time, although in 21 percent of the cases there was an immediate improvement. Parents with traditional values seem liable to reconsider those values when they apply to their own child. Aside from the obvious question regarding whether older adults who disclose would be found to experience similar rates of acceptance, a more interesting question arises: Might older adults be better judges of their family members' reactions than adolescents and young adults? If this were found to be true, it would have important implications for counselors and other service providers.

A number of authors also cite improved self-esteem (Hammersmith & Weinberg, 1973; Nemeyer, 1980; Cramer & Roach, 1988), "enhanced identity formation" (Coleman, 1982) and better psychological adjustment (Gonsiorek, 1977) as potential effects of disclosure (Cramer & Roach, 1988). It is intuitively easy to imagine that these benefits might accrue from disclosure by an adolescent or young adult, given the often central role parents still play in their lives as well as their stage of development. However, it is not equally intuitive with older adults. That is, would one necessarily expect Cousin Harry's adjustment to suddenly improve, or that he would feel noticeably better about himself as a person, or that his "identity formation" would be enhanced? One would need to substantiate such an assertion before it could be accepted at face value.

More significantly, if an older adult's psychological well-being does improve, the more interesting question might be *how*. Psychological well-being is intimately tied to one's developmental stage in life. For an adolescent or young adult, establishing a clear, positive sense of who he or she is—an identity—is central at this point in development. Parents' approval and support can not only facilitate this process, but may be crucial. In later life, however, Erikson's task of generativity or ego integration may be a more salient measure of psychological well-being. Consequently, disclosure may improve Cousin Harry's psychological well-being because he finds himself taking on new roles in the family, feels more a part of the larger gay community, and begins to feel increasingly like he is "giving back" to the world around him, providing a sense of generativity. Alternatively, coming out may allow him to begin to review his life with important family members and develop a degree of acceptance, not of *who he is* but of *what his life has been*, providing an opportunity for ego integration. In short, any assertion of psychological benefits must be framed, studied, and understood within a developmental context.

What are the benefits of disclosure? Mattison and McWhirter (1995) and others (Ben-Ari, 1995a,b; Mahoney, 1994) suggest that disclosure may result in increased intimacy as well as a sense of relief, at least in some people. Does this finding hold true for older adults as well as adolescents? An implicit premise in much of the literature is that the concealing of homosexuality shapes the character of interactions between various family members. Although there would be no reason to doubt this, we wonder exactly how much disclosure might change patterns that have been consistent possibly for decades. Relationship patterns, positive and negative, may continue even when the original cause of these patterns is removed. Again, further study is indicated here.

Most lesbian couples report that disclosure decreased feelings of isolation from family and increased feelings of identity congruence (Murphy, 1989). Moreover, Murphy found that positive valuations of a lesbian's partner by her parents tended to enhance her partner in her eyes. Fifty percent of those in her sample whose parents were positive toward their daughter's partner reported that parental attitudes helped the relationship. These findings are particularly interesting because in a social structure where there are few legitimizing opportunities for gay or lesbian unions, parental acceptance, support, and validation *of the relationship* may be an important aspect of coming out to family in later life. And of note, being involved in a long-term relationship at the time of disclosure to parents or siblings may have a considerable impact on the family's response. More study is needed here.

Change in family relations seems to follow certain paths. Mahoney (1994) interviewed parents who not only accepted their son's or daughter's sexual orientation but also became politically active through advocacy. Six steps seemed to characterize their change: (1) emotional reaction to child's disclosure; (2) restorying the past; (3) using external sources; (4) life events as motivation; (5) social justice: and (6) feeling proud. Two of these are of particular interest. First, he found that his subjects had to "restory" the past. Parents of older gay men and lesbians have much more past to restory, and this is a large task. At the same time, however, disclosure may seem increasingly *less anomalous* with passing time (or more so in the case of gay men and lesbian who married heterosexually). Second, he identified a step of "feeling proud." The crisis-oriented model prevalent in the current literature may impede an understanding of how families of gay and lesbian individuals develop positive feelings about their son, daughter, or sibling following disclosure. Certainly family members may come to respect individuals for having lived their lives successfully in spite of hate and homophobic obstacles placed before them. The sense of "social justice" Mahoney describes in these parents may be characteristic of a shift in perception from consigning gay men and lesbians to social stigma to a commitment to liberating them from that stigma. In article upon article that focuses upon grief and crisis, we see negative assumptions unquestioningly repeated, and Mahoney's work suggests that there may be other areas worth investigating beyond crisis and grief. One of us (Beeler) has interviewed a family with an 85-year-old grandfather suffering from dementia who, upon finding out his grandson was gay, was immediately supportive. During his more lucid periods he reads the local newspapers and cuts out articles related to gay rights and other gay issues. Although this may not be common, it may represent a heretofore underexplored aspect of the family member's re-action to disclosure: the transformative potential disclosure has on the recipient's awareness of social and political structure and its effects on individual lives. A shift from the paradigm of crisis to one of transformation may yield rich rewards.

This brief review of the literature on disclosure of older lesbians and gay men reveals innumerable differences between the two generations, suggesting that it is hazardous to generalize from younger cohorts. Older lesbians and gay men are at a different point in their life course and development, as are their family members, which suggests that their motivations for coming out, as well as the consequences, may be quite divergent. Likewise, the process of disclosure and the family's response and adjustment—sandwiched as it were between the initial motivation and the consequences—is also likely to be significantly different. In particular, a family member's reaction to an older adult's disclosure is likely to be more oriented to the past, as opposed to the parent of a younger adult, who is likely to be more future oriented. Moreover, developmental differences between older and younger gay and lesbian adults, and their families should be considered within the context of a changing cultural milieu. We must study older gay and lesbian individuals in their own right, and not conflate their lives with those of younger gay and lesbian adolescents and young adults.

Throughout this chapter we have examined differences between older and younger lesbians and gay men. We should note, however, that older lesbians and gay men themselves constitute a quite diverse group. In fact, there is likely to be more diversity among older than younger gay men and women. While few gay adolescents are likely to be involved in a heterosexual marriage, a substantial portion of older gay men and women have been or are currently heterosexually married. The life experience of a retired gay man who spent forty years in a heterosexual marriage and has adult children will be dramatically different from Cousin Harry's life experience. Researchers must consider this diversity when studying the lives of older gay men and women (see Herdt, Beeler, & Rawls, 1997). Additionally, few studies to date have taken into account cultural and ethnic differences. Importantly, the effect of culture may vary by cohort and age. For example, the impact of culture on an older, first-generation gay Asian male may be quite different from the impact of culture on a second- or third-generation Asian American. It is our hope that future studies of older gay and lesbian adults will incopororate the question of diversity into their work.

Conclusion

The gay and lesbian movement has experienced rapid and dramatic social change over the last three decades, fundamentally altering its status and perception in American society. Not every gay and lesbian individual has been actively involved in these changes. Many older gay men and lesbians, in fact, may be far removed from these sociopolitical events, even though their lives may have been changed by them. However, it is likely that many of these changes reach them through a process of backward socialization (Hagestad & Neugarten, 1985; Cook & Cohler, 1986): they become socialized into new perspectives, values, and possibly behaviors vis-à-vis the activities of younger cohorts, whenever they encounter each other.

For example, Cousin Harry may have kept his sexuality hidden for decades, generally considering it to be a "dreadful secret." Imagine Harry at the Thanksgiving dinner table when somehow the topic of homosexuality comes up. Imagine an older adult using a euphemism to refer to homosexuality only to have a younger adult at the table say, "You mean 'gay'?" A discussion ensues in which Harry's college-age niece reports one of her best friends is gay and "he's not weird at all." Within this discourse, the younger generation has as much opportunity to socialize the older as the reverse. This concept is important because older adults are often viewed as "more set in their ways." This assumption may be unfair. Backward socialization, as a concept, allows researchers an opportunity to study the pathways through which older adults continue to respond and adapt to their changing environments. This process may be more important to older gay and lesbian adults than to most older adults. It is this backward socialization that brings about the "new opportunities" we pointed to in the introduction. But what is the result of this?

Kenneth Plummer's (1995) book, *Telling Sexual Stories,* sketches a "sociology of stories" that is informative here. People are embedded in a web of narratives that shape how they see and understand their lives and significant others. Stories of secrecy and disclosure, repeated again and again over time, can begin to give voice to a previously disenfranchised and powerless group. One example Plummer explores is the now well-documented "coming out story" of gay men and lesbians (Herdt & Boxer, 1996). This story has been the Archimedean point leveraging gay and lesbian identity for the individual and visibility and rights for the community. For many gay and lesbian individuals, "coming out" (or "being closeted") is often viewed as the most important context in which to understand their lives. With older gay and lesbian adults, the question may be to what degree are they backwardly socialized into these narratives of coming out and a newer perspective?

Perhaps part of the answer lies in the recognition that identity is a system of contexts, nested within each other. Herdt's (1982) work on the Sambia of New Guinea advanced the notion of "identity contexts." In Sambia rituals, the expected outcome of development for a 10-year-old boy was culturally anticipated, and the various rituals and initiations through which he advanced into adolescence served as progressive developmental "identity contexts" enacted for the purpose of assuring the expected outcome. Later, Herdt (1992) studied the rituals of coming out in a similar way. In our culture there is no predetermined outcome to development; rather, the result is *emergent* or fluid, the product of changing contexts (Herdt, 1990). That the outcome of development is emergent, however, means that the identity contexts of lesbian or gay lives are still changing, the end goals still evolving. The identity context that has developed over the past thirty years is precisely the "coming out" context and its narratives. Recapitulating a variant of the coming out story in one's own life is the route to establishing a clear gay or lesbian identity—and a place within the lesbian and gay community (Herdt & Boxer, 1996).

We opened our chapter by alluding to the potential for a "second act." By this we meant an opportunity for *individuals* to dramatically redefine their relationships with the world around them, particularly their families, and specifically through coming out in the later years of life. A "second act," however, may also carry collective and historical connotations. Collectively, the second act refers to the second *half* of gay or lesbian lives—that there *is* a second half and it deserves attention. Historically, the coming out story has served to *unify* the gay or lesbian voice; in a historical second act, the coming out story may serve to *diversify* the gay or lesbian voice. While coming out has so far served well as a liminal rite of passage, the metaphor has thus far spoke little to long-term *outcomes:* coming out *but going where?*

In an earlier study, Herdt and Boxer (1996) found that many gay, lesbian, and bisexual adolescents in Chicago were unable to imagine the future course of their lives beyond the age of 32. They had no role models or stories to call upon. Continuing our metaphor, they could anticipate no second act in their lives. Coming out and establishing their identity as a lesbian or gay man was as far as they could go into the future. Older gay men and lesbians are thus crucial to creating social continuity and the promise in gay and lesbian lives of a richer and fuller life course across generations. The "second act" of older lesbians and gay men is of great import not only for older lesbians and gay men but also for the progress of gay and lesbian lives in our culture generally. This, we believe, is *our* collective second act.

References

Ben-Ari, A. (1995a). Coming out: A dialectic of intimacy and privacy. *Families in Society, 76*, 306–314.

Ben-Ari, A. (1995b). It's the telling that makes the difference. In R. Josselson, & A. Lieblich (Eds), *The narrative study of lives* (pp. 153–172). London: Sage Publications.

Berger, R. (1982). *Gay and gray: The older homosexual man.* Urbana: University of Illinois Press.

Borhek, M. (1983). *Coming out to parents.* New York: Pilgrim Press.

Boxer, A. M., & Cohler, B. (1989). The lifecourse of gay and lesbian youth: An immodest proposal for the study of lives. In G. Herdt (Ed.), *Gay and lesbian youth* (pp. 315–355). New York: Harrington Park.

Boxer A. M., Cook, J. A., & Herdt. G. (1991). To tell or not to tell: Patterns of self disclosure to mothers and fathers reported by gay and lesbian youth. In K. Pillemer & K. McCartney (Eds.), *Parent-child relations across the lifespan* (pp. 59–63). New York: Oxford University Press.

Cass, V. C. (1979). Homosexual identity formation: A theoretical model. *Journal of Homosexuality, 4*, 219–235.

Chodorow, Nancy J. (1992). Heterosexuality as a compromise formation: Reflections on the psychoanalytic theory of sexual development. *Psychoanalysis and Contemporary Thought, 15*, 267–304.

Cicirelli, V. (1995). *Sibling relationships across the lifespan.* New York: Plenum Press.

Coleman, E. (1982). Developmental stages of the coming out process. *Journal of Homosexuality, 7*, 31–43.

Cook, J. A., & Cohler. B. J. (1986). Reciprocal socialization and the care of offspring with cancer and with schizophrenia. In N. Datan, A. L. Greene, and H. W. Reese (Eds.), *Life-span developmental psychology: intergenerational relations* (pp. 223–243). Hillsdale, NJ: Erlbaum.

Cramer, D., and Roach, A. (1988). Coming out to mom and dad: A study of gay males and their relationships with their parents. *Journal of Homosexuality, 15*, 79–91.

D'Emilio, J. D., & Freedman, E. B. (1988). *Intimate matters: A history of sexuality in America.* New York: Harper & Row.

Derlega, V. J., & Grzelak. J. (1979). Appropriateness of self-disclosure. In G. J. Chelune (Ed.), *Self-disclosure origins, patterns, and implications of openness in interpersonal relationships.* San Francisco: Jossey-Bass.

DeVine, J. (1984). A systemic inspection of affectional preference orientation and the family of origin. *Journal of Social Work and Human Sexuality, 2*, 9–17.

Driskill, P. (1994). Family counseling without the family: Working with an individual client. In C. Huber (Ed.), *Transitioning from individual to family counseling* (pp. 75–84). Alexandria: American Counseling Association.

Feldman, S., Biringen, Z., & Nash, S. (1981). Fluctuations of sex-related self-attributions as a function of family life cycle. *Developmental Psychology, 17*, 24–35.

Gonsiorek, J. (1977). Psychological adjustment and homosexuality. *JSAS Catalog of Selected Documents in Psychology, 7*(45), (Ms. 1478).

Gutmann, D. (1975). Parenthood: A key to the comparative study of the life cycle. In N. Datan & L. Ginsberg (Eds.), *Life-span developmental psychology* (167–184). New York: Academic Press.

Hagestad, G., Neugarten. B. (1985). Age and the life-course. In R. Binstock and E. Shanas (Eds.), *Handbook of aging and society*, 2nd ed. (pp. 35–61). New York: Van Nostrand-Reinhold.

Hammersmith, S., & Weinberg, M. (1973). Homosexual identity: Commitment, adjustment, and significant others. *Sociometry, 36*, 56–79.

Herdt, G. (1982). Sambia nose-bleeding rites and male proximity to women. *Ethos, 10*, 189–231.

Herdt. G. (1990). "Developmental continuity as a dimension of sexual orientation across cultures," In D. McWhirter, J. Reinisch, & S. Sanders (Eds.), *Homosexuality and heterosexuality: The Kinsey scale and current research* (pp. 208–238). New York: Oxford University Press.

Herdt, G. (1992). 'Coming out' as a rite of passage: A Chicago study. In G. Herdt, (Ed.), *Gay culture in America* (pp. 29–67). Boston: Beacon Press.

Herdt, G., Beeler, J., & Rawls, T. (1997). Life course diversity among older lesbians and gay men: A study in Chicago. *Journal of Gay, Lesbian, and Bisexual Identity, 2,* 231–246.

Herdt, G., & Boxer, A. (1996). *Children of Horizons: How gay and lesbian teens are leading a new way out of the closet.* Boston: Beacon Press.

Herrell, R. (1992). The symbolic strategies of Chicago's Gay and Lesbian Pride Day parade. In G. Herdt (Ed.), *Gay culture in America* (pp. 225–252). Boston: Beacon Press.

Isay, R. (1996). *Becoming gay. The journey to self-acceptance.* New York: Pantheon Books.

Jones, C. (1978). *Understanding gay relatives and friends.* New York: Seabury Press.

Jourard, S. M. (1971). *The transparent self.* New York: Van Nostrand Reinhold.

Kelvin, P. (1977). Predictability, power and vulnerability in interpersonal attraction. In S. Duck (Ed.), *Theory and practice in interpersonal attraction.* New York: Academic Press.

Komarovsky, M. (1976). *Dilemmas of masculinity: A study of college youth.* New York: Norton.

Kooden, H., Morin, S., Riddle, D., Rogers, M., Sang, B., & Strassburger, F. (1979). *Removing the stigma.* Final report, Task Force on the Status of Lesbian and Gay Male Psychologists. Washington, DC: American Psychological Association.

Laird, J. (1996). Invisible ties: Lesbians and their families of origin. In J. Laird & R.-J. Green (Eds.), *Lesbians and gays in couples and families: A handbook for therapists* (pp. 89–122). San Francisco: Jossey-Bass.

Levinger, G. K., & Shoek. J. D. (1972). *Attraction in relationship: A new look at interpersonal attraction.* Morristown, NJ: General Learning Press.

Mahoney, D. (1994). Staying connected: The coming out stories of parents with a lesbian daughter or gay son. Unpublished master's thesis, University of Guelph, Canada.

Mattison, A., & McWhirter, D. (1995). Lesbians, gay men, and their families. *The Psychiatric Clinics of North America, 18,* 23–137.

Muller, A. (1987). *Parents matter.* New York: Naiad Press.

Murphy, B. (1989). Lesbian couples and their parents: The effects of perceived parental attitudes on the couple. *Journal of Counseling and Development, 68,* 46–51.

Neymeyer, L. (1980). Coming out: Identity congruence and the attainment of adult female sexuality. Unpublished doctoral dissertation, Boston University.

Plummer, K. (1995). *Telling sexual stories: Power, change and social worlds.* New York: Routledge.

Reid, J. (1995). Development in late life: Older lesbian and gay lives. In A. R. D'Augelli & C. J. Patterson (Eds.), *Lesbian, gay, and bisexual identities over the lifespan: Psychological perspectives* (pp. 215–224). New York: Oxford University Press.

Robinson, B., Walters, L., & Skeen, P. (1989). Response of parents to learning that their child is homosexual and concern over AIDS: A National Study. *Journal of Homosexuality, 18,* 59–80.

Rosenfeld, L. B. (1979). Self-disclosure avoidance: Why I am afraid to tell you who I am? *Communication Monographs, 46*(10), 63–74.

Savin-Williams, R. (1989). Coming out to parents and self-esteem among gay and lesbian youths. *Journal of Homosexuality, 18,* 1–35.

Silverman, C. (1996). The history of treatment. In R. Cabaj and T. Stein (Eds.), *Textbook of homosexuality and mental health* (pp. 3–16). Washington, DC: American Psychiatric Press.

Strommen, E. (1989). You're a what?: Family member reactions to the disclosure of homosexuality. *Journal of Homosexuality, 18,* 37–58.

Tobin, S. (1991). *Personhood in advanced old age.* New York: Springer.

Troiden. R.. R. (1989). The formation of homosexual identities. *Journal of Homosexuality, 17,* 43–73.

Valiant, G. (1977). *Adaptation to life.* Boston: Little, Brown.

Weston, K. (1993). Lesbian/gay studies in the house of anthropology. *Annual Review of Anthropology, 22,* 339–367.

Weinberg, G. (1972). *Society and the healthy homosexual.* New York: St. Martin's Press.

Williams, M., & Weinberg, C. W. (1974). *Male homosexuals: Their problems and adaptations.* New York: Oxford University Press.

10

Invisible Ties: Lesbians and Their Families of Origin

Joan Laird

My life partner, Ann, and I recently celebrated the thirty-second anniversary of our lives together. My son, Duncan, born during my eight-year marriage to his father, was 16 months old when Ann came into our lives. He called her "Baboo" and loved her very much, while she returned that love and showed it by fully sharing the child care, the responsibilities, the joys, and the pains of parenthood. It took many years (indeed, decades) for us and the world to change enough for her to claim parental legitimacy, but she now calls him "my son," experimenting somewhat hesitantly but proudly with a language long disallowed by the social world around us.

Four years ago, Duncan, now a social worker, married Meg, herself a social worker from a family with a strong social work tradition. Although the *New York Times* would not allow Ann's name to be included in the engagement announcement, Ann's and my names were on the wedding invitation, along with our daughter-in-law's father and stepmother. The wedding ritual was wonderfully expressive of the cultures of both families, blending the traditional, the innovative, and the young couple's hopes for the future, all witnessed by a larger kinship network that included Ann's and my families, as well as our old and newer friendship families. The fact that both Ann and I walked Duncan down the aisle, wished him well, and danced together at his wedding, modeled—for younger lesbians and for the heterosexual world—one way that lesbian relationships can be enacted in the larger family context and how central rituals can be adapted to express particular definitions of kinship. Two years ago, Meg and Duncan had their first child and Ann and I our first grandchild, a beautiful, sturdy little girl, Hannah. I bought them a baby book and one day, when I was visiting, began to look through the first entries. Meg had drawn in new branches on the published version of the family tree—an illustration on which there was no room for nonbiological or nonheterosexual kin—branches for Ann and her roots. Several pages later, inserted in the illustrated pages for intergenerational information on parents and grandparents, was a beautifully drawn and painted page for Ann's biography.

I begin with this very personal story to illustrate the central point in this chapter, a point that would seem simple and obvious but has been all but neglected in both popular culture and in the professional literature and research on lesbians, gay men, and bisexual people. Ours is not an unusual story. Lesbians, gay men, and bisexual people come from families and are connected to these original families. Many of us live in families of choice as well. ("Family of choice" is a political and ideological term used by gay men and lesbians to describe the families they have created outside of legal marriage that may include a partner, adopted or biological children, and/or an extended network of friends, usually but not exclusively lesbian and gay, who perform functions similar to those of close, extended biological families.) Most of us are *not* cut off from our families—not forever rejected, isolated, disinherited. We are daughters and sons, siblings, aunts and uncles, parents and grandparents. Like everyone else, most of us have continuing, complicated relationships with our families. We participate in negotiating the changing meanings, rituals, values, and connections that define kinship. Lesbians, gay men, and bisexual people *do* have role models (and those role models may be straight, gay, or bisexual) and themselves serve as role models for others in their families; they are not bereft of ritual lives, of culture, of histories. Like everyone else, they have parts of themselves they openly share and parts they keep silent about—choosing between what will be said and what will be unsaid as they move from one context to another in their daily lives.

This chapter is about intergenerational family relationships, primarily about lesbians' relationships with their families of origin. Two themes seem to dominate in common impressions and assumptions about lesbians and their families. First, since the family relationships of lesbians are so invisible and knowledge about them so unavailable, the first theme is a nonimpression, a theme of invisibility. We might be led to believe that lesbians do not have family connections, since these connections are so rarely portrayed or discussed. Second, when they are acknowledged, the relationships are usually viewed as tortured. Families of origin are portrayed as hurt, dismayed, and confused at best when they learn their child is lesbian, gay, or bisexual; or angry, hostile, and utterly rejecting—even violent—at worst. The major metaphor is one of loss, of mourning all that has gone wrong and all that might have been.

Generally viewed as a source of rejection and homophobia and as negatively affecting the psychological and social life of lesbians, the family of origin also is seen to lack relevance to the here-and-now life of the adult gay, lesbian, or bisexual person with or without a family of creation. How often have we heard or read that gay men, lesbians, and bisexual people have had no role models, no family experiences that prepare them for coupling, for role division, for parenting? But a family is about far more than sexual orientation—it is about values, morality, human connectedness and relationship, legacy and generativity, and much, much more. As lesbians, gay men, and bisexuals, we would not wish to promote the idea that we are incapable of providing role models for our own (usually heterosexual) children, for passing on family and cultural values, ethics, and skills for living to our heterosexual children and grandchildren. Lesbians, in fact, are pioneering both coupling and family ideas that may be useful to our heterosexual siblings and that may gain the admiration and respect of our heterosexual parents. Similarly, we are very much psychologically and culturally part of our (probably heterosexual) families and they part of us. Our (probably heterosexual) parents and grandparents have taught us who to be and how to be, who not to be and how not to be, through both positive and negative example.

My effort here is to look more closely at the narrative of family invisibility, rejection, and alienation that prevails in popular culture and in the professional literature, contrasting this narrative with what lesbians themselves say about their relationships with their families. In this work, I focus primarily on adult lesbian daughters' relationships with their parents. Since these relationships are virtually unexplored in any systematic way in the professional literature, my sources of information are eclectic. First, since our personal stories are shaped, influenced, and to a great extent limited by the repertoire of available narratives and the dominant social discourses in the larger surround, I briefly explore popular film for its portrayals of gay and lesbian family of origin connections. This is one way of trying to expose the dominant narrative, in this case how family relationships are viewed in the larger culture. A tiny effort here, it nevertheless suggests how lesbians are reminded every day of their invisibility and the invisibility of their family relationships—or worse yet, if they do not deconstruct the homophobic dominant discourse, how they may come to believe themselves that such relationships do not exist—that is, that lesbian sexual orientation means disconnection from family. Second, I examine the professional literature, which is primarily a literature from psychology, for insight into these relationships. Third, I comment on some of the popular lesbian literature for the same purposes. Finally, I turn to 19 transcribed interviews with lesbians that I have completed over the last three years. I am interested in what lesbian intergenerational relationships (particularly with parents) look like and how they seem to work, in their complexity and their quality. I end with some thoughts about the implications of this work for clinical practice.

Gay Men, Lesbians, and Families in Popular Film

In an exploration of lesbians and lesbian images in popular film that began with Marlene Dietrich's cross-dressing adventures in the 1930 film *Morocco*, I failed to find a single instance of lesbians portrayed in the context of their families until 1995. Lesbians have been depicted as self-loathing, doomed creatures whose ultimate solution was death, a fate that Shirley MacLaine suffered in the 1961 film *The Children's Hour*. Sandy Dennis, in *The Fox* (1967), a homophobic, ironic, and phallocentric film suggesting that all a lesbian really needs is a man, is crushed to death when a giant tree falls between her legs. To be sure, one of the two women in the sexually ambiguous French film *Entre Nous* (1983) returns to family, broken and in despair, but we learn nothing of her family relationships. She and her woman friend (lover?) both have children from their heterosexual marriages but are portrayed as neglecting them, as their intense friendship consumes them. Lianna, the heroine of the 1982 John Sayles's Canadian film of the same name, forfeits her children to her cruel and philandering husband after she tells him of her affair with a female college teacher. She is subsequently alienated from her best friend and, indeed, from everyone around her. In one scene, Lianna is heard talking to her mother on the telephone, a perfunctory conversation in which she shares nothing of her troubles. Although this film contains seeds of hope and the promise of repair of relationships, until very recently the future for the lesbian couple or parent in film was indeed grim.

Gay men have suffered similar fates in popular film over the decades. They have been portrayed not at all or as sick, exotic creatures, as drag queens, but never as men in stable couple relationships or as men connected to their families. Nevertheless, gay men have fared better than lesbians in the family department. They began to be awarded families beginning with the 1978 French farce *La Cage aux Folles*. Readers may remember that Renato has an-about-to-be-married son, a rite of passage that serves as the centerpiece for this marvelous romp. Who can forget Alban's booming "Here's Mother!" as he appears in drag at the first meeting with the prospective daughter-in-law's parents? We learn nothing of the two men's parents, however. *La Cage* was followed in 1988 by an American film, *Torch Song Trilogy*, a party autobiographical story that originated in the theater. Harvey Fierstein's powerful portrayal of a gay man's attempts to build a family and to stay connected with and demand respect from his critical and guilt-making but ultimately caring mother represents a breakthrough in American film. Arnold, a female impersonator by profession, and his lover are in a committed relationship. In a commentary on the extreme homophobia in our society, the young lover is brutally murdered on the street below by a gang of gay haters. Arnold later takes in a foster child, a 15-year-old gay boy—a move that is beyond his mother's comprehension—and continues his struggles to forge a connection with his mother that is authentic and that recognizes his right to mourn the loss of his lover and to form a family of his own.

Philadelphia, to my knowledge, was the first film to give a gay person, in this case a son living with and then dying of AIDS, a loving and supportive family that welcomes and includes his partner. Some gay people themselves were critical of this film, for they found it diffcult to believe such families exist. Most recently, a 1995 Australian film, *The Sum of Us,* pivots around a loving relationship between a gay man and his straight father, who is worried that the young man isn't settled down with a life partner and keeps trying to fix him up.

In recent years there have also been some excellent popular and documentary films portraying gay men in the context of their families of choice— films such as *Parting Glances* and *Longtime Companion.* But what about lesbians? In keeping with the combined forces of homophobia, heterosexism, and sexism that plague lesbians, it is even rarer for the lesbian to be granted a family of origin, choice, or creation in popular culture. The first film to show in some depth the relationships between a lesbian, her children, and her family of origin, in this case her father, was the award-winning made-for-television biographical account *Serving in Silence: The Marguerite Cammermeyer Story.* This is the story of a courageous woman who successfully defies the military's injunction of "don't ask, don't tell," with the support of her children and, finally, her usually critical father as well.

Not only are gays and lesbians themselves largely invisible in popular film and rarely envisioned in the context of intergenerational relationships with parents or children, but lesbians and gay men of color were virtually beyond the collective imagination as represented in popular film—until *The Wedding Banquet.* In this 1993 Taiwanese-Chinese-U.S. comedy, we see contrasted the lavish cultural celebration of the (false) heterosexual wedding and the (true) silent, secret love between two young men—Simon, an American, and Wai Tung, a Taiwanese American. The film represents a fascinating juxtaposition of the meanings of filial piety, kinship norms, and the values of the traditional Chinese family and the new cultural ingredients of Wai Tung's couple relationship with a white American gay man. It is a rare and wonderful moment when Wai Tung's traditional Chinese father, in spite of his powerful cultural values that prescribe traditional marriage, figures out how to have his kinship cake and eat it too, in this case his son, his son's lover, his new daughter-in-law, and the grandchild on the way.

The first American film portraying lesbians in the contexts of their families made its debut in 1995. Again, the film centered on an interracial relationship. A low-budget, art theater delight, *The Incredible Adventures of Two Girls in Love* is about a white working-class teenager who knows she is lesbian and dresses the part—wrinkled man's shirt, vest, and baggy jeans— who is ready for love. She is a loner—isolated, marginalized, and seen as a weirdo by her peers. This young woman lives with her aunt, a leatherjacketed lesbian, and her aunt's partner. The boundaries of this family are quite permeable, as various assorted other characters from time to time join this caring, flamboyant, and slightly chaotic family of choice; it is a household in which everyone contributes to the politically correct vegetarian stew and everyone has advice for the teenage heroine. The young lesbian begins to pursue a friendship with an African-American girl in her school, a girl from an upper-middle-class professional family. This girl is popular, beautiful, and immaculately dressed in preppie style. She goes home to a loving, divorced mother, a successful professional woman who runs a well-organized, well-decorated home where nothing is out of place, life is highly ritualized, and meals are quiet, orderly affairs. Differences in race, social class, and lifestyle fade away as these two young women tentatively begin to explore their feelings for each other, upending their families and the entire community in the process.

These few films penetrate the wall of invisibility and the myth of isolation from family that has characterized the portrayal of lesbians and gays in popular film. It is a beginning. Other hopeful signs that the discourse is changing may be seen in the increasing presence of lesbian or gay characters in television sitcoms and dramas highlighted by the recent, much publicized coming out of Ellen DeGeneres on *Ellen* as well as in real life. And Ellen has a visible and supportive family, on and off television. Sandra Bernhardt's role on the long-running show *Roseanne,* and the increasingly "daring" traditions of writing gay and lesbian lives on and off Broadway and in other theaters, such as in Tony Kushner's two-part play, *Angels in America.* Nevertheless, there still are almost no openly gay male performers in the media, short of those tragically exposed by AIDS. There are, of course, rumors.

Lesbians and Family in the Professional Literature

The ideas of "lesbian" and "family," then, have rarely been joined in popular film. In the professional literature, the dominant theme in work on lesbian relationships with family focuses on disclosure or "coming out" (e.g., Berzon, 1979; Brown, 1989; Kleinberg, 1986; Krestan, 1988; Strommen, 1989; Zitter, 1987). There is virtually no exploration of lesbian relationships with families of origin over time other than in the isolated clinical vignette, although DeVine (1984) and others comment on the developmental stages a family must go through to move toward acceptance of their child's homosexuality. Slater's (1995) comprehensive and otherwise excellent work on the lesbian family life cycle, except for the isolated comment, virtually ignores the family of origin, as does Benkov's (1994) fine account of lesbians with children. An exception is to be found in Walker's (1991) pioneering work with families of gay men with AIDS.

There is, in fact, a small but growing collection of research on lesbians with children, both children from heterosexual marriage and children born to or adopted by lesbians as single parents and in same-sex couple relationships, as well as a modest body of clinical literature that weaves together theory and example (Patterson, 1996). There also have been numerous studies of lesbian and gay couple relationships, a few of which include some data on family of origin connections (e.g., James & Murphy, this volume; Kurdek & Schmitt, 1987; Levy, 1989; Murphy, 1989).

Nevertheless, if the lesbians' families of origin have been largely invisible in the media of popular culture, they are also ignored in the professional research and clinical literature. There are five probable reasons for this state of affairs.

First, as scholars and practitioners, lesbian researchers and clinicians are not immune from the knowledge or power arrangements and the larger social stories that form the cultural depository from which we can select our own personal and professional narratives. In those social stories, lesbians and gay men are assumed to have few if any meaningful connections to their families.

Second, in the early days of the women's movement, more radical feminists and lesbian feminists declared the family the seat of patriarchy. In some circles, lesbian politics substituted the lesbian community for family and frowned on long-term coupling and monogamy. Choosing children through birth or adoption, although not storied in social discourse, was rare but did occur. Lesbians with children, and particularly lesbians who felt their ex-husbands and families should play a meaningful role in their children's lives, were often treated as "politically incorrect" by the lesbian community and isolated from their peers. Family, including the so-called rejecting family of origin, belonged to the hated and feared heterosexual culture and supposedly had little to offer.

Third, our individualistic society, with its emphasis on the inner life and self-fulfillment, drew attention away from an emphasis on community, family, and kinship.

Fourth, psychoanalytic and psychodynamic psychologies, with their focus on the therapist-client relationship and the phenomenon of transference, paired with the virtual ignoring of the client's lived experiences in the real world where the self is constructed intersubjectively, fostered inattention to current family relationships, focusing, rather, on childhood family experiences.

Finally, in the family field, the traditional nuclear family, in spite of its growing obsolescence, remained the central metaphor for "family."

Even as various other kinds of diversity gradually became recognized—diversity in ethnic or racial heritage and identity, in social class, in family structure—heterosexuality was assumed for all families. Through the 1980s, the gay- or lesbian-headed family was surely beyond the pale during an era when we had barely begun to notice how important gender was in constituting family relationships. Even when feminist family therapists began to critique the lack of attention to gender and the patriarchal features of systemic models, lesbians and their families of origin and creation, with a few notable exceptions, remained invisible.

In fact, the entire field of "family," both in family research and in the application of family theory to the clinical professions, has ignored and neglected the lesbian and gay family. Allen and Demo (1995), in a comprehensive review of the leading family research journals from 1980 to 1993, as well as a number of journals in related fields over the same period, found that lesbian and gay families were rarely studied. And when they were included as part of larger studies, they were regarded as problematic or deviant, and their diversity was ignored. Allen and Demo conclude, among other things, that "lesbian and gay kin relations offer new conceptual inroads into older concepts in the family literature" (p. 14) and believe that investigations of intergenerational and extended family relations beyond the procreative family life cycle should become a priority.

A similar picture emerges from a statistical analysis of the mainstream family therapy literature. The first article I know of appeared in 1972 in *Family Process*, the flagship clinical journal, and was titled "My Stepfather is a She" (Osman, 1972). The clinical solution to a problem of an adolescent boy being raised in a lesbian household was to place him elsewhere, a solution we seldom see in the family therapy literature. The pioneering article by Krestan and Bepko (1980), "The Problem of Fusion in the Lesbian Relationship," which drew from Bowen's family of origin theory, appeared in *Family Process* a few years later. Several years passed before Roth's (1984) chapter was published. Both quickly became classics and have been reprinted in several collections. In 1988, Krestan published a second article, on lesbian mothers and daughters; Roth teamed with Murphy (1986) for further exploration of family system issues. Until very recently, we would not need all ten fingers to count the journal contributions in the family therapy field. Occasionally, writers in the more generic journals in social work, psychology, psychiatry, and other counseling professions addressed family themes, but the list is short (see Laird, 1993a).

When the family of origin is mentioned in what might be called the heterosexual clinical literature, which of course is always sensitive to problem and pathology, and in the psychological literature on gay and lesbian identity making, it is often portrayed solely as the thing that one does or does not "come out to." The prevailing picture that emerges is often one of disappointment, rejection, compromise, loneliness, and physical and/or emotional distance. It is, of course, often the nightmarish family that attracts attention in the press, as in the case of the Sharon Kowalski story, in which a homophobic and neglecting family reclaimed custody of Sharon after she suffered a head injury in an automobile accident (Griscom, 1992). More recently, lesbian mother Sharon Bottoms was sued for custody of her son by her own mother in a case heard eventually in the Virginia Supreme Court. The trial judge concluded that Sharon's lesbianism and the fact that she had had oral sex—a felony in Virginia—contributed to making her an unfit mother (Bull, 1995).

These kinds of stories captivate the press. We are less likely to hear stories like that of the Filipino-American mother who made a beautiful, traditional Filipino wedding gown and prepared the wedding party dinner for her lesbian daughter Trinity's marriage to Desiree, a woman of Japanese, Chinese, Native Hawaiian, and German ancestry (Ordona & Thompson, 1990). Nor do we hear stories like that of Kathy, one of the women I interviewed, now in her late 40s, who came out to herself and to her family of origin just a few years ago. Not long after, her Mormon father said to her life partner, as the two women visited him in his hospital room during the last days of his life, "Dorothy, I am so happy for the two of you and so grateful that Kathy has you to take care of her and to love her."

Brown (1989), highlighting clinical issues in coming out to family, describes common patterns for juggling the closet and the family. In the first scenario, the person may maintain rigid geographical and emotional distance from the family of origin, the lesbian feeling more or less estranged, and the family often hurt and puzzled. In a second adaptation, which she calls the "I know you know" pattern, there is a conspiracy of silence—no one will ask about the gay person's personal life and he or she is afraid to tell. In this situation, the gay or lesbian individual is usually treated as single and available to the family of origin for holidays, extra help, and so on. In yet a third situation, the "don't tell your father, it would kill him" story, the secrecy supports various family coalitions and keeps the lesbian daughter's life hostage to the family. In all of these adaptations, as Murphy (1989) points out in her study of the effects of perceived parental attitudes on the lesbian couple, the couple relationship may be rendered more vulnerable, as one individual may blame her partner for all she has lost and for all their togetherness is costing. Brown (1989), Murphy (1989), Krestan (1988), and others have helped to articulate the possible effects of disclosure to families on the lesbian daughter and lesbian couple relations, offering useful implications for clinical practice. But the initial disclosure—coming out—while certainly an important event and an important part of the evolving self and family narrative, is far from the whole story. Family relationships are about much more than coming out, and coming out, although it can be a painful and debilitating process for some, for others is a most self-authenticating and differentiating process that can result in very positive growth for both the individual and the family. We rarely hear about that side of family life.

We need to know more about the everyday lives, the stories, the kinship and community connections, the special rituals of lesbians, gay men, and bisexual people in their families of choice and in connections with their wider kinship networks. What is missing from the professional clinical literature and the social science literature (with a few notable exceptions) is the ethnographic study of lesbian and gay life in the United States and, more particularly, the ethnographic study of the cultural life of the lesbian and gay family. It is in "culture" that, in recursive fashion, we both learn who we are and continually construct and reconstruct ourselves. In a sense we construct our psychology, our "selves," as we participate in larger cultural surrounds, from family to society. And relationships with the families of origin, families of choice, and extended kin networks are essential parts of the cultural.

Anthropologist Gilbert Herdt has led the way in calling our attention to the "cultural" in lesbian and gay studies. His stunning book, *Gay Culture in America* (1992), although not particularly about families or lesbians, demonstrates how the use of cultural and constructionist metaphors can open up new dimensions for understanding lesbian and gay life. It moves us away from an exclusive focus on the psychological and away from deficit perspectives. Although this kind of research effort in lesbian and gay studies is in its infancy, recently there have been at least three major ethnographic studies of lesbian culture that shed new light on lesbians and their family relationships.

First, Weston's (1991) study of the kinship relationships of 80 lesbians in the San Francisco Bay area explores what "family" means to lesbians. She became convinced, as she pursued her research, "that gay families could not be understood apart from the families in which lesbians and gay men had grown up" (p. 3). Her work represents a tremendous breakthrough in examining the complexity of kinship meanings and arrangements in lesbian lives, as she captures the creativity. Second, Kennedy and Davis (1993) conducted a fascinating ethnographic and historical study of lesbian bar culture in Buffalo, New York, from the late 1930s to the early 1960s. These scholars go beyond conversations with the white, middle-class, well-educated, and often professional lesbians over represented in the research in order to capture the richness of and the contributions to lesbian culture of the lives of women of color and working class and poor women as well. A third work is Ellen Lewin's (1993) study of lesbian mothers, again an ethnographic adventure that explores the everyday lives, experiences, meanings, and relationships of lesbians. These three works combine to give us an emergent portrait of lesbians in family relationships that takes us beyond the trauma of disclosure, beyond hostility and emotional distance to redefinition and recreation, to a much more complex view of how lesbians define and construct kinship networks.

Interestingly, and supportive of a point I made earlier, it becomes clear in these studies of nonclinical populations that the physical and emotional cutoff of the lesbian from her family is much rarer than commonly assumed. (In fact, that may be true among clinical populations as well). Kennedy and Davis, for example, in their study based on the oral histories of 45 working-class lesbians, found that there were various degrees and forms of family disapproval that ranged from avoidance to, in one case, severe beatings. None were warmly accepted, yet none were completely rejected by their families. In fact, within several years of coming out, each woman had established a truce and was maintaining contact with her family—this in an era when out lesbianism was far more dangerous and largely confined to bar culture and when no woman was expected to move from home until she married. Many of these women fought to maintain connections *and* to protect their families from the social stigma and ridicule they knew were inevitable, were it to become known a daughter had become lesbian. Some families were openly supportive. For instance, one conservative Italian Catholic mother insisted that her daughter bring her friends home for Sunday dinner and invited her daughter's friends who were visiting from out of town to stay with the family.

Lewin (1993), in her study of lesbian mothers, found that mothers regarded family members, especially their parents, as the most reliable sources of support when times were bad. Even when cutoffs occurred, neither lesbian daughters nor their parents could endure permanent ruptures—family ties were too profound, she believes. Becoming a mother oneself seems to enhance the need for stronger kinship ties for both the new mother and her parents, and the sense of commonality and identification of the younger woman with her own mother. Lewin's findings fly in the face of much of the lesbian literature, which suggests that families of lesbians will not be helpful and that they have little to offer these newly created families.

These lesbian mothers also tended to identify and spend time with other young mothers—heterosexual mothers—more than they did with single lesbians, contradicting the notion that only other lesbians, peers, or parents, may serve as role models for daily living. Clearly, Lewin's work points to the need to know more about how lesbian mothers and their children construct kinship and community relationships with both heterosexuals, gay men, and lesbians and, similarly, how lesbian mothers and grandmothers are connected to their children and grandchildren as well as to the wider kinship network.

Lesbians, Gay Men, and Family in Popular Literature

It is often the nonprofessional, nonacademic person who carves out new paths, raising consciousness and pointing the way for new professional learning and practice. Clinical practice and research have been influenced, for example, by the various self-help movements in the fields of sexual abuse, alcoholism, and adoption. Ordinary people tell their stories, breaking longstanding silences and questioning long held "truths" in what Foucault (1980) has called the insurrection of subjugated knowledge, and we "experts" finally listen, inventing new professional languages and models of practice and investing them with expertise.

One rich source to be mined in exploring the ethnography of lesbian, gay, and bisexual life is the personal narrative, as it is told in biography, autobiography, novels, poetry, memoir, oral history, and in the self-help literature. Again, much of the popular literature on lesbians' relationships with their families of origin focuses on coming out. But there are also a number of works that demonstrate that lesbians and gays do indeed come from families and that they are connected, sometimes ambivalently or painfully, with families in the present, and haunted by ghosts from the past (for examply, Hall Carpenter Archives, 1989a, 1989b). The popular and self-help literatures attest in a way the professional literature does not to both the importance of families of origin and their presence in the lives of gay sons and lesbian daughters. For example, Bernstein (1995), in his account of the parents in Parents, Families, and Friends of Lesbians and Gays (P-FLAG), begins with horror stories of violence against gays, high rates of adolescent suicide among lesbians and gays, family rejection and isolation, all by way of prelude to the stories of family courage and, indeed, heroism, of parents in P-FLAG who have come to join the marches and to lead in fighting the new initiatives against gay civil rights, often at great personal risk and cost. This is a side of families we rarely see in the professional literature. Other parents have shared their joys and heartaches in living with and loving gay and lesbian sons and daughters (for example, Dew, 1994; Griffn, Wirth, & Wirth, 1986). Butler's (1990) anthology of lesbian commitment ceremonies recounts many stories of how families of widely varying ethnic and social class backgrounds participated in their children's weddings and other unions. Martin, in her *Lesbian and Gay Parenting Handbook* (1993), translates the expertise of the psychologist into highly readable language available to all gay and lesbian families and includes attention to families of origin in many places throughout her work. And stories of coming to terms with family, sometimes precipitated by impending death from AIDS, often lie at the heart of biography and anthology—witness the works of Monette (1991, 1992, 1994) or Preston (1992).

Here I can suggest only some of the themes appearing in the popular literature. But this literature offers us one way to listen to the narratives of the "subjugated" themselves, to listen and to move beyond the biases built into the heterosexist and homophobic social discourses in which professional assumptions are shaped. Those assumptions, in turn, can shape our preunderstandings in such a way that we cannot listen to and do not hear the "family" stories in the life of the lesbian or gay client, or the gay and lesbian stories in families. How many of us, for example, find the lesbian or gay couples on family genograms or explore further the stories of the "maiden" aunt or the "confirmed bachelor"? How many of us, as therapists, have dared to say the unsaid or ask the unasked?

Lesbian Family of Origin Narratives

My own observations about ongoing family of origin connections in the lives of lesbians come from my personal experience, from the experiences of others in my social network, from some twenty-five years of clinical experience as a family therapist working with both heterosexual and lesbian individuals, couples, and families, and from a series of research interviews conducted with lesbians and lesbian couples. It is the latter source of data that I report on in the following pages. These observations in sum contradict the impression generated in popular culture and in the professional literature of the isolated, rejected lesbian, disconnected from her family and from her roots, adrift without models for living or sources of support.

The purpose of my study was to explore the uses of the language of lesbianism in varying contexts, with a view toward better understanding the impact of secrecy, the unsaid, and the unspoken, on lesbian lives. I wanted to know how these women storied their lives, in exchanges with family, work, community, and so on. For one thing, I had become impressed over the years with how, in spite of the secrecy, silence, and homophobia that seemed to characterize their lives, so many lesbians I had come to know through clinical work and through friendship had such clear strengths and were leading such productive lives. In the field interview process, I learned a good deal about their relationships with their families, the norms for language use, the rewards, as well as the accommodations and compromises made.

My sample, which was one of convenience, consisted of 19 lesbians. Eight of the women were interviewed in couple format, although each woman had the opportunity to tell her own story. Six were living alone, and were not in committed relationships at the time of the interview. All of the women were white, and all had completed high school. All but two had completed college, and most had advanced degrees. Contrasted with these commonalities, there was wide variation in ethnic, religious, and social class backgrounds. Two women had grown up on public assistance and one of them, whose family had been on public assistance for two or three generations, was receiving assistance herself. At the other end of the economic continuum, one of my informants was reared in a very privileged, wealthy family in Great Britain in which her father was a diplomat and her mother a champion amateur athlete. Raised primarily by nannies and governesses, she was sent to boarding school at an early age. The women ranged in age from 26 to 68, their stories reflective of very different eras and very different social contexts. The audiotaped interviews averaged two hours each; they were subsequently transcribed, and a copy was sent to each informant for comments and editing. The following major themes have emerged from these conversations.

Separations and Connections

First, my research supports the conclusions of research cited earlier: Kennedy and Davis (1993), Kurdek and Schmitt (1987), Levy (1989), Lewin (1993), Murphy (1989), and Weston (1991)—namely, that lesbians typically are not cut off from their families. Every woman in my sample remains very much in complex connection with her family of origin, although certainly the nature and quality of those connections varied a great deal, as they do in all families. For some of the women, there were periods of conflict and distancing from their families of origin after coming out or during periods of trying to come out, particularly during late adolescence and early adulthood. For some, there were brief periods of alienation and emotional cutoff. Sometimes parents made rather extreme moves to erase the homosexual possibility. Two of the women I interviewed, Lila and Cheryl, in a practice that was not and may still not be uncommon, were ejected from their families in late adolescence by being committed to mental hospitals. Both believe that their personal stress during that period, as well as the solutions of their families and mental health professionals, resulted from larger social forces that defined homosexuality as a sickness or mental illness.

A third woman, Deborah, of Jewish origin and now in her sixties, reminisced:

> I think they never wanted me to be at college in the first place . . . [and then] I came back with a degree . . . and with this woman and on top of everything else. She was Japanese, and we took an apartment in New York, and so my mother's way of breaking this up . . . [was] my father had a cold, which she decided was pneumonia, and so they had to move back to the city and into my apartment. I asked, "What do you expect me to do with Gail? It's her apartment too." My mother said, "You can send her to The Y." My grandfather sent me a telegram . . . saying that my parents were dying of heart attacks, and were mailing themselves to me in separate coffins. Well, when they moved into the apartment and discovered we were gone, that's when my mother had hysterics and I was out of touch with my family for two years.

Deborah's mother is still going strong at 98, living independently and financially supported by Deborah, who takes her some place very special every year on her birthday and keeps in close contact.

Robin, 43, a woman who so far has survived leukemia and lives in a small house in the woods built by herself and a community of women, cleans houses and sells her weaving to make a living. This former hippie and political radical reports a difficult childhood and a long period of cutoff from a family that neglected her during her years of severe medical crisis. When she was about 35 and about the time she came out to herself and others, she reconnected with her mother and brother (her father had died ten years earlier) and, like Beth, Lila, and Deborah, Robin has become a most dutiful daughter during her mother's later years. Robin's mother, who now has Alzheimer's disease, easily accepted and in fact expected Robin's lesbianism, seeing that as perhaps just one more aspect of her earlier "60s rebellion" against her family's values. Robin feels that during the last few years, even with her mother's illness, she and her mother have become close for perhaps the first time.

Although the stories of Beth, Lila, Deborah, and Robin are more dramatic than some, the pattern of leaving and resuming is typical—leaving physically for a period of time or emotionally distancing in order to come to terms with independence and choices for living that are troubling for the family, later returning to renegotiate the terms of the relationship when the women themselves feel more secure in their choices. This is a common phenomenon in the lives of young heterosexual women as well.

In Robin's case, the lesbian theme mirrors an earlier struggle for independence and individuation, probably ancillary to other, even more powerful, family themes that may or may not have been resolved. Janet, now 56, was raised in a Southern Baptist farm family in which overt racist language and practice was the norm. Family loyalty, family pride, and family values were very clear, and the ties very strong, but Janet became an early, active participant in the civil rights movement. She made it clear then that she loved her family and would maintain close connections, but would march to a different drummer. And sometimes the lyrics to her music would be her own, unspoken but enacted.

Early on, she wrote to her parents from college, "Even though our *definition* of what's right and what's wrong may differ, I appreciate that you taught me that there *is* a right and a wrong." Racist beliefs and practices were part of family culture, but at some point, during a family conversation, Janet said, "We have very different beliefs, a different position on these things, but I'm not going to argue with anybody, I'm not going to fight with you about it, but I just want you to know that I'm here and you're there. And, said Janet, "I never discussed it again."

She recounted an exchange with her father, when some of her sisters were visiting:

> And he started one of his tirades about niggers. And I just sat opposite him at the table, and I just looked at him. And he stopped. And later, I don't remember how I heard this story, he was sitting around the store with the boys, and someone was ranting and raving—as they were playing checkers—about this nigger-lovin' guy who's running for governor and my father said, "Aster, now we had our day, and we did it our way. Now it's time for somebody else to do it their way. . . ." And that was a big change.

Janet handled her positioning as a lesbian in much the same way. She is much respected in the family and maintains close ties with her mother, siblings, their children, and the extended family.

One of the things Janet's story, and the stories of most of the women I interviewed, suggests is that these are women individuating-in-connection, questioning some of the politics, gender prescriptions, values, and lifestyles of their families of origin. The "lesbian" theme is an important one, and can become for a time the pole around which the daughter's struggles for self-definition pivot. But it is not an issue powerful enough, over the long haul, to supersede the importance of family connection. In fact, for many of the women I interviewed, whatever else the lesbian choice may imply about their fundamental sexual orientation, it has also meant a way to escape society's constraining gender expectations for women. Many of these women talked of how important the women's movement and feminist thinking has been in their lives, allowing them freedom to construct a story for their lives that is different from those prescribed for their female predecessors—a story that opened up many options, including the possibility that one could choose a woman rather than a man for a life partner.

Folk wisdom suggests that it is even more diffcult for men or women from certain ethnic or racial groups to choose a gay or lesbian identity, particularly gay men and lesbians from families with Old World values or from families of color. Certainly, definitions of family and what it means to be a family vary among groups, and the issues for the lesbian daughter can vary as well. Although all of the women I interviewed were white, several writers have described how cultural-racial themes and meanings intersect with the meanings of gay or lesbian choices (e.g., Greene, this volume; Greene & Boyd-Franklin, 1996; Liu & Chan, 1996; Morales, 1996). Different cultural values about such issues as gender, sexuality, individuation, the meanings of "family," and loyalty to family will have an impact on the son's or daughter's choices and subsequent relationship with the family. Furthermore, lesbians and gay men of color can find themselves abandoned or neglected by both the family and community of origin and the gay community, making it more difficult to build new families of friendship.

Nevertheless, Tremble, Schneider, and Appathurai (1989), in a study of the influence of ethnicity on the relationships of gay and lesbian young people and their families, found that "when apparently intractable cultural strictures collide with the facts of life, the parents' response was more flexible, complex and subtle than we had expected" (p. 256). Interestingly, one would think that more traditional values and expectations for traditional marriage and family would predict a more negative family response to the lesbian or gay child. As these researchers point out, these same values point to the importance of family, to maintaining ties, and to reconciliation. They found that both parents and children developed various strategies of accommodation that might not be optimal but prevented cutoff. For example, families storied the lesbian and gay behavior as a bad habit, an addiction, or a seduction, externalizing the blame and removing responsibility from themselves or the child, while their children kept their gay friends and lives separate from their families and ethnic communities, sometimes feeling lonely and isolated.

Lesbianism as the Family "Red Herring"

Relationships in all families must be continually renegotiated, family values embraced or discarded, stands taken, and compromises made or refused on all sides. The lesbian daughter's attempts to become more the author of her own life are no different from any other daughter's, except that she chooses an identity and a course for her life that may be painful or initially unacceptable for her family, an identity that is socially stigmatized. Not unlike the daughter who chooses to marry someone from a different and presumably less socially valued racial, ethnic, social class, or religious grouping or the daughter who rejects her family's politics, the lesbian daughter challenges the family's closely held expectations for its children. Some families, like Janet's or Kathy's, although concerned and worried about what the future may hold—for their children and for themselves—are accepting and supportive from the beginning. Most families, although there may be some initial conflict and separation, at the very least accommodate over time, gradually absorbing and at least tolerating their daughter's choices. A few, like that of Louise, dig in and use the lesbian narrative for other purposes.

Louise, 28, the youngest of eight siblings from a working-class Irish Catholic family, at age 18 became aware of her attraction to Gerry, her long-time best girlfriend in high school. When the two began to spend more and more time together and Louise began to think about moving in with Gerry, Louise's mother became frantic. She intercepted phone calls and letters, screaming that Gerry was a "devil" and the relationship the "work of the Devil, an attack on God." One of Louise's brothers, 22, living at home and drunk at the time, told her it was a stage she was going through. "If you weren't my sister," he said, "I would take you upstairs and fuck you and then you'd get over this lesbian thing." Her siblings sided with Mom, while her Dad was silent. Louise left home rejected, sad, and angry—at once uncertain about what being with another woman might mean for her self-definition and her future but fiercely determined to make her own choices.

Louise believes that her choice to self-identify as a lesbian, to leave home, and to move in with Gerry allowed her to escape what were extremely limiting constraints for the women in her family. In this family, gender roles were highly traditional and the family boundaries extremely rigid. Girls were to marry and to have children, but to maintain primary loyalty to their parents; spouses were included, but never really welcomed. College for girls would not be supported or even discussed. Louise believes that it was her lesbian choice and the support of her partner, Gerry, that allowed her to differentiate enough from her family to move beyond the limited possibilities for the females in her family. After working for a few years, she attended a prestigious college on the West Coast (where she won many awards for her scholarship) and has launched a promising professional career. It has taken ten years for Louise—who maintained rather superficial and rigidly ritualized contact with her family during this period, compromising as necessary to maintain the connection—to take a stand with them on defining her as part of a lesbian couple and including Gerry as part of the family. Her parents had not allowed Gerry in their home, had forbidden her contact with any of the many children of Louise's siblings, and had never visited Louise and Gerry in their home. Nevertheless, this family has reluctantly accepted Louise's recent pronouncement that Gerry will be accompanying her on visits to her family, if they wish to see Louise at all. It is a significant move for a family that, at Louise's college graduation, was utterly bewildered by the unknown educational and professional worlds their daughter had entered, changes that threatened the family's coherence as much if not more than the lesbian connection.

This is a family in which it is extraordinarily difficult for any of the children to break a rule, a home that was extraordinarily difficult to leave. Louise's lesbianism afforded a convenient target for warding off any challenges to the parents' grip on their children's lives or any threats to the only story they could recognize, as well as a way to escape the constraints of traditional marriage and roles for women as conceptualized in her family. Her marginal choice has allowed her to question the center in ways that seem to have been healthy and growth-producing for her. In other families of the women I interviewed or have known in other contexts, parents, with more or less subtlety, use the daughter's own anxieties and sensitivity about her lesbianism, what has been termed "internalized homophobia" in the professional literature, and her fears of losing her ties to her family, to bind her loyalties. In these situations, it may be difficult for the lesbian daughter to form other central attachments; when she does, it introduces tension and conflict in the lesbian couple relationships, as it would if she were to "leave home" in the context of a heterosexual relationship. But in the case of lesbianism, the homophobia in the larger community, like racism or sexism, can support the family's efforts to thwart any innovative choices.

One couple, when I began to see them clinically several years ago, had lived together for thirty-five years and had yet to spend a major holiday together. Neither was invited, on these occasions, to the home of the other's parents, and each felt she must spend the holiday with her family of origin. These women had not openly defined their coupleness in their families of origin, and their families had never asked about it. These were women who, when the family of origin made demands, made serious compromises and repeatedly jeopardized their own relationship to retain family approval. It is difficult to know whether either woman, if she had not somehow found the other, might ever have been able to marry and leave home. I wondered whether husbands would have been included within the family of origin emotional system; in the context of the unrecognized lesbian relationship, everyone concerned could define each of them as "single" when necessary.

Voicing the "L" Word

Some narrative and constructionist theorists believe that, until something is "languaged," it does not exist. One of the themes I explored at some length in these interviews was how, in what ways and in what contexts, women differentially languaged—gave words to—their lesbianism and the nature of their love relationships. "Outness" has typically been defined in the literature as verbal disclosure and is seen as vital to the development of a healthy gay or lesbian identity. Nondisclosure, secrecy, and silence are seen as problematic, signs of unresolved developmental issues and internalized homophobia, risks to mental health. Using verbal criteria, several studies indicate that self-disclosure rates are very low, and that gay men and lesbians are "invisible."

But meanings are communicated in many powerful ways, through ritual, story, metaphor, and everyday action. As Healy (1993) points out, behavior can and does often speak louder than words. The language of action can conceal or reveal lesbian identity, affirm or invalidate relationships, recognize or disqualify commitments. It is during ritual times that families most vividly define themselves, through words but also through actions and symbols, constructing and shaping their definitions. All of the lesbians in my research were "out" to their families of origin nonverbally or behaviorally—that is, in the ways they wore their lives for family to clearly interpret the signals, and to make whatever meanings of their situations they chose. Some, however, rarely use the "L" word, so associated with sexuality in public discourse, much as most heterosexual couples do not go around using sexual language or highlighting the sexual parts of their relationship for their parents. But lesbians may clearly occupy one bedroom, co-own a home and a car with another woman, spend their major rituals as a couple with their respective extended families, and in most actions make clear they are partnered and committed.

And though some of their families might wince at the word *lesbian*, sending powerful "don't use that awful language" messages, most of these same families show through their actions that they care deeply about and remain tied to their daughters. When the daughter is partnered, they acknowledge and validate the lesbian relationship to the extent that they open up their family boundaries to include the partner and to define her as "family member" in various ways. If there are children, there is even more reason in both generations to remain solidly connected.

All but one of the women I spoke with felt she was out to her family, but this sense of outness had different meanings. Maureen, at 68 the oldest woman with whom I spoke, said that she had been a lesbian all of her life and thought her parents and siblings probably had known, but used the "L" word for the first time in our conversation. Since that opportunity to review her life and to think about her family relationships, she has come out to her brother, who in turn shared some of his own secrets and life disappointments with her. Maureen told me in a later conversation that she has become much closer to her brother, as they seem now to be able to talk more openly about many things. Most women reported that they rarely used the "L" word in their families or in work contexts. For most, it was part of a special language used with lesbian and gay friends, and in gay culture contexts.

Most of these women had at some point verbally disclosed to their parents and siblings, and saw themselves as out to their families. That is, they had made it clear at some point that they loved women and continued to demonstrate that implicitly in their life choices and actions. For those who were partnered, for the most part their partners were defined as "family," and included in nuclear and extended family gatherings and important family rituals. Most women indicated that their partners had gradually become included in gift-giving and card exchanges with their families of origin. This is even the case for Marilyn, the one woman I interviewed who has not come out to her family verbally. Marilyn was raised in a poor family and she spent several years on public assistance after her husband abandoned her and her three children. She has now completed a master's degree, and she and her children live with Judy. She has come out verbally to her three children, a process that was extraordinarily difficult and painful and she is, tentatively and gradually, enacting her new coupleness in contacts with her family of origin, inviting them to her home on special occasions. She is gradually introducing them to her new world, but does not feel they could accept or even tolerate an overt "lesbian" definition.

Most of the women who came out verbally to their families have learned, in the years following initial disclosure, to screen their language. Using the "lesbian" descriptor generated tension and sometimes a visible shrinking back or flinching on the part of a parent or sibling, even after many years of knowing the daughter's lesbian identity. Often an awkward silence would follow, or the subject would be changed.

Of course, the daughter's not languaging her lesbianism allows families to story her and her relationships in whatever ways they choose. Although this situation is often represented as deplorable and asks for too many compromises on the part of the lesbian daughter, it also seems to allow for family connections, however precarious, to be maintained. And this is a compromise all seem willing to make or at least resigned to making for the sake of maintaining peace and family connectedness.

> Deborah has never minced words with her now 98-year-old mother, but her mother has ingenious strategies for transforming lesbian language. A few years ago, Deborah and her mother were visiting a lesbian couple, longtime friends of Deborah's, for the weekend. Deborah had explained to her mother that the women were lesbians, and had lived together for forty years. As she was taking her mother home after the visit, Deborah asked whether her mother had enjoyed the visit. She said, "Yes, dear, but you are mistaken about them. I'm sure they are sisters, they look so much alike." "Yes, mother," sighed Deborah, "they are indeed Sisters."

In one of my efforts to language my own relationship, some years ago I ventured to say to my mother over the telephone, "Ann and I will be celebrating our twenty-fifth anniversary together next week." A long and uncomfortable silence ensued. Not to be quite so easily discouraged, the next week I described to my mother the beautiful ring Ann had given me. Again, there was a long pause and my mother finally said, with some asperity, "Don't you have enough jewelry?"

My mother, myself, and all but the youngest of the women I interviewed, and their families, have grown up in a world that has forbidden the naming of the lesbian relationship, as Oscar Wilde called it, "the love that dares not speak its name" (Sanders, 1993). "Lesbian," for most of us, conjured up deep, dark, dirty, and forbidden part-images or resided even beyond the imagination. Several of the women with whom I spoke, even at very young ages when they suspected they might be different, knew enough not to tell anyone or to use the forbidden word, even to themselves. It was common to go the library to find a book or an article on homosexuality that might tell them about themselves. That, too, was a painful experience, since what little they could find was full of dismal forebodings for their futures. Most of us growing up never met anyone who was a lesbian or we heard, in our families, some woman or couple pointed at or whispered about. I went to a women's college reputed to be a hotbed of lesbianism, but never knowingly met a lesbian.

Priscilla, the daughter of socially liberal, highly educated parents, reported that her parents "accept" her partner, welcome her into the family, but maintain silence about the relationship outside the family. She wishes, for example, that her parents could be joyful for her, would show her family pictures to friends and neighbors, could brag about her publicly the way they do about their other children and grandchildren. The lesbian relationship, accepted and sometimes even languaged inside the family, is rarely spoken of beyond the family borders.

Although naming the relationship seems to raise the tension level in most of these families even when, in general, the communication patterns seem relatively comfortable and open, sometimes the lesbian language theme fits into a larger pattern of constrained or problematic family communication. Several of the women reported, for example, that no conflictual or negative conversation was allowed in their families. In other families, such as Gerry's, which has been relatively accepting and inclusive of Louise, there is a concern that younger children not be exposed to lesbian language or openly expressed affection, as if lesbianism were infectious.

Sometimes parents seem to understand about their daughter's sexual orientation even before their daughters have any language. In two situations, when the daughter finally disclosed to her mother, each mother said something like. "I wondered how long it would take you to find out. I've known for years."

Certainly, the experience of self-disclosing, of coming out in contexts where one previously has been censored or has censored oneself, can be enormously self-empowering—and the terror of being discovered can be debilitating. Certainly there can be serious costs to silencing and censoring oneself and being silenced by others. But all of us make choices about what we will share or not share about ourselves everyday. In every sentence, we select what we wish to bring into the conversation—in our body language, through dress, in the ways we organize our homes, and in other uses of the said and the unsaid. Most of us wish to present ourselves well, to construct stories of self that are marketable and communicate a coherent sort of self to others. There are always rules and strategies for conversation in any family; the things we talk about and do not talk about with varying people; even the genres for speech are prescribed, differing by gender, age, ethnicity, social class, education, family and community culture, and so on.

We have tended to assume that silence and secrecy are problematic for individual identity development, but every human being manipulates language. We all use it strategically and intersubjectively, constructing together with our families and others how we will talk together and be together, editing and reediting our personal narratives for ourselves and for those around us (Laird, 1993b).

The lesbian literature, I believe, often exaggerates the differences between lesbians and others and overlooks the tremendous diversity within lesbian culture. These narratives demonstrate both the commonalities these women share with all women defining connections with their families and the considerable diversity in the forms these connections take. One can speculate that these women are as close to or distant from, as involved or uninvolved, as one might find in any sample of 19 heterosexual women.

Strength and Resilience

One reason I undertook this study was that I perceived an enormous gap between the people I knew, and the generally dismal impressions many people have of the gay and lesbian individual and the ravages of heterosexism and homophobia. Gay men and lesbians I was meeting in my own life were among the most interesting, talented, strongest people I had ever had the privilege to know. Who was writing about them, about their strengths and their creativity? What gave them such resilience in a world that finds homosexuality deviant and even disgusting?

Many of the lesbians I know seem to me to often be the strongest and most differentiated members of their nuclear families. I have been interested in the fact that there is so little writing on the tremendous strength and resilience exhibited by gay men and lesbians, *in spite of* experiences of oppression and having to negotiate one's life in negatively defining, homophobic environments. My own impressions and personal experiences seemed to belie the dismal portrayals of maladjustment and pathology in the clinical literature and popular media. The women I interviewed, regardless of social class, seemed to support my impression. For example, Cheryl, 26, whose family is characterized by generations of alcoholism, unemployment and underemployment, and welfare, is the first person in her twelve-member family to attain sobriety, and the first to attend college. She takes one or two courses at a time at a community college, and is hoping to get her associate's degree next year. Louise, described earlier, defied her family's gender prescriptions and with the support of her partner Gerry graduated Phi Beta Kappa from a top college, winning five separate major awards. Grace, who grew up in a rejecting and critical family with two seriously dysfunctional alcoholic parents, has gone on to become a well-known writer and expert on work with alcoholic families.

The lesbian issue affords not only simply conflict but also possibility and opportunity. It is often the pivot around which the tasks of individuation or differentiation occur and continue to occur throughout life, not in some neat and tidy arrangement of stages. We never, in my view, "resolve" our lesbian identities; it is a narrative without end, always being edited and reshaped as we and our contexts change.

Judy, 46, a graduate school professor and clinician herself, was on a car trip with her mother. Her mother was talking about one of Judy's sisters, who had been going through a very difficult phase in which she was expressing a great deal of anger at their mother, and had recently said some things the mother found very hurtful.

> And so my mother said, "Well, do you feel that way [about me]?" And I thought, well, I don't want to just dismiss this, to leave my sister looking like she owns this whole problem. But neither did I have the same degree of feeling about it as my sister. Anyway, I said, "You know, Mom, sometimes I think that all of us in the family suffer from a great amount of judgementalness. And that you have it too, and that sometimes when I talk to you, I feel the first place you're coming from is some sense of moral judgement about things . . . and that can really make it hard to want to talk to you sometimes."

Judy went on, in this conversation with her mother, to use the example of how her mother, when talking about lesbian or gay issues, always begins with something like, "Well, of course I don't really quite understand, uh, what it's like." This really bothered her, she told me, her mother always acting if a gay relationship is some *"totally* foreign animal! "So she said to her mother, "I feel like when you say that, you've been married to my father for fifty-two years, you know something about loving somebody, and when you say that, you're totally distancing yourself from something that you *do* know about, and putting me in this category that's . . . totally foreign, and it isn't." And she went on to say, "And, I think you can do better than that."

Said Judy to me,

> I'm not sure she completely got it, but I knew she was going to go home and think about it. . . . And I felt like at that point, I had a right to expect more from her in terms of understanding my relationship. Even if she wouldn't choose it for me, even if she didn't think it was great—she did have some human experience to connect with me about it. And she wants to connect with

me about it, that's really the whole context of what the discussion was about. *It wasn't about being gay, it was about how she connected with her children* [Emphasis added].

In another example, Janet, from the rural Southern Baptist family described earlier, has not hidden her lesbian orientation, but as in matters of race, she does not attempt to convince others—her style is not to argue or to provoke rupture. Her family is too important to her, but she does not compromise her own convictions—about race or about sexual orientation. Her partner and she frequently travel to Tennessee to spend time with her mother (her father is now deceased), and her mother and adult siblings often visit her. *Family* is more important here than politics or sexuality, and she manages well what we might think of as biculturality. One senses that she has taught her family a great deal as she has, in her actions, steadfastly made clear who she is and what she believes in relation to, not separate from, family.

The daughter's lesbianism, then, can be used by the family as a rationalization for binding her loyalties and preventing her from authoring a life too different from that of the family, or it can be used by the daughter herself as a marker of angry rebellion and demands for quick and complete acceptance of difference. But in most cases, as Judy's and Janet's narratives both illustrate, the lesbian theme is just one facet of the ongoing complex task of working on family relationships. With another son or daughter, a different theme may emerge as pivotal.

Certainly, many of the women I interviewed wish for more. They wish their families could more openly admire and affirm them and could brag about *their* families as well as their individual accomplishments to their neighbors and friends. They wish they could do more than often reluctantly accept the inevitable. But they understand how both history and social context continue to make this leap into affirmation and voice extraordinarily difficult, and they forgive their families for their failures to stand up against social homophobia because they know how hard it was for them, and they know their families do not have the same supports they have— that is, another context in which they can use the language of lesbianism.

Families of Choice

Although this chapter is about families of origin, I do not believe that lesbians *need* their original families to forge meaningful, rich, and full family lives—I do believe we can also choose and build new families that may work better for us. But it may mean tremendous costs that, if we worked harder at it, we might not have to suffer (Bowen, 1978; Hartman & Laird, 1983). In Butler's (1990) work on commitment ceremonies, if families did not attend, the couple often lamented the fact they were not or could not be there; it was often a great sadness that their special commitment could not be shared. The costs to Louise of maintaining her lesbian position and maintaining a distanced and ritualized relationship with her family may be greater than the costs of the compromises she has had to make to stay in connection. We do not have to like our relatives or agree with them or even spend much time with them; but, if Bowen (1978) is correct, we do have to come to terms with our own emotional reactivity in the family of origin system, and to differentiate sufficiently for our new relationships to be free of what he has termed the "emotional baggage" of the past.

Family therapists, however, tend to overemphasize the dire consequences of cutoff from families of origin, and at the same time minimize the richness and importance of families of choice. Most of the women I interviewed both maintain connections with blood families *and* have forged new and meaningful extended networks of friends that come to behave like close extended families. Priscilla, Sheila, and Robin, for example, live in a small, rural, politically radical enclave in which a community of women serve as extended family for each other. This family seems to be forged around similar political beliefs such as nonmaterialism, and shared activities such as exchanges of labor and extensive recycling of material goods. Deborah, who finds little in common with most of her blood relatives, has constructed an extended family pieced together from the families of former lovers and connections with other lesbians from all over the country.

The area in which this study was conducted and 14 of the women live, particularly the small city of Northampton, Massachusetts, and environs, is known as a lesbian-friendly and lesbian-affrmative community. This means that most of the women have formed extensive lesbian (although not exclusively lesbian) friendship networks that, at least some of the time, serve similar functions as those served by extended families—participating in "family" rituals, helping out at times of illness or other crisis, lending money or sharing other resources, and so on. We know too little about how such networks operate, and it is clear that we rarely ask about them in our clinical work (Siegel & Walker, 1996).

Implications for Clinical Practice

In this chapter, I have visited the prevailing narrative of family of origin invisibility in the life of the lesbian, examining popular film, family studies, and the family therapy literature, as well as the popular literature concerning their portrayals of these ties (or lack of ties). The picture that emerges—largely one of invisibility, rejection, loss, and cutoff—is contrasted with what lesbians themselves have told me in a series of interviews. I find that lesbians are not usually cut off from their families, and that their patterns of separating and connecting seem similar to those of daughters in general. Furthermore, the issue of the daughter's lesbianism becomes just one of the salient issues in her individuation-in-relation process and, as was the case with some of the women I talked with, can sometimes actually be very helpful in that process, offering both opportunity and new possibilities for self-definition and for couple and family life.

It is also clear that coming out is not simply a matter of verbal disclosure. Commitment to a lesbian relationship may be demonstrated in many ways, behaviorally and verbally, in the family of origin and in other contexts. Lesbians, like everyone else, make careful judgments about how and in what contexts they will communicate, about what they will say, and about what they will leave unsaid, to themselves and to others.

The family's response to the daughter's lesbianism reflects its more enduring patterns of organization and the extent to which the autobiographical family narrative is available for reauthoring. Families who tend to be inflexible concerning rules for behavior and visions for their children are often inflexible about many things. Families that have difficulty talking about sensitive or controversial issues of any kind will have more trouble talking about this one. Families that have difficulty allowing their children to leave or to grow up, for whatever reasons, can use the convenient red herring of lesbianism to stall their child's leaving or to insist on loyalty to traditional social, religious, or political ideas.

To the extent that relationships with families of origin are important or relevant to clinical work with any client, so are they in work with lesbians. Family of origin relationships may become part of the therapeutic conversation in any clinical modality—in individual, couple, child, family of origin, family of choice, and group interviews.

What the narratives of lesbians themselves most clearly reveal is (1) that these family connections are important and ongoing, and (2) that the "lesbian" theme is very much intertwined with and expressive of other relational issues. How well the lesbian daughter and family together are able to integrate the lesbian story into their lives and to embrace new definitions for couple and family life is expressive of how well parents are able to come to terms with their daughters becoming the authors of their own lives as independent women.

Certainly, "lesbianism" adds an important ingredient to the family stew. These women have experienced some of the pain, rejection, isolation, and anger from families we commonly hear about, and their families have undergone periods of anger, confusion, anxiety, concern, and loss over the daughter's lesbian identity. But it is clear that these women and their families travel beyond the rocky road of initial disclosure and forge more or less satisfying ongoing relationships, maintaining connections and continuing to negotiate how familiness will be defined. These are tasks in all families.

The lesbian daughter must deal with her family's heterosexist assumptions and their homophobia, as well as her own; and all concerned must face how they will support each other in a more or less homophobic context, one which does not ordinarily allow for the sharing of either joy or pain outside of the family. The family must learn to live with and perhaps to fight against a sense of marginality they never expected.

Most of the family of origin issues lesbians bring into therapy are, as White and Epston (1990) would frame it, "problems with problems," and they look like the problems anyone might bring—everything from how to hold one's own with a critical mother, how to set limits with an interfering father, how to cope with a parent's failing health, to how to recover from a childhood of abuse and despair or how, as a couple, to deal with different family of origin cultural styles and levels of acceptance, or how to define grandparent relationships.

What is crucial is that the therapist be able to bracket and to move beyond his or her own prior understandings and assumptions that probably have been shaped in a heterosexist and homophobic context. These understandings and assumptions or "maps" not only can keep us from hearing what the lesbian client is saying but can mean that we fail to ask the good questions. For instance, we may fail to fully explore the meanings of "family" for the lesbian and lesbian couple. On the one hand, we may ignore family of choice relationships, colluding with feelings of hurt and rejection, or on the other hand, we may too easily fail to question and more deeply explore cutoffs from family of origin.

We may make either the alpha error of exaggerating the differences between lesbians and heterosexual women or the beta error of minimizing the differences (Hare-Mustin, 1987), leading us to behave clinically with lesbians in ways we would never otherwise consider. The alpha error can happen in the case of therapists who, for example, may have stereotypical assumptions about lesbian culture and how lesbians are "different" from other women, failing to explore themes or appreciate relationships in ways that they ordinarily would with women clients. Clinicians who make the beta error may underestimate the power of homophobia, thus perhaps prematurely urging lesbians to come out to their families and in other contexts and underestimating the potential negative reactions of others. Both groups may fail to note the tremendous diversity of lesbian experience among lesbian clients, by virtue of social class, race or ethnicity, age, geography, and other social markers, or simply because of profoundly different life experiences and life contexts.

In general, lesbian women seem to be more like heterosexual women, for example, than they are like gay men. Gender, seemingly, is a more powerful determinant of certain kinds of values and behaviors than sexual orientation (Blumstein & Schwartz, 1983). If Gilligan (1982), the Wellesley College Stone Center researchers (see, for example, Jordan & Surrey, 1986), and other women scholars are correct, women more than men, for whatever reasons, nature or nurture, tend to forge relationships in connection. In this regard, it would be very interesting to know whether the relationships of gay men with their families of origin follow different patterns from those of women. Since the literature and research on homosexuality, as well as popular cultural narratives, have centered on the lives of gay men, it is possible that the portrayal of gay men and lesbians as separate and isolated from family better reflects gay male than lesbian experience.

In sum, as clinicians we need to be as knowledgeable as possible about lesbian culture and lesbian experience, not so as to lead from our own knowledge or theory in a way that makes prior assumptions but so as to be able to fully listen—to ask the questions and listen to the answers in a way that lack of knowledge or fixed ideas can prevent us from doing. Only then will we be able to help lesbians, in the context of their families of origin, creation, and choice, move ahead in ways that recognize their strength and resilience, and that make the most of their potential for positive connection and mutual support. There are, of course, many sources for this "knowledge," but none better than the narratives of those who have lived the experience, from the "native's point of view," if you will. We need to listen to the stories of lesbians themselves and to the stories of their families, who have been neglected by heterosexually and homosexually oriented scholars. As a mother of a lesbian daughter said recently in the question period after a series of presentations by therapists on lesbian families, "We're out here, we want to support you, and you need to listen to us." At another conference in which I presented a paper, a Mennonite couple with a lesbian daughter described how they had formed a church group to support parents of gay and lesbian children and to educate fellow church members, and how this idea had spread to several congregations. They *are* out there, and they are willing to bear witness to their experiences in a way that can be helpful to clinicians and to the larger community.

I want to end this chapter with another moment from my own experience—a moment that attests to the richness and complexity of life in the lesbian family. This moment is part of a family transition, an intergenerational and kinship ritual centered around a child's bat mitzvah, a time in most families when individual and family narratives are edited to reauthor the old and to incorporate the new. In this case, we as therapists can learn a great deal about how we might help lesbian daughters and families with lesbian members to express their connectedness through narrative and ritual.

Lila, whom I interviewed, is also a longtime friend and the first lesbian I knew to choose to become a mother through donor insemination. I regard her as a courageous pioneer. Lila gave birth to her daughter, Edith, in the context of what she thought at the time was a lifetime partnership with Elaine, a formerly married lesbian with a son of her own. The two later separated and, again, were pioneers in figuring out, in spite of the hurts and disappointments, how to co-parent in the best way possible the children they had shared, and how to maintain ties with their own and their partners' families of origin and their own extended family of choice.

Now it was time for Edith, the daughter of Lila and Elaine, to enter young womanhood through the ritual of the bat mitzvah. The congregation was filled with family and friends—lesbian couples and their children, straight couples and their children, and family members. Although Lila's parents are now deceased, her sisters and their families came, an aged friend of her father's from New York arrived to represent the grandparent generation, and Elaine's father and stepmother came from three thousand miles away to be present.

Edith moved through her parts of the bat mitzvah perfectly, singing and speaking the traditional Hebrew words in a clear and beautiful way. Toward the end, when it came time for her own reflections, she spoke of the meanings her participation in the Jewish faith has had for her and the questions she continues to probe. She ended by speaking of her family:

> Through the years, when describing my *different* family situation, I have gotten a wide variety of responses, some consisting of disbelief, some of total amazement, and an occasional few of disgust. One thing that I have come to understand is that it makes no difference *what* the family consists of, as long as there is love, honesty, and humor. . . .
>
> My family consists of my biological mother, Lila, my other parent, Elaine, my stepmother, Helen, and my nonbiological brother, Doug. I have no shame that my parents are, [and here there was a smile and a twinkle in her 13-year-old dark, bright eyes, as she said, loudly and crystally clear] well, shall I say it? Lesbians! The only problem I have with it is that they are sometimes discriminated against. Just for loving who they want to love. It bothers me that in this day you are discriminated against just for being who you are.
>
> Having my parents be lesbians makes *me* stronger. Now when I see someone being discriminated against for who they are and not hiding it, I make sure that the discriminator knows that they are the wrong one. Denying someone the right to be who they are is like telling someone that they cannot have water.
>
> Discrimination is dependent upon fear. . . . I believe that if you do not agree with someone's sexual preference, race, class, gender, size, age or looks you should still respect them for who they are. As many people say, don't judge a person by who they are on the outside, but instead who they are on the inside.

Her mother, Lila, in her talk, remarked on the load that Edith carried—in her backpack and on her shoulders—her talents, her grace, her marvelous sense of humor, her generosity, her rage, and her forgiving spirit, and Elaine spoke of the unusual challenges Edith has been presented with in her 13 years and how courageously she has met them.

What courtroom judge, given half the chance, might have awarded custody of this wonderful young woman to a challenger of her mothers' sexual orientation? What is "family," if not the strength and beauty that flourishes in this kind of social arrangement?

References

Allen, K. R., & Demo, D. H. (1995). The families of lesbians and gay men: A new frontier in family research. *Journal of Marriage and the Family, 57,* 1–17.

Benkov, L. (1994). *Reinventing the family: The emerging story of lesbian and gay parents.* New York: Crown.

Bernstein, R. (1995). *Straight parents/gay children: Keeping families together*. New York: Thunder's Mouth Press.

Berzon, B. (1979). Telling your family you're gay. In B. Berzon & R. Leighton (Eds.), *Positively gay* (pp. 88–100). Millbrae, CA: Celestial Arts.

Blumstein, P., & Schwartz, P. (1983). *American couples: Money, work, sex.* New York: Morrow.

Bowen, M. (1978). *Family therapy in clinical practice*. Northvale, NJ: Aronson.

Brown, L. (1989). Lesbians, gay men, and their families: Common clinical issues. *Journal of Gay and Lesbian Psychotherapy, 1*(1), 65–77.

Bull, C. (1995, May 20). Losing the war: The courts disregard evidence in denying lesbian mother custody of her son. *The Advocate*, p. 33.

Butler, B. (Ed.) (1990). *Ceremonies of the heart: Celebrating lesbian unions*. Seattle: Seal Press.

DeVine, J. L. (1984). A systemic inspection of affectional preference orientation and the family of origin. *Journal of Social Work and Human Sexuality, 2*, 9–17.

Dew, R. F. (1994). *The family heart: A memoir of when our son came out*. New York: Ballantine Books.

Foucault, M. (1980). *Power/knowledge: Selected interviews and other writings*. New York: Pantheon Press.

Gilligan, C. (1982). *In a different voice*. Cambridge, MA: Harvard University Press.

Greene, B., & Boyd-Franklin, N. (1996). African American lesbians: Issues in couples therapy. In J. Laird & R-J. Green (Eds.), *Lesbians and gays in couples and families: A handbook for therapists* (pp. 251–271). San Francisco: Jossey-Bass.

Griffin, C. W., Wirth, M. J., & Wirth, A. G. (1986). *Beyond acceptance: Lesbians and gays talk about their experiences*. New York: St. Martin's Press.

Griscom, J. (1992). The case of Sharon Kowalski and Karen Thompson: Ableism, heterosexism, and sexism. In P. R. Rothenberg (Ed.), *Race, class and gender in the United States: An integrated study* (pp. 215–225). New York: St. Martin's Press.

Hall Carpenter Archives. Gay Men's Oral History Group (1989a). *Walking after midnight: Gay men's life stories*. London: Routledge.

Hall Carpenter Archives. Lesbian Oral History Group (1989b). *Inventing ourselves Lesbian life stories*. London: Routledge.

Hare-Mustin, R. (1987). The problem of gender in family therapy theory. *Family Process, 26*, 15–27.

Hartman, A., & Laird, J. (1983). *Family-centered social work practice*. New York: Free Press.

Healy, T. (1993). A struggle for language: Patterns of self-disclosure in lesbian couples. *Smith College Studies in Social Work, 63*(3), 247–264.

Herdt, G. (Ed.) (1992). *Gay culture in America: Essays from the field*. Boston: Beacon Press.

Jordan, J. V., & Surrey, J. L. (1986). The self-in-relation: Empathy and the mother-daughter relationship (pp. 81–104). In *The psychology of today's woman: New psychoanalytic visions*. Hillsdale, NJ: Analytic Press.

Kennedy, E. L., & Davis, M. D. (1993). *Boots of leather, slippers of gold: The history of a lesbian community*. New York: Routledge.

Kleinberg, L. (1986). *Coming home to self, going home to parents: Lesbian identity disclosure*. Work in Progress Series, No. 24. Wellesley, MA: Wellesley College Stone Center for Women's Development.

Krestan, J. (1988). Lesbian daughters and lesbian mothers: The crisis of disclosure from a family systems perspective. In L. Braverman (Ed.), *Women, feminism, and family therapy* (pp. 113–130). New York: Haworth Press.

Krestan, J., & Bepko, C. (1980). The problem of fusion in the lesbian relationship. *Family Process, 19*(3), 277–289.

Kurdek, L., & Schmitt, J. P. (1987). Perceived emotional support from family and friends in members of homosexual, married, and heterosexual cohabiting couples. *Journal of Homosexuality, 12*(2), 85–99.

Laird, J. (1993a). Lesbian and gay families. In F. Walsh (Ed.), *Normal family processes*, 2nd ed. (pp. 282–328). New York: Guilford.

Laird J. (1993b). Women's secrets—women's silences. In E. Imber-Black (Ed.), *Secrets in families and family therapy* (pp. 243–267). New York: Norton.

Levy, E. (1989). Lesbian motherhood: Identity and social support. *Affilia, 4*(4), 40–53.

Lewin, E. (1993). *Lesbian mothers: Accounts of gender in American culture*. Ithaca, NY: Cornell University Press.

Liu, P., & Chan, C. S. (1996). Lesbian, gay, and bisexual Asian Americans and their families. In J. Laird & R-J. Green (Eds.), *Lesbians and gays in couples and families: A handbook for therapists* (pp. 137–152). San Francisco: Jossey-Bass.

Martin, A. (1993). *Lesbian and gay parenting handbook: Creating and raising our families*. New York: HarperPerennial.

Monette, P. (1991). *Halfway home*. New York: Avon.

Monette, P. (1992). *Becoming a man: Half a life story*. New York: HarperCollins.

Monette, P. (1994). *Last watch of the night*. San Diego, CA: Harcourt & Brace.

Morales, E. (1996). Gender roles among Latino gay and bisexual men: Implications for family and couple relationships. In J. Laird & R-J. Green (Eds.), *Lesbians and gays in couples and families: A handbook for therapists* (pp. 272–297). San Francisco: Jossey-Bass.

Murphy, B. C. (1989). Lesbians and their parents: The effects of perceived paternal attitudes on the couple. *Journal of Counseling and Development, 68*(1), 46–51.

Ordona, T., & Thompson, D. (1990). A thousand cranes. In B. Butler (Ed.), *Ceremonies of the heart: Celebrating lesbian unions* (pp. 81–90). Seattle: Seal Press.

Osman, S. (1972). My stepfather is a she. *Family Process, 11*, 209–218.

Patterson, C. J. (1996). Lesbian mothers and their children: Findings from the Bay Area families study. In J. Laird & R-J. Green (Eds.), *Lesbians and gays in couples and families: A handbook for therapists* (pp. 420–437). San Francisco: Jossey-Bass.

Preston, J. (1992). *A member of the family: Gay men write about their families*. New York: Dutton.

Roth, S. (1984). Psychotherapy with lesbian couples: The interrelationships of individual issues, female socialization, and the social context. In E. Hetrick & T. Stein (Eds.), *Innovations in psychotherapy with homosexuals* (pp. 90–114). Washington, DC: American Psychiatric Press.

Roth, S., & Murphy, B.C. (1986). Therapeutic work with lesbian clients: A systemic therapy view. In J. C. Hansen & M. Ault-Riche (Eds.), *Women and family therapy* (pp. 78–89). Gaithersburg, MD: Aspen Press.

Sanders, G. (1993). The love that dares to speak its name: From secrecy to openness—Gay and lesbian affiliations. In E. Imber-Black (Ed.), *Secrets in families and family therapy* (pp. 215–242). New York: Norton.

Siegel, S., & Walker, G. (1996). Connections: Conversations between a gay therapist and a straight therapist. In J. Laird & R-J. Green (Eds.), *Lesbians and
gays in couples and families: A handbook for therapists* (pp. 28–68). San Francisco: Jossey-Bass.

Slater, S. (1995). *The lesbian family life cycle.* New York: Free Press.

Strommen, E. F. (1989). "You're a what?" Family members reactions to the disclosure of homosexuality. In F. Bozett (Ed.), *Homosexuality and the family*
(pp. 37–58). Binghamton, NY: Haworth.

Tremble, B., Schneider, M., & Appathurai, C. (1989). Growing up gay or lesbian
in a multicultural context. In G. Herdt (Ed.), *Gay and lesbian youth* (pp. 253–
264). New York: Haworth.

Walker, G. (1991). *In the midst of winter: Systemic therapy with families, couples, and
individuals with AIDS infection.* New York: Norton.

Weston, K. (1991). *Families we choose: Lesbians, gays, kinship.* New York: Columbia
University Press.

White, M., & Epston, D. (1990). *Narrative means to therapeutic ends.* New York:
Norton.

Zitter, S. (1987). Coming out to Mom: Theoretical aspects of the mother-daughter
process. In Boston Lesbian Psychologies Collective (Eds.), *Lesbian psychologies: Explorations and challenges* (pp. 177–194). Urbana: University of Illinois
Press.

III

Community and Contextual Issues

11

The Economic Well-Being of Lesbian, Gay, and Bisexual Adults' Families

M. V. Lee Badgett

Families and households formed by lesbian, gay, and bisexual people have become increasingly visible to the larger U.S. public. In recognizing that lesbian, gay, and bisexual people might create their own families (outside of their families of origin), the public's attention has mainly been on lesbian couples and gay male couples.[1] And that attention has spotlighted often contradictory so-called facts about those couples. On the one hand, those relationships are extremely unstable, and on the other hand, such couples can amass unusual wealth and discretionary income without children to support—even during the short duration of those relationships, apparently (Weston, 1991: 157):

> The homosexual lifestyle is inconsistent with the proper raising of children. Because homosexual relationships are characteristically unstable, they are less likely to provide children the security they need. (Knight & Garcia, 1994)

> Homosexual households had an average income of $55,400 compared with a national average of $36,500. . . . This is not the profile of a group in need of special civil rights legislation in order to participate in the economy or to have an opportunity to hold a decent job. It is the profile of an elite. (Broadus, 1994)

---

1. Some explanation of terminology is in order at this point. I use "gay family" to refer to a family formed by a lesbian, gay male, or bisexual individual. (Obviously not every member of such families will be lesbian, gay, or bisexual.) The most visible form of such families, and arguably the most common form, is that of a couple. For the sake of convenience, I use "gay couples" or "lesbian couples" to refer to same-sex couples, although the self-identified sexual orientation of individuals in such couples could certainly be bisexual or even heterosexual.

Still, in gay households, "you're talking about two people with good jobs, lots of money and no dependents. This is a dream market." (Rigdon, 1991)

At this point in U.S. economic history, when average real income growth has stagnated while income inequality among individuals has increased, and when the two-earner family has become the primary strategy for many families attempting to improve their standard of living, it is no surprise that much of the attention to gay families has focused on economic matters. And it is probably no coincidence that the particular "facts" that are often cited suggest that gay families are doing well on their own (amassing wealth and earning high incomes) or are the victims of their own choices (if instability causes economic damage). Those conclusions imply that increasingly scarce public resources need not be spent worrying about the well-being of gay families.

But these stereotypes are rooted in and are maintained by three basic problems: (1) the inappropriate use of data in studying gay households; (2) incorrect or incomplete assumptions about the composition of gay people's families; and (3) ignorance of the influence of adverse legal and social treatment on the economic status of lesbian and gay individuals and their families. This chapter seeks to correct these misunderstandings. At least part of the first two problems stems from the lack of scientifically collected data available for the study of lesbian, gay, and bisexual people and their families. Fortunately, some recent surveys provide a better understanding of gay households. The third factor involves analysis of employment and family policies and requires considering the economic position of lesbian, gay, and bisexual people as individuals as well as family members. When these problems are addressed, we are left with a different image of gay families. Contemporary findings, in fact, suggest that rather than being privileged, gay families face many of the same economic stresses as all families, but they lack the underlying social and economic supports available to heterosexual families. In addition, an appreciation of the limitations of our current information leads to recommendations about further research, which will be detailed at the end of the chapter.

Data Issues in Studying Lesbians and Gay Men

Studying a stigmatized group is never an easy task, particularly since obtaining a representative sample of the group is necessary to make broad inferences about that group. Readily available probability samples, such as those conducted by the federal government, rarely ask questions about sexual orientation, but samples of gay people obtained by other methods, such as convenience or snowball samples, are likely to result in biased samples. Constructing more inclusive survey instruments for probability samples poses the difficult problem of encouraging forthright responses to questions on sensitive topics. All of these issues arise in the study of lesbian, gay, and bisexual people, and the lack of awareness of some of these problems has resulted in a distorted picture of gay people in the United States (see Badgett, 1997).

Students of lesbian, gay, and bisexual people have long relied on convenience and snowball samples. Those studies often revealed important aspects of gay life even though the conclusions could not properly be generalized beyond the groups that seemed to be well represented by those samples, usually white, urban, male, and middle-class homosexuals.

Unfortunately, the care with which many academics interpret their results from such samples has disappeared in public reports of more recent marketing surveys of gay people in the United States. Driven by the economic self-interest of the marketing entrepreneurs or the political self-interest of opponents of gay equality, the economic image promoted by both groups is one of gay affluence, both of individuals and of households. The results of the most recent marketing surveys are summarized in Table 11.1. These surveys find lesbian and gay households with much higher income levels than the typical U.S. family. Also, members of gay households have been found to have higher levels of education, take more vacations, and have other characteristics desirable to advertisers who are seeking out new niche markets for their products.

From a research perspective, the findings of affluence are deeply flawed because of problems in sampling. The methods used to construct samples were likely to attract high-income people, resulting in a biased sample. Data from the marketing firm Overlooked Opinions are pulled together from the firm's samples of lesbians and gay men from various sources, including those attending the 1993 March on Washington. The potential for bias is clear in the use of attendees of the march. Given the expense involved in travel and accommodations, lesbians and gay men with relatively high incomes would have been more likely to attend the march, making the marchers an unrepresentative sample of lesbian and gay America. Even a random sample of marchers would itself be biased toward higher income

Table 11.1. Lesbian, Gay, and Bisexual Household Income in *Nonrandom* **Samples**

SURVEY	YEAR	N	L/G/B HOUSEHOLD INCOME	U.S. HOUSEHOLD INCOME
Overlooked Opinions[1]	1991	7500	42,689 (gay men) 36,072 (lesbians)	30,126
Overlooked Opinions[2]	1991	?	51,325 (gay men) 45,927 (lesbians)	36,520
Simmons Mkt. Research Bureau[3]	1988	?	55,430	32,144

Note: "U.S. Household income" from each source, in US $.

Sources: [1]Cronin, 1993; [2]*Courier-News*, 12/1/91; [3]Rigdon, 1991; Gravois, 1991.

people, given the underlying population—of marchers, not gay people in general—being sampled. The Simmons Market Research Bureau survey sought out gay men and lesbians by placing surveys in gay newspapers and magazines in urban areas. But this method is no more likely to result in a representative sample of gay America than a "national sample" garnered from a survey inserted in the *Wall Street Journal*. Consider a similar example from African Americans, a group known to have lower incomes from reputable government surveys. A Simmons study of readers of *Ebony* and *Jet*, magazines targeted at African Americans, shows that those readers earn 41 to 82 percent more than the typical African American (Badgett, 1997).

To put it simply, research starting with the high-income end of the gay population will show high average incomes. The limitation of this method—and a more accurate economic description of gay people—is also evident from examining four recent surveys that do not share the problem of nonrepresentative samples. These other surveys are based on probability samples of the population (often called "random samples") and include questions about sexual orientation that allow for income comparisons. The four surveys discussed here have different measures of sexual orientation and somewhat different methods of sampling. They share two important characteristics—the use of scientific sampling methods and ways of asking about sexual orientation that are likely to prompt more truthful responses. Unfortunately, they may also share a common problem in that some gay people may not answer questions about sexual orientation truthfully. The effect of this potential misresponse is difficult to predict and depends on whether the misresponse is systematically related to the variables of interest, such as income or children. Where appropriate, the discussion below will consider this issue. (For a further discussion of the effect of misresponse, see Badgett, 1995b.) Finally, in discussing these surveys, it is also important to distinguish individual incomes from household incomes that combine earnings from more than one adult. Close examination of individual incomes often reveals a gap between gay incomes and heterosexual incomes that is obscured when combining two persons' earnings into household income figures.

The first detailed comparison of incomes by sexual orientation was Badgett (1995b), which used data from the 1989–91 General Social Surveys (GSS). The GSS is a national face-to-face survey based on a full probability sample, so that each household in the United States has an equal probability of being surveyed. A self-administered questionnaire asked each respondent to give the number of male and female sex partners since his or her 18th birthday, allowing classification of respondents into sexual orientations based on their adult sexual behavior. In the GSS subsample of full-time workers, 4.6 percent of female respondents could be classified as lesbian or bisexual, and 4.9 percent of male respondents could be classified as gay or bisexual. On average, individual lesbians earned $15,056 per year, while heterosexual women earned $18,341. Gay men averaged $26,321, compared to the $28,312 averaged by heterosexual men. After controlling for individual differences in education, experience, occupation, marital status, race, and urban and regional residence, gay and bisexual people working full time still earned less than heterosexual people working full time. Gay or bisexual men earned as much as 27 percent less than similarly qualified heterosexual men. Lesbian or bisexual women also earned less than heterosexual women in this sample, but that difference was not statistically significant. In other words, such a wage gap could occur in a sample of women by chance, and a different sample might show no difference.

The Yankelovich Monitor is a face-to-face survey of attitudes and demographics given to a national probability sample. In 1993, this survey asked respondents, "Which of the following words or phrases describe you?" Respondents called out a code for any personal characteristics from a list of 50 possibilities printed on a card, which included "idealistic," "competitive," "a leader," and "gay, lesbian or homosexual." From the 2,503 total respondents, Yankelovich found 143 respondents (5.7 percent who self-identified as "gay, lesbian, or homosexual." The household incomes of those gay men and lesbians were statistically indistinguishable from the incomes of heterosexual households: heterosexual men averaged $39,300 in their households, while gay men averaged $37,400 (Lukenbill, 1995). Heterosexual women reported an average of $34,400, just under the average lesbian household income of $34,800.

Another source of data is voter exit polls that include questions on sexual orientation and family income. Voters were randomly selected when leaving the polling place in 1992 and were asked to fill out an anonymous questionnaire, which they then placed in a box. One question was, "Do any of the following apply to you," followed by a list of nine descriptors such as "first-time voter," "Born-again Christian/Fundamentalist," or "gay/lesbian/bisexual." Respondents answered by checking a box for yes or no. Although those voters were not representative of the larger U.S. population, as voters are better educated and have higher incomes than nonvoters, there is no reason to think that gay voters are systematically different from heterosexual voters in terms of income. Of the 15,000 voters randomly surveyed in 1992, 466 self-identified as gay, lesbian, or bisexual (3 percent). Comparisons of family income by sexual orientation presented in Table 11.2 show that gay voters tended to be in lower family income categories than heterosexual voters.

Although no official government surveys ask for respondents' sexual orientation, the 1990 census allowed unmarried people to indicate if they had an "unmarried partner" as well as the gender of that partner. Thus we can identify men who have male partners and women who have female partners, whom we might reasonably presume to be lesbian, gay, or bisexual. Unfortunately, the census form did not ask unpartnered lesbian or gay people any identifying questions, and suspicions of a serious undercount seem reasonable given that very few people indicated a same-sex partner

Table 11.2. Lesbian, Gay, and Bisexual Family Income in Voter Exit Polls

FAMILY INCOME	GAY MEN (%)	ALL MEN (%)	LESBIANS (%)	ALL WOMEN (%)
Less than $15,000	18	12	26	16
$15,000–30,000	26	23	26	25
$30,000–50,000	28	30	29	29
$50,000–75,000	16	20	12	19
More than $75,000	12	14	6	11

Source: Cronin, 1993.

(only 0.16 percent of all households). Those concerns notwithstanding, in the census the average female same-sex couple's income was $45,166, male same-sex couples received $58,366, and married couples averaged $47,193 (Klawitter & Flatt, 1996). Therefore, the census data findings for gay men seem closer to the findings of the market surveys summarized in Table 11.1. But Klawitter and Flatt also performed a more detailed analysis of the census data, comparing *individuals* in same-sex couples to married individuals and controlling for differences in education, location, racial or ethnic status, age, disability status, language, and children. In their expanded analysis, they observed a pattern similar to my GSS findings: the men in same-sex couples earned less than married men, but full-time working women in same-sex couples did not differ in earnings from married women.

Overall, the conclusions about the economic status of gay and lesbian households crucially depend on the source of data. Evidence from methodologically flawed samples gives a very different picture from more statistically appropriate samples. Using appropriate data, lesbian and gay households appear to be similar to heterosexual households. Indeed, the gay households may be disadvantaged because the individuals within them face the threat of unfair treatment in the labor market and might end up with lower individual contributions to their households.

Incorrect and Incomplete Assumptions About Gay Family Structure

The second source of confusion about the economic status of gay families derives from underlying assumptions about the nature of these households. In particular, two major problems are apparent in public discussions: (1) an incomplete understanding of the importance of gender in determining household income, and (2) the assumption that, unlike the typical heterosexual family, the typical gay family or household contains no children.

The gender issue is obviously related to the household income question raised above. Because the average woman working full time in the United States earns about 71 percent of a man's income (Economic Report of the President, 1994), gender differences in household composition are crucial.

And the fact that women are less likely to work at all and to work full time increases the gender gap in overall earnings. In 1989, 76 percent of men but only 57 percent of women in the United States were either employed or looking for work (Economic Report of the President, 1994). Of those working, 7 percent of men and roughly 23 percent of women were working part-time (Mishel & Bernstein, 1993). As a result, any household with two average male earners will earn more than a married couple or a two-woman couple, even if both members of the heterosexual or lesbian couple work full time.

The impact of gender composition can be seen using the census data because the census is the one more reliable survey showing higher incomes for male same-sex couples. Table 11.3 shows both average household incomes and average individual earnings. Male same-sex couples had higher incomes than married couples, while female same-sex couples had lower household incomes than either male couples or married couples. But disaggregating household incomes into individual earnings components removes the gay male advantage and demonstrates that male same-sex couples earn more than married couples because men earn much more than women. When Klawitter and Flatt (1996) controlled for differences in household members' education and other relevant factors, they found that the income advantage for male same-sex couples disappears. Thus, the alleged advantage of male couples is purely a gender composition effect, disguising the underlying disadvantage faced by individual gay men. Many commentators conveniently ignore this gender effect when they want to "prove" that gay households are economically better off than heterosexual households (e.g., Duncan & Young, 1995: 100). And the apparent individual lesbian advantage in Table 11.3 reflects the higher rate of labor-force participation and more working time by lesbians. Klawitter (1995) found that women in same-sex couples worked more hours and more weeks per year than did married women. In the voter exit polls, 49 percent of heterosexual women worked full time while 56 percent of lesbians did (Badgett, 1994).

The other major misconception in discussions of gay families and households is that gay families are childless. The prevalence of this assumption

Table 11.3. Average Household Incomes and Individual Earnings from the 1990 U.S. Census of Population

		Couples	Men	Women
L/G/B	Male	$58,366	$23,037	
	Female	$45,166		$17,497
Heterosexual (married)		$47,193	$24,949	$ 9,308

Note: Individual averages do not add up to the couple average because household income includes sources of income other than earnings.

Source: Klawitter & Flatt, 1995.

probably stems from a naive biological determinism that assumes only opposite-sex couples could directly produce offspring and, perhaps, from a heterosexist perspective that only opposite-sex couples *should* produce offspring. Whatever its source, the childlessness assumption ignores the personal histories of many lesbian or gay individuals, as shown in the other chapters in this volume.

A more sophisticated version of the childlessness assumption suggests that while some gay couples might have children from past heterosexual relationships or from using alternative reproductive technologies, a smaller proportion of gay families than heterosexual families will include children. This argument highlights the relative difficulties involved in conceiving a child for lesbians or of "producing" a child (for instance, with a surrogate mother) to raise for gay men. (This perspective probably overestimates the difficulties for lesbians, given multiple possible sources of sperm; see Patterson, 1994). In addition, lesbians and gay men often face formal and informal biases in the adoption of children. Ultimately, the number of gay families with children is an empirical question.

Unfortunately, the same empirical problems that arise when measuring household income are present in estimating the number of children of gay men or lesbians. Without a representative sample, reliable conclusions are unlikely. Three surveys discussed earlier, the Voter Research and Surveys (VRS), Yankelovich Monitor, and 1990 census provide some insight into the number of children in lesbians' and gay men's households and are summarized in Table 11.4. The first two surveys found that the proportion of lesbian households with children is roughly equal to the proportion of children in heterosexual women's households (Badgett, 1994; Lukenbill, 1995). In the VRS, 31 percent of lesbians and 37 percent of heterosexual women had children under 18 in their households. In the Yankelovich Monitor, 67 percent

Table 11.4. Proportion of Lesbians and Gay Men with Children

	Lesbians (%)	Heterosexual Women (%)	Gay Men (%)	Heterosexual Men (%)
Yankelovich[1]				
Children in household	32	36	15	28
Parents	67	72	27	60
Voter Exit Poll[2]				
Children in household	31	37	22.5	32.5

	Lesbians	Married couples	Gay Men
1990 Census[3]	20	57	5

Note: Differences between lesbians and heterosexual women are not statistically significant; differences between gay men and heterosexual men are statistically significant.

Sources: [1]Lukenbill, 1995; [2]Badgett, 1994; [3]Klawitter & Flatt, 1996.

of lesbians and 72 percent of heterosexual women were parents; 32 percent of lesbians and 36 percent of heterosexual women had children under 18 in the household (Lukenbill, 1995: 97). For women, the differences in both surveys are not statistically significant. The picture is very different for men, however. Only 22.5 percent of the gay men in the VRS had children under 18 in the household, while 32.5 percent of heterosexual men did; and 15 percent of gay men in the Yankelovich Monitor reported children while 28 percent of heterosexual men did. The Yankelovich data also showed that 27 percent of gay men were parents compared to 60 percent of heterosexual men. The differences between gay and heterosexual men are statistically significant. Using the 1990 census data, Klawitter and Flatt (1996) found fewer same-sex households with children: 20 percent of female couples and 5 percent of male couples reported children, compared to 57 percent of married couples. This difference could reflect the exclusion of single lesbians and gay men or a different reporting pattern. For instance, same-sex couples with children might have been more fearful that disclosing their relationship on a government-sponsored survey could result in custody challenges.

The wording of the question about children in these surveys is important in interpreting these findings. The question does not allow for distinctions between the respondent's biological or adopted children, children for whom the respondent has legal responsibility, and the biological or adopted children of another household member. In other words, the respondent's level of child-raising responsibility is uncertain. For instance, is the respondent a legal parent, a co-parent, or a roommate with no lasting attachment to the child? Further, we do not know whether the child is the product (in its various meanings) of a heterosexual relationship or of a homosexual relationship. And finally, except for the Yankelovich findings, we know nothing about children residing outside the respondent's household. This last issue is especially important since lesbians and gay men who have children from prior heterosexual marriages face difficulties getting and maintaining custody of such children (Editors of Harvard Law Review, 1990: 120–121). However, they may continue to bear considerable financial responsibility for these children.

In spite of these caveats, the data on children are a striking reminder that conventional images of gay families are limited. The fact that so many lesbian and gay households contain children suggests, at the very least, that individual lesbians and gay men have some interaction with children on a regular basis, even if the gay adult is not a parent or co-parent. And while the quality of that interaction is unknown, it seems reasonable to suppose that adults who are present in children's households will exert influence over children. This parenting may range from minimal child care to serving as significant role models to sharing equally in child rearing, as it does in other families. Thus even without knowing more about the relationships, we can assume that many gay people have some responsibility in the upbringing of children.

The Impact of Public Policy and Legal Institutions

The final general problem with public discussions of gay families is the failure to place gay families in the context of legal and economic institutions. Thinking about gay families as abstractions or just comparing household incomes overlooks important questions of differential access to economic resources, such as jobs and benefits, and to legal institutions that confer advantages, such as marriage. If we want to know about the overall economic position of lesbians' and gay men's families, we must consider the impact of institutions on economic status and on family behavior.

One important difference concerns the labor market's treatment of lesbians and gay men. Two of the income studies cited earlier (Badgett, 1995b; Klawitter & Flatt, 1996) found that gay men (and possibly lesbians) have lower earnings than heterosexuals after controlling for education, age, experience, location, race, and gender. Why should that difference exist? Labor economists and sociologists generally conclude that discrimination is present if observably similar people have different earnings levels (Cain, 1986), suggesting that the studies are documenting discrimination against lesbian, gay, and bisexual people. Other evidence of discrimination comes from surveys of self-identified lesbians and gay men who report losing jobs or promotions because of their sexual orientation (Badgett, Donnelly, & Kibbe, 1992). Some employers readily admit that they would discriminate against employees or job applicants known to be gay (Brause, 1989). Such discrimination is possible because employment discrimination against lesbian, gay, and bisexual people is illegal in only eleven states (Hawaii, California, Wisconsin, Maine, Minnesota, New Hampshire, New Jersey, Rhode Island, Connecticut, Massachusetts, Vermont) and the District of Columbia, and in some local jurisdictions, demonstrating the lack of a public policy consensus on the importance of equal treatment in the workplace. The fact that many gay, lesbian, and bisexual people might experience discrimination and have no legal recourse diminishes not only a gay family's current household income and economic standing but their job security and their ability to plan for the future.

Other differences derived from public policy treatment are also related to a family's economic well-being, the most important difference probably being the inability of same-sex couples to marry legally. Because, as Posner (1992) states, "marriage is a status rich in entitlements," the prohibition of same-sex marriage deprives same-sex couples (and other family configurations) of many economic resources (see LaCroix & Badgett, 1995), such as

- Social Security benefits for "spouses" who are not eligible for their own Social Security benefits (in 1993 this averaged $347 per month, plus survivors' benefits if the insured spouse dies first)
- Possible tax benefits, including the use of a potentially more advantageous tax schedule, claiming an exemption for a spouse, and ex-

cluding an employer's payment of a spouse's health insurance benefits from taxable income (payments for domestic partners' benefits are taxable)

- Various income security–related benefits, including the ability to sue for wrongful death of a spouse
- Lower transaction costs for establishing certain aspects of a relationship, such as rights of inheritance, division of property if the relationship ends, or designating someone to make important decisions on an incapacitated individual's behalf
- Valuable benefits extended to spouses by custom, especially employer-provided health and pension coverage
- Discounts related to marital status on other privately provided goods and services, such as lower auto insurance rates

Many other benefits exist that cannot be readily valued in dollar terms, such as hospital visitation rights, the right to live in residential areas zoned for "families," preferences for spouses in immigration quotas, or rights with respect to adopting children (Duclos, 1993). These benefits are clearly important to couples despite the uncertainty of their economic value. Of course, marriage also comes with some potential economic "costs" for individuals, including some disadvantageous income tax situations and obligations for support (Duclos, 1993: 166), although some see the support obligations as a benefit as well. But at least opposite-sex couples inclined toward a cost-benefit approach to marriage can make economically rational choices based on their own situations.

Although some of those benefits might be created by same-sex couples through written contracts or through the recognition of same-sex domestic partnerships, those extensions are very limited. In the case of contracts, marriagelike agreements about the intermingling of finances and assets can be drawn up and might specify the division of property if the relationships ends. Partners can draw up wills designating the other as an heir and can give powers of attorney to a partner in case of incapacitation. But in all of these cases, such documents are costly and depend on a couple's understanding the need for such documentation and their access to knowledgeable attorneys. Furthermore, such agreements may be subject to court challenges (Editors of Harvard Law Review, 1990: 113–114). Domestic partnership registries sometimes give partners public hospital or prison visitation rights (Gossett, 1994), but registered partners do not receive any of the more economically valuable benefits such as health insurance unless one of the partners is a public employee of a jurisdiction providing domestic partner benefits. (For instance, employees of the City of New York must register their domestic partnerships at City Hall to be eligible for employment benefits for their partners.)

The lack of access to the many economic benefits of marriage puts gay and lesbian couples and their families at a disadvantage relative to similar heterosexual married couples and their families. Aside from the direct impact of the above benefits on the well-being of families, economic theory suggests further effects of institutions like marriage on economic behavior in the family, specifically with respect to the household division of labor, family stability, and fertility (Badgett, 1995a; Becker, 1991). The adaptations by lesbians and gay men to their inability to marry might result in further disadvantages that are economic in nature (i.e., dealing with the production and allocation of goods and services), but are not immediately apparent in data on incomes or from access to employer-provided health-care benefits.

An analysis of these less obvious disadvantages for gay families is strengthened by considering a common economic model of the family (Becker, 1991). In this model, the family produces (and consumes) goods and services, either directly producing them in the home (meals and child care) or by working in the wage labor market and buying products with earned income. In an economically rational household that is attempting to maximize its overall material and psychic well-being, members will specialize in tasks for which they are relatively well suited. Being "well suited" to a task might mean having skills as a result of biology, formal training, or socialization (a kind of informal training). External market conditions will also be important by informing household members of the value of their services in terms of wage income. In a household with a male-female couple, Becker (1991) predicts that the biological ability to bear and breastfeed children, plus labor market discrimination against women, will give women a relative advantage in domestic work. Men, whose reproductive services are more limited and whose wages are higher, will have a relative advantage in market work. This kind of decision making, Becker argues, explains the traditional division of labor in heterosexual families where women work in the home and men in the wage labor market.

Others such as Bergmann (1986) have argued, in contrast, that the observed division of labor between men and women in heterosexual families can be better explained by the existence of powerful norms about appropriate gender behavior. Indeed, it is difficult to distinguish empirically between the norm model and the economic efficiency model, and perhaps both factors are relevant for heterosexual families. (For lesbian or gay male couples, a difference in gender norms would not be expected to play much, if any, role in the household division of labor; see Kurdek, 1995.) Furthermore, economically "rational" calculations might only partly explain the decision-making process of actual families, but the impact of these considerations makes them worthy of attention for lesbian and gay families, as well as for heterosexual families. The role of economic efficiency is likely to be apparent in making decisions about such matters as who will take an unpaid parental leave to care for a new child or whether a family should move if one partner is offered a lucrative job elsewhere.

The institution of marriage encourages the household division of labor in several ways. One obvious issue for an individual considering the economic rationality of specialization in either home or market work concerns the possible dissolving of the household. Specialization means that one could be left single with a set of skills valuable in the home context but not in the labor market. One possible solution is to create a long-term agreement between the parties. Becker (1991), in fact, defines marriage as "a written, oral, or customary long-term contract between a man and a woman to produce children, food, and other commodities in a common household" (p. 43). And divorce laws, in theory at least, can take specialization into account through alimony or property settlements. From the contractual perspective, marriage enhances a couple's willingness to specialize and take advantage of economic efficiencies of larger households, enhancing economic well-being. This creates a further disadvantage for gay or lesbian couples. Their relative abilities might make specialization advantageous, but they cannot make such a contract because of the uncertainty about its enforceability.

Many of the economic benefits of marriage create additional incentives to specialize. The federal income tax code, for instance, favors married couples that specialize (Nelson, 1991). The so-called marriage penalty actually only penalizes *nontraditional* marriages. The penalty arises when members of a couple earn roughly similar money incomes, resulting in their paying more in total taxes than would two unmarried individuals with the same incomes. A traditional married couple with a wife working in the home and a husband in the paid labor market actually receives a marriage "bonus" in the form of lower taxes than they would pay as two individuals (Feenberg & Rosen, 1995). The employment benefits often provided to married employees further enable specialization. A member of a married couple who decides to work at home is likely to still have some form of health insurance through a spouse's employment, but very few partners of employed lesbians or gay men would have the same advantage if working at home. And, finally, other benefits of marriage described earlier provide similar incentives to specialize, such as the Social Security spousal benefit.

Some might argue that specialization is itself either undesirable or increasingly impractical in the current economy. The second objection certainly appears to be true (Mishel & Bernstein, 1993) and the first is at least arguable. The point is not to celebrate a pattern of lifelong specialization, but to suggest that the *terms of choice* among desired household arrangements are unequal. A lesbian who wants to work in the home either does so under unequal terms or decides that she and her partner cannot afford to do so given possible career risks or health insurance considerations, for instance. This difference in available options hinders a same-sex couple's ability to choose an economically enhancing household arrangement, another institutional disadvantage for gay families. The influence of these different constraints and incentives is apparent in the higher labor-force participation of lesbians compared to heterosexual women.

A final effect of prohibiting same-sex marriage is exacerbating the difficulties for lesbians and gay men to be engaged in child rearing. (See Martin and Patterson, this volume.) For instance, lesbians and gay men face problems adopting children because of their single status and because of their sexual orientation. Furthermore, the legal institution of parenthood is as much rooted in marriage as in biology. In a 1989 decision, *Michael H. v. Gerald D.*, the U.S. Supreme Court upheld a California law presuming that a baby born in wedlock is the biological child of the husband. (While such a principle could be revisited by the Supreme Court should same-sex couples win the right to marry, it is hard to imagine a scenario in which marriage would result in a worse situation than gay people currently face with regard to children.) Given the legal problems and the uncertainty of whether parents will be seen as having legal parental rights, lesbians and gay men who are willing and able to make the *same* sacrifices as heterosexuals to raise children will not be able to do so because of legal constraints or because the actual tradeoff faced by potential gay parents is very different. In mainstream economic terms, the "demand curve" for children could be the same for lesbians, gay men, bisexuals, and heterosexuals, but gay people will have fewer children because of the higher price of conceiving, adopting, and raising children. The resulting uncertainty about parental rights to make decisions for children or to have visitation and custody rights is matched by uncertainty about obligations to provide for children, reducing the economic security of children who do not have guaranteed access to two parents' income or health-care coverage if the parents' relationship ends. Again, this reduction of choice for gay families puts such families—adults and children—at a disadvantage relative to married couples and other heterosexual families.

Directions for Future Research

The picture sketched out in this chapter should be thought of as a starting point for a realistic and accurate analysis of the economic position and challenges of families formed by lesbians and gay men rather than the final word on the subject. Considerably more research will be necessary to develop a clearer sense of where and why gay families are distributed across the range of economic well-being measures. The biggest challenge for future research, however, will be in obtaining the kind of data necessary to analyze subtle questions: large-scale probability samples. Larger data sets will be necessary to examine more closely the impact of race and ethnicity on gay families' economic position. Similarly, understanding the economic challenges of low-income gay families—a group invisible in almost all studies of gay families—requires a much larger sample size (or targeted oversampling) than is available in existing surveys that include questions on sexual orientation.

Unfortunately, most surveys of very large samples are usually conducted by the federal government. My own preliminary efforts to lobby government statisticians have revealed many barriers to convincing government agencies to include questions on sexual orientation on their surveys, including political fear, political biases, and methodological ignorance. Overcoming these barriers will require an intensive effort by social scientists from across the disciplinary spectrum who can apply their experience in collecting and analyzing survey data on sexual orientation to convincing government officials that it can and should be done on a larger scale. Until then, the smaller scale data sets that are privately collected or are under less federal control are researchers' best bets. In addition to the data sources described in this chapter, researchers should urge their data-collecting colleagues to include questions on sexual orientation whenever possible.

A second research challenge comes in expanding our ideas of how families are configured. Even the expanded image of gay families sketched out here overlooks the multiplicity of family structures present in the lesbian, gay, and bisexual communities. Weston (1991) studied what she termed "families we choose" of gay people, which showed considerable variability in structure. Such gay families might include a lesbian couple and a gay male couple raising children together. Or they might not be based on couples at all, with groups of friends, ex-lovers, and even biological kin forming families. Similarly, Nardi (1992) notes, "For gay people, friends often provide the role of maintaining physical and emotional well-being, especially when difficulties arise when soliciting social support from their families and other kin" (p. 110)

But relatively little is known about these other variations of gay family structure. To a certain extent, they may be adaptations to the economic, social, and emotional requirements of the people involved. Or they might be responses to increasing external economic stress that could not be met by the more traditional two-adult economic and social unit. For instance, Stacey (1992) found that the notion of "family" among working-class people in Silicon Valley has expanded beyond the nuclear family to include ex-spouses, adult children, and neighbors from other households. She argued that these developments stem from the decline of the welfare state, increased economic insecurity, and the need for multiple earner families. Those families, unfortunately, fall completely out of the view of standard large-scale surveys and are rarely directly contemplated in public policy discussions. Indeed, it is difficult to know exactly how social scientists should measure the economic well-being of these alternative family structures or what policies would be necessary to support such families. The invisibility of such families in existing research suggests a fruitful area of future research, one that would be enhanced by expanding survey sampling units to allow families to cross households.

A third general area for future research effort seeks a deeper understanding of the economic position of gay families by asking basic questions, perhaps starting with questions asked of heterosexual families: Why do individuals form families? Why are some couples' relationships more stable than others? What determines why, how, and when families raise children? How do individuals decide to enter the labor market, and how does discrimination affect their financial contribution to the family? How do family members divide household responsibilities? What should the role of the state be with regard to gay families? These are questions that economists have only begun to ask about lesbian, gay, and bisexual people and their families, but psychologists, sociologists, and anthropologists have been working on these issues longer. Economists can contribute an analysis of the material incentives and constraints to this larger discussion.

And finally, a focus on economics also allows for ready applications to policy questions. For instance, what happens to the economic position of a lesbian couple engaged in a child custody dispute? What happens to a gay family if a judge makes child custody contingent on the partner of the biological parent moving out of the household? Or consider the question of alternative formal definitions of relationships, such as same-sex marriage or domestic partnership. What are the larger effects of these policies on family structure and decision making'? Will the larger "families we choose" disappear when gay couples are legally and socially recognized? Will the number of domestic partners taking advantage of partner benefits increase over time as gay families adapt to this new opportunity? Although these questions focus on economic behavior and measures, any analysis of the underlying behavioral and social processes at work would benefit greatly from interdisciplinary research projects.

Such research projects will add depth to the emerging picture of gay families. As this chapter has shown, reconsidering the economic status of lesbians' and gay men's families using more scientifically sound data and in the context of legal institutions provides a different description from the stereotype of an affluent, consumer-oriented gay population. The image that emerges is both familiar and unexpected. Families with children being raised by one or two parents are, of course, quite familiar in the United States. And families with children are likely to share the same hopes and fears for their children, including concerns about their intellectual and moral development. Families without children are also fairly common in the United States. Most families, with or without children, face the same worries about paying bills, keeping jobs, creating homes, and providing for old age. But gay families face all of these challenges with added burdens such as the threat of employment or housing discrimination, potentially lower individual and/or family incomes, uncertainty about parenting arrangements, diminished flexibility in allocation of household members' time, and exclusion from most public policies supporting families. An accurate understanding of gay families must include these disadvantages.

Such an understanding is required for discussion of policies that will influence gay families in the future.

References

Badgett, M. V. L. (1994, October). Civil rights and civilized research: Constructing a sexual orientation nondiscrimination policy based on the evidence. Paper presented at Annual Research Conference, Association for Public Policy Analysis and Management, Chicago, IL.

Badgett, M. V. L. (1995a). Gender, sexuality, and sexual orientation: All in the feminist family? *Feminist Economics, 1*(1), 121–139.

Badgett, M. V. L. (1995b). The wage effects of sexual orientation discrimination. *Industrial and Labor Relations Review, 49*(4), 726–738.

Badgett, M. V. L. (1997). Beyond biased samples: Challenging the myths on the economic status of lesbians and gay men. In A. Gluckman & B. Reed (Eds.), *Homo economics.* New York: Routledge.

Badgett, L, Donnelly, C., & Kibbe, J. (1992). Pervasive patterns of discrimination against lesbians and gay men: Evidence from surveys across the United States. Washington, DC: National Gay and Lesbian Task Force Policy Institute.

Becker, G. (1991). *Treatise on the family,* Cambridge, MA: Harvard University Press.

Bergmann, B. (1986). *The economic emergence of women.* New York: Basic Books.

Brause, J. (1989). Closed doors: Sexual orientation bias in the Anchorage housing and employment markets. In *Identity reports: Sexual orientation bias in Alaska,* Anchorage, AK: Identity Incorporated.

Broadus, J. (1994, July 29). Statement before the Committee on Labor and Human Resources, U.S. Senate, on S. 2238, the Employment Non-Discrimination Act.

Cain, G. G. (1986). The economic analysis of labor market discrimination: A survey. In O. Ashenfelter and R. Layard, (Ed.), *Handbook of labor economics, 1.* New York: Elsevier Science Publishers.

Cronin, A. (1993, June 27). Two viewfinders, two pictures of gay America. *New York Times,* section 4, p. 16.

Courier-News (Bridgewater). (1991, Dec. l). Companies aim for gay market.

Duclos, N. (1993). Some complicating thoughts on same-sex marriage. In M. Minow (Ed.), *Family matters: Readings on family lives and the law.* New York: New Press.

Duncan, R. F., & Young, G. L. (1995). Homosexual rights and citizen initiatives: Is constitutionalism unconstitutional? *Notre Dame Journal of Law, Ethics, and Public Policy, 9,* 93–135.

Economic Report of the President (1994). Washington, DC: U.S. Government Printing Office.

Editors of the Harvard Law Review. (1990). *Sexual orientation and the law.* Cambridge, MA: Harvard University Press.

Feenberg, D. R., & Rosen, H. S. (1995). Recent developments in the marriage tax. *National Tax Journal, 48*(1), 91–101.

Gossett, C. (1994). Domestic partnership benefits. *Review of Public Personnel Administration, 14*(1), 64–84.

Gravois, M. (1991, Nov. 7). President, Rivendell Marketing Company. Personal communication.

Klawitter, M. (1995, April). Did they find each other or create each other? Labor market linkages between partners in same-sex and different-sex couples. Presented at Annual Meeting of Population Association of America, San Francisco, CA.

Klawitter, M., & Flatt, V (1996). The effects of state and local antidiscrimination policies for sexual orientation. Unpublished manuscript, Graduate School of Public Affairs, University of Washington.

Knight, R. H., & Garcia, D. S. (1994). Homosexual adoption: Bad for children, bad for society. *Insight,* Family Research Council, Washington, DC.

Kurdek, L. (1995). Lesbian and gay couples. In A. R. D'Augelli & C. J. Patterson (Eds.), *Lesbian, gay, and bisexual identities over the lifespan* (pp. 243–261). New York: Oxford University Press

LaCroix, S. J., & Badgett, L. (1995). A brief analysis of important economic benefits accruing from same-sex marriage. Revised testimony before Commission on Sexual Orientation and the Law, State of Hawaii.

Lewin, E. (1993). *Lesbian mothers. Accounts of gender in the American culture,* Ithaca, NY: Cornell University Press.

Lukenbill, G. (1995). *Untold millions.* New York: Harper Business.

Mishel, L., & Bernstein, J. (1993). *The state of working America, 1992–93.* Armonk, NY: M. E. Sharpe.

Nardi, P. M. (1992). That's what friends are for: Friends as family in the gay and lesbian community. In K. Plummer (Ed.), *Modern homosexualities* (pp. 108–120). New York: Routledge.

Nelson, J. (1991). Tax reform and feminist theory in the United States: Incorporating human connection. *Journal of Economic Studies, 18*(5/6), 11–29.

Patterson, C. T. (1994). Lesbian and gay couples considering parenthood: An agenda for research, service, and advocacy. *Journal of Gay and Lesbian Social Services, 1,* 33–55.

Posner, R. (1992). *Sex and reason.* Cambridge, MA: Harvard University Press.

Rigdon, J. E. (1991, July 18). Overcoming a deep-rooted reluctance, more firms advertise to gay community, *Wall Street Journal,* pages B1–B2.

Rubenstein, W. B. (Ed.) (1993). *Lesbians, gay men, and the law.* New York: New Press.

Stacey, J. (1992). Backward toward the postmodern family: Reflections on gender, kinship, and class in the Silicon Valley. In B. Thorne & M. Yalom (Eds.), *Rethinking the family. Some feminist questions,* revised ed. (pp. 91–118), Boston: Northeastern University Press.

Weston, K. (1991). *Families we choose: Lesbian, gays, kinship.* New York: Columbia University Press.

12

Cultural Heterosexism and the Family

J. Roy Gillis

Heterosexism has been defined as "an ideological system that denies, denigrates, and stigmatizes any non-heterosexual form of behavior, identity, relationship or community" (Herek, 1992: 89). Cultural heterosexism represents the manifestation of this ideological system in societal customs and institutions (Herek, 1992). As a consequence of cultural heterosexism, homosexuality has traditionally remained hidden in American society, and gay men, lesbians, and bisexual people continue to be objects of ridicule and scorn. This invisibility has resulted, in part, in a proliferation of myths in society that result in the association of negative characteristics with lesbians, gay men, and bisexual people. Like other unpopular groups in society, gay men, lesbians, and bisexual people have been variously stereotyped as "anti-family, sexually deviant, gender role deviant, mentally ill, and subversive" (Diamond, 1995; Herek, 1996a). The characterization of gay men, lesbians, and bisexual people as threats to the traditional family has been a prominent, and politically effective, strategy of conservative Christians (Diamond, 1995). The so-called threat to the traditional family posed by lesbians, gay men, and bisexual people has been used most recently to pass anticipatory federal legislation that would prohibit the recognition of same-sex marriages by individual states should a favorable ruling be obtained in the current court case in Hawaii (Baker, 1996; Ad Touts Clinton's, 1996).

A consensus is beginning to emerge from theory, clinical experience, and empirical investigations about the cumulative impact of negative life experiences on the lives of lesbians, gay men, and bisexual people. Some of the consequences of cultural heterosexism such as discrimination, and hate crimes have been studied for their effects on the lives of adult lesbians, gay men, and bisexual people (Cogan, 1996; Herek, 1995; in press; Herek, Gillis, Cogan, & Glunt, in press), and gay, lesbian, and bisexual youth (Martin &

Hetrick, 1987; Hunter & Schaecher, 1987; Rotheram-Borus, Reid, Rosario, VanRossem, & Gillis, 1995; Zera, 1992). However, this line of research that recognizes the negative impact of cultural heterosexism could not have developed without the influence of the gay and lesbian liberation movement. The success of the modern lesbian, gay, and bisexual liberation movement (see Altman, 1982; Adam, 1995, for excellent reviews) led to changes in laws regarding same sex behavior, and provoked reconsideration of the mental illness explanation of homosexuality. In this chapter, I will cite modern examples of cultural heterosexism, explore some of the societal roots of cultural heterosexism, review some longitudinal data suggesting changes in attitudes toward lesbian, bisexual, and gay people, and offer some direction for research aimed at reducing cultural heterosexism.

Contemporary Heterosexism

A major victory for the early gay, lesbian, and bisexual movement occurred in 1973, when the Trustees of the American Psychiatric Association endorsed the following motion removing homosexuality from the diagnostic nomenclature of the *Diagnostic and Statistical Manual of Mental Disorders-Version II*:

> Whereas homosexuality in and of itself implies no impairment in judgment, stability, reliability or vocational capabilities, therefore, be it resolved, that the American Psychiatric Association deplores all public and private discrimination against homosexuals in such areas as employment, housing, public accommodation, and licensing, and declares that no burden of proof of such judgment, capacity, or reliability shall be placed upon homosexuals greater than that imposed on any other persons. Further, the APA supports and urges the enactment of civil rights legislation at local, state, and federal levels that would insure homosexual citizens the same protections now guaranteed to others. Further, the APA supports and urges the repeal of all legislation making criminal offenses of sexual acts performed by consenting adults in private. (Bayer, 1981: 137)

However, despite this decision by the American Psychiatric Association to remove homosexuality from the *DSM-II*, there are still psychiatrists and psychologists who hold that homosexuality represents psychopathology. These individuals actively promote a pathological model of homosexuality, and claim that gays, lesbians, and bisexual people can be cured (e.g., Nicolosi, & Freeman, 1993; Socarides, & Volkan, 1991). Others with overtly political agendas dedicate their efforts to publish and distribute misleading information about gays, lesbians, and bisexual people (e.g., Cameron, & Cameron, 1995; Cameron, Playfair, & Wellum, 1994, Cameron, Proctor, Coburn, & Forde, 1986; Pietrzyk, 1994).

Coincident with these changes in societal and institutional responses to lesbians, gay men, and bisexual people, the early 1980s saw the emergence in the United States of the AIDS epidemic among urban gay men living in New York, San Francisco, and Los Angeles. The early government response to the AIDS epidemic was characterized by a denial of the scale of the problem and a refusal by then President Reagan to even mention the word *AIDS* in any public speeches (Shilts, 1987). Since the early groups identified as affected by AIDS included gay men and intravenous drug users, right-wing Christian groups were quick to attribute AIDS to the "wrath of God," who was punishing these groups, especially gay men, for their sinful behavior (Diamond, 1995; Herek, in press; Herek & Glunt, 1988). Despite clear indications of prejudice toward gay and bisexual men with AIDS (Herek, in press), the overall influence of the AIDS epidemic on societal attitudes toward gay men, lesbians, and bisexual people has been hard to measure (Herek, in press). A 1985 Gallup poll on the effect of the AIDS epidemic on the general public's view of lesbians, gay men, and bisexual people constitutes some hard data on the issue (Gallup, 1986). When asked "Would you say the AIDS epidemic has changed your opinion about homosexuals for the better, for the worse, or has it not made any difference in the way you feel?", 59 percent indicated it had made no difference, 37 percent indicated their opinion changed for the worse, and only 2 percent indicated that it changed their opinion changed for the better (Gallup, 1986).

Another major setback for the lesbian, gay, and bisexual movement came in 1985 with the Supreme Court decision in *Bowers v. Hardwick*, which upheld the right of states to prohibit specific types of consensual sexual behavior—specifically in this case, anal and oral sexual intercourse (sodomy). A subsequent Gallup poll in July 1986 revealed that 51 percent of the general public approved of the intent of this ruling (Gallup, 1987). As of June 1995, there were twenty states with fully enforceable laws prohibiting consensual sodomy (oral and anal sex) (Eskridge, 1996). Though sixteen of these states also prohibit consensual nonmarried heterosexual oral and anal sexual activities, the laws have most frequently been used to intimidate gay men, lesbians, and bisexual people (Eskridge, 1996). However, some hope for progress in the legal arena for gay, lesbian, and bisexual human rights has been engendered by the recent Supreme Court ruling that overturned Colorado's attempt to prohibit local ordinances protecting lesbians, gay men, and bisexual people from discrimination (Sample, 1996).

In our current era, the conservative Christian agenda is still very popular, and it is difficult to avoid hearing the phrase "family values" in any discussion of political or social issues. The decline of "family values" is cited for being responsible for the majority of social ills including unemployment, violent crime, AIDS, women living in poverty, child abuse, sex offenses, and alcoholism. This decline in family values is attributed by conservative and fundamentalist Christian sources (Adam, 1995; Diamond, 1995; Nava & Dawidoff, 1994; Pharr, 1988; Robison, 1980) largely to several forces or groups in society, these often being identified as liberals, feminists, lesbians, gay men, and bisexual people, and big government spending. These groups are characterized as having a primary social agenda to destroy the family (Adam, 1995; Diamond, 1995: Robison, 1980). Feminists are said to be responsible for encouraging women to leave the home, their children, and their spouses, and take jobs in the marketplace instead. This shift to more women in the job market is said to be responsible for increasing divorce rates, child abuse and abandonment, domestic violence, and juvenile delinquency. Likewise, openly gay, lesbian, and bisexual people are said to recruit other individuals and to give the message that homosexuality is an acceptable lifestyle. Homosexuality is variously described by Christian fundamentalists as unnatural, against the Bible, antifamily, a mental illness, immoral, and unhealthy (Adam, 1995; Diamond, 1995; Robison, 1980). Since Christian fundamentalists and many others who condemn lesbians, gay men, and bisexual people cite the Christian Bible as their authority, it is to a consideration of the relevant biblical texts and theological interpretations that we turn next to uncover one of the origins of cultural heterosexism.

Cultural Heterosexism and the Biblical Tradition

Conservative Christians, Jews, and Moslems have traditionally cited eight passages in the Bible as indicating direct condemnation of homosexual activity and, thus, by implication bisexual people, lesbians, and gay men. Consistent with the sexist traditions of the authors of the Bible, only one of the eight passages can be construed as applying to women. These passages are: Deuteronomy 23:17–18 (Revised Standard Edition), which condemns "sodomites", Genesis 19:4–11; Judges 19:22; and Jude 7, which contain the story of the destruction of the city of Sodom whose crime gave rise to the term "sodomite"; Leviticus 18:22, and 20:13, known as the "Holiness Code" which forbids "a man to lie with a man as a woman"; and I Corinthians 6:9, 10 and Timothy 1:10, which have been translated to indicate that homosexuals are among those people who are not, by their actions, part of God's realm. These passages have been used to great advantage by fundamentalist Christians and others to argue against civil rights for lesbians, gay men, and bisexual people. It is also clear that biblical passages and related concepts of "natural law" (Sullivan, 1995) continue to be used to justify discrimination against gay men, lesbians, and bisexual people, as evidenced by the quotation of biblical text in the *Bowers v. Hardwick* Supreme Court decision, and in support of the military's policy ban on lesbians, gay men, and bisexual people in the Armed Services (Shilts, 1993).

General theologians and lesbian, gay, and bisexual scholars have argued that the above biblical passages have been incorrectly translated from original Greek and Hebrew texts, and do not, in fact, refer to homosexual behavior (Boswell, 1980; Jung & Smith, 1993). They also point out that the concept of a gay, lesbian, or bisexual identity, as opposed to homosexual behavior, would be unfamiliar to the authors of the Bible. Jung and Smith

(1993) make the argument that the focus of religious activities around lesbians, gay men, and bisexual people should be to eliminate discrimination and hate crimes, rather than to condemn and stigmatize sexual behavior. They believe that gay, lesbian, and bisexual unions and heterosexual unions must be held to the same standards of faithfulness, love, monogamy, and commitment to be considered valid in the eyes of God. Jung and Smith describe five models of moral positions regarding homosexuality that represent a spectrum of religious views of homosexuality.

The most negative position, endorsed by conservative Christians, Jews, and Moslems, views homosexuality and gay men, lesbians, and bisexual people as possessed of an "unnatural and evil" orientation that developed as a series of immoral choices. Homosexuality, in this view, is giving into a temptation to commit evil behavior. Homosexuality is not an inborn characteristic of the individual, but reflects a misdirection of appropriate life goals. Abstinence is preferable to homosexual behavior, but a faithful heterosexual marriage is the only acceptable life goal.

Another moral position, common among the general population, views homosexuality as an illness (Jung & Smith, 1993). In this model, homosexuality is similar to alcoholism and results in similar negative consequences. Homosexuality is viewed as primarily a disorder, rather than a sin. The abstinence model is endorsed, and expressions of sexuality represent relapse. Advocacy of a gay, lesbian, or bisexual lifestyle is not acceptable. Violence or unwarranted discrimination against lesbians, gay men, and bisexual people, however, is not justified. A different moral position views homosexuality as a serious defect, such as congenital blindness. People do not chose homosexuality, as people do not chose to be blind. Unlike alcoholics, people are not held accountable for their blindness, and it is not seen as a sign of moral weakness. Homosexuality, in this view, would not be a preferred way of living, but the cost associated with lifelong abstinence would be considered too great. Some types of just, loving and faithful homosexual relationships could be permissible (Jung & Smith, 1993).

A more liberal perspective is captured in a fourth model, which views a homosexual orientation as a minor defect, similar to color blindness. Being gay, lesbian, or bisexual, in this view, represents an inferior state of being. Homosexuality is not an ideal orientation, and if treatment were easily available, it should be taken. One cannot be blamed for being lesbian, bisexual or gay because it is simply part of what one is. According to Jung and Smith (1993), advocates of this position would privately support and bless homosexual unions, but would be opposed to civic or ecclesiastical recognition of same-sex unions.

The most gay, lesbian, or bisexual affirmative position described by Jung and Smith (1993) describes homosexual orientations as natural. Advocates of this position view homosexuality as a natural variation, similar to left-handedness. As we currently see nothing wrong or inferior about left-handedness, so we would accept homosexuality. A gay, lesbian, or bisexual orientation represents a gift from God and as such should be celebrated, rather than changed. One would evaluate homosexual behavior and unions with the same norms of justice, love, and fidelity used to evaluate heterosexual behavior and unions (Jung & Smith, 1993).

An additional moral perspective has been offered by Walter L. Williams of the University of Southern California (Williams, 1995). Williams, based on his reviews of cross-cultural research on homosexuality, proposes a model wherein a homosexual orientation is celebrated, and homosexual attraction is valued as a special gift. Expanding this line of thought, the discovery that a family member has a homosexual orientation would be cause for celebration, and would increase the social status of the family under William's model. Homosexual unions and behavior would be seen as sacred, and would serve as a model for heterosexual unions.

Variants of these moral positions on homosexuality are endorsed by the spectrum of Christian, Jewish, and Moslem denominations. The prevalent moral position regarding homosexuality in the denomination guides positions on such issues as whether the denomination welcomes or accepts openly lesbian, gay, or bisexual members; whether gay, lesbian, or bisexual individuals would be suitable clergy, priests, or religious officials; whether same-sex unions can receive ecclesiastical blessing; and whether the denomination supports civil rights legislation for gay men, lesbians, and bisexual people. Understanding the moral position about homosexuality of a denomination is critical because it allows the gay-positive theological, activist, or politician to effectively challenge the belief system of the individual. This point is well stated by the liberal theologians Jung and Smith:

> All who wish to reform Church teachings must recognize that no scientific evidence about the origins and changeability of sexual orientation will solve the normative questions at stake in these deliberations. This evidence *is not relevant* to the questions of whether or not this de facto variation is pathological. The mere existence of a phenomenon or its intractability do not make it natural or normatively human. The reform of any moral tradition will rest on a normative base not disconnected, but clearly distinguishable, from these facts. For Christians, the Bible forms the cornerstone of that base. Thus, the reform of Church teaching regarding human sexuality must find its roots in Scripture. (Jung & Smith, 1993: 63)

Attitudes toward Homosexuality: The Opinion Poll Data

The extent to which these beliefs or attitudes about gay men, lesbians, and bisexual people fostered by Judeo-Christian traditions are endorsed by the general public is one measure of the prevalence of cultural heterosexism in society. Attitude has been defined as "a psychological tendency that is expressed by evaluating a particular entity with some degree of favor or disfavor" (Eagly & Chaiken, 1993: 1). An attitude is an inferred construct characterized by a set of cognitive, affective, and behavioral components toward the attitude object (Eagly & Chaiken, 1993). Attitudes formed on the basis of personal interactions with the target group have been termed experiential, while attitudes formed about an unfamiliar group have been termed symbolic (Herek, 1988, 1995, 1996a). Since only about one-third of the adult general population know an individual who is lesbian, gay, or bisexual (Herek & Capitanio, 1996), attitudes formed about these groups are, thus, largely symbolic. Symbolic beliefs endorsed about lesbians, gay men, and bisexual people by heterosexuals are believed to fulfill three purposes. These have been described by Herek: (1996a) as (1) value-expressive, wherein the attitude serves to reinforce important values and concepts of self; (2) social expressive, wherein the attitude serves to strengthen one's sense of group identity and gain group acceptance; and (3) ego-defensive, wherein the attitude serves to diminish anxiety resulting from conscious or unconscious conflicts surrounding sexuality and gender identity. An examination of existing attitude data will provide estimates of the prevalence of negative, stereotypical, and prejudicial opinions about homosexuality and how these opinions have changed over time.

The primary sources of attitude data concerning lesbians, gay men, and bisexual people have been the Gallup Organization polls (Gallup, 1993, 1994), and the General Opinion Survey of the National Opinion Research Center (NORC) (Wood, 1990), which have been polling members of the general public about their attitudes toward homosexuality since the 1970s. The Gallup and NORC surveys are both random national surveys drawn from the forty-eight contiguous states with sample sizes of at least 1,000. The Gallup polls are conducted by telephone while the NORC surveys involved face-to-face interviews. Some of the survey questions asked by these organizations have remained the same over time. Therefore, the examination of these historical data will allow the estimation of change of attitudes over time. Unfortunately, the questions were not asked at regular time intervals, and some questions were repeated infrequently, so the number of data points per opinion item and time frames per response are different.

The opinion poll data from the 1970s to the 1990s show several identifiable trends when changes in attitudes concerning civil rights for lesbians, bisexual people, and gay men, the morality of homosexual behavior, and the causes of homosexuality are examined. Opinion poll data from three main areas—employment rights, causes of homosexuality, and the morality of homosexuality—have been included for illustrative purposes.

Employment Rights

A very strong trend toward increasing support for equal job opportunities for gay men, lesbians, and bisexual people has been evident in the Gallup poll data since the 1980s, and has been particularly strong in the 1990s. The question "In general, do you think homosexuals should or should not have equal rights in terms of job opportunities?" was favorably endorsed by 56 percent of the Gallup poll sample when the question was first asked in 1977. Support for this item increased slightly to 59 percent in 1982, increased substantially to 71 percent in 1989, and remained constant at 74 percent in 1992. In the latest available survey data from 1993, the percentage responding yes rose again to 80 percent. The Gallup poll organization has also looked at support for equal job rights for specific professions. Despite a general trend for equal job rights to increase over time, the item reveals some interesting differences in the public's support of job rights for gay men, lesbians, and bisexual people (see Table 12.1). The greatest support for equal job rights in 1992, as well as in all other years, is for lesbians, gay men, or bisexual people working in the sales profession. Sales is a profession that is often of lower status and has lower pay, where the nature of the social contact is brief and impersonal, and is not likely to involve influence over children or moral authority. Support for equal job rights for lesbians, gay men, or bisexual people in the profession of teaching or the clergy received the least support in 1992 (41 percent and 43 percent, respectively), as in other years. Support for equal job rights within the military (57 percent) and among doctors (53 percent) in 1992 was between that of sales and teaching, with the relative ranking of all professions remaining constant over the period 1977–1992. Interestingly, sales and teaching are the professions showing the largest increase in support for equal job rights in 1977–1992, with both increasing by an absolute amount of 14 percent. Given the lower initial approval rating for equal job rights for teachers, this gain represents a greater proportional gain for support for equal employment opportunities for lesbians, gay men, and bisexual people as teachers.

Beliefs About the Morality, Legality, and Cause of Homosexuality

Conversely, items measuring attitudes about the morality of homosexuality ("Adult homosexual relations are always wrong?") have changed little over the 26-year time span of the polls. In 1973, 73 percent of the NORC

Table 12.1. Percentage of Sample Endorsing Support for Gay/Lesbian Job Rights by Specific Professions and by Year of Survey

YEAR OF RESPONSE	% ENDORSING FOR SALES	% ENDORSING FOR MILITARY	% ENDORSING FOR DOCTORS	% ENDORSING FOR CLERGY	% ENDORSING FOR TEACHERS
1977	68	51	44	36	27
1982	70	52	50	38	32
1987	72	55	49	42	33
1989	79	60	56	44	42
1992	82	57	53	43	41

Note: Data are excerpted from Gallup poll surveys data summarized in Gallup (1993, 1994).

sample believed that "adult homosexual relations are "always wrong" while 74 percent of the sample endorsed the same belief in 1989 (see Table 12.2). Similarly, there has been little change in the proportion endorsing the belief that homosexual relations are "never or sometimes wrong." However, recent Gallup poll data indicated that there has been a slight increase in the proportion of the general public that agree that "Homosexuality is an acceptable lifestyle," with 44 percent of the Gallup sample in 1996 agreeing with the item (Moore, 1996), compared to 38 percent agreeing in 1992 and 34 percent agreeing with the item in 1982 (Gallup, 1994). Agreement with the opinion item "Adult homosexual relations should be legal" has also remained relatively unchanged, and was endorsed by 43 percent of the Gallup sample in 1977 and by 48 percent in 1992 (Gallup, 1993). However, there has been considerable change in the belief about whether people are "born homosexual," with the percentage of the Gallup poll sample endorsing this belief rising from 12 percent in 1977 to 31 percent in 1992 (Gallup, 1993). The increase in the belief in the genetic or biological origins of homosexuality is of interest, and is probably related to the extensive media coverage given to studies suggesting genetic contributions to homosexuality (Bailey & Dawood, this volume; LeVay, 1991, Hamer, & Copeland, 1994; Hamer, Hu, Magnuson, Hu, & Pattatucci, 1993; Swaab & Hofman, 1990).

Social psychological research has demonstrated that negative attitudes toward lesbians, gay men, and bisexual people are associated with strong conservative religious ideology, more support for traditional gender roles, and being older and less educated (Herek, 1996a, Kite & Whitley, 1996). Heterosexual men, compared to heterosexual women, have been shown to be more negative in their attitudes toward gay men, but not toward lesbians (Kite, & Whitley, 1996). However, heterosexual men and women do

Table 12.2. Percentage Endorsing Various Responses by Year of Sample to Question "Are Adult Homosexual Relations Wrong?"

YEAR OF RESPONSE	% RESPONSE "ALWAYS WRONG"	% RESPONSE "NOT WRONG AT ALL"	%RESPONSE "ONLY SOMETIMES"	%RESPONSE "NEVER/ SOMETIMES"
1973	73	11	8	19
1974	70	13	8	21
1976	70	16	8	24
1977	72	15	8	23
1980	73	15	6	21
1982	73	15	7	22
1984	73	14	7	21
1985	75	14	7	21
1987	77	12	7	19
1988	77	13	6	19
1989	74	16	6	22

Note: Data are excerpted from National Opinion Research survey summarized in Wood (1990).

not differ in their support for gay civil rights (Kite & Whitley, 1996). Cross tabulations of data from the 1993 *NY Times* / CBS News poll (Schmaltz, 1993), and two Gallup poll samples taken in 1993 (Gallup, 1994) provide further insight into the associations of negative and prejudicial beliefs about homosexuality. As can be seen in Tables 12.3 and 12.4, more negative beliefs about homosexuality (that it is immoral, an unacceptable lifestyle, should be illegal, opposition to civil rights, and the belief that homosexuals want special rights) are associated with the endorsement of beliefs indicating that homosexuality is "chosen" or that "people prefer homosexuality." In contrast, more positive views about homosexuality and endorsement of civil rights for homosexuality are associated with endorsing the beliefs that "people are born homosexual" or that "homosexuality cannot be changed" (see Tables 12.3 and 12.4).

Although cross-tabulations by religious affiliation for the data were not available, it would probably reveal that religious conservatism is associated with beliefs that homosexuality is chosen or preferred. It is also probable that religious conservatism would have been a strongly predictive item for negative beliefs about homosexuality and denial of civil rights. Supporting this contention, the Gallup poll found that belief in the biological causation of homosexuality was lowest in the geographic areas of the South and Midwest, traditionally associated with religious conservatism (25 percent and 26 percent, respectively) (Gallup, 1993). Correspondingly, endorsement of the genetic origins of homosexuality was highest in the East (42 percent) and intermediate in the West (35 percent) (Gallup, 1993). The South and the Midwest were also the regions where the belief that "homosexuality is preferred" was the highest (37 percent and 40 percent, respectively) (Gallup, 1993). Increasingly, public opinion data, such as the data reviewed above, have played important roles in public policy and Supreme Court decisions involving the lives of gay men, lesbians, and bisexual people (Herek, 1996b). Public opinion data have also been important in determining the objectives of leading lesbian, gay, and bisexual rights organizations such as the Human Rights Campaign (Marinucci, 1997). Re-

Table 12.3. Endorsement of Positive Response to Items Concerning the Legality, Morality, and Acceptance of Homosexuality by Beliefs About the Cause of Homosexuality for New York Times/CBS News Sample

Responses To Items	Homosexuality is Chosen	Homosexuality Can't Be Changed	Full Sample
Gay relationships should be legal	32	62	46
Homosexuality is an acceptable lifestyle	18	57	36
Homosexuality is morally wrong	78	30	55

Note: Data are derived from the *New York Times* / CBS News Poll (Schmaltz, 1993).

Table 12.4. Endorsement of Positive Response to Items Concerning the Legality, Morality, and Acceptance of Homosexuality by Beliefs About the Cause of Homosexuality for Gallup Poll Sample

Responses To Items	People Are Born Homosexual	Homosexuality Develops	People Prefer Homosexuality	Full Sample
Should have equal job rights	95	74	73	80
Favor gays in military	65	33	34	44
Gay rights coming too quickly	45	59	64	56
Oppose civil rights for gays	28	58	59	48
Gays want special rights	27	50	53	44
Prefer gays stay in the closet	24	49	43	37

Note: Data are derived from two Gallup Poll surveys conducted in 1993 (Gallup, 1994).

cently, the Human Rights Campaign has chosen to focus on the passage of employment nondiscrimination legislation and increased support for AIDS/HIV drug programs and research as some of their top priorities, topics which their polling indicated had high levels of support in the general population (Marinucci, 1997). Despite the attempts of human rights and lesbian, gay, and bisexual rights organizations to reduce discrimination, cultural heterosexism impacts the lives of lesbian, gay, and bisexual people and their families in many ways. A consideration of some of the specific instances of oppression that lesbians, gay men, and bisexuals experience will serve to highlight the severity and extent of the problem.

Cultural Heterosexism: Instances of Systematic Oppression

Hate Crimes Against Lesbians, Gay Men, and Bisexual people

Hate crimes against lesbians, gay men, and bisexual people represent the most extreme and violent expression of cultural heterosexism (Herek, 1995). Hate crimes based on sexual orientation can vary from abusive and threatening verbal behavior to aggravated sexual assaults and murder. These hate crimes have in common the defining feature that an individual is targeted for victimization primarily for his or her perceived membership in a devalued social group—in this case, because the individual was believed or perceived to be a gay male, lesbian, or bisexual person (Herek, 1986, 1992, 1995). Hate crimes are a physical manifestation of the intolerance and prejudice of the dominant heterosexual majority, and young, disenfranchised, males are most often the perpetrators (Herek, 1986, 1992, 1995). The purposes of a hate crime from the perspective of the perpetrator are varied and include intimidation of the selected group, self-esteem enhancement of the perpetrator, and establishing group identity for the perpetrators (Herek, 1992, 1995). The negative consequences for the victim of a hate crime continue after the initial attack. A secondary trauma can occur when the individual reports the hate crime to unsympathetic or biased police, receives substandard medical or psychological assistance because of his or her sexual orientation, or receives little support from friends or family (Cogan, 1996; Herek, 1995).

While no definite survey of hate crimes among lesbians, gay men, and bisexual people exists, the experience of verbal harassment appears almost universal, and substantial percentages of individuals report experiencing serious physical and sexual assaults (Berrill, 1992; Herek et al., in press). Some authors have suggested that the incidence of hate crimes against lesbians, gay men, and bisexual people has increased over the past decade (Dean, Wu, & Martin, 1992; Herek, 1992, National Gay and Lesbian Task Force, 1991). Several factors at work in society combine to make this increase in hate crimes a likely occurrence. First, many people believe a climate of intolerance and desensitization to violence has become increasingly prevalent in American society (Hampton, Jenkins, & Gullotta, 1996). Second, the increasing visibility and public acts of lesbians, gay men, and bisexual people marks their presence and identifies them as potential targets to perpetrators (Herek, 1995). Additionally, the empowerment of gay men, lesbians, and bisexual people brought about by the gay, lesbian, and bisexual liberation movements is believed to have facilitated the readiness of individuals to report hate crimes (Herek, 1992, 1995).

Legislation designed to monitor the occurrence of hate crimes and community-based organizations formed to assist survivors of hate crimes and organize community advocacy efforts around hate crimes have also increased the awareness of hate crimes in the gay, lesbian, and bisexual communities (Cogan, 1996; Herek, 1995). However, much work remains to be done to prevent and reduce the occurrence of hate crimes (see, for example, Cogan, 1996), and hate crimes remain one of the most troubling manifestations of cultural heterosexism affecting all members of lesbian, gay, and bisexual families.

Gay Men, Lesbians, and Bisexual People in the Military

Hope for change was created within the gay, lesbian, and bisexual community when, nine days after his presidential inauguration, President Bill Clinton announced his intention to end the military's policy of excluding gay men, lesbians, and bisexual people from the armed forces (Herek, 1993; Herek, 1996b; Korb, 1996). This policy to discharge homosexuals had been formally in place since 1982, and in the decade 1980–1990 had resulted in the discharge of 16,919 men and women for suspected homosexuality (Herek,

1993). The announcement to draft a new policy was met with a storm of protest and resistance from the Pentagon, from the Joint Chiefs of Staff, from the Senate and Congress, from veterans groups, and from religious groups (Herek, 1996b; Korb, 1996; Shilts, 1993). The chair of the Joint Chiefs of Staff, General Colin Powell, threatened to resign if the new policy was put into effect (Korb, 1996; Shilts, 1993), and at least one member of the Chiefs of Staff circulated copies of a Christian Right's antihomosexual propaganda videotape to other generals (Shilts, 1993). Overwhelmed and defeated by the aggressive response of his opponents, Clinton in July 1993 introduced the "Don't Ask, Don't Tell, Don't Pursue" policy, which was essentially an affirmation of the status quo in current military policy (Herek, 1996b; Korb, 1996; Shilts, 1993). The policy was perceived as disingenuous and a breach of promise by gay, lesbian, and bisexual activists (The Covers, 1994; Marinucci, 1997).

Despite considerable controversy and adverse legal rulings on the policy, "Don't Ask, Don't Tell" at this time remains the official policy of U.S. government because of the refusal of the U.S. Supreme Court to consider the constitutionality of the policy (Greenhouse, 1996), and is likely to remain so for the near future (Herek, Jobe, & Carney, 1996). The "Don't Ask, Don't Tell" policy continues to be used by the military to discharge gay, lesbian, and bisexual people, and has not resulted in a decrease of discharges of lesbian, gay or bisexual military personnel (Korb, 1996). Claims have been made that the intent of the policy has been violated by directly asking military personnel about their sexual orientation and conducting wide-ranging investigations to uncover personnel suspected of being lesbian, gay, or bisexual (Priest, 1996). The most recent figures from the Defense Department indicated that in fiscal year 1995, a total 722 gay, lesbian, and bisexual military personnel were discharged on the basis of their sexual orientation, compared to 597 discharged in fiscal 1994, and 682 discharged in fiscal 1993 (Priest, 1996).

The Rush to Pass Legislation Barring Recognition of Same-Sex Marriages

The likelihood that the state of Hawaii, as the result of a State Supreme Court ruling, may permit the civil sanctioning of same-sex marriages has resulted in anticipatory legislation in other states (Essoyan, 1996). A recent favorable lower court ruling by Circuit Court Judge Kevin Chang in Hawaii in the case of *Baehr v. Miike* has increased the political maneuvering on the issue, and the verdict will most likely be appealed to the State Supreme Court (Salinas, 1996). Even legislators in Hawaii are attempting to amend the state constitution to ban same-sex marriages, though a separate bill that would grant domestic partnership benefits to same-sex couples has been approved by the Hawaiian State Senate (Bill Gives Some Rights, 1997). However, not all of these legislative attempts to prohibit same sex marriage have met with success, and some have been defeated by clever political maneuvers. In 1996 in California, legislation prohibiting same-sex marriages failed to pass in the state senate after "poison pill" amendments, which provided limited rights for unmarried domestic partners, were added (Matthews, 1996). The reason for the urgency of the legislation is the fear that other states will be forced to recognize same-sex marriages performed in Hawaii because of the concept of reciprocity, wherein marriages or other legally binding contracts originating in one state are recognized in other states (Eskridge, 1996). These legislative efforts come far in advance of the Hawaiian court's ruling on the matter, are likely to be declared unconstitutional if passed, and reflect the panic of legislators over the possibility of having to allow same-sex marriage in their state (Eskridge, 1996). Conservatives fear that the granting of legal marriage status to same-sex partners will legitimize gay, lesbian, and bisexual same-sex relationships, as marriage is not only a private contract between two individuals but also a public recognition of a private relationship (Sullivan, 1995).

It would seem that the general public is not yet ready to sanction same-sex marriages. A recent Gallup poll on the issue (Moore, 1996) was conducted on March 15–17, 1996, and 1,008 adults were asked the following question: "Do you think marriages between homosexuals should or should not be recognized by law as valid, with the same rights as traditional marriages?" The survey revealed that 68 percent of the public were opposed to same-sex marriage rights while only 27 percent were in support. Even among those individuals surveyed who indicated that "homosexuality was an acceptable lifestyle," 43 percent were opposed to legally sanctioned same-sex marriages (Moore, 1996). Opposition to same-sex marriages was higher for men (76 percent) than for women (61 percent), with the gender difference greatest under age 30 (Moore, 1996).

Political affiliation was also an important correlate of opposition to same-sex marriage with 80 percent of Republicans versus 61 percent of Democrats opposed. Despite support in some media, as evidenced by an editorial endorsement for same-sex marriage civil rights in the conservative economic journal The Economist (Let Them Wed, 1996), public opinion tends to be negative about same-sex marriages or even same-sex couples adopting children. A recent telephone poll by Louis Harris also found that the majority were opposed to same-sex marriage, and same-sex couples adopting children (Gay Marriage, 1996). Opposition to same-sex marriage did not differ by the gender of the couple, with 63 percent opposed to same-sex marriage of female couples and 64 percent opposed to same-sex marriage of male couples (Gay Marriage, 1996). Similarly, the survey found that 61 percent of the sample disapproved of a female couple adopting a child while 65 percent disapproved of a male couple adopting a child (Gay Marriage, 1996).

The topic of gay marriage also arouses strong feelings in the lesbian, gay male, and bisexual communities. Some community and political activists have argued that the legalization of same-sex marriage is a denial of the goals of feminism and radical gay, lesbian, and bisexual liberation (Dunlap, 1996; Eskridge, 1996; Thorpe & De La O, 1995). In the general lesbian, gay male, and bisexual communities, however, same-sex marriage is not seen so much as a political act but rather simply as "an expression of our feelings for one another" (Thorpe & De La O, 1995: 59). The majority of the lesbian, gay, and bisexual communities appear to view the prospect of same-sex marriage positively, as indicated by readership surveys by the *Advocate* magazine (Lever, 1994, 1995). In that survey, two-thirds of the lesbians and gay men surveyed indicated a desire to marry someone of the same sex (Lever, 1994, 1995).

The looming battle over same-sex marriage legislation promises to dwarf the machinations of the "gays in the military" debate because no one issue is more central to the conservative Christian agenda than preserving the status quo on marriage and the family (Diamond, 1995; Howe, 1996). The overwhelming opposition to same-sex marriage among the general public and support for the Defense of Marriage Act, as evidenced in opinion polls, is likely to encourage legislators to draft more laws prohibiting same-sex marriage (Marinucci, 1997). The larger question of whether legalization of same-sex marriage would represent a major moral and social victory over cultural heterosexism or another step into integration in the dominant heterosexual cultural (Sullivan, 1995) remains to be answered.

Implications for Future Research

Though a considerable body of research literature and public opinion data about attitudes toward lesbians and gay men has emerged in the last two decades (see Kite & Whitley, 1996; Herek, 1996a; & Herek, in press; for reviews), the research literature in this area is deficient because it fails to include people with bisexual identities, is cross-sectional in scope, and focuses solely on the individual while ignoring the context of family and community. These deficiencies are most pronounced in national public opinion polls, such as the Gallup and NORC polls, which even fail to make the most basic distinctions between attitudes toward lesbians and gay men and continue to use the term "homosexual." Furthermore, the premise of many of the questions is leading (i.e., "Should homosexuals have equal job rights?" or "Should adult homosexual behavior be legal?"). These types of questions infer that basic human rights can be denied to certain unpopular groups, and that consenting sexual behavior between adults should be proscribed. This is vividly illustrated by substituting the word *black* or *Jew* when asking the questions and observing the justified anger.

Attitude research conducted by more sensitive and informed investigators (e.g., Herek, 1988) has also failed in the test of bisexual, family, and community inclusiveness. By not assessing attitudes toward bisexual people as a separate category, and determining what the participants understanding of bisexuality is, the research contributes to the invisibility of the bisexual person (Lang, 1996) and fails to uncover potentially important research findings (Fox, 1995). As the researcher studying the general population is admonished to have sufficient representation of minority populations and to exercise cultural sensitivity (Okazaki, & Sue, 1995), so should she or he avoid promoting stereotypes of gay, lesbian, and bisexual people; recruit a representative sample that includes self-identified bisexual people; and appropriately distinguish among the various methods of assessing sexual orientation (Herek, Kimmel, Amaro, & Melton, 1991).

The majority of the psychological research on lesbian, gay, and bisexual people is also limited by a cross-sectional design. Data are collected at only one point in time, and there is no chance to observe the developmental process of change. This lack of longitudinal research is a particular concern for studies of erotic attraction and sexual-orientation identity formation, and can lead to discontinuous models of these processes (Fox, 1995). Several researchers have used the context of community or the family in their research with and writing about lesbian, gay, and bisexual participants (e.g., D'Augelli, & Garnets, 1995; Friend, 1989; Strommen, 1989). Unfortunately, consideration of the role of the family, community, or organization in research has tended to be the exception. This failure to consider the broader social context can lead to an underestimation of the social support that an individual has, an underestimation of the stressors the person experiences, and a failure to understand the complexity of his or her social relationships and values. The neglect of a family and relationship context in research also contributes to stereotypes of lesbian, gay, and bisexual people as "isolated, sexually deviant, and antifamily" because the attitudes and behavior of the individual are presented without acknowledging the support of family members or the peer norms of the community.

The most promising and potentially beneficial line of research, however, is that of preventing heterosexism (see Rothblum & Bond, 1996). With an impressive accumulated knowledge base of theory and empirical data about heterosexism, social scientists are now in a position to design interventions to reduce and prevent heterosexism. Some attempts have been made at this goal, but these interventions have been typically with college-level students and have involved only single-session interventions such as panels of speakers or required enrollment in a specific course (e.g., D'Augelli, 1991; Geasler, Croteau, Heineman, & Edlund, 1995; Schreier, 1995). Working with Australian young offenders, Van de Ven (1995) described the results of a promising educational intervention that resulted in reductions of homophobic behavior and beliefs. It is likely that these intervention programs and others would benefit from considering the implications of the public opinion data reviewed. The most effective way of changing negative attitudes about lesbians, gay men, and bisexual people in the general population is likely to be an appeal to the widely endorsed concept of equal civil rights for all, which includes lesbians, gay men, and bisexual people, rather than an attempt to normalize same-sex behavior. The Christian Right has recognized the success of this strategy, and has attempted to subvert the message into one of "special rights" for lesbian, gay, and bisexual people (Diamond, 1995). Similarly, it would be important to understand the moral position regarding homosexuality, as described by Jung & Smith, assumed by an individual or group before attempting to influence its attitudes. As has been recognized in HIV/AIDS intervention research (Walters, Canady, & Stein, 1994), it is probably necessary to tailor intervention programs to specific characteristics of the target population, such as age, gender, ethnic and racial background, and religious affiliation, for the programs to be effective in reducing heterosexism.

The most critical venue for preventing heterosexism, however, is the elementary classroom. In the classroom, children can be exposed to unbiased material about lesbian, gay, and bisexual people in a supervised environment and at an age when it may be possible to promote acceptance and tolerance more effectively. A striking example of the success of such a program is detailed in the documentary film *It's Elementary* by filmmaker Debra Chasnoff, which examines how educators are teaching elementary schoolchildren about gays, lesbians, and bisexual people (Brune, 1996). With innovative programs and integrated attempts to educate our youth, combined with the positive influence that "coming out" has on changing the attitudes of those close to us (Herek & Capitanio, 1996), we may some day achieve a reduction in prejudice, discrimination, and denial of civil rights for all lesbian, gay, and bisexual people. Cultural heterosexism and its consequences for the family will, we hope, become a subject of historical, rather than contemporary, interest.

References

Ad touts Clinton's opposing gay marriages (1996, October 15). *New York Times*, p. A24.
Adam, B. D. (1995). *The rise of a gay and lesbian movement*, (revised ed.). New York: Twayne Publishers.
Altman, D. (1982). *The homosexualization of American, the Americanization of the homosexual*. New York: St. Martin's Press.
Baker, P. (1996, September 22). President quietly signs laws aimed at gay marriages. *Washington Post*, p. 21.
Bayer, R. (1981). *Homosexuality and American psychiatry: The politics of diagnosis*. New York: Basic Books.
Berrill, K. T. (1992). Anti-gay violence and victimization in the United States: An overview. In G. M. Herek & K. T. Berrill (Eds.), *Hate crimes: Confronting violence against lesbians and gay men* (pp. 289–305). Newbury Park, CA: Sage Publications.
Bill gives some rights to same-sex couples (1997, January 25). *San Francisco Chronicle*, p. A6.
Boswell, J. (1980). *Christianity, social tolerance, and homosexuality: Gay people in*

Western Europe from the beginning of the Christian era to the fourteenth century. Chicago: University of Chicago Press.

Bowers v. Hardwick, 106 S. Ct. 2841 (1986).

Brune, B. (1996, October 13). Teaching teachers to talk about gay issues. *New York Times,* pp. N12, L22.

Cameron, P., & Cameron, K. (1995). Does incest cause homosexuality? *Psychological Reports, 76,* 611–621.

Cameron, P., Playfair, W. L., & Wellum, S. (1994). The longevity of homosexuals: Before and after the AIDS epidemic. *Omega: Journal of Death & Dying, 29,* 249–272.

Cameron, P., Proctor, K., Coburn, W., & Forde, N. (1986). Child molestation and homosexuality. *Psychological Reports, 58,* 327–337.

Cogan, J. (1996). The prevention of anti-lesbian/gay hate crimes through social change and empowerment. In E. D. Rothblum & L. Bond (Eds.), *Preventing heterosexism and homophobia* (pp. 219–238). Thousand Oaks, CA: Sage Publications.

D'Augelli, A. R. (1991). Teaching lesbian/gay development: From oppression to exceptionality (Special Issue: Coming out of the classroom closet: Gay and lesbian students, teachers, and curricula). *Journal of Homosexuality, 22,* 213–227.

D'Augelli, A. R., & Garnets, L. D. (1995). Lesbian, gay, and bisexual communities. In A. R. D'Augelli & C. J. Patterson (Eds.), *Lesbian, gay and bisexual identities over the lifespan: Psychological perspectives* (pp. 293–320). New York: Oxford University Press.

Dean, L., Wu, S., & Martin, J. L. (1992). Trends in violence and discrimination against gay men in New York City: 1984 to 1990. In G. M. Herek & K. T. Berrill (Eds.), *Hate crimes: Confronting violence against lesbians and gay men* (pp. 46–64). Newbury Park, CA: Sage Publications.

Diamond, S. (1995). *Roads to dominion: Right-wing movements and political power in the United States.* New York: Guilford Press.

Dunlap, D. W. (1996, June 7). Some gay rights advocates question effort to defend same-sex marriage. *New York Times,* pp. A8, A12.

Eagly, A. H., & Chaiken, S. (1993). *The psychology of attitudes.* New York: Harcourt Brace Jovanovich College Publishers.

Eskridge, W. N. (1996). *The case for same-sex marriage: From sexual liberty to civilized commitment.* New York: Free Press.

Essoyan, S. (1996, September 8). Hawaiian wedding bells ring alarm bells, as court looks at same-sex unions, debate crosses the ocean. *Los Angeles Times,* p. A1.

Fox, R. C. (1995). Bisexual identities. In A. R. D'Augelli & C. J. Patterson (Eds.), *Lesbian, gay and bisexual identities over the lifespan: Psychological perspectives* (pp. 48–86). New York: Oxford University Press.

Friend, R. A. (1989). Older lesbian and gay people: Responding to homophobia. *Marriage and Family Review, 14,* 241–263.

Gallup, G. (1986). Jobs for homosexuals. *Gallup poll: Public opinion 1985* (pp. 287–288). Wilmington, DE: Scholarly Resources.

Gallup, G. (1987). Homosexuality. *Gallup poll: Public opinion 1986* (pp. 213–216). Wilmington, DE: Scholarly Resources.

Gallup, G. Jr. (1993). Homosexuality and gay rights. *The Gallup poll: Public opinion 1992* (pp. 101–103). Wilmington, DE: Scholarly Resources.

Gallup, G. Jr. (1994). Homosexuality and gay rights. *The Gallup poll: Public opinion 1993* (pp. 83–89). Wilmington, DE: Scholarly Resources.

Gay marriage, male or female, equally opposed (1996, August 19). *San Francisco Chronicle*, p. A5.

Geasler, M. J., Croteau, J. M., Heineman, C. J., & Edlund, C. J. (1995). A qualitative study of students' expressions of change after attending panel presentations by lesbian, gay, and bisexual speakers. *Journal of College Student Development, 36,* 483–492.

Greenhouse, L. (1996, October 27). Justices defer a review. *New York Times*, p. E2.

Hamer, D. H., & Copeland, P. (1994). *The science of desire: The search for the gay gene and the biology of behavior.* New York: Simon & Schuster.

Hamer, D. H., Hu, S., Magnuson, V. L., Hu, N., & Pattatucci, A. M. (1993). A linkage between DNA markers on the X chromosome and male sexual orientation. *Science, 261,* 321–327.

Hampton, R. L., Jenkins, I., & Gullotta. J. P., (Eds.) (1996). *Preventing violence in America.* Thousand Oaks, CA: Sage Publications.

Herek, G. M. (1986). The social psychology of homophobia: Toward a practical theory. *Review of Law & Social Change, 14,* 923–934.

Herek, G. M. (1988). Heterosexuals' attitudes toward lesbians and gay men: Correlates and gender differences. *Journal of Sex Research, 25,* 451–477.

Herek, G. M. (1992). The social context of hate crimes: Notes on cultural heterosexism. In G. M. Herek & K. Berrill (Eds.), *Hate crimes: Confronting violence against lesbians and gay men* (pp. 89–104). Newbury Park, CA: Sage Publications.

Herek, G. M. (1993). Sexual orientation and military service: A social science perspective. *American Psychologist, 48,* 538–547.

Herek, G. M. (1995). Psychological heterosexism in the United States. In A. R. D'Augelli, & C. J. Patterson (Eds.), *Lesbian, gay, and bisexual identities over the lifespan: Psychological perspectives* (pp. 321–346). New York: Oxford University Press.

Herek, G. M. (1996a). Heterosexism and homophobia. In R. P. Cabaj & T. S. Stein (Eds.), *Textbook of homosexuality and mental health* (pp. 101–113). Washington, DC: American Psychiatric Press.

Herek, G. M. (1996b). Social science, sexual orientation, and military personnel policy. In G. M. Herek, J. B. Jobe, & R. M. Carney (Eds.), *Out in force: Sexual orientation and the military* (pp. 3–14). Chicago: University of Chicago Press.

Herek, G. M. (in press). The HIV epidemic and public attitudes toward lesbians and gay men. In M. P. Levine, P. Nardi, & J. Gagnon (Eds.), *The impact of the HIV epidemic on the lesbian and gay community.* Chicago: University of Chicago Press.

Herek, G. M., & Capitanio, J. P. (1996). "Some of my best friends": Intergroup contact, concealable stigma, and heterosexuals' attitudes toward gay men and lesbians. *Personality and Social Psychology Bulletin, 4,* 412–424.

Herek, G. M., Jobe, J. B., & Carney, R. M. (1996). Conclusions. In G. M. Herek, J. B. Jobe, & R. M. Carney (Eds.), *Out in force: Sexual orientation and the military* (pp. 303–308). Chicago: University of Chicago Press.

Herek, G. M., Gillis, J. R., Cogan, J. C., & Glunt, E. K. (in press). Hate crime victimization among lesbian, gay, and bisexual adults: Prevalence, psychological correlates, and methodological issues. *Journal of Interpersonal Violence.*

Herek, G. M., & Glunt, E. K. (1988). An epidemic of stigma: Public reactions to AIDS. *American Psychologist, 43*, 886–891.

Herek, G. M., Kimmel, D. C., Amaro, H., & Melton, G. B. (1991). Avoiding heterosexist bias in psychological research. *American Psychologist, 46*, 957–963.

Howe, R. G. (1996). *Homosexuality in America: Exposing the myths.* Charlotte, NC: Issachar Institute.

Hunter, J., & Schaecher, R. (1987). Stresses on lesbian and gay adolescents in schools. *Social Work in Education, 9*, 180–190.

Jung, P. B., & Smith, R. F. (1993). *Heterosexism: An ethical challenge.* Albany: State University of New York Press.

Kite, M. E., & Whitley, B. E. (1996). Sex differences in attitudes toward homosexual persons, behaviors. and civil rights: A meta-analysis. *Personality and Social Psychology Bulletin, 4*, 336–353.

Korb, L. J. (1996). The President, the Congress, and the Pentagon: Obstacles to implementing the "Don't Ask, Don't Tell" policy. In G. M. Herek, J. B. Jobe, & R. M. Carney (Eds.), *Out in force: Sexual orientation and the military* (pp. 290–302). Chicago: University of Chicago Press.

Lano, K. (1996). Bisexual history: Fighting invisibility. In S. Rose & C. Stevens (Eds.), *Bisexual horizons: Politics, histories, lives* (pp. 219–226). London, England: Lawrence & Wishart.

Let Them Wed (1996, January 6). *The Economist,* pp. 13–14.

LeVay, S. (1991). A difference in hypothalamic structure between heterosexual and homosexual men. *Science, 253*, 1034–1037.

Lever, J. (1994, August). Sexual revelations. *The Advocate,* pp. 17, 24.

Lever, J. (1995, August 22). Lesbian sex survey. *The Advocate,* pp. 22–31.

Marinucci, C. (1997, February 2). Gays focus on job protection. *San Francisco Chronicle,* p. A2.

Martin, A. D., & Hetrick, E. S. (1987). The stigmatization of the gay and lesbian adolescent. *Journal of Homosexuality, 15*, 163– 183.

Matthews, J. (1996, August 20). State senate foils gay-marriage foes. *Sacramento Bee,* pp. Al, A12.

Moore, D. W. (1996, April). Public opposes gay marriages: Major generational gaps on issue of homosexuality. *Gallup Poll Monthly, 367*, 19–21.

National Gay & Lesbian Task Force (1991). *Anti-gay/lesbian violence, victimization, and defamation in 1990.* Washington, DC: Author.

Nava, M., & Dawidoff, R. (1994). *Created equal: Why Gay rights matter to America.* New York: St. Martin's Press.

Nicolosi, J., & Feeman, L. (1993). *Healing homosexuality: Case histories of reparative therapy,* Northvale, NJ: Jason Aronson.

Okazaki, S., & Sue, S. (1995). Methodological issues in assessment research with ethnic minorities (Special issue: Methodological issues in psychological assessment research). *Psychological Assessment, 7*, 367–375.

Pharr, S. (1988). *Homophobia: A weapon of sexism.* Little Rock, AR: Chardon Press.

Pietrzyk, M. E. (1994, October 3). Queer science: Paul Cameron, professional sham. *New Republic, 211*, 10–13.

Priest, D. (1996, February 28). Military, despite policy shift, discharged more gays in '95. *Washington Post*, p. A2.

Robison, J. (1980). *Attack on the family*. Wheaton, IL: Tyndale House Publishers.

Rothblum, E. D., & Bond, L. (Eds.) (1996). *Preventing heterosexism and homophobia*. Thousand Oaks, CA: Sage Publications.

Rotheram-Borus, M. J., Reid, H., Rosario, M., VanRossem, R., & Gillis, R. (1995). Prevalence, course, and predictors of multiple problem behaviors among gay and bisexual male adolescents. *Developmental Psychology, 31*, 75–85.

Salinas, M. (1996, December 5). Hawaii judge rules for gay marriage. *Bay Area Reporter, 26*(49), 1, 27.

Sample, H. A. (1996, May 21). Court rules against anti-gay rights law. *Sacramento Bee*, p. A1.

Schmaltz, J. (1993, March 5). Poll finds an even split on homosexuality's cause. *New York Times*, A 14.

Schreier, B. A. (1995). Moving beyond tolerance: A new paradigm for programming about homophobia/biphobia and heterosexism. *Journal of College Student Development, 36*, 19–26.

Shilts, R. (1987). *And the band played on: Politics, people, and the AIDS epidemic*. New York: St. Martin's Press.

Shilts, R. (1993). *Conduct unbecoming: Gays and lesbians in the U.S. military*. New York: Fawcett Columbine.

Socarides, C. W., & Volkan, V. D. (Eds.) (1991). *The homosexualities and the therapeutic process*. Madison, CT: International Universities Press.

Strommen, E. F. (1989). Hidden branches and growing pains: Homosexuality and the family tree. *Marriage & Family Review, 14*, 9–34.

Sullivan, A. (1995). *Virtually normal: An argument about homosexuality*. New York: Knopf.

Swaab, D. F., & Hofman, M. A. (1990). An enlarged suprachiasmatic nucleus in homosexual men. *Brain Research, 537*, 141–148.

The covers (1993 *Advocate* covers) (1994, January 25). (Special double issue: The year in review) *Advocate*, pp. 31–36.

Thorpe, D., & De La O, M. (1995, May/June). Holy matrimony. *10 Percent, 3*, 56–70.

Van de Ven, P. (1995). A comparison of two teaching modules for reducing homophobia in young offenders. *Journal of Applied Social Psychology, 25*, 632–649.

Walters, J. L., Canady, R., & Stein, T. (1994). Evaluating multicultural approaches in HIV/AIDS educational material. *AIDS Education & Prevention, 6*, 446–453.

Williams, W. (1995, June 3). Personal communication.

Wood, F. W. (Ed.) (1990). *An American profile: Opinions and behavior 1972–1989*. Detroit: Gale Research.

Zera, D. (1992). Coming of age in a heterosexist world: The development of gay and lesbian adolescents. *Adolescence, 27*, 849–854.

13

Clinical Issues in Psychotherapy with Lesbian-, Gay-, and Bisexual-Parented Families

April Martin

Families headed by lesbian, gay, and bisexual parents have only very recently acquired visibility on the sociological landscape. Until perhaps two decades ago the popular media, the legal literature, and the mental health fields seemed almost universal in their identification of parenthood as the exclusive province of heterosexuals (Coontz, 1992; Lewin & Lyons, 1982). Despite estimates of lesbian and gay parents in the millions (Bozett, 1987; Gottman, 1990; Patterson, 1992), there has been little, if any, mention of them until recently. Indeed, the two words, *lesbian* and *mother*, were only put together for the first time in the 1970s, as lesbian mothers began tentatively to emerge from enforced secrecy and invisibility (Martin & Lyon, 1991; Pollack and Vaughn, 1987). The concept of a gay father seemed to many an oxymoron (Bigner & Bozett, 1990; Bozett, 1993), and this population still lags behind lesbian mothers in representation in the research literature (Patterson, 1995). Even more significantly, the concept of family is only now being broadened to encompass the full variety of parent-partner-child groupings that lesbians and gay men create (Benkov, 1994; Markowitz, 1995; Patterson, 1994a; Slater & Mencher, 1991; Weston, 1991).

Yet by now, families headed by lesbian and gay parents have achieved some significant recognition (Cavaliere, 1995; Kolata, 1989). The fact that they are now frequently represented on television and radio talk shows, in newspaper articles, and even on sitcoms reflects a sea change in visibility.

One consequence of this increased openness and visibility is that more lesbian-, gay-, and bisexual-parented families are presenting themselves for mental health services. Indeed, there are probably more such families in existence as lesbians and gay men are creating families with children through adoption and donor insemination in unprecedented numbers (Martin, 1989a; 1993; McPherson, 1993; Patterson, 1994b; Pies, 1990; Ricketts & Achtenberg, 1990). It is safe to say, however, that the mental health needs of these families are still very much underserved. Many psychotherapists are still inclined to view homosexuality as an illness or a moral failing (Garnets, Hancock, Cochran, Goodchilds, & Peplau 1991; Hancock, 1995). Even therapists who express tolerance or support for diverse sexual orientations may become critical when there are children involved (Garnets et al., 1991). In addition, many well-meaning therapists are simply handicapped by not having specialized knowledge of these families, and are therefore basing treatments upon inaccurate assumptions (Hancock, 1995). Because of the real possibility that they will be misunderstood and mistreated in the mental health profession, lesbian, gay, and bisexual parents are often understandably reluctant to seek help when they have individual, relationship, parenting, and child-development problems.

Families parented by lesbians, gay men, and bisexuals seek treatment for a variety of difficulties that have nothing specifically to do with their sexual orientations. Yet they also have unique issues, circumstances, and problems that may be the focus of treatment or that may form the lens through which other problems are experienced (Carter, 1995). These unique issues may result from the problems of belonging to a stigmatized sexual minority (Berzon, 1988; De Monteflores, 1993; Hammersmith, 1988; Herek, 1995; Martin, 1982); from the unique features of same-gender relationships (Clunis & Green, 1988; Peplau, 1993; McWhirter & Mattison, 1984); from circumstances pertaining to membership in any of a variety of gay, lesbian, or bisexual communities (D'Augelli & Garnets, 1995); or from their dual or even triple membership in several minorities (Chan, 1993; Espin, 1987, 1993; Garcia, Kennedy, Pearlman, & Perez, 1987; Loiacano, 1993; Morales, 1990). It behooves the therapist to become familiar with the myriad issues that are specific to such families in order to work in an ethical and effective manner.

This chapter first considers questions of family membership as they apply in lesbian- and gay-headed homes. How is it determined who is and who is not a member of such a family? Next, issues of families with heterosexual beginnings are discussed. When children have been born in the context of heterosexual marriages, lesbian and gay parents often face questions about disclosure of sexual identities to their children, who must then cope with these new circumstances. The next section concerns parents who had children after identifying themselves as gay or lesbian, including the influence on family dynamics of the complicated legal and social pressures with which these families are coping. Unless otherwise noted, clinical examples have been composited from cases in the author's own practice.

Identifying the True Family

To begin with, it is important to know that family constellations among lesbian- and gay-parented families are different in certain respects from the heterosexually parented nuclear family. The biological family has been the basis for virtually all of psychology's assumptions about family dynamics and child development. Until recently, the notion in most of the mental health field has been that a proper family consists of two parents, one of each gender, each biologically related to the children, with children who are all biologically related to each other, and unless there has been a mishap, all living under one roof (McPherson,1993; Patterson, 1995). Even heterosexually parented families formed by adoption are often seen as problematic imitations of the biological model, rather than truly alternative structures with strengths of their own, as evidenced by the degree of secrecy that has traditionally surrounded most adoption placements. Not only has the biological family been considered to be the normative model against which all other family constellations must be compared, but it is also assumed to be an optimal structure for child development, compared to which other constellations are seen as deficient (Patterson, 1995).

In order to work effectively with lesbian- and gay-parented families, though, the psychotherapist must often discard the heterosexual model. Effective treatment of lesbian- and gay-parented families must proceed from the premises that (1) there is no definite requirement for the number of parents a family must have in order to be healthy; (2) there are no requirements about what genders those parents should be; (3) healthy families may comprise many combinations of biological or nonbiological relatedness between parents and children, and among siblings; (4) a healthy family may intentionally comprise more than one household; and (5) the psychological health of a family is unrelated to the sexual orientation of the parents or of the children (Achtenberg, 1987; American Psychological Association 1993; Green, Mandel, Hotvedt, Gray, & Smith, 1986; Golombok et al., 1983, Kirkpatrick, Smith, & Roy, 1981; Martin, 1989b; Patterson, 1992, 1994a, 1995; Polikoff, 1990). Psychotherapists working with individual family members or with family groupings are better off when they proceed on the assumption that it is quality of care, not any particular family constellation, that determines what is optimal for children's development.

There is considerable variety in the family constellations of gay-, lesbian-, and bisexual-parented families. For example, consider an 8-year-old boy who lives in two households. In one household is his lesbian biological mother and in the other are his two gay dads, neither of whom is biologically related to him. In fact, they entered his life only a few years ago, when he was 4. The fathers share half-time custody, including very active involvement in school activities, yet have no legal rights to the child if anything should happen to the mother. His mother has a partner, but she is not a designated parent in this family system. The biological father is unknown.

In another family, 12-year-old Joshua's two lesbian mothers conceived him through donor insemination. The women's relationship broke up when Joshua was a baby, but they continued to co-parent from separate households, and he has always called both of them "Mom." In addition, each one now has a lesbian partner, and those partners have also become his parents, though he calls them by their first names. Each of those partners has also given birth to a child through donor insemination, and Joshua considers those children to be his siblings, despite their having no biological relation to him. His family thus consists of two households containing four mothers and two siblings. His biological father is known to everyone in the family, but this man is considered a sperm donor rather than a family member. In addition, Joshua's biological father was the sperm donor for another lesbian in Joshua's acquaintance, making that woman's daughter a biological half-sister to Joshua. Psychologically, however, she not a sibling in Joshua's family.

In yet another family, a lesbian was inseminated with sperm from her partner's brother. The child she gave birth to thus has two mothers, one of whom is her biological mother with full legal rights and responsibilities, and the other of whom is her biological aunt with no parental rights or responsibilities, in the legal sense. Her biological father is, functionally speaking, not a father at all but an uncle, yet he has full parental rights and responsibilities under the law.

It should be clear from examples like these that in dealing with lesbian- and gay-parented families we often need to rethink definitions of family that are based on biology, gender, or legal assumptions about parenthood. Instead, the therapist should attempt to identify a child's functional, psychological family—that in which the parents are those people committed to raising him or her, regardless of how many parents there are, what their genders or sexual orientations may be, whether or not they are biologically related to the child, whether or not they have legal rights and responsibilities of parenthood, and whether or not they have sexual relationships with each other. Most of the time, lesbian- and gay-parented families that are identified in this way will fail to meet the definitions of family required by most of this culture's institutions. Indeed, lesbian- and gay-parented families regularly encounter difficulties based on interfacing with a society not yet prepared for them. Simply filling out a form that asks for the identities of family members, for example, raises questions of definition. As a result, much clinical work with these families can center on conflicts between the true psychological family constellation and the legally defined family structure.

The composition of the true family may not be immediately apparent when a family presents itself in the consulting room. Many families who come for therapy may themselves be limited by heterosexist definitions of family that make them unable to value and fully explore the potential of the family they have created. Helping them to think more imaginatively about family structure is not merely necessary in order to proceed with therapy, it may often be a therapeutic intervention in and of itself.

For example, a lesbian couple, Sheila and Lucy, came because of frequent bitter fighting. Sheila was raising her biological daughter from a previous heterosexual marriage when she met Lucy, who moved in with them. They had been together for three years and Sheila's daughter was now 9. A typical argument might be triggered when Sheila had to interact with her ex-husband around visitation or child support and would express some frustration about it to Lucy. Lucy would respond by threatening to beat up or kill Sheila's ex-husband, ostensibly in support of Sheila, but with a level of agitation that was quite upsetting. Sheila felt frightened and abandoned by Lucy's rages and would respond by telling her to get out.

The dynamics in this family were perhaps not so different from what often happens in stepfamilies, in which a new parent feels insecure about his or her role. But they were made far worse by the fact that it had not occurred to either Sheila or Lucy to define Lucy's role as that of stepparent. Lucy had always assumed that being a lesbian meant she couldn't be a mother, and neither woman could quite imagine a child's having two mothers.

What emerged over time, however, was that Lucy, for all her defensive tough-guy posture, had invested a great deal of time and loving energy in teaching, playing with, and feeling responsible for Sheila's daughter. She did it, however, in a very inconsistent way, as every reminder that she was not really a member of the family caused her to withdraw defensively. Sheila similarly invited Lucy to share the parenting work, but periodically pushed her away because she felt guilty about not doing it all herself, and because she wanted to protect her daughter from Lucy's inconsistencies. Sheila's ex-husband was merely salt in Lucy's wounds as a painful reminder that she was not important in this child's life.

The therapist offered them the possibility of defining Lucy as a stepparent—of fully vesting her with decision-making power and responsibility. They began to understand that their conflicts resulted from not recognizing Lucy's parenting. The child responded by letting Lucy know emphatically that she would be thrilled to have her as a second mother. Over time, as Lucy saw herself as a mother, she shed her gruff, defensive manner and was able to be a more consistent parent. Sheila resisted at first, but was ultimately relieved to yield her position as sole parent and share responsibility with Lucy. In the process, Lucy also came to understand that one of her functions as a stepmother was to respect the role of the child's father and support his position as Dad, and she was able to let go of her anger at him. None of this would have been possible had the therapist accepted the premise that Sheila is a single mother with a lesbian lover and ignored the fact that this is a family.

The way a family defines itself is often shaped by societal and legal definitions, including the facts that (1) nonheterosexual orientations have for so long been deemed incompatible with parenting; and (2) parenting relationships are usually recognized only where there is biological relatedness, legal marriage (which is at present unavailable to same-sex couples), or both. The lack of societal and legal recognition for lesbian and gay parents sometimes causes the parents themselves to devalue their roles or to fail to define them as parental (Baptiste, 1987). Some families with same-gender parents, believing that the family constellation is irrelevant to, for example, the child's school problems, or wishing to hide the fact of a same-gender relationship, will appear for psychotherapy without the nonbiological or nonlegal parent and omit mention of him or her altogether. Sensitivity to the possibility that any family may contain a gay, lesbian, or bisexual member requires that the therapist inquire about any other adults who may participate regularly in the family's life. When a lesbian- or gay-parented family has an adult who is not designated as a parent, but merely as the parent's partner, or perhaps also as a friend to the child, the therapist needs to assess what that really means. The critical clinical issue is to determine whether that person's designation as a nonparent reflects the realities and considered preferences of all involved, or whether it has been largely determined by heterosexism and internalized homonegativity.

The therapist inquiring about why an adult in the family has not elected to be a parent to the child should be alert to answers like, "Well, she already *has* a father" or "I just never saw myself as a parent" or "I just don't think it's right" or "I don't want to confuse the child" or "How would I ever explain that to my family? to my job? to the school? to the neighbors?" Remarks such as these may be indicators that the family may have been structured more by heterosexism and homonegativity than by the true desires of everyone involved.

Restructuring the family's self-definition may involve asking them to use their imaginations, to envision a world where all forms of family are respected, and in such a setting to focus on how they actually feel about the details of caring for the child, sharing responsibility, being celebrated as a parent on Mother's Day or Father's Day, relating to each other as co-parents, and so on. The therapist should encourage the adults to identify their feelings of parental closeness and concern, with the implicit or explicit reassurance that there will be some way to make such an unconventional family structure viable in the world.

Increasingly, it appears that families are affirming their structures by calling two or more female parents "Mom," or two or more male parents "Dad," or some variants of those labels (Martin, 1993). The advantages of doing so are that a parent without legal rights or biological ties can be continually affirmed in his or her role with respect to the child. The disadvantages, of course, are that it takes a fair amount of courage and energy to withstand the befuddled looks and raised eyebrows in the most benign of social situations, and in the worst of settings it can expose the family to real dangers of violence or discrimination. On the other side, however, failing to give the title of Mom or Dad to someone who is a functional parent in the family may deprive him or her of needed recognition from extended family and community. It may also deprive the child of permission to bond fully with that parent (a child is taught by our culture to have a different feeling about someone called Dad from someone called Uncle Bob). In addition, it may interfere with the untitled parent's identity as a parent. In general, it is often easier for families to perceive the risks of being too visible than to recognize the more subtle psychological damage caused by trying to hug the shore of conventionality. Raising consciousness about the true risks and benefits of calling all parents by a title allows families to make informed decisions that genuinely suit them.

Not all relationships to children, however, are easily categorized as either parental or nonparental. Some lesbian- and gay-parented families will include people who consciously and deliberately choose to have a limited, secondary caregiving status for which we have no name. The therapist should help the family articulate what the parameters of such a semiparenting role might be. It is also important to acknowledge its contribution to the child's life, particularly since lack of acknowledged status may lead to its devaluation by the family. At present, however, our legal system sees only two possibilities: parenthood with full legal rights and responsibilities, which is conferred primarily on the basis of biology and legal marriage; or complete nonparenthood. It may therefore be useful to reserve the term "parent" for those people who are prepared to assume the full responsibility for raising a child that legal parenthood requires, whether or not they actually have legal parental rights.

The issue of legal parental rights has profound psychodynamic implications in a family. Parents who take on the work and worry of raising a child without any legal rights of parenthood are taking enormous risks. Some people are reluctant to invest themselves emotionally in a child they could lose if the relationship breaks up or if the legal parent dies. More often, however, people do become intensely bonded with a child, but the insecurity of their position may get reflected in family tensions.

When a family with lesbian or gay parents separates, there are few safeguards to ensure that the custody and visitation arrangements that are made will be in the child's best interests (Martin, 1993). When a same-sex relationship is working happily, it's easier to affirm an unconventional family structure as equal co-parents. At the time of a breakup, though, there may be considerable pressure from family and friends to redefine the family relationships along heterosexist lines. A biological mother, for example, in a crisis of anger and hurt, may resort to legal privilege and view the child as solely hers, thereby ignoring the child's need for emotional continuity of an emotional connection with his other mother. A nonbiological mother often knows that she has very little chance of succeeding in a court challenge, and so may just withdraw from or get pushed out of the child's life. The therapist who has the opportunity to intervene in such a situation may prevent destructive actions from being taken by affirming the reality of this child's psychological family, and facilitating visitation negotiations that respect the nonlegal parent's position in the child's life.

Beyond identifying the true family structure in a gay- or lesbian-parented family, many other issues can also be important in treatment. For purposes of discussion, it is useful to make a distinction between families in which lesbians, gay men, or bisexuals have children within a heterosexual marriage, perhaps later divorcing and forming stepfamilies with same-sex partners, and families in which gay men or lesbians choose parenthood outside of the conventions of the heterosexual model, usually through donor insemination, surrogacy, or adoption (Kirkpatrick, 1996; Martin, 1993; Patterson & Chan, 1996). The two types of families present generally different concerns in therapy. This discussion will first focus on families with heterosexual beginnings, and then address the issues of families of the current lesbian and gay baby boom.

Families with Heterosexual Beginnings

In families that start out in a heterosexual marriage, many treatment issues center on disclosure of a parent's sexuality (Barret & Robinson, 1990; Bigner & Bozett, 1990; Corley, 1990; Dunne, 1988; Schulenberg, 1985). A gay parent may struggle with how to tell a spouse. If there is a separation or divorce, one or both parents may wrestle with how to tell the children that Daddy is gay or Mommy is a lesbian. Because the children have taken for granted that they have heterosexual parents in a conventional family, they may hear the news with the awareness that they have been lied to for some time. If they are old enough to have absorbed the prevailing culture, they have also learned that gay people are highly stigmatized. The fact that their parents have lied to them may suggest that even their parents think being gay is embarrassing or bad. If, in addition, the parent's sexual orientation is seen as the reason for a divorce, the news may come in the context of severe crisis, significantly complicating the child's ability to comprehend what it means. Despite all of these difficulties, it is generally advisable to help a family move toward full disclosure as quickly as possible. Considerable damage is done by maintaining family secrets, as it leaves children reacting to the situation, but with no means for communicating or even conceptualizing their feelings about it (Pennington, 1987).

There are two preconditions for coming out to the children, however. The first is that custody arrangements must be as secure as possible. Lesbian mothers and gay fathers still risk losing custody and visitation of their children simply because they are lesbian or gay (Rivera, 1987, 1991). If the other parent or the in-laws are homonegative and vindictive, coming out can pose a significant danger. In cases where the gay or lesbian parent's sexuality has not yet been disclosed to the heterosexual parent, it is often best to withhold the information from children until there has been time to consult a knowledgeable attorney about custody (Rivera, 1981). As painful as it may be to keep this information from children, it is not good for children to be asked to keep one parent's secret from the other parent.

Where custody has been decided on the presumption that a parent is heterosexual, the arrangements can never be considered totally secure. Subsequent revelation of the custodial parent's homosexuality can constitute changed circumstances that could reopen custody proceedings. Nevertheless, parents sometimes find it necessary to obtain custody under a false presumption of heterosexuality, just to protect the child's continuity with that parent for as long as possible (Rivera, 1987). Therapists in such situations may be primary sources of support for a parent who is under the severe stress of having to hide a newly emergent sexual orientation in fear of losing her child. The therapist should be informed about and prepared to make referrals to legal resources like Lambda Legal Defense and the National Center for Lesbian Rights, as well as sources of community support such as the Gay and Lesbian Parents Coalition International. By contrast, custody can be presumed to be relatively secure where the parent's lesbian or gay sexual orientation is openly known by all parties prior to a custody decree, and neither the ex-spouse nor the court was negatively disposed toward it.

The second precondition for coming out to children is that the parent must be able to present a positive viewpoint about his or her sexual orientation (Barett & Robinson, 1990). It is never advisable for a parent to confess shamefully to a hated sexuality. It gives the child no tools for dealing with societal prejudice and burdens him or her unduly with parental suffering. It is extremely important that the parent work on his or her own feelings about being gay or lesbian and arrive at a degree of positive acceptance before trying to tell the child. The therapist should be aware of support services in the gay, lesbian, bisexual, or transgendered communities and make appropriate referrals. Meanwhile, therapy should focus on exploring the parent's shame and guilt about having a stigmatized sexuality, dispel myths about issues of sexuality and gender, raise consciousness about the nature of societal prejudice, and help to evaluate realistically the patient's fears of societal homonegativity.

Beyond those two preconditions (i.e., securing custody and having a positive gay consciousness), there are many individual situations that affect when and how to disclose one's sexual orientation to children. For any individual child, there may be circumstances that make it advisable to delay coming out for a while, such as a death in the family or other trauma, a move to a new home, or a change of school. If the child is in the throes of emotional upheaval, it is probably wise to wait. In general, however, it is not advisable to attempt to wait for the child to attain some optimal age. The child's age will indeed affect the way the news is received and processed, and disclosure must be done in age-appropriate language, but nothing is gained by trying to wait for a different developmental period (Bigner & Bozett, 1990; Miller, 1987).

For the most part, the younger a preadolescent child is, the less prejudice he or she already has been exposed to and the easier it is for him or her to comprehend men loving men and women loving women without a sense of stigma (Barret & Robinson, 1990; Huggins, 1989). For young children, the relevant concepts are about affection and family relationships, rather than about sexuality per se. They can easily understand that Mom loves Rachel, in the context of reassurance that Mom continues to love them.

For a variety of reasons, adolescents may have a more difficult time coping with the news than younger children. For one thing, they are likely to have already absorbed more negative attitudes from the culture. In addition, they comprehend the sexuality involved in same-gender relationships, and may be dealing with concerns about their own sexuality or their own masculinity or femininity. Furthermore, at an age when peer groups demand a high degree of conformity, they may have fears of being ostracized by their peers if word gets out. The therapist may function as a coach to the parent, sensitizing him or her to the particular concerns coming out may raise for the child, and helping to choose the circumstances and language of disclosure. Additionally, the therapist may offer support to help the parent tolerate the response of those adolescents who may be angry or withdrawn.

There are some parents, caught up in the exhilaration of releasing a long-suppressed sexuality, and also perhaps in the fear of embarking on such a revolutionary path in their lives, who come out to their children impulsively and without regard to the child's state of mind at the moment. In a state of need themselves, they may believe that their openness is in the child's best interests, and fail to be sensitive to the child's grief over divorce, difficulties adjusting to a new school, and so on. The therapist should support the parent, providing referrals to gay, lesbian, and bisexual parenting support groups wherever possible, so that the parent can resume a more nurturing and protective role with the child.

More often, however, parents are resistant to the idea of telling the children. Parents' internalized homonegativity may lead them to imagine that their children will be harmed by the news of their sexual orientation. Parents of preschool children, for example, sometimes mistakenly imagine that coming out to their children is the same as disclosing details about adult sexual behavior. Such parents might say, "A four-year-old shouldn't be told about sex," or "My father never told me about his sex life so I don't see why I should tell my kids I'm gay." They get much reinforcement for these ideas from the pervasive cultural stereotype that gay or lesbian sexuality has to do with sexual acts while heterosexuality is seen to represent family and relationships. In this case, the therapist should function as an educator and raiser of consciousness, pointing out that babies as young as a few months observe the ways in which people may be related in affection, that it is healthy for children to see their parents in loving relationships, and that it is important that such relationships get talked about openly and positively.

Parents of school-age and older children may express concerns that coming out may influence the child's sexuality. Despite research indicating that sexual orientation of offspring is unrelated to the sexuality of the parents (Green & Bozett, 1991; Golombok, Spencer, & Rutter, 1983; Huggins, 1989), some gay and lesbian parents are influenced by the popular cultural misconception that one's sexuality can be somehow "caught" from others. In addition to providing the information that one's sexuality appears to be unrelated to the sexuality of one's parents, the therapy should question why the parent feels that a nonheterosexual orientation would be undesirable. The therapist's goal, through education and supportive exploration, is to enable the parent to locate the problem in society, as prejudice, and not in the parent's individual sexual and affectional orientation.

Much of the time, however, parents' resistance to disclosure results from deep fears of being rejected by their children, though it may be disguised in language of concern for their children's mental health. They may insist, for example, that they cannot inflict such a disruptive communication on their child while the child is having troubles with his fourth-grade teacher, or so soon after the grandmother's death, or while waiting for admission letters from colleges. These may, indeed, be realistic reasons to delay disclosure, but they may also reflect underlying fears that need to be explored and articulated. Therapy can help the parent understand that failure to disclose creates a distance that inevitably undermines the parent-child relationship, resulting in reduced contact, limited areas of communication, and a poverty of intimacy that is painful to both parties. The benefits of coming out, including the chance to have an open dialogue, may then appear worth the risk of rejection.

In one family, for example, the father is gay and HIV positive. He and his wife have a loving relationship and have agreed to stay together in the marriage, allowing him two nights a week in his apartment in the city in which to pursue gay relationships and community. It is a difficult solution to their discordant sexuality, especially since there is virtually no social support for it from either the heterosexual or the gay communities, but the therapist has encouraged them to redefine it as their unique and courageous choice, rather than the result of weakness or conformity (see Matteson, 1987). They have a daughter in college and a son graduating from high school, to whom they have so far disclosed nothing. Therapy initially addressed the father's shame about being gay, his guilt about what he viewed as "inflicting all this on my wife," her shame about being married to someone gay, and their profound isolation from any support (see Cadwell, 1994).

As this couple gradually felt more esteem for the quality of their marriage and less negative about his sexuality, the therapist repeatedly but gently raised the issue of coming out to the children. This was unthinkable to them, all for reasons that had to do with the children's welfare. Both parents tended to infantilize the children, wanting to protect them from anything unpleasant. The father gradually came to realize that he feels increasingly distant from and impatient with his daughter's preoccupations with her social life, which appear to him as self-centered and trivial when his daily concerns revolve around serious health management. He has been referred to and is participating actively in HIV support groups. The therapist has also suggested that the children should probably learn about his HIV status while he is in relatively good health, and not have to confront that news at the moment of a medical crisis, should one arise. He is coming to believe that disclosure to the children would indeed cause pain, but would also respect their ability to share in and contribute to the family's reality. As his guilt diminishes, so does his fear that his children will reject him. Meanwhile, he has begun taking a more assertive stance with his wife, advocating disclosure to a few select friends. His wife remains reluctant to tell the children anything, but is also enjoying his more active participation in family decisions. Together, they have considered telling the children about the HIV but claiming it resulted from a transfusion. We continue to explore their shame about gay sexuality, and they are making progress toward an eventual self-acceptance that can include the children as well.

Children with gay and lesbian parents may need help to sort out their feelings on a variety of levels. The fact of a parent's being gay or lesbian may become the focus for anger and hurt about family separation and divorce, for example. It may be easier and more socially acceptable, for example, for a boy to say "I hate my father because he's gay" than to admit that his father has broken his heart, and perhaps his mother's heart as well, by leaving the home. Children may similarly express their resentment of a new stepparent in the family system in antigay language ("I love my mother, but I can't stand that lesbian she brought home"), for which they may find support among their peers or relatives. Therapy can help young people develop an understanding of the nature of prejudice, locating the problem in society and not in their family structure, and separating it from other feelings. It can similarly educate young people about sexuality in general, addressing their anxieties about their own sexualities.

Even children who have no difficulty accepting that their parent is gay or lesbian, however, may need help dealing with the antigay sentiments of their peers. Among adolescents, homonegativity appears to be the most severe of the various prejudices (Goleman, 1990; Radkowsky, 1995). Young people may worry about being teased or rejected for having gay parents. They may want their parents to help them keep the "family situation" private.

Parents may need guidance in how open to be about their sexuality around their child's peers, balancing their needs for visibility against their child's wish for privacy. In one family, for example, the mother felt that wearing lesbian-affirmative T-shirts and having other open displays of lesbian pride around the house were deeply important to her own sense of identity, and were a hard-earned right. She also reasoned that her pride and openness modeled integrity and courage, and were therefore in her daughter's best interests. Her 15-year-old daughter, however, was trying desperately to fit into a peer group in which even having the wrong blue jeans, much less a stigmatized sexuality, could lead to rejection. The therapist helped the mother understand that her daughter's conformity to her peers was not a rejection of her mother, nor an indication that her daughter would grow up to be a bigoted adult, but a normal developmental stage that would not last forever. The mother was able, reluctantly, to agree to being less obvious in the presence of the girl's friends. Her willingness to yield on this issue allowed the daughter to have more empathy for the mother's position, and to thank her for her sensitivity to the daughter's concerns.

The situation may be more complex when the parent has a same-sex partner in the home, as the adults want respect for their relationship but the adolescent may feel ashamed about explaining the partner's presence to friends. Family therapy that includes the adolescent, the parent, and the partner may assist in developing ways of presenting the family members publicly and establishing guidelines for conduct with which everyone can live. One family agreed that the mother's partner could be represented as "Aunt Sally," and that if asked, the daughter could say that Aunt Sally slept in the den. The daughter was helped to understand that her parents were willing to make this painful denial of family relationships as a loving accommodation to her needs to fit into an imperfect world.

In general, it appears that many teenagers find at least some friends to whom they can disclose the fact that their parent is gay or lesbian (Tasker & Golombok, 1997). They learn to distinguish who is "cool" on gay issues and who isn't. In addition, they should be reassured that once past high school it becomes easier to find open-minded peer groups. The best therapy for adolescents, however, is often the opportunity to get to know other kids with gay parents, and they should be referred to the national support organization Children of Lesbians And Gays Everywhere (COLAGE), as well as to local support groups in their area.

Families Created through Donor Insemination, Adoption, and Surrogacy

Families that did not start in a heterosexual context present a substantially different profile. One major difference is that there are generally no issues about coming out to the children. Gay men and lesbians who become parents through adoption, donor insemination, or surrogacy generally create a family in which their sexuality is as openly taken for granted as that of heterosexuals in traditional families. The children grow up with a natural and comfortable awareness of their parents' affectional lives. While these families still face problems helping the children interface with a homonegative world, such challenges are generally not confounded by the children's own prejudice.

Another difference in these families is that they are generally created through a great deal of planning and decision making (Martin, 1993). Conscientious couples often seek therapy for some guidance in the process. The therapist, in addition to exploring psychodynamic factors affecting the situation, may be called on to supply information about legal considerations, health issues, and insemination options, and referrals to support groups, written materials, and community.

As part of the extensive preparation for parenthood that many lesbians and gay men undergo, they often seek therapy to assess their ability to adapt to the challenges and stresses of parenthood (Martin, 1993). The fears generally center on whether parenting as a lesbian or gay man will isolate them or their children from relatives, friends, community, and society in general, or expose them unduly to the harmful effects of prejudice. Without minimizing these concerns, it is useful for the therapist to point out that anyone who has the very considerable emotional resources necessary to deal with raising children is likely to also be able to rise to the specific challenges that lesbian or gay parenthood presents. There is no better antidote to such fears than contact with other lesbian- and gay-parented families, through local parenting groups and/or through the Gay and Lesbian Parents Coalition International.

The overwhelming number of lesbians and gay men, however, have had their ability to include parenthood as an ordinary part of their life cycle planning deeply undermined by a lifetime of messages that gay life is unwholesome for children and that gay people are unsuited to have contact with children (Falk, 1993). They may have been affected by the heterosexist presumption that the effects of growing up in an unconventional family are harmful for a child. Many lesbians and gay men have not even entertained the possibility that they could become parents. This is an area in which therapeutic neutrality, which generally dictates addressing only those issues that the client has raised, is misplaced. People will not bring up and discuss what they do not believe is possible. The therapist should take a proactive stance, raising the question of whether parenthood has been considered. When clients have desires to nurture children but say things like "You can't do that to a child," the therapist has a crucial role in exploring homonegativity, presenting options, offering information, education, and referrals to support organizations. While the therapist has no investment in whether or not someone ultimately chooses to become a parent, the provision of positive encouragement may be essential in overcoming the repressive influences of societal censure, and therefore allowing the patient to make a truly informed decision.

A unique feature of this kind of family is that there is usually an opportunity to define the family structure and articulate each person's role in it before a child arrives. For couples planning biological parenthood, some crucial questions have to do with the identities and roles of the biological parent of the other gender. Lesbians, for example, must decide whether to obtain sperm from an anonymous donor pool or to choose a man they know as a donor (Martin, 1993; Pies, 1985). If they work with someone they know, they will need to define his role. They must be aware that the law will generally grant a known donor full parental rights to custody of the child if a conflict arises, whether or not he participates actively as a father (Martin, 1993; Polikoff, 1990). If he is to be a functioning father, there is a great deal of negotiating and communicating that has to occur for everyone involved to be sure that they can, in fact, co-parent together. It is not easy to share the child you love and protect with someone in another household, whom you don't necessarily love; some temperaments are more suited to it than others. It is important to discover ahead of time if someone in the system would become anxious or uncomfortable at not having sole control over his or her child's environment and care. It is also important to assess whether the parties involved have the conflict-resolution skills to deal with the inevitable differences that will arise. Where the biological father will be known and may have some involvement, it is helpful to work with the couple alone on articulating their needs and wishes, then see the donor alone to discuss his feelings and intentions, and then have them all come in together to clarify their expectations of one another.

Alternatively, the use of anonymous sperm donors solves legal problems and reduces family complications at least in the short run, but it is not without its own difficulties. At present, established legal and medical procedures deprive almost all children conceived through anonymous sperm donors of the opportunity to contact (or even obtain basic information) about their biological fathers. If sperm banks set up registries similar to those used in adoption situations, allowing the grown children access to identifying information on (consenting) biological fathers once the age of parental rights and responsibilities was passed (there are two sperm banks that do this currently), all parties would have the safety of anonymity when it counts. Similarly, if laws were changed to define family relationships based on the intentions of those creating the family rather than on biology, there would be no need for anonymity (Hollandsworth, 1995; Polikoff, 1990). Until laws and policies change, however, the price of legal safety is most often complete lack of access. Therapy may need to address the parents' guilt about not being able to provide such access, or their fears that children may suffer or resent them for choosing anonymous donors. The opportunity to talk with other parents who have chosen this option is usually valuable for prospective parents.

In exploring the unique set of options open to this group of parents, the therapist may be called upon to present the risks and "what if" scenarios that an enthusiastic couple may have failed to notice, or similarly to identify strengths and solutions that a pessimistic couple have failed to appreciate. For example, one lesbian couple was planning to use a known donor from among their social circle, but intended not to tell the child about the biological father's identity. They needed help to think through questions like, "Is the donor permitted to tell his friends that this is his biological child? If the donor enters into a relationship with a life partner, may he disclose to him that he has a biological child? May he tell his mother? If he may, are all these people going to be sworn to secrecy, and what is the likelihood that they will maintain it? If they decide instead to tell their child openly who his or her biological father is, how can they help their child and the world understand that, despite biology, he is not one of the functional parents in this family system?"

In another family, however, the adults were distraught because they were caught up in imagining every possible future scenario. The lesbian couple and single gay man who were planning to conceive a child together had spent three years negotiating and clarifying what everyone's expectations would be. They shared similar views on education, nutrition, religion, ethics, and the function of parents. They valued the different things each could contribute to family life. They had already drawn up all the relevant legal documents and secured whatever legal protection was available to the family in their jurisdiction. Yet they would periodically have flareups of mistrust, concerned that one of the other parents would undermine his or her relationship with the child in some way. They made efforts to anticipate every possible catastrophe and to write a contract that would cover it. In therapy it became possible to reframe all the mistrust as a function of the deep and abiding investment each had already committed to this endeavor. Documents can never be a guarantee against heartbreak, and having done all the work, they were simply going to have to trust each other. They were relieved to discover that they could rely on their love and goodwill rather than attempt legal certainty.

Gay men who are considering becoming sperm donors should be encouraged to think carefully about their motivations. It is not uncommon for men to have much stronger feelings about a child they helped conceive than they expected, and the role of an uninvolved sperm donor could prove to be extremely painful. In therapy, inquiry should address such questions as how the donor would feel if he discovered that he did not approve of the way the mothers were raising the child. If there were conflict between the child's mothers, or evidence of substance abuse in the home, would it be possible for the donor not to feel responsibility toward the child? Sometimes men will consider donating sperm when what they would really prefer is fatherhood, believing that to be a sperm donor is as close to fatherhood as they could get (Martin, 1993). Once such men realize that parenthood is a real option, they are often able to seek ways of becoming fathers instead.

Gay men who become fathers through the use of surrogate mothers must consider the role that the child's birth mother will have. She cannot be thought of as the female equivalent of an anonymous sperm donor because of the fact that she will conceive, carry, give birth to, and say goodbye to the child. She is therefore someone with whom the child has already had a relationship. Questions of how much contact to have, however, and the nature of that contact, can evoke insecurities for all parties. The best of commercial surrogacy agencies address these concerns, support the surrogate's position, and help everyone in the family to be able to talk openly about the situation to the child. Unfortunately, however, other surrogacy agencies offer no such guidance, and many surrogacy arrangements are made independently, necessitating that the parties involved deal with the issues themselves. A knowledgable therapist at such a juncture can do a great deal to prevent catastrophe and / or facilitate the creation of a family.

For example, one gay man has asked his sister to bear a child for him and his partner, conceived with his partner's sperm. The sister was married with three children of her own. The therapist has helped raise issues for the lengthy discussions they are having with her and her husband about what the insemination and pregnancy would be like, how to explain to their children that Mommy is having a baby for Uncle Steve, how the family could answer the questions of neighbors and coworkers, and how to ensure that the sister's agreement, secured in the presence of three men (her husband, her brother, and his partner) and an offer of financial assistance, has not in any subtle way been coerced.

Lesbians and gay men who are considering becoming parents by adoption may need an informed therapist's help to access the network of adoption resources open to them. They may also need help in understanding the psychological issues involved in transracial or transcultural adoption, raising a child with disabilities, or perhaps committing themselves to parenting a child who may not survive to adulthood. Prospective parents may fear that for a child to have gay or lesbian parents who are also of a different race or ethnicity and perhaps from a different country than the child might be more than any child could handle. Therapy can help to assess realistic concerns involved in creating such a family, while exploring what feeling "different" meant for clients in growing. This may include an exploration of how the pain of "difference" can be projected onto the vision of a child.

Finally, it is important to remember that lesbian- and gay-parented families also present themselves for mental health services for issues that have nothing to do with the nature of their family composition. They are in danger, however, of having their family structure be seen as the central issue or even the cause of the problem. Especially if it is the child who is being presented for evaluation, perhaps for any of the ordinary range of problems that are common in heterosexually parented families, the family is likely to be told that the parent's sexuality or the unconventionality of the family constellation is the real underlying problem. One lesbian couple in my acquaintance, for example, brought their 7-year-old daughter to a psychologist to evaluate her school difficulties. They were told that the child's problems resulted from the absence of a father in the home and a resultant feeling of being different from other children. This couple was able to seek help elsewhere before too much damage was done, and their child's school problem was correctly diagnosed as dyslexia.

Lesbian-, gay-, and bisexual-parented families exist in a homonegative culture. In a perverted twist of reasoning, however, they are often blamed for society's prejudice. For example, their child-rearing desires and efforts are condemned as damaging to children, on the grounds that the children in those families will be exposed to prejudice. Perhaps the therapist's most vital function in working with lesbian-, gay-, and bisexual-parented families is to affirm their legitimacy and to respect the resources they have to offer children. This includes supporting the family's ability to give the children the tools they need to deal with prejudice, and offering reassurance that their family can be as wholesome and healthy as any other.

In the interests of space, this article has been limited to issues of parents' relationships with each other and with their children. No family, however, exists outside of a social and familial context. Gay- and lesbian-parented families will be powerfully affected by, and have effects on, their immediate and extended families of origin. In addition, many gay men and lesbians create lasting familial relationships with close friendship circles (Weston, 1991). Such relationships should not be underestimated when assessing a family's resources and stresses. The inclusion of biological and/or chosen extended family in the treatment may be pivotal in the therapy process.

Finally, the treatment of lesbian- and gay-parented families must be understood as the intersection of the psychological with the sociological and the political. Homonegativity is a societal disorder, and the remedy is ultimately to be found in social change. The task of the therapist, at this point in history, is very often one of compensating for the lack of lesbian and gay visibility, for the absence of support for nonheterosexual relationships, and for the gaps in education for young people on issues related to sexual orientation. Until lesbian- and gay-parented families are visibly commonplace in the media, until the schools are familiar with, accepting of, and willing to educate about these families, and until these families find definition and protection within this country's legal system, we can not expect psychotherapy alone to be a cure for their problems. In our treatment rooms, we must consider gay and lesbian organizations and support groups as our co-therapists in addressing both internalized and external homonegativity and heterosexism. As therapists we often must be a source of referrals to local and national resources for gay- and lesbian-parented families. In addition, on a larger level, we should be prepared to use our expertise to offer guidance and advocacy within the legal, political, educational, and medical establishments so that, one day, the well-being of these families will not be jeopardized by fear and ignorance.

References

Achtenberg, R. (1987). *Lesbian and gay parenting: A Psychological and legal perspective.* San Francisco: National Center for Lesbian Rights.

American Psychological Association (1993). Amici Curiae brief, *Sharon Lynne Bottoms v. Pamela Kay Bottoms,* Court of Appeals, Virginia.

Baptiste, D. A. (1987). The gay and lesbian stepparent family. In F. W. Bozett (Ed.), *Gay and lesbian parents* (pp. 112–137). New York: Praeger.

Barret, R. L., & Robinson, B. E. (1990). *Gay fathers.* Lexington, MA: Lexington Books.

Benkov, L. (1994). *Reinventing the family.* New York: Crown.

Berzon, B. (1988). *Permanent partners.* New York: E. P. Dutton.

Bigner, J. J., & Bozett, F. W. (1990). Parenting by gay fathers. In F. W. Bozett and M. B. Sussman (Eds.), *Homosexuality and family relations* (pp. 155–175). Binghampton, NY: Harrington Park Press.

Bozett, F. W. (1987). Children of gay fathers. In F. W. Bozett (Ed.), *Gay and lesbian parents* (pp. 39–57). New York: Praeger.

Bozett, F. W. (1993). Gay fathers: A review of the literature. In L. D. Garnets and D. C. Kimmel (Eds.), *Psychological perspectives on lesbian and gay male experience* (pp. 437–457). New York: Columbia University Press.

Cadwell, S. A. (1994). Twice removed: The stigma suffered by gay men with AIDS. In S. A. Cadwell, R. A. Burnham, Jr., and M. Forstein (Eds.), *Therapists on the front line: Psychotherapist with gay men in the Age of AIDS* (pp. 3–24). Washington, DC: American Psychiatric Press.

Carter, B. (1995). Looking at families through the gay lens: An interview with Betty Carter. *In the Family,* 1, 12–15.

Cavaliere, F. (1995, July). Society appears more open to gay parenting. *APA Monitor,* p. 51.

Chan, C. S. (1993). Issues of identity development among Asian-American lesbians and gay men. In L. D. Garnets & D. C. Kimmel (Eds.), *Psychological perspectives on lesbian and gay male experience* (pp. 376–387). New York: Columbia University Press.

Clunis, D. M., & Green, G. D. (1988). *Lesbian couples.* Seattle: Seal Press.

Coontz, S. (1992). *The way we never were.* New York: Basic Books.

Corley, R. (1990). *The final closet: The gay parents' guide for coming out to their children.* Miami: Editech Press.

D'Augelli, A. R., & Garnets, L. D. (1995). Lesbian, gay, and bisexual communities. In A. R. D'Augelli & C. J. Patterson (Eds.), *Lesbian, gay, and bisexual identities over the lifespan* (pp. 293–320). New York: Oxford University Press.

De Monteflores, C. (1993). Notes on the management of difference. In L. D. Garnets & D. C. Kimmel (Eds.), *Psychological perspectives on lesbian and gay male experience* (pp. 218–247). New York: Columbia University Press.

Dunne, E. J. (1988). Helping gay fathers come out to their children. In E. Coleman (Ed.), *Psychotherapy with homosexual men and women: Interated identity approaches for clinical practice* (pp. 213–222). New York: Haworth Press.

Espin, O. M. (1987). Issues of identity in Latina lesbians. In The Boston Lesbian Psychologies Collective (Eds.), *Lesbian psychologies* (pp. 35–51). Chicago: University of Illinois Press.

Espin, O. M. (1993). Issues of identity in the psychology of Latina lesbians. In

L. D. Garnets & D. C. Kimmel (Eds.), *Psychological perspectives on lesbian and gay male experience* (pp. 348–363). New York: Columbia University Press.

Falk, P. J. (1993). Lesbian mothers: Psychosocial assumptions in family law. In L. D. Garnets & D. C. Kimmel (Eds.), *Psychological perspectives on lesbian and gay male experience* (pp. 420–436). New York: Columbia University Press.

Garcia, N., Kennedy, C., Pearlman, S. F., & Perez, J. (1987). In The Boston Lesbian Psychologies Collective (Eds.), *Lesbian psychologies* (pp. 142–160). Chicago: University of Illinois Press.

Garnets, L., Hancock, K., Cochran, S., Goodchilds, J., & Peplau, A. (1991). Issues in psychotherapy with lesbians and gay men: A survey of psychologists. *American Psychologist, 46,* 964–972.

Goleman, D. (1990, July 10). Homophobia: Scientists find clues to its roots. *New York Times,* pp. C1, 11.

Golombok, S., Spencer, A., & Rutter, M. (1983). Children in lesbian and single-parent households: Psychosexual and psychiatric appraisal. *Journal of Child Psychology and Psychiatry, 24,* 551–572.

Gottman, J. S. (1990). Children of gay and lesbian parents. In F. W. Bozett & M. B. Sussman (Eds.), *Homosexuality and family relations* (pp. 177–196). New York: Harrington Park Press.

Green, G. D., & Bozett, F. W. (1991). Lesbian mothers and gay fathers. In J. D. Gonsiorek & J. D. Weinrich (Eds.), *Homosexuality: Research implications for public policy* (pp. 197–214). Newbury Park, CA: Sage Publications.

Green, R. (1989). Sexual identity of 37 children raised by homosexual or transsexual parents. *American Journal of Psychiatry, 135,* 692–697.

Green, R., Mandel, J. B., Hotvedt, M. E., Gray, J., & Smith, L. (1986). Lesbian mothers and their children: A comparison with solo parent heterosexual mothers and their children. *Archives of Sexual Behavior, 15,* 167–184.

Hammersmith, S. K. (1988). A sociological approach to counseling homosexual clients and their families. In E. Coleman, (Ed.), *Integrated identity for gay men* (pp. 173–190). New York: Harrington Park Press.

Hancock, K. A. (1995). Psychotherapy with lesbians and gay men. In A. R. D'Augelli & C. J. Patterson (Eds.), *Lesbian, gay, and bisexual identities over the lifespan: Psychological perspectives* (pp. 398–432). New York: Oxford University Press.

Herek, G. M. (1995). Psychological heterosexism in the United States. In A. R. D'Augelli & C. J. Patterson (Eds.), *Lesbian, gay, and bisexual identities across the lifespan: Psychological perspectives* (pp. 321–346). New York: Oxford University Press.

Hollandsworth, M. J. (1995). Gay men creating families through surro-gay arrangements: A paradigm for reproductive freedom. *Journal of Gender & the Law, 3,* 183–246.

Huggins, S. L. (1989). A comparative study of self-esteem of adolescent children of divorced lesbian mothers and divorced heterosexual mothers. In F. W. Bozett (Ed.), *Homosexuality and the family* (pp. 123–135). New York: Harrington Park Press.

Kirkpatrick, M. (1996). Lesbians as parents. In R. P. Cabaj & T. S. Stein (Eds.), *The textbook of homosexuality and mental health* (pp. 353–370). Washington, DC: American Psychiatric Press.

Kirkpatrick, M., Smith, C., & Roy, R. (1981). Lesbian mothers and their children: A comparative survey. *American Journal of Orthopsychiatry, 51,* 545–551.

Kolata, G. (1989, January 30). Lesbian partners find the means to be parents. *New York Times*, p. A-13.

Lewin, E., & Lyons, T. A. (1982) Everything in its place: The coexistence of lesbianism and motherhood. In W. Paul, J. D. Weinrich, J. C. Gonsiorek, & M. E. Hotvedt (Eds.), *Homosexuality: Social, psychological, and biological issues* (pp. 249–273). Beverly Hills, CA: Sage Publications.

Loiacano, D. K. (1993). Gay identity issues among black Americans: Racism, homophobia, and the need for validation. In L. D. Garnets & D. C. Kimmel (Eds.), *Psychological perspectives on lesbian and gay male experience* (pp. 364–375). New York: Columbia University Press.

Markowitz, L. (1995). Editor's note. *In The Family, 1*(1), 2.

Martin, A. (1982). Some issues in the treatment of gay and lesbian patients. *Psychotherapy: Theory, research and practice, 19*, 341–348.

Martin, A. (1989a). Lesbian parenting: A personal odyssey. In J. Offerman-Zuckerberg (Ed.), *Gender in transition: A new frontier* (pp. 249–262). New York: Plenum.

Martin, A. (1989b). The planned lesbian and gay family: Parenthood and children. *Newsletter of the Society for the Psychological Study of Lesbian and Gay Issues, 5*, 6, 16–17.

Martin, A. (1993). *The lesbian and gay parenting handbook: Creating and raising our families*. New York: HarperCollins.

Martin, D., & Lyon, P. (1991). *Lesbian woman*. Volcano, CA: Volcano Press.

Matteson; D. R. (1987). The heterosexually married gay and lesbian parent. In F. W. Bozett (Ed.), *Gay and lesbian parents* (pp. 138–161). New York: Praeger.

McPherson, D. (1993). *Gay parenting couples: Parenting arrangements, arrangement satisfaction, and relationship satisfaction*. Unpublished doctoral dissertation, Pacific Graduate School of Psychology, Palo Alto, CA.

McWhirter, D. P., & Mattison, A. M. (1984). *The male couple: How relationships develop*. Englewood Cliffs, NJ: Prentice-Hall.

Miller, B. (1987). Counseling gay husbands and fathers. In F. W. Bozett (Ed.), *Gay and lesbian parents* (pp. 175–187). New York: Praeger.

Morales, E. S. (1990). Ethnic minority families and minority gays and lesbians. In F. W. Bozett & M. B. Sussman, (Eds.), *Homosexuality and family relations*. (pp. 217–239). Binghampton NY: Harrington Park Press.

Patterson, C. J. (1992). Children of lesbian and gay parents. *Child Development, 63*, 1025–1042.

Patterson, C. J. (1994a). Lesbian and gay families. *Current Directions in Psychological Science, 3*, 62–64.

Patterson, C. J. (1994b). Children of the lesbian baby boom. In B. Greene & G. Herek (Eds.), *Lesbian and gay psychology: Theory, research and clinical applications* (pp. 156–175). Thousand Oaks, CA: Sage Publications.

Patterson, C. J. (1995). Lesbian mothers, gay fathers, and their children. In A. R. D'Augelli & C. W. Patterson (Eds.), *Lesbian, gay, and bisexual identities over the lifespan: Psychological Perspectives* (pp. 262–290). New York: Oxford University Press.

Patterson, C. J., & Chan, R. (1996) Gay fathers and their children. In R. P. Cabaj & T. S. Stein (Eds.), *The textbook of homosexuality and mental health* (pp. 371–393). Washington, DC: American Psychiatric Press.

Pennington, S. B. (1987). Children of lesbian mothers. In F. W. Bozett (Ed.), *Gay and lesbian parents* (pp. 58–74). New York: Praeger.

Peplau, L. A. (1993). Lesbian and gay relationships. In L. D. Garnets & D. C. Kimmel (Eds.), *Psychological perspectives on lesbian and gay male experience* (pp. 395–419). New York: Columbia University Press.

Pies, C. (1985). *Considering parenthood: A workbook for Lesbians.* San Francisco: Spinsters/Aunt Lute.

Pies, C. (1990). Lesbians and the choice to parent. In F. W. Bozett & M. B. Sussman (Eds.), *Homosexuality and family relations* (pp. 137–154). Binghampton, NY: Harrington Park Press.

Polikoff, N. D. (1990). This child does have two mothers: Redefining parenthood to meet the needs of children in lesbian-mother and other nontraditional families. *Georgetown Law Journal, 78,* 459–575.

Pollak, S., & Vaughn, J. (1987). *Politics of the heart.* Ithaca, NY: Firebrand Books.

Radkowsky, M. (1995). *The effects of peer support on gay and lesbian youth.* Unpublished doctoral dissertation, Ferkauf Graduate School of Psychology, Yeshiva University, New York.

Ricketts, W., & Achtenberg, R. (1990). The adoptive and foster gay and lesbian parent. In F. W. Bozett (Ed.), *Gay and lesbian parents* (pp. 89–111). New York: Praeger.

Rivera, R. R. (1981, Spring). Some practical advice for lesbian and gay parents. *News From Lambda,* Newsletter of Lambda Legal Defense, p. 4.

Rivera, R. R. (1987). Legal issues in gay and lesbian parenting. In F. W. Bozett (Ed.) *Gay and lesbian Parents* (pp. 199–227). New York: Praeger.

Rivera, R. R. (1991). Sexual orientation and the law. In J. C. Gonsiorek & J. D. Weinrich (Eds.), *Homosexuality: Research implications for public policy* (pp. 81–100). Newbury Park, CA: Sage Publications.

Schulenberg, J. (1985). *Gay parenting.* Garden City, NY: Doubleday.

Slater, S., & Mencher, J. (1991). The lesbian family life cycle: A contextual approach. *American Journal of Orthopsychiatry, 61,* 372–382.

Tasker, F., & Golombok, S. (1997). *Growing up in a lesbian family.* New York: Guilford, 1997.

Weston, K. (1991). *Families we choose.* New York: Columbia University Press.

Index

AA (Alcoholics Anonymous), 106, 128
abortion, 64
abstinence, sexual, 253
ACA. *See* American Counseling
 Association
achnucek (Kodiak androgynous male),
 59
additive genetic variance, 5, 13
adoption
 by gay couples, 65–67, 262, 271,
  282–84, 286
 legal issues, 241, 244
 by lesbian mothers, 159–61, 164
 of same-sex relationship partner, 58
 social benefits of, 65–67
 traditional societal secrecy about,
  272
adoption studies
 behavioral genetics designs, 4, 6, 20
 of environmental factors, 12, 22
 of heritability, 21
 sibling trait analysis, 6, 24
Advocate, The (magazine), 81, 263
Africa, 60
African Americans, 40–51
 coming-out issues, 91, 92
 extended family and, 44, 46, 49
 gay youths, 79, 85, 91
 gender roles, 46, 49–50
 homophobic attitudes, 47–48
 income surveys, 234
 motherhood's importance to, 46
 other-race friendships, 129
 relationship cultural issues, 100

sexual myths and stereotypes, 43,
 46–51
and Western Christian religiosity,
 47
AFTA. *See* American Family Therapy
 Association
ageism, 57
aging. *See* elder care
AIDS/HIV, 99, 178, 259
 family concerns about, 187, 202, 208
 friendship network support, 125,
  131–33
 heterosexist attitudes and, 251
 Hollywood film depiction, 201
 impact on sexual activity, 110–11
Alaska, 59
Alcoholics Anonymous (AA), 106, 128
alcoholism
 among gay men and lesbians, 103,
  106, 128
 parental, 5
Aleuts, 59
alienation, in family relationships,
 199, 206, 210–11, 221
alumni organizations, 105
American Counseling Association, 113
American Family Therapy
 Association, 113
American Orthopsychiatric
 Association, 113
American Psychiatric Association, 250
American Psychological Association,
 113
Am Tikva, 112